A NEW INTRODUCTION TO CHAUCER

LONGMAN MEDIEVAL AND RENAISSANCE LIBRARY

General Editors:
CHARLOTTE BREWER, Hertford College, Oxford
N. H. KEEBLE, University of Stirling

Published Titles:

Derek Brewer

A NEW INTRODUCTION TO CHAUCER

Second edition

LONGMAN
LONDON AND NEW YORK

Addison Wesley Longman Limited
Edinburgh Gate
Harlow
Essex CM20 2JE
United Kingdom
and Associated Companies throughout the world

*Published in the United States of America
by Addison Wesley Longman, New York*

© Addison Wesley Longman Limited 1998

The right of Derek Brewer to be identified
as author of this Work has been asserted
by him in accordance with the Copyright,
Designs and Patents Act 1988.

First edition 1984
Second edition 1998

ISBN 0 582-09348-1

British Library Cataloguing-in-Publication Data

A catalogue record for this book is available from the British Library

Library of Congress Cataloging-in-Publication Data

Set by 35 in 10.5/12pt Bembo
Produced by Longman Singapore Publishers (Pte) Ltd.
Printed in Singapore

Contents

Contents   vii

Preface

This book is so radical a revision of my earlier *Introduction to Chaucer* (1984) that it is certainly different, though it retains some sections from the earlier book, mainly those providing basic information on which in many cases a new structure is built. There is now a largely new and much more extensive discussion of the poetry and prose. More attention is paid to the sheer difference of Chaucer's culture from modern Western culture. In attempting to give a full introductory account of Chaucer's life and works the emphasis is on the writing. Chaucer himself wrote to entertain, interest and instruct, and in so far as I could I have followed his example.

Developments in the criticism of Chaucer's work over the past 25 years have introduced many new topics and attitudes. I have greatly benefited from these, but I believe some of them to be wrong, and I have taken an independent line in many interpretations. In my attempts to identify what is common to human nature and what is caused by changing human values and assumptions, I may of course be wrong. It will be for the reader to decide. Works of art may have many meanings, and not all different interpretations are incompatible. Furthermore, Chaucer is often deliberately enigmatic, reserved, or ambiguous, not to say occasionally ironical. But complete relativism of judgement is impossible, even in literary studies. Some views and interpretations are downright wrong and can be shown to be so. It is important to get things right when we can, even in literary studies.

In so far as they concern literature I have, as in the past, turned to other disciplines including social anthropology, for help. I have made what use I can of modern literary theory. It has opened up interesting new prospects for literary perception. Not all of it applies to traditional pre-seventeenth-century literature in English, including Chaucer, but some modern views provide or provoke either new insight or a better statement of older views. Some literary theory, explicit or implicit, is present in all criticism, though while I have tried to make such theory as I possess explicit, this book is empirical and written in plain English, directed not only to the specialist but to those with an interest in yet no previous knowledge of Chaucer.

It has become something of a *topos* in the Preface to books like this on Chaucer to name a hundred or so persons to whom one is indebted. It is a useful device, cutting out a lot of potential reviewers and in a medieval way invoking a crowd of 'compurgators' in one's own defence (cf. p. 119). Like Chaucer himself, one hopes that 'with this swerd shal I sleen envie' (*Astrolabe*, 64), and I would not wish to be guilty of ingratitude. But the number of those to whom I am indebted would go beyond even the usual limits and I restrict myself to very few names. I am particularly grateful to those eminent modern critics named in the text who have stimulated me to such pleasurably strong disagreement. I owe much to the volumes of *The Oxford Guides to Chaucer*.

I am greatly obliged to the co-editor of the series, Dr Charlotte Brewer, for her creative criticism and encouragement, and to her and the publishers for their patience with my delays in what proved a much more difficult task than I expected. Miss Gillian Kirk of Mansfield College, Oxford, generously volunteered to read the earlier version with a fresh eye for what seemed especially dated. Mrs Linda Allen has typed my old-fashioned scrawl with her usual exemplary perception and accuracy. I owe a more general but nonetheless warmly felt debt of gratitude to all those indefatigable conference speakers and listeners, all the scholars and critics of medieval European literature and Chaucer, all the university students, from Japan to Europe to the United States, an international community of learning, whose friendliness and generosity over many years, even when they have suffered my lectures, have constituted one of the social pleasures of my life. I have benefited from the friendly company of the Cambridge English Faculty for many years, and especially from my brilliant medievalist colleagues. A more specific debt is owed to the Master and Fellows of Emmanuel College, Cambridge, in their successive incarnations of which I have had the great privilege for many years to be a part, for company and conversation, and for the 'solid joys' of Research Grants for typing and a study in College. My greatest debt is to my wife.

Acknowledgements

All quotations have been taken from *The Riverside Chaucer*, edited by L. D. Benson, and I wish to acknowledge my indebtedness to the many scholars who have edited the various works in that indispensable volume. Like all others who have written on the life of Chaucer, I have also made full use of the equally indispensable *Chaucer Life Records*, edited by Martin M. Crow and Clair C. Olson. Where particular use has been made of books or articles I have noted them, but my main debt to other scholarly and critical work is listed in the Select Bibliography.

Prelude

Chaucer speaks to us directly from fourteenth-century England. His work still lives, though only a few physical fragments of that time remain, such as parts of the Tower of London, where the Queen Mother of the 15-year-old king, Richard II, and grown-up courtiers cowered in fear as peasants rampaged through London in 1381 and insulted the royal family. Richard II's great Hall of Westminster, a couple of miles away, can still be seen with the glory of its hammer-beam roof; and parts of Westminster Abbey. A few churches survive, at least in part – not the great Gothic St Paul's, destroyed in the Fire of London in 1665 to be replaced by Wren's masterpiece, but the already ancient St Bartholomew the Great, in the City, whose huge twelfth-century chancel survives. Scattered through England are the footprints of the past. Some of the Pilgrims' Way between London and Canterbury can still be walked, though the heavy incrustations of later centuries and the bulldozers and concrete of recent times have hidden much.

Something remains too of the initiatives and mental structures of the remarkable fourteenth century, when in England as in Europe so much was growing which still affects us. Much of our religious feeling dates from then; much commercial enterprise; and much that was valued then, as the spirit of love both secular and divine. Dire catastrophe – the Great Plague, later called the Black Death, of 1348–9 – was endured and did not crush. Building continued.

There is continuity and change. The climate was much the same. The English language is essentially the same, with many differences. How different were the people? There are some human constants. One is reminded of Shakespeare's Shylock: 'Hath not a Jew eyes? Hath not a Jew hands, organs, dimensions, senses, affections, passions . . . If you prick us, do we not bleed? If you tickle us, do we not laugh?' (*The Merchant of Venice*, III, i, 67–70), and more to the same effect. All humanity has the same basic qualities, which we share with all other periods and cultures. But the directions and nature of passions and feelings and ideas and social compulsions all change, and there is very considerable change between fourteenth-century English society and modern post-industrial post-Christian societies. Fascination lies in the change, based on human similarity, as with foreign travel.

England in the second half of the fourteenth century was a small agrarian society of around two million people all told. Ninety per cent of people were peasants, many tied to the land, necessarily involved in back-breaking labour most of the year. Of the rest, 1 or 2 per cent were nobility and gentry. The remainder lived in towns or villages, practising a variety of crafts and services. The only significantly large town was London City, of about 45 000 people (and some 400 churches). The countryside came close to the town. Travel was by foot or horseback or slow clumsy carts.

It was what we might call a Third World or, better, a developing society. Very low-level technology led to low productivity, high mortality, especially of children, constant danger of famine and much human brutality. Yet there were glorious buildings and beautiful art and music. Such societies also have elaborate social codes and structures very different from the modern. They are hierarchical. Few members are shocked by the coexistence of widespread grinding poverty for the many and fantastic wealth and extravagance for the very few. Territorial possessiveness and aggressiveness encourage war. The presence of death, the lack of control over nature, encourage religion and superstition, which soak through the whole fabric of society, ameliorating harshness in general but sometimes worsening it. Devotion, asceticism, splendour, honour, self-sacrifice, in that small part of society above peasant level in particular (but also sometimes within it) flourished very vividly, like the variety of clothes. The roles of men and women were sharply defined. Internal contradictions abound as they still do.

England was smaller than France, but even France was much smaller than now. Burgundy joined with part of the Low Countries to form another entity. The English claimed a dynastic right to rule France and, indeed, held Calais and the large area of Aquitaine from Bordeaux southwards to the Spanish kingdom of Castile. England also claimed sovereignty over Wales, Scotland, Ireland, which was fiercely resisted. There were many more European countries than now, many small courts. Italy was a jigsaw puzzle of city-states. And they all fought each other, or sought alliances, and all shared much the same general culture, a culture of honour, chivalry, war, but also of a form of Christianity. Medieval Christianity had too its internecine conflicts, with for a long while two rival Popes, one at Avignon, one at Rome, each variously supported by French, English, Italian, German kings and dukes. Piety fought with piety.

Within all the turmoil, great works of art, great intellectual developments, major changes in sentiment, also took place. The resourcefulness of the human spirit, goodness beside horrible brutality, asserted undying hopefulness. Moreover, in England, three of the greatest English poets survived the Black Death: Chaucer, William Langland, the *Gawain*-poet (as we may call one whose name is not known) and not far behind there comes John Gower.

In this book Geoffrey Chaucer is our interest, a poet both highly individual and widely representative. His poetry can still speak directly to us, and through it we learn of another world which yet is our world. We learn more of the poetry by seeing how it interacts with the culture of which it is a part.

Chaucer's poems present a continuous quest throughout his life for the meanings in experience and authority. He seems always to be seeking an answer to the explicit question at last formulated in *The Knight's Tale*

> What is this world? What asketh men to have?
> Now with his love, now in his colde grave,
> Allone, withouten any compaignye.
>
> *(CT,* I, 2777–9)

There are many possible responses to this question, some of them surprisingly comical or satirical. The plangent line about the lonely grave was used again by Chaucer in a comical context (*CT, The Miller's Tale*, I, 3204). There were plenty of would-be authoritative theological answers available to the questioning about the world and what happens beyond the grave. But in the noble *Knight's Tale*, after having struck this poignant note about the contradictions of joy and sorrow in the human condition, the poet continues, of Arcite's death, which has just been described in painful detail,

> His spirit chaunged hous and wente ther
> As I cam nevere, I kan nat tellen wher.
> Therfore I stynte: I nam no divinistre.   *stop: theologian*
>
> *(CT,* I, 2809–11)

The poet stops at the end of the known world. This is a more common, and commonsense, observation than might be expected. Even Margery Kempe, the fascinatingly hysterical woman mystic of late fourteenth-century Norfolk, makes a similar remark. As for Chaucer, he will later tell saints' lives and a sort of sermon, but now, after pay-ing respect to what is beautiful, solemn and uplifting, having shown a stoical acceptance of good and bad, and paying tribute to the divine principle, he will later in *The Canterbury Tales* enjoy the heartless derisive comedy of the everyday world, as well as religious pathos and serious advice.

The poems and the prose works record a questing eager spirit and intellect, as interested in astronomy as amused by the bawdy mis-adventures of the lower classes or the pathos of lost love. The poet's quest, driven by interest rather than anxiety, by sympathy for human-ity, carries us with him through an extraordinarily varied landscape of history, everyday life, learning and fantasy. It is indeed a pilgrimage, with a characteristically ambiguous glimpse of the heavenly Jerusalem at the end of it, at the end of his own Canterbury pilgrimage and his own life.

The poems to be fully understood and enjoyed must be seen in the context of Chaucer's own life and times. We can trace much of his own family and his own career at a key point of the emergence of the outlines of the modern world. He was no revolutionary, but his views were *avant-garde* for his own time. Society was developing rapidly from archaic structures (still part of our own humanity) to modern structures and attitudes.

This is not to argue that Chaucer can or should be made into 'our contemporary'. That would be self-defeating. Much of the value of reading his work depends on recognising its difference.

> Important works of the past, imbued with human intelligence, have a durable content which survives repeated encounters with new cultures. In uncovering their own meaning, they acquire new life. In the same way, different cultures are mutually enriched in the course of history, and as a result of historical knowledge, without losing their inner unity and integrity.[1]

Gurevich, whom I have just quoted, follows M. Bakhtin who says (as translated in Gurevich's essay)

> In an encounter through dialogue two cultures do not merge and blend: each keeps its uniqueness and open integrity, but both are enriched.[2]

One need not take this thought too far. We all have hands, eyes, feel pain and joy at some of the same things, we love and hate, and all must die. It is because human beings have so much in common in all periods and places that we can (if we want) understand in part, see in part, though as through a glass darkly, and therefore there is indeed some merging and blending. Without it there would be little hope of understanding 'from the inside' of the other culture. We need to empathise while still maintaining some critical detachment.

Such a mixture of empathy and detachment is particularly needed when reading any literature, but particularly that of the past, and even more so when for English readers (including myself) that past is one's own, and to some extent still a part of oneself.

Chaucer's poetry and prose to a quite extraordinary extent reflect and express the breadth and depth of fourteenth-century English and European culture. His writings can still speak directly to us, yet they also have an intriguing, stimulating difference. Love, sex, war, religion, character are all the same yet different. Chaucer was not only a serious prose writer and a poet who took poetry seriously, but also an entertainer and a jester, who needed to catch at his audience. His poetry has a bright surface, easy to understand, once the not very great historical differences of language are overcome. His poetry is particularly rewarding because there is remarkable subtlety in his language. The bright surface has sometimes unsuspected depths and implications. He is very rarely an allegorist – he does not need to be. Metaphor is brief, traditional and not, as with the Romantics, the heart of his poetry. The depths come from ironies, jests, the further implications of what is literally described, the play with contents and expectations, the convolutions of story structure. The following chapters attempt to introduce and suggest some of the many interests and pleasures of Chaucer's writing, leaving much more for the reader to discover.

Some of the content of Chaucer's life and times needs to be appreciated in order to grasp more readily the fuller meanings of the work, and some preliminary information follows before we come to the poems.

NOTES

1. Aaron Gurevich, *Historical Anthropology of the Middle Ages*, ed. Jana Howlett (Oxford, 1992) 7.
2. M. Bakhtin, *Estetika* (*The Aesthetics of Verbal Creation*) (Moscow, 1979).

In the Beginning

THE NEW AND THE OLD, ARCHAIC AND MODERN

Geoffrey Chaucer, the most varied of our half-dozen greatest English poets, is well documented as a courtier, customs officer, diplomat, occupant of a flat over Aldgate in London Wall, traveller to France and Italy, married, with children, and so forth. His poetry tells us about him as a poet. Put together the records, the poetry, and the history of the fascinating fourteenth century, and we find a remarkably full and interesting picture of a man and an age. It was a great creative period. Many new things were starting or, having started, were gaining strength. The modern world was beginning. Towns were established, capitalist enterprise raised standards of living, serfdom was being eroded, new inventions such as clockwork and a new numeracy and power to calculate, were developing. New feelings, for the family, for the individual, a new tenderness for suffering, were being experienced. These have to be seen against a background of special sorrows and troubles. Things went badly for England in much of Chaucer's lifetime, even when they prospered for him personally, and he was fully responsive to the sadness of life. Ancient sorrows continued: those caused by mankind, the savage warfare, the brutal rapine of cities; and those caused by nature, starvation and disease from poor harvests, illnesses unmitigated by medicine, and plague. Religion ancient and new offered consolations. The message of Christianity has always been the conquest of suffering and death, the triumph of love and significance. Religious experience increased the emphasis on the individual's internal values. The very success of Christianity in preaching higher ideals, more gentleness, more pity, led to men judging the Church unfavourably by its own divinely inspired ideals as inefficient and corrupt. On the other hand the higher value which was being set on secular life gave that more vividness, more splendour, and consequently, because it was so swiftly passing and so full of suffering, gave it more pathos.

One of the driving engines of all these developments was the spread of schooling derived from the Church, which created literacy and the multiplication of books. Books were still in manuscript, painfully copied with many errors, for the last great medieval invention, printing, was still a century away. But there were many books, the more powerful ones in Latin – the Bible, the great theological tomes, and the classics of Antiquity themselves, still used as schoolbooks. There were also many books in French, which was still, since William of Normandy's Conquest in 1066, one of the main languages of England, though it was now more of a local dialect, limited to the upper classes, and losing its hold. There was a rapidly increasing flow of books in English: sermons, romances, encyclopedias, works of instruction, often translated, but with more original work also. The steady advance of literacy had been at first limited to the clergy. To be literate was indeed to be a cleric, a clerk. But now in the second half of the fourteenth century the literate layman, secular, advanced in thought, appears, and his supreme manifestation is Geoffrey Chaucer.

For all his advanced interests, Chaucer was solidly a part of traditional culture. The mixture of tradition and innovation which he supremely illustrates is one of his great qualities. Literate, son of a citizen of London, numerate, secular in his occupations, and thus a part of what was new, he was also a 'courtman all his life', as one of his characters says. The court, with its fierce loyalties and betrayals, its focus on the king, its basis in the ethos of fighting, its interest in sexual love, was a flourishing example of traditional archaic patterns of thought and feeling. The court flourished partly because it was so well allied with the city. The court at Westminster, and two miles away the City of London, with the law courts on the way, sum up the spread of Chaucer's life, an axis which gave unique opportunities to a unique genius.

THE LIFE OF A PAGE AT COURT

Chaucer first appears in a court record. Medieval England is notably rich in administrative records of many kinds, but this record has survived by a marvellous accident. It is a couple of pages which were later used for binding up another book and were preserved by pure chance. They are pages from the accounts, kept as usual in a curious mixed jargon of Anglified Latin and French, mingled with actual English words, of the household of Elizabeth, Countess of Ulster, wife of Lionel, Duke of Clarence, who was the third son of the glamorous and long-reigning King Edward III. From these scraps we learn that various people were given ribbons and robes worth so much, and that 'Galfridus' (Latin for Geoffrey) Chaucer was given, on Monday 4 April 1357 a 'paltok' or short cloak, costing four shillings, and a pair of red and black breeches and a pair of shoes which cost his lady a further three shillings. He must have been a page, probably now 17 years old, and was being set up in bright new clothing for Easter, which fell on 9 April. His outfit was quite expensive to the Countess. Twelve pence made a shilling, and 20 shillings a pound. We would have to multiply these sums at least 300 or 400 times to get their rough modern equivalents, though on the other hand labour was terribly cheap and the gap between rich and poor immensely greater than in modern Britain. A ploughman was paid about 12 shillings a year, while the Black Prince when at war drew pay of 20 shillings a day, and an archer sixpence a day.

Our sight of Chaucer in this princely household shows his connection, at his most impressionable age, with all the splendour, elegance and sophistication of Edward III's court – the most magnificent in Europe and also the most efficiently run. It was the Edwardian court rather than the 'Ricardian' (of Richard II, Edward's grandson) which formed Chaucer's poetic nature, though his later poems were produced in the youthful Richard's court. Chaucer's lady, the Countess Elizabeth, travelled about the country a great deal, and probably took Chaucer with her. London, Southampton, Reading, Hatfield, Windsor, Hertford Castle, Anglesey, Liverpool all saw her and her train in those four years, some places several times. State weddings and funerals held at Edward's court, as well as the normal feasts of the year, were duly kept by her, and no doubt by Chaucer in her train. As her page he helped to serve her at table, and attend her at various ceremonies, according to the strict and elaborate etiquette of a great household, which he had to learn. Some slight care would be taken of his general education, as well as of his manners. Much of what he learned, of politeness, of good manners, of noble behaviour (as well, doubtless, as scandalous talk and comic stories) came to him by watching and waiting at table, talking with his fellow pages and the older squires, and so forth. The chaplain might supervise his serious reading. He picked up an interest in music. He listened to, and read for himself, the current songs and romances, both English and the fashionable French ones. French was losing its domination as the language of the court, but the royal family spoke it. However, Chaucer learned Continental French, the 'French of Paris', and any influence from Anglo-French was indirect and general. Chaucer had a remarkable memory for the poems of the fashionable Continental French poet Machaut, as *The Book of the Duchess* shows. The last item of this courtly education by living was instruction in military exercises, given by the knight or gentleman in the Countess Elizabeth's household to whom this important duty was assigned. Chaucer is never cynical about fighting.

What was Chaucer's background for this courtier's life?

CHAUCER'S FAMILY

Chaucer came, like a number of other courtiers, from a well-to-do merchant family whose progress can be traced from modest beginnings in Ipswich, and whose increasing prosperity depended on being equally at home, in a modest way, in both Court and City.

Both Chaucer's father and grandfather were prosperous men, with varying amounts of property, whose principal income came from their connection with the wine trade. Apart from their own business as wholesale importers and wine merchants, they were both (like Chaucer himself) employed at various times in the collection of the king's customs. The family had property in Ipswich and had probably lived there, but before Chaucer was born his father had moved to London. He was drawn, doubtless, by that city's increasing importance as a financial and business centre, and by its nearness to the king's court and administrative offices.

About the poet's grandfather, Robert, little is known. He owned property in Ipswich and was a vintner. In 1308 and 1310, he was deputy to the king's chief butler (an important official, who was sometimes a man of considerable wealth). Part of the butler's duties was the collection of taxes on imported wines, and this was Robert Chaucer's department. His wife Mary came from the prosperous Ipswich family of the Westhales, and when he married her she was already a widow, presumably with property.

Robert and Mary Chaucer had a son, John Chaucer (who became the poet's father), born in 1313. He inherited his father's Ipswich property and carried on the family business as a vintner. A curious sidelight is thrown on the fourteenth century by an incident in his childhood, when at 11 years of age his aunt (Robert Chaucer's sister), and others, abducted him with the intention of marrying him to her daughter Joan, thereby joining his Ipswich property to hers. This was no unusual event at the time, but fortunately for us she and her accomplices were prevented. They were then sued at law. Her principal accomplice was very heavily fined. Having escaped this early marriage, John Chaucer is next seen at the age of 25, as a member of the great and splendid retinue which the king took to the Continent in 1338, though we do not know in what capacity John Chaucer travelled. Probably around this time he married a widow, Agnes Northwell, who also owned property. John Chaucer prospered. He became one of the main vintners in the City of London; for two years he, like his father, was deputy to the king's chief butler in the collection of duty on wines, and he was also deputy to the same person in April 1347 in the collection of export duties on woollen cloths. By this time he was an important figure in the general affairs of the City. To this wealthy wine merchant, man of affairs, connected with the court, Geoffrey Chaucer was born; perhaps in his father's house in Thames Street, about 1340, to judge from his own remarks about his age made in the Scrope-Grosvenor trial in 1386.

THE CITY OF LONDON

London was Geoffrey Chaucer's earliest experience. It was unique among English cities, being the centre of commercial power, with a special relationship to the king. It was that square mile on the north bank of the Thames, still called in English *the* City, and thus near the main seat of the royal power, which was the city of Westminster, further along the river. London was the biggest of English cities with a population of about 45 000. (Estimates for other towns are: York, about 11 000; Bristol, about 10 000; Plymouth and Coventry, about 7000; no other town is thought to have had above 6000; by contrast, contemporary Florence, one of the biggest cities in Europe, had about 90 000.) London also had substantial suburbs south of the Thames, especially at Southwark, by London Bridge. From Southwark, just over the river, the Dover Road, and the Pilgrims' Way to Canterbury began. In Southwark was the Tabard Inn, at which Chaucer's pilgrims gathered, and the church (now the Cathedral) where the effigy of the poet John Gower, a friend of Chaucer, can still be seen. North of the river, the road which is still called the Strand (or Bankside) ran between London and the palace of Westminster, passing the law courts, and then the large town houses owned by rich merchants and nobles, including the Savoy, John of Gaunt's palace already mentioned. To get to Westminster from the City you could go along the Strand from London, but the Exchequer and Privy Seal clerks, like Chaucer's younger friend and poetic follower Hoccleve, who worked at Westminster and usually lodged in London, often preferred, like many others, to go by water, especially in winter when the roads were so muddy.

The River Thames was a fine highway, though the famous bridge, with houses on it (like the Ponte Vecchio still to be seen in Florence) was a dangerous hazard with its great supports which caused a six-foot drop in the water level when the tide was running strong. It also bore grim reminders of the rough punishments of the times, with its rotting heads of offenders stuck upon spikes. Within the city many houses had their gardens, often with vegetable plots and fruit trees. Since the houses were mostly of no more than two storeys it must have been easy to see the blossom in spring, and church towers everywhere, with over all the Gothic spire of Old St Paul's, destroyed in the seventeenth-century Great Fire of London. There were big markets, and masses of shops, all governed by complex laws. There was a sewage-system, advanced for the times, a number of public latrines, and despite arrangements for street-cleaning, much filth in the streets, with pigs rooting about in the rubbish, and streams that were open sewers. It must have smelt like a farmyard in summer. We cannot estimate the city by our own standards of comfort and cleanliness; the great medieval European cities, of which London was a small example, were a remarkable achievement, with all their faults, in the art of living, won against heavy odds: of physical difficulty in an age without machines; of administrative difficulty in an age when communication was slow and limited; of disciplinary difficulty in an age when men were often as violent, unruly and unstable as children; and of the sheer difficulty of survival in an age of primitive medical science, ignorant of microbes. The fourteenth century saw the growth of some great cities such as Hamburg, Paris, Florence, on the Continent. London, alone of all English cities in the fourteenth century, achieved something of their quality.

In the great cities of Europe in the fourteenth century a new urban consciousness was developing, of which we are the direct heirs. Many of the things we now take for granted in cities and towns, like the common services of street-cleaning and sewerage, and complex matters of shopping regulations, uniformity of measures and proper time-keeping, were being established. They relied on a greater communal sense, a certain amount of democratic self-government, and created more privacy, less domination of the collective over the individual. Out of them emerged the most powerful social structures the world has devised, of bourgeois liberal democracy, the ultimately triumphant foe of tyranny and hierarchy. In the fourteenth century, however, this was far in the future, though the seeds were sown. Despite social mobility like that of Chaucer's family, authority, hierarchy, inherited inequality were the norm. Chaucer's questing spirit was to some extent the result of tensions between ancient and modern. For things were changing.

There were many other influences encouraging the privacy of the individual. Many came from religion, and the education in literacy that the Church gave, and some came from the court, especially in the sentiment of love, 'derne' (secret) love, as the poets called it. But the sense of privacy and individuality in Chaucer must be considerably due to his rich bourgeois background. The city was the place of trade, of specialised work, of regular time, and a serious concern for this world. We shall see that Chaucer became a kind of accountant, and with this urban numeracy we can associate what eventually became his strong sense of regular metre, and his unusual sensitivity to the passage of time in his poetry. Chaucer's secular humanism and realism, which were not at all anti-religious (for the cities were very pious in their worldliness) must be related in a general way to that strand in his make-up represented by his City background, as were his rationalism, his individualism and his self-awareness. All these aspects will be summed up in that great original work of a series of portraits, *The General Prologue* to *The Canterbury Tales*. Worldliness, work, social experience, a concentration on the rich centre of society (the middle classes), privacy, a loosening of feudal personal bonds, and at the end a certain loneliness; these are the gifts of the city. There must also have been an emphasis on vernacular English, to be discussed later.

The gifts of the city must be seen in context, especially in the case of Chaucer. The countryside with its alternating seasons of harshness and joy was never far away. There was a certain social mobility among all classes, much of it prompted by the presence of cities and towns, leading to a general mingling of country, city and court. It was becoming possible for peasants to enrich themselves and to rise in society, even apart from the Church which had for long offered the only chance of escape from the ignorant, sweated poverty which was the lot of the peasantry. Even a knight might have a serf as ancestor, while at the end of the century John Greyndor, a yeoman from the Forest of Dean, rose by his capacity as a ruthless captain (he beheaded 300 captives after a battle with the Welsh in 1405) to become Member of Parliament, sheriff of Glamorgan and of Gloucester, and constable of four border castles. In later life he turned merchant of Bristol (and was in fact guilty of something like piracy), and this is yet another example of the way in which, among the upper classes in England, trade and the professions (including that of war), merchants and the nobility, found it easy to mix. When Gaunt, the greatest noble in England (and about this time the most hated), was pursued by the mob in 1381, he was having dinner with a great merchant, Sir John Ypres. Sir John Montague, later Earl of Salisbury, was the third husband of a rich mercer's daughter. Nicholas Brembre, the grocer, was rich enough to make loans to Richard II and John of Gaunt. He was knighted for his bold behaviour during the Revolt, and was closely associated with the ruling court faction which was displaced by the barons in 1388. He paid for his social mobility and his financial and political power by being executed for political reasons.

The older upper classes often resisted the new tendency to move from class to class, and Parliament in 1363 passed a 'sumptuary' law, regulating the food and clothing that each class should have. Naturally, it was not obeyed. A chronicler complains that yeomen dress like squires, squires like knights, knights like dukes, and dukes like kings. Chaucer, in his description of those social climbers *par excellence*, the city merchants, or gildsmen, describes them, no doubt deliberately, as wearing clothing above their station.

All this shows that along with much unease (there were often riots in London), and much oppression, English society by the second half of the century was reasonably well mixed and united, if not harmonious. The legal distinction between a crime committed by an Englishman, and one committed by a Norman, introduced by William the Conqueror for holding down a defeated English nation with a small Norman–French force, had long been out of date when it was abolished by Parliament in 1340. Of this sense of unity London was a signal example. That did not mean that it was not often in conflict with the Court. But neither Court nor City could do without each other.

Though Chaucer's origins were 'bourgeois', city-man as he was, he remained also a 'court-man'. There is no need to think of him as an embarrassed 'middle-class' person in a servile position in an 'aristocratic' court. Court and City had many levels, many mansions; Chaucer was at home in all.

Chapter 2

Chaucer's Education

There is first-class evidence that Chaucer went to school – his poetry. It is full of school-learning, like the passage from the Latin author Claudian, used as a school-text, in *The Parliament of Fowls*, 99–105, and dozens of others, including school jokes, like the reference to 'dulcarnoun' put in Criseyde's mouth, with Pandarus's tart reply (*Troilus and Criseyde*, III, 930–5). Chaucer's references in *The Prioress's Tale* to the 'song-school', that is, the primary school for choirboys attached to a cathedral, suggest personal knowledge. Chaucer's own knowledge of Latin is likely to have been acquired at a grammar school.

There were at least three schools in London at the time: St Paul's (a grammar school, with an almonry or song-school as a semi-independent attachment), the Arches (at St Mary le Bow), and St Martin's le Grand. St Paul's was nearest Chaucer's father's house in Lower Thames Street, and he may well have gone there. The hours were long, and the holidays none except the festivals of the Church, which would, however, have amounted to at least one day a week, apart from Sundays.

LATIN

The instruction at such a school may be summed up in one word: Latin. Latin was the language of the Church, and of much of the country's administration (which was largely run by clerics). It was the language of the Holy Bible; it was the language of philosophy, and of science; and in it was also the most impressive single body of literature known to the Middle Ages, the Classics of Antiquity. First, however, at the most elementary level of teaching (which they were supposed to have passed through before they came to a grammar school), children were taught to read in English the Ave Maria ('Hail Mary', which is the beginning of the Annunciation of the birth of Christ to the Virgin Mary, Luke I, 28, used as a prayer); the Lord's

Prayer; and the Creed (the essentials of belief), with a few psalms. Such might be learned from a primer which would contain first the alphabet in large and small letters, then the exorcism, and the Lord's Prayer, followed by the Ave Maria, the Creed, the Ten Commandments, and the Seven Deadly Sins. The child thus learned to read Latin, often without being able to understand it – like the little boy in *The Prioress's Tale*, who had just started at such a school.

Chaucer would have learned his 'grammar' at the grammar school. Grammar meant something more than it does today. Not only did it signify grammar in the modern sense of 'the structure of the language', but also, when this was acquired, much information of various kinds. The most common way of starting the actual Latin grammar was for the master to dictate it, and the children to write it down and learn it off by heart. There were versified Latin grammars to help this. This method of learning and of acquiring books was in use even in the university. The extreme shortage of books in the fourteenth century has always to be remembered. Memory had to play a far larger part in all schooling and all scholarship than it does now. Professor Mary Carruthers has shown how fundamental to attitudes of mind towards many things, and how systematic, were methods of memorising. They went far beyond mere rote-learning, though some of that was basic. There were systems for storing and retrieving knowledge in the mind as it might be in a computer – but the brain was more active than a computer on its own. Memory even in modern times is essential to intellectual power. How much more so when physical aids to memory, such as paper and writing implements, were scarce and expensive. Memory was therefore rated very highly. The 'creative imagination', which we rate so highly (and is based on memory), was much less valued. Originality was therefore less valued. Yet a writer with a richly stored memory, like Chaucer, had vast resources for creativity. Chaucer's works in particular reveal an astounding memory for what he had read.[1]

As soon as children had acquired some knowledge of Latin an attempt was made in some schools to enforce Latin speaking at all times. Some of the better pupils at any rate acquired some fluency in speaking Latin. Some simple textbooks, such as Aesop's *Fables*, were read after the elements of grammar, and then some classical authors, especially parts of Virgil and Ovid. No classical authors were read thoroughly. Aside from Virgil, who was considered to be almost a Christian, they were often looked upon with suspicion by some and Christian authors were often preferred. The extremely pious nature of the educational system is one of its most notable characteristics.

This is noticeable in some Rules for Conduct for the boys of Westminster School, which, although written in the thirteenth century, probably applied in the fourteenth, and were similar to those in other schools:

> In the morning let the boys upon rising sign themselves with the holy cross, and let each one say the creed, namely, I believe in God, etc., and the Lord's prayer three times, and the salutation to the Blessed Virgin five times, without shouting and confusion; and if anyone neglects these good things, let him be punished.[2]

By such repetition piety, though almost automatic, and not necessarily affecting actual behaviour in other spheres, becomes ingrained, a second nature.

If Chaucer went to the song-school attached to the grammar school at St Paul's he remembered it in the early parts of *The Prioress's Tale*, where the little boy of seven attends a song-school. The realism and precision of detail, though so brief, are entirely convincing. At St Paul's there were books of exactly the kind that Chaucer's poetry shows him to have read, as we know from a rare piece of documentary evidence, in a will. About the middle of the century the song-school of St Paul's had an unusual schoolmaster, William Ravenstone, who had a large collection of books in Latin. Although he was a chaplain, he seems to have had very few theological books, but a great many other books of various interest, including some practical teaching books and a large number of Latin classics. When he died he left these books to the school, to the number of 84, a chest to keep them in, and provision for an annual gift of money to the boys. There are some 76 000 wills surviving from the fourteenth and fifteenth centuries in England. Of these Miss Deanesly examined 7568 and found only 388 which bequeath books; yet this was a period when books were valuable and so likely to be mentioned in wills. The wills containing books are far fewer in the fourteenth than in the fifteenth century, and usually only one or two books are mentioned in each will. So Ravenstone's 84 are really outstanding. Furthermore, it was extremely difficult to get the use of a library. Most of those that existed were in monasteries, were mainly devotional and theological, and restricted to the use of monks. On the other hand, Chaucer himself from an early period shows a quite unusual knowledge of the classics, while his parents' house was not far from the song-school of St Paul's. So it is possible that Chaucer got his unusual knowledge from Ravenstone's collection, and that the learned and kindly Ravenstone may have been Chaucer's own teacher, either at the song-school, or retained as a private tutor by Chaucer's father. It is an encouraging thought to all teachers.

Chaucer is exceptional as an English poet in his range of learning. He must have learned Latin quite well, and it made him free of a world of great intellectual riches, from poetry to philosophy, via a good deal of humdrum instruction and much moralising. Latin opened up to him the world of science, especially astronomy, in which he became so much interested. Even so, Latin is a hard language, and Chaucer never disdained a French crib when he could find one, as for example in translating Boethius's *Consolation of Philosophy*, which is a difficult text.

FRENCH

Someone must have taught Chaucer French quite formally. There were already phrase books and word lists that would have helped. The reason for supposing this is that Chaucer, as we can judge from his own work, could read Central, Continental French, the French of Paris, very well, for he shows intimate knowledge of *Le Roman de la Rose*, and Machaut's poems. He could also read, if he wanted to, many works written in Anglo-Norman, or Anglo-French, which was the language which had developed from the French conquerors of England, and was now a distinct but dying dialect, of a decidedly provincial kind. Chaucer rarely shows interest in Anglo-Norman though the main source of *The Man of Law's Tale* is in that language. In *The General Prologue* Chaucer gently sneers at the socially pre-tentious Prioress who speaks the French of 'Stratford-atte-Bowe', a village near London, virtually a suburb. She did not know, says Chaucer, the French of Paris. Since he obviously did, he did not speak French at home, for that would have been Anglo-Norman. Therefore, he spoke English at home and was taught the 'proper' French of the Continental French poets whom he enjoyed so much.

ITALIAN

There would have been no formal teaching of Italian at school and though there was considerable intercourse with the group of Italian city-states that make up what is now modern Italy, there do not seem to have been many English speakers of Italian and there was hardly any knowledge of Italian literature in fourteenth-century Eng-land. Yet Italy (as we may call the states for short) was the leader of European culture in the fourteenth century, as will be mentioned below. That Chaucer was in later life sent on special Italian visits may indicate that he already knew some Italian. If so he would have learned through acquaintances of his father, who as a merchant could have had dealings with the group of Italian merchants in Southampton and also in London. Italian bankers were important in London. Lombard Street is named after them.

Whether Chaucer learned Italian as a boy or later cannot be known. A speaking knowledge could have been picked up in London. The first evidence in his poetry of a knowledge of Italian literature comes in *The House of Fame* written some time in the 1370s, that is, when Chaucer was in his thirties. It took him time to digest Italian poetry, notably that by Boccaccio and Dante, but he came to know it well. Opinions differ as to whether he ever read Boccaccio's famous collection of 100 short stories, *Il Decamerone*. They are based on European-wide folktale plots, though told with incomparable laconic wit and elegance. Chaucer used some of the same plots, but in my opinion the balance of probability is that he did not know Boccaccio's collection. At all events, knowledge of Italian was a rare accomplishment for an Englishman in Chaucer's day, and knowledge of Italian poetry, though commonplace in the more advanced culture of Italy, was virtually non-existent in England. Chaucer's genius shows up not least in his recognition of the greatness of Dante, in his use of some of Boccaccio's work, and his knowledge, though limited, of Petrarch's greatness. This knowledge immensely extended his range and ability.

ARITHMETIC AND NUMEROLOGY

Besides his literary training somebody at some time taught Chaucer arithmetic. Chaucer was unusual in his command of what was already developing as 'the two cultures', one scientific, the other in the Humanities. A little bit of arithmetic might have been learned at school, but he may have had to have private lessons. Only in Italy in the middle of the fourteenth century was there large-scale serious teaching of arithmetic, given in many schools which specialised in secular training for business. Religious people normally distrusted arithmetic, no doubt because it seemed too worldly, too abstract, and morally neutral.

The teaching of arithmetic was gaining ground in England. Merchants needed it, and towards the end of the fourteenth century a teacher of arithmetic appears in Oxford. Maybe there was one earlier in the century in London who is not recorded. London, the business centre of the kingdom, would be a natural place for a teacher of the commercial skill of arithmetic. Or perhaps Chaucer's own father taught him, for as a prosperous business man he would both need and be able to carry out arithmetical calculation. He must have set a value on it. Knowledge of arithmetic did not in Chaucer's case lead to trade but to astronomy. When he himself was 50 he started to write a textbook on the astronomical instrument, the astrolabe, for 'little Lewis, my son', who he tells us is ten years old. Perhaps he himself at a similarly tender age had been taught by a similarly enthusiastic father. Knowledge of arithmetic was still relatively rare in the fourteenth century but it was developing and it changed men's mentalities more than we may realise. It was part of the modern, measurable, impersonal world, promoting habits of accuracy and attention to detail. These habits when transferred to literature lead to the precision, literalism, 'realism', and moral neutrality or relativism which are such notable characteristics, though not the only ones, of Chaucer's later writing.

Arithmetic was then new. It contrasted with the archaic use of numbers now called numerology (and ancient as it is, still to be noticed in some modern habits and superstitions). The essence of numerology lies in the use of numbers in symbolic patterns, thus satisfying an aesthetic sense we have now largely lost and signifying further meanings. It was used not only in some literature but in, for example, sacred buildings like Chartres Cathedral or the late twelfth-century Baptistery at Parma. Such numbers were used not for practical reasons (such as stress, load–bearing) but religious meaning. Many people still feel, in less serious mood, that the numbers three and seven, for example, have some 'magic', that 13 is unlucky, etc. The underlying psychology is the same.

Numerology would not have been taught at school, except perhaps incidentally as a part of 'grammar', but Chaucer could have come across it in examples of Latin poetry, and could also have picked up some knowledge of it from an enthusiastic teacher.

The great and most obviously accessible source of number-symbolism which Chaucer could not have avoided is in the Bible. Biblical writing is not in itself organised in numerological patterns, but it makes considerable use, in some parts, of symbolic numbers. One that used to be well-known is the number, 153, of the miraculous draught of fishes recorded in one of the Resurrection appearances of Jesus in John XXI, where it is said that the net did not break. This number is the sum of its component digits ($1 + 2 + 3$ etc. up to 17), which is also a significant number as $10 + 7$ was regarded as the sign of perfection and completion. The passage received various allegorical interpretations including the completeness of death (Shippey 1996). The last book of the Bible, *The Revelation of Saint John the Divine*, is full of allegorically significant numbers, usually neglected by modern commentators but not by medieval men. Twelve is a significant number (2 × 2 × 3) (hence probably the number of disciples, most of whom are shadowy figures). So is 11, because of Judas's betrayal, and hence the sign of death. While a number of medieval Latin poems are based on number patterns, the only certain medieval English example is the poem *Pearl*, by the *Gawain*-Poet, based on the number 12.

It has been argued that there are at least traces of number symbolism in *The Book of the Duchess* and *The Parliament of Fowls*. It may be that Chaucer in his younger years had not fully emancipated himself from numerology. In his later years he seems to have dabbled occasionally in the not dissimilar astrological symbolism, if any of J. D. North's arguments are correct, but even if he did so he seems to have tired of them and not carried them through. Perhaps an empirical, arithmetical bent of mind made him in the end impatient of them, though he was always willing to experiment first.

BOOKS AND SPEECH

The dual nature of education based both on books (literacy) and speech (orality) has already been noticed. The relation between the two crops up constantly in the enjoyment and understanding of Chaucer's poetry and need be only briefly touched on here. Speech depends on personal relationships and situations, from between two persons to groups listening (say) to a poem, to speeches given to a crowd. This situational character of orality allows much more to be conveyed than the bare words. Knowledge of the speaker, of the reason for that meeting, tone, gesture, immediate response, and also the need for repetition, hyperbole, traditional expression (so as not to puzzle the hearers) all make orality warm, immediate, personal and evanescent. The context is all important, and the context disappears with the occasion.

By contrast books are more solitary. They can be read aloud to a group, as Chaucer describes in *Troilus*, II, 78–112, but even so there is less spontaneity and immediacy. A book can be read in quiet and solitude, with reader and writer unknown to each other. In this case the context has to be built into the text, so to speak. The reader cannot rely on the impulsion of an actual speaker and reference to a particular occasion without that being suggested in some way in the words themselves. It must be remembered that all books up to Chaucer's time and a 100 years later in England were manuscripts, not printed. Writing is in a way divided between orality and the full literacy of print. No two copies of a text in manuscript are absolutely identical. Handwriting varies. The process of writing is laborious, so books were scarce, though we must not exaggerate this, for there were hundreds of thousands of manuscripts of all shapes and sizes around in the fourteenth century, copies of copies of copies.

Yet books were relatively scarce because they were so toilsome to produce. Paper was slowly coming into use, but the skin of sheep or calf was still the usual material of books. The supply was short and the preparation elaborate. Ink and pens were not easily to be bought: the ink had to be made up, and the quill pens cut from a goose's feather. Scribes sometimes complain about the quality of the pen, or the paper, or the cold of the cloister, in the margins of the books. Serious literature was still almost entirely in Latin, sometimes contained in huge tomes which included many separate items. One book might constitute almost a small library. Other books were small; all were without title-pages. Each item was written in folded sheets, like a pamphlet, which were then bound together to form the book. Sometimes discoloured sheets inside a book show that one of the pamphlets which make it up was left for a long time before being bound up with others, and its outer page had become dirty.

Scribes wrote on sloping desks, with a stick in one hand to hold the page steady without smudging it, and pen in the other. Much writing was still done in the monasteries, but stationers are recorded in England from the beginning of the century, and by the middle of the century there may have been a commercial bookshop in London, perhaps the only one in England, though Florence had several. The London shop could have employed as many as half a dozen scribes, who busily copied out various items which were then bound together. Professional scriveners, who copied out books for people, are recorded from the middle of the century, and probably existed before. They often made mistakes, and some scribes may have left mistakes uncorrected, because a correction spoiled the look of the page. For this reason a beautiful manuscript may be less reliable in its text than a manuscript untidily written out by a careful amateur. One is bound to make mistakes when copying out by hand. None of Chaucer's own manuscripts survives, but those of his Italian contemporary, Boccaccio, are still preserved, and he made plenty of mistakes when copying out his own poetry.

Sometimes parts of Chaucer's poems, for example, were copied from different manuscripts, of varying reliability, which makes texts even more complicated when you have copies of copies. All manuscripts are different, and vary from the original copy, though some less so than others. English spelling varied wildly. Punctuation was erratic or non-existent. That is why the reconstruction of Chaucer's or Langland's text is a highly technical and laborious job, when, as in the case of *Piers Plowman* or *The Canterbury Tales*, more than 80 manuscripts or fragmentary manuscripts have to be taken into account and compared. Recognition of the 'slipperiness' of texts is vital and affects our judgement.

Most manuscripts, like most books today, had little adornment, and were much less beautiful than most books are today. In the fourteenth century the style of handwriting is what has come to be called Gothic script, which was imitated in type when printing was introduced (the so-called 'blackletter'), and which continued in some books until the seventeenth century in England and the twentieth in Germany. It is markedly mannered and different from modern script and print, and can be very beautiful in its elaborate way. Books were very expensive when professionally produced. The cheapest, of only a few leaves, cost about a shilling (five new pence), which today must be multiplied 300 or 400 times at least to find its equivalent. Few good books cost less than ten shillings then, and standard works of philosophy etc., of the kind of which Chaucer's Clerk had 20 by his bed, cost two to three pounds. No wonder his overcoat was threadbare. The book which the Wife of Bath threw into the fire, because her young husband read to her stories unfavourable to women from it, must have cost one to two pounds. Splendidly decorated books cost a very great deal more, since they might mean the employment of several skilled men for several years, although naturally in all these cases the costs varied greatly with the books and the conditions of sale.

Being without information on preliminary pages, and often very miscellaneous in content, books were often anonymous unless by very famous, usually religious authors. There was no copyright. It is virtually certain that even with Boccaccio, so famous and prolific an author, in so literate a society as that of Italy, so many of his works circulated in anonymous manuscripts that Chaucer, his slightly younger contemporary, and a visitor to Italy, did not know his name. Books had authority, power and mystery. They were difficult to master.

Many important books in Latin had the text written in the centre of the page surrounded by commentary and annotation, known as the 'glose' or 'Gloss'. This was particularly true of the Bible, whose text accumulated so much commentary that it took on as it were a life of its own, and in its dominant form came to be known as the *Glossa Ordinaria*, the 'Ordinary Gloss'. Chaucer uses the word 'glose' (= gloss) quite neutrally to mean 'commentary' in *The Book of the Duchess* and his translation of Boethius's *Consolation of Philosophy*, of about 1385. Thereafter he uses the word sarcastically, for commentaries had become in some cases so extravagant that the very verb 'to glose' came to mean 'flatter' or 'deceive'. Hence Chaucer says he will declare 'the naked text' (*Prologue* to *The Legend of Good Women*, G. 86) of his stories, and this apparent preference well accords with his literalism and modernism. He has little taste for allegory. Medieval texts in English, particularly stories, by whomever they are written, are without a glose. The manuscripts of Chaucer's poems, from first to last, have very little in the way even of reference to certain Latin texts, and there are no interpretations, allegorical or otherwise, to accompany them. This perhaps represents the less grand status of the vernacular, though by the last quarter of the fourteenth century there was much serious writing in English, notably the Wycliffite Bible, and much other devotional and scientific matter in English. English had become again a significant literary language and a brief look at its position and history is necessary.

THE ENGLISH LANGUAGE

The status of English was both 'natural', a mother-tongue, spoken by almost everybody, and inferior. No one taught Chaucer English. Grammar books in and about English were not written until the seventeenth century. The deficiency was less felt because literate people had to learn some Latin grammar, in order to acquire the language of learning, and though the grammar of Latin with its word-endings and different sentence structure is not entirely well suited to English, the two languages have a basic relationship. The not entirely adequate terms and concepts of 'noun', 'adjective', 'verb', 'preposition', and 'subject' and 'object', etc. are still more useful for most purposes than the many substitutes suggested in recent times. It is valuable to have a language with which to describe language, i.e. to have a knowledge of grammar and a dictionary. In the absence of a native grammar and dictionary in the fourteenth century the exercise of translation into Latin was a very useful substitute.

Of course we do not learn our own native language through grammar books and dictionaries, helpful as they may be at a later stage. Chaucer's poetry shows him to have been a native speaker of English, and no doubt his parents and grandparents were too. He would have learned his first prayers in English before turning to Latin. Though not part of his formal schooling he would also have heard plenty of songs and stories in his mother tongue. It was on these that his own later songs and stories were based, though with so much greater richness from his breadth of formal knowledge and of foreign languages.

Up to the end of the thirteenth century, the first language of the aristocracy in many parts of the country was often French, or rather, Anglo-Norman, the variant of French that had developed in England among the upper classes. The reason for this was the Norman Conquest (1066). But the conquerors, though they took over the higher levels of administration and displaced some of the English gentry stock, were relatively few in number, and the defeated English were always a majority. Most people even of the upper classes spoke English, though much influenced by Anglo-Norman vocabulary.

English has always been the language of the English. The French that was imposed by the Conquest had greater social prestige, and was used for law and administration, but it never displaced English as the general spoken vernacular. The question was not, except for the very highest nobility, did a man speak English, but did he speak French as well, or Latin? Many learned men were versed in all three, like Chaucer himself, and his friend Gower, without displacing English as the cradle-tongue of the majority.

Chaucer was presumably of long-established English stock. The surname 'Chaucer' (variously spelt 'Chaucers', 'Chaucier', 'Chaucy', etc.) is indeed French and probably means 'shoemaker', suggesting the level of skilled craftsmen from which the family arose. A great-grandfather was Andrew de Dinnington (the name of an English village from which he must have come), who was sometimes known as Andrew le Taverner, 'Andrew-who-keeps-a-pub', who lived in Ipswich. His son Robert acquired the surname 'le Chaucer'. It was a skilled trade, and Robert must have done well from it, but the name had nothing to do with Robert's own family origins, which could have been both humble and totally English from before the Conquest.

In a curious way the recovery of the English language from the heavy blow struck against it by the Conquest is paralleled by the rise of the Chaucer family, as far as we can see it, even to the extent of acquiring a glossy French surname.

As a result of the Conquest, French became by the thirteenth century in England the language of high culture, law and administration, and English lost prestige. It was therefore less used for educated purposes. It had lost the standard spelling which had been evolved in late Anglo-Saxon times. It became written more phonetically, according to local dialects. Spelling varied confusingly. The powerful general and abstract words in native English, requiring education to acquire, needing to be used at the higher levels of culture, slowly fell into disuse. For such English words, French words were usually substituted. Thus the English word for 'peace' was *grith*, but *peace* was one of the earliest French borrowings. There are many hundreds of examples. On the other hand, those down-to-earth words by which we live, eat bread and drink beer, make love, sleep, dream, wake and so forth, are all native English. Chaucer's forefathers and he himself, spoke them, to the language born.

Chaucer's English had changed from its Old English form. It had lost most of the endings of words except those which show the difference between singular and plural. Instead of endings such prepositions as *of, to, for,* etc. (though these are English too) came to be used to indicate the meaning of the words and the part they played in the sentence. These endings partly remained in Chaucer's time, but were mostly reduced to an obscure vowel-sound indicated by the letter -*e*. Thus word-order became much more important for establishing meaning. But the ending -*e* often retains meaning in Chaucer's English, for example as the plural of an adjective, and when historically justified (not just added by a scribe) needs to be pronounced for the verse to have the rhythm intended by Chaucer. Most of the vowels remained 'pure', that is, single sounds, not, as so often in modern English, diphthongs, that is, double sounds. So 'time' was pronounced not as now, where the *i* represents a diphthong *ah-ee*, but *teem*. Chaucer's English was more beautiful in this respect, and more like modern Italian, French, German, etc., than modern English. Almost all the consonants that were written were pronounced, as for example the *k* in *knight*, or *g* in *gnaw*. The English used by Chaucer is called for scholarly purposes Middle English, to indicate its period. Modern English begins around 1500.

Although these changes in large part came from a lowering of status, a defeat and a deprivation, they can be seen more positively. The basis of the English language remained essentially unaffected. In common with the other European languages it developed a direct word-order based on the sequence subject + verb + object. It absorbed from French and Latin a new vocabulary. It became in general adaptive and flexible and throughout the fourteenth century rose, like the Chaucer family and many other English families, especially in towns, in social status, and in power to deal with varied subject-matter. Its vocabulary was more mixed than either the modern Germanic languages or the modern Romance (i.e. the Roman, i.e. Latin-derived languages). This had some disadvantages, for example a rather arbitrary spelling, which made learning more difficult. There was a division in origins of vocabulary which may have promoted class-division; yet it also opened up many linguistic possibilities, and a vast range of meanings which Chaucer and in his time Shakespeare were able to exploit to remarkable effect, and has continued to make English diction extraordinarily rich and adaptable.

The development of the vocabulary of English and some of the word-order, from Old English to Chaucer's day, can be summed up in one line by Chaucer from *Troilus and Criseyde*, when Criseyde says to Troilus:

Welcome, my knyght, my pees, my suffisaunce.

(III, 1309)

Welcome my knyght are all native English words, warm and concrete, though *knight* has developed in meaning to take on all the rich significance of chivalry. *Peace*, more general, was, as already noted, one of the earliest French words to be borrowed and is first recorded in English in the mid-twelfth century. *Suffisaunce* is more abstract, learned and rare. It means what we now call *sufficiency*. It combines a physical with almost spiritual senses. Chaucer is the first to be recorded using it, and he seems to have been fond of it, using it for a jest as well as perfectly seriously here and elsewhere.

TO MAKE HIS ENGLISH SWEET UPON HIS TONGUE

This subheading is a little unfair to Chaucer in that it is part of his sardonic description of the smooth, highly educated, unscrupulous Friar in *The General Prologue*, who lisped to make his speech attractive, especially to the young and well-to-do (*CT*, I, 265). The Friar is described particularly in terms of his speech and manner, and perhaps Chaucer a little resembled him in his self-ingratiating manner and 'fair language' – an unconscious partial self-portrait. Chaucer gave much thought to making his language pleasing and fair, and registered the difficulty of writing verse in English to rhyme as fluently as in French, 'Syth rym in English hath such skarsetee'

(*Complaint of Venus*, 80) – though as we might expect Chaucer's rhyming is extraordinarily skilful. The Germanic languages, such as Old English, have fewer endings that rhyme than are found in the Romance languages descended from Latin, especially French and Italian.

The Norman Conquest, the consequent loss of a written standard for English, with scribes representing more or less their own dialects, with different conventions, led to a great variety of spelling in English reflecting different dialects and scribal habits, so that even by Chaucer's time, when the dialect of the South East Midlands as found in London had begun to dominate, there was still much difference. Chaucer was acutely aware of the problem and at the end of *Troilus* he writes with obvious sincerity and no irony about the problems of the varieties of English and English spelling:

> And for ther is so gret diversite
> In English and in writyng of our tonge
> So prey I God that non myswrite the,
> Ne the mysmetre for defaute of tonge:
> And red wherso thow be, or elles songe
> That thow be understonde, God I biseche.
>
> (V, 1793–8)

Three problems are addressed here. One is that of variety (diversity) in itself; the second is the unreliability of scribes. No one can copy out a long piece in writing (or typing or wordprocessing or printing) without making mistakes. A laborious process of correction is necessary. Standards of scrupulous revision for accuracy are extremely hard to attain, and in writing are very messy. Moreover in a society still moving between orality and literacy the need for precision in repetition is both harder to obtain and less desired. Only with print do we get the possibility of absolute accuracy in repetition, and even that took centuries – printed copies of the same edition of books by Caxton vary. Chaucer wrote an exasperated little poem to his scribe, Adam, cursing him for his inaccuracy in copying *Troilus* and *Boece*, thereby causing Chaucer to have to scrape the parchment, a laborious process, in order to rewrite correctly.

The third problem Chaucer addresses in the stanza quoted is that of metre: a complicated subject with an interesting history, for which some historical knowledge is necessary. The basis of English is the Germanic, that is, the northern European languages, which are heavily stressed. Old English verse, the extreme example, is composed of lines of four stresses, each of one long syllable, plus two light stresses in each half-line, separated by a brief pause (caesura). The light stresses are made up by unstressed syllables between each stressed syllable. This movement is still natural to native English speakers and is a sort of undercurrent throughout English verse until regular rhythms were largely abandoned after the middle of the twentieth century. Many of Shakespeare's or even Milton's ostensibly five-stress, ten-syllable lines can be scanned in the old way. So of course can Chaucer's, and in Chaucer's own time his great contemporaries Langland and the *Gawain*-poet, as well as many other poets in the north and west of England, wrote in this type of stressed verse. It has the added decoration of alliteration, beginning each of the first three stressed syllables with the same sound, usually the same letter.[3]

Chaucer knew this style and distantly imitates it in a couple of battle pieces, which shows the associations it had for him as a 'Southern man', not a northerner, as the Parson remarks (*CT*, X, 42–3), though the Parson holds rhyme to be little better than the alliterative 'rum, ram, ruf'. The Parson's disapproval of all verse was by no means shared by all clerics, and least of all by Chaucer.

So Chaucer devoted most of his writing life to verse of a continental type derived first from earlier English romances and lyrics, then from French, and a little from Italian. He developed a rich poetic language ranging from ordinary everyday English to high and eloquent diction. Historically he was, or more correctly, we are, unlucky, in a sense, with his language. His Middle English is beautiful and interesting. But English has changed more radically in a thousand years than any other European vernacular. Chaucer would not have understood Old English, and modern English people find Middle English more difficult than, say, French people find their own language of the corresponding period to be. But let us not exaggerate our difficulties. Chaucer's English is still close to modern English; its differences are intrinsically interesting, and it is much easier for us to learn his language than it was for him to learn Latin or French, without proper dictionaries or grammar books.

THE END OF SCHOOLING AND THE DEVELOPMENT OF THE LITERATE LAYMAN

When a boy went to a grammar school, what was his aim, or his parents' aim for him? That the impassioned pursuit of knowledge for the sake of understanding was as strong then as now we are bound to believe, if only from Chaucer's portrait of the Clerk of Oxford. That is the noblest portrayal of that ideal anywhere in English literature, and wonderfully free from the embarrassment that tinges later attempts by English writers to describe the high calling of teaching and learning that any man might be proud to follow. It is not likely, however, that the pursuit of pure knowledge was any stronger then than now, and the general opinion was perhaps even less in favour of it. All learning, and especially Theology, the Queen of the Sciences, as it was called, was useful learning, to save souls, to administer the law, to cure the sick. And the three professions of the Church, law and medicine were the likely aim of anyone who entered a grammar school at least up to the time of Chaucer. Latin was the foundation of all three. The practitioners of all three professions were usually what it is now convenient to call clerics: that is to say, members of one or other of the official ranks of the Church, though not necessarily all priests.

The reason for this is that when Classical civilisation went under to the barbarians, in the fifth and sixth centuries AD, it was the Christian Church alone which preserved in the West what learning and civilisation there was. In the Dark Ages, with very few exceptions, only churchmen could read or write. The whole story of the European mind from the sixth to the sixteenth centuries may be summed up as the attempt, against appalling difficulties, to preserve, to rediscover, and to extend the almost lost civilisation of the classical world of Greece and Rome. The so-called Renaissance of the fifteenth and sixteenth centuries is really not a rebirth but the most triumphal stage of that process. In Italy, where continuity was strongest (and leaving out of consideration the Arab and Byzantine worlds, which for long preserved more than the West), there may always have been a few laymen who could read and write. But to the barbarian nations of the north of Europe, including the English, it was Christianity itself which brought knowledge of words along with the Word. And both were in Latin. A cleric (the word itself is Latin), or clerk, was a minister of the Church, and so inevitably, because Christianity is the religion of the Book, he was one who could read. And still, at the end of the fourteenth century, to be able to read was in itself regarded as evidence that a man belonged to the official ranks of the Church. This could be an important privilege, for if accused of a serious crime such a man might demand to be tried by canon law rather than by the law of the land, and canon law was often more lenient. If a man were convicted of murder, he would hang by the ordinary law. But if he could claim 'Benefit of Clergy' he received a lighter punishment. And he proved his 'clergy', which meant both his learning and his clerical status, by showing he could read Latin.

Thanks to the Church's own programme of teaching, mainly derived from the Lateran Council of 1215–16, this monopoly of literacy slowly changed and by the middle of the fourteenth century we note in England the coming into existence of literate laymen: men, not in religious orders, who could read both English and Latin, and who could probably write both at a pinch. The prime example of the new literacy is Chaucer himself. Another is Gower, who composed poetry in English, French and Latin. Henry IV knew Latin. None of these could or would claim to be in even minor clerical orders. Most of the knights and ladies of Richard's court could read English. Many of them, at least until right at the end of the century, could read and speak French, though doubtless with a provincial English accent.

It is impossible to know what was the purpose of Chaucer's schooling, whether it was received at school or, less likely, given by private tutor. Maybe his father, the prosperous merchant, proud of his quick, clever, book-learned son, designed for him a university career. On the whole that seems unlikely. The two English universities of Oxford and Cambridge had not then the social prestige they began to acquire in the sixteenth century. They were rather utilitarian in approach, in that they prepared men for the canon law, i.e. church law (not civil law in England), for medicine, and for the church. It is true that mathematics and science, particularly astronomy, were strong at Oxford in the beginning of the century, and in the second half of the century Oxford was riven by theological controversy, especially that initiated by Wycliffe, who inspired the Lollards. There was much here to attract Chaucer. He is notable for his interest in science and astronomy. His sympathies were drawn to the Lollards, as will be shown, and in later life he had a number of connections with Oxford. But the universities were primarily seminaries for priests and theologians. Chaucer was young, secular-minded, realistic, with an eager interest in love and life, inclined to mock fine-drawn theological argumentation ('I cannot bolt it to the bran,' that is, 'I can't be bothered to sort it out,' he says of theological controversy in *The Nun's Priest's Tale*). Though he was a genuine intellectual (or *because* he was a genuine intellectual), he cannot be imagined as ready to cloister himself in celibate abstract studies. He honoured them in the Clerk of Oxford, but they were not for him.

So what else could he do? He was no doubt quick at figures. Trade gave the impetus for the development of arithmetical skills, which were so important for later science, and indeed, in the background, for Chaucer's own poetry. But Chaucer was a boy too much interested in reading, in poetry, in history, and again, too much of an intellectual, to be a merchant like his father, though his later career drew him at times perilously close to such activities, as he was to complain.

Maybe there was something in him of Perkin Revelour, the charming, idle, lecherous, dancing, gambling apprentice of the unfinished *The Cook's Tale*; or at least something in him that sympathised with Perkin; but such sympathies would themselves lead him away from trade, not towards it. Perhaps it is symbolic that *The Cook's Tale* of Perkin is unfinished. For such a boy as we might imagine Chaucer to be, of rich parents, immensely talented, eager, intellectual, pleasure-loving, the only careers could be either at Court, or in the civil law, for the legal Inns of Court were a kind of secular university. He might even combine both, as some young courtiers did. Whatever Chaucer's father's ambitions were for his son, he must have done as other rich merchants did, and procured him a place as a page in as good a court as he could manage, which was pretty good, even if not the king's. Chaucer must have been about 16 when he went there, and must have felt joyously in his own element. What a glorious change from school.

NOTES

1. Mary Carruthers, *The Book of Memory: A Study of Memory in Medieval Culture* (Cambridge, 1990).
2. Quoted by E. Rickert, *Chaucer's World* (1948), 116–17.
3. For an elaborate analysis of the *Gawain*-poet's metre, and full reference to that of other poets, see Hoyt N. Duggan, 'Meter, Stanza, Vocabulary, Dialect' in *A Companion to the* Gawain-*poet*, edited by Derek Brewer and Jonathan Gibson (Cambridge, 1996), 217–38.

Chapter 3

The Courtly Life

The most glowing description of the world of the English courts comes from Jean Froissart, the man who, of all men, was most enamoured of the brilliance and romance of fourteenth-century chivalry. Unlike Chaucer, he was a professional man-of-letters, rewarded by gifts from patrons and by sinecures in the Church. But his career offers some interesting parallels to that of Chaucer, who must have known him, and who certainly copied his verse. Froissart's early days are even more obscure than Chaucer's. First, we note that in his poetry he makes three references to his age, and thereby gives us the choice of three different birth years – 1333, 1337, 1338. Froissart was a Fleming and, like Chaucer, seems to have been born to a wealthy middle-class family and to have early moved in courtly, aristocratic circles. He began Latin at 12, which was later perhaps than an English boy would have done. But, he says with un-Chaucerian complacence, he was more interested in the little girls, and in fighting the other boys, than in his lessons. In 1362 he came to England, to find as his patron his fellow-countrywoman, Edward's Queen Philippa, whose praises he so warmly tells wherever he finds occasion.

The young Froissart, enamoured of chivalry, was enraptured by the English court, then at the height of its glory. London was delightful, with a splendid and honourable court, a king feared by three kingdoms, with a noble queen, whom Froissart served with beautiful songs and treatises of love. This court, with its well-spoken knights, aroused in him a youthful enthusiasm which he never lost. The English knighthood was in the full flush of its early splendid successes in the Hundred Years War. The court was full of the heroes of both sides, including Prince Edward, 'the first knight of the world', whom later ages have called the Black Prince; with his Princess, Joan, the Fair Maid of Kent, 'the most beautiful woman in the whole realm of England' says Froissart, 'and the most loving', with her strange, rich, new fashions of dress which the moralists so condemned. His first visit was the most brilliant moment of Froissart's life, and one he never forgot. 'I could not tell nor recount in a day the noble dinners, the suppers, the festivals, the entertainments, the gifts, the presents, the jewels, which were made, given and presented,' he cries. He was astonished and delighted by the courtly manners of the English knights. They had an absolute faith in a knight's word of honour. To the many captured French knights who remained at the English court awaiting their ransoms and passing the time in sports, and feasting with their captors, that court was no place of exile and desolation; it was more like some important town today during an international congress. In this court it was Froissart's delight to collect the materials for his great *Chronicles*, to write fashionable verse, and to talk with gallant lords and ladies of those two 'eternal' themes, Arms and Love.

There was another side to all this. Froissart himself, later in life, said hard things about the English. The Hundred Years War appears to us now as a long-drawn-out horror of desolation and suffering inflicted on the fair land of France and her wretched peasants. Even within the limits of his own chivalric ideal Froissart sees easily enough, and describes clearly enough many instances of bad faith and wanton cruelty. But though much that was said about chivalry in the fourteenth century was lip-service, the ideal itself was a potent and glittering one, and for all its faults it has enriched the human mind. It gave the basic structure of accepted feelings and ideas for courtiers, and for Chaucer, in the secular and even the religious realms of the mind. Its genuine power over the actions of men was limited, and sometimes failed completely, as can be easily seen in Froissart's *Chronicles* themselves. But there are also many examples where the ideal did not fail. Perhaps the most striking brief example of the ideal, because of the person who expresses it, and at such a late date, is the sentence which the unhappy and disastrous King Richard II was said to have uttered, when very near the time of his death: 'Je suis loyal chevalier et oncques ne forfiz chevalerie.' Whatever his faults, the king *believed* in the chivalric ideal.

THE MATERIAL AND PRACTICAL BASIS OF COURT CULTURE

The court was a mixture of ceremony and practical usefulness in which the one often supported the other. All the same there was a distinction between ceremony and amusement on the one side, and practical usefulness on the other, and this distinction is reflected in the records we have. The life of leisure, the fine flow of court culture which is the chief subject of this chapter, had roots in utility. But all too often the records show us only roots or flower and, as in the court game of the competing parties of the Flower and of the Leaf, the two often seem in opposition. We cannot see the connections. Our knowledge of Chaucer's life suffers. His poetry is the finest aspect of the flower of court culture, and he was famous as a poet in his day even in France. Yet the records show him only as a minor courtier; a diplomatic envoy; a Comptroller of Customs; Clerk of the Works; member of commissions such as that which inquired into the state of the Thames embankments; subject to writs for small debts. What a portrait of England's famous poet! Yet in such details, interesting enough in themselves, we must ground ourselves, if we are to recreate in imagination that beautiful but transient flower of court culture which in the fifteenth century so quickly faded and fell.

Chaucer knew that

> al nis but a faire
> This world, that passeth soone as floures faire.

> (*Troilus*, V, 1804–1)

It is Vanity Fair that we shall be describing.

The king's court was in origin the household of the greatest of the 'magnates' or great lords. There were vast estates to be administered, rents and debts to be collected, justice to be done, a thousand daily decisions large and small to be taken. All magnates had such big households, comprising all ranks from the humblest kitchen-helper to the magnate's personal council, which in John of Gaunt's case was 150 strong. But the king's household was now something more than that of the greatest magnate; it was turning into the administrative centre of the kingdom. Originally, domestic departments, like that of the wardrobe, were becoming departments of government. The wardrobe became divided into the king's wardrobe, the great wardrobe, and the privy wardrobe. The great wardrobe became responsible for supplies. The privy wardrobe became an armaments store, settled in the Tower of London, where it was responsible for stocks of bows and arrows, pikes, lances, equipment for horses, tools – and even that new material which was to destroy knighthood, gunpowder. Departments such as these were becoming detached from the court proper, but their dependence on it was still close. The same is true for other departments of the king's government, such as the law courts. The king had been the chief law-giver, but he no longer sat on the bench of justice. Parliament had grown out of the council of great men who advised the king, though it was also a court of law, but the developments of the century, notably the king's need of money from the nation for the nation's wars, which he could not finance out of his own estates, forced him to make Parliament more representative of the nation at large. Members of Parliament, judges, heads of great departments of state, were many of them courtiers also; so, in his minor way, was Chaucer, Justice of the Peace, and in one Parliament a Knight of the Shire for Kent.

The economic basis for all this has been the subject of vast study of which the detail would be irrelevant here. Like all economic bases it ultimately rested on assumptions largely unquestioned. They were very different from those of the modern state. Agrarian pre-industrial societies rest on a wide basis of laborious physical labour on the land, to which the huge majority of the people were willy-nilly committed. They had to pay much of their produce to their social superiors and the feeding and well-being of all derived from this. From time immemorial, but especially in the Middle Ages, it was accepted that there was a vast labouring class whose rewards were small, whose duty it was to feed all. They were 'the ploughmen', often literally so. Chaucer describes one (only one) among his Canterbury Pilgrims, and he is a rather superior, idealised figure, in contrast with what the contemporary Langland represents in his passionate, intellectualised and allegorical poem *Piers Plowman*, which is much more conscious of the plight of the poor than is Chaucer's courtly work. The bitterness of the ploughman's plight is represented even more vividly in the alliterative poem *Pierce the Ploughman's Crede*.

The (to us) manifest social injustice of this system always aroused resentment among the victims, and among a few better educated and more sensitive people, like Langland himself. Hence the Peasants' Revolt of 1381, produced by an unfair and heavy tax on the populace, added to the normal exactions.

Even those who most resented the injustices inevitably made current assumptions about society. Langland himself accepts the ancient, if very rough and ready, division of society into three orders: of ploughmen to provide food, clergy to pray for men's (and the word includes women's) souls, and knights to defend the realm and preserve law and order. Even John Ball, leader of the Peasants' Revolt, proposed that he himself should be king.

It was virtually impossible to imagine society as not being hierarchical, with the king and his court at the apex of a social pyramid. There was a natural reverence for the idea of kingship, and a readiness to support it, that did not at all prevent hostility to the actual person who happened to be king at the time. The king had 'two bodies': one the regal continuing entity, the other the actual man. Barons and courtiers, concerned with good government and greedy for power and wealth were quite capable of murdering what might be called the current incumbent of regality, and did so twice in the fourteenth century, in the persons of Edward II (d. 1327) and Richard II (d. 1400).

The king's superiority in the realm (though always vulnerable to turbulent barons, especially when the king was a boy like Richard, who came to the throne aged 11) was matched at lower levels by men, and occasionally women, all down the scale, repeating the hierarchical pattern. Ideally, the movement of wealth and reverence upwards was matched by a corresponding respect and generosity downwards. The king had to give great gifts to his courtiers, and the records are full of them. Less mighty subjects were called on to reward those below them and to give to the poor. Although great churchmen tended to behave like great nobles, the doctrine of Christianity has always insisted on the duty to help the poor, as Chaucer's Parson repeats. He condemns extravagant display of wealth (such as was found in the court (*CT*, XII, 416ff.) and even implicitly condemns hierarchy when he repeats the familiar injunction to be humble (*CT*, XII, 480ff.). Sovereignty is to be maintained, but a lord must be just to his servants (*CT*, XII, 770ff.). No doubt there were many just and good lords: equally surely there were many who were not, all down the scale, just as there must have been many lazy, violent, incompetent peasants among many who were kind and dutiful. Almost all traditional societies have similarly hierarchical systems. They are natural to agrarian societies with low productivity, little formal education, and poor technological and medical resources. The forces of nature are mysterious and largely beyond control. Supernatural powers are close and they and nature are often hostile, needing propitiation. Change of all kinds is often feared, is hard to imagine, and harder to implement.

RELIGION IN COURT LIFE

Virtually all traditional societies are for these reasons as it were soaked in religion. Granted the assumptions, religion is 'natural' for them as it is not for most people in science-based, technologically advanced societies. Since life in the court, whatever its hardships and limitations, was at the apex of society, and enjoyed leisure, conservative forces were strong, but so also were some newer forces even when occasionally, like Lollardy, in some respects subversive. There is always a subversive element in Christianity. The New Testament arises out of the Old, but often subverts it. Christian otherworldliness could and often did condemn the practices of this world. Medieval Christianity had its own multiple and sometimes self-contradictory characteristics.

The fourteenth century was no exception. The earlier flowering of spirituality in Europe continued. In England, always a little later and a little cooler than the Continental leaders, there was a rich development of different kinds of spirituality and mysticism (Pollard and Boenig 1997). It was the great period of the English mystics. Some of this feeling reached part of the court and had some association with the group around Joan of Kent, mother of Richard II. An example was the growth of the Carthusian Order. Founded in the eleventh century, it was severely ascetic and contemplative, and attracted men of high spiritual, intellectual and social quality, whose quality never deteriorated. They were very few but almost fashionable in the court. Sir Walter de Manny founded the London Charter-House (where his body was found intact after the Second World War) in 1371 (Dickinson 1979, 281). Sir John Holland founded the priory of Mount Grace in Yorkshire, which remains their most striking memorial today. Holland was a ruthless scoundrel who got his friends to contribute funds without giving a penny himself. Yet he seems not to have been a conscious hypocrite, and his religious feeling, in so far as it existed, was no doubt of the kind illustrated by Edward III.

One of the priors of Mount Grace was Nicholas Love (fl. 1410) who before 1410 wrote the influential translation *The Mirrour of the Blessed Lyf of Iesu Christ* from the famous thirteenth-century Latin work at that time attributed to the Italian Saint Bonaventura. This develops a vein already begun to be worked by the English mystical writer, Richard Rolle, of the early fourteenth century. Here, ascetism becomes a morbid concentration on the Passion of Christ, i.e. the events immediately leading to his suffering and death upon the cross. The Gospels give a very laconic unsensational account. The developing forms of spirituality proceeded to invent and elaborate the most horrible kinds of torture inflicted upon Jesus, to increase sympathy and devotion, emphasising one aspect of his humanity. It became a form of spirituality widespread in Europe and some devout persons, mainly women on the Continent, went to quite extraordinary lengths of physical self-mortification in claiming to imitate Jesus's sufferings (Aers and Staley 1996). In the latter part of the fourteenth century in England, Margery Kempe and Julian of Norwich share the same tendencies though Julian had also a generous commonsense.

The movement is widely represented in the art of the thirteenth and fourteenth centuries, where the twisted agonised figure of Jesus on the cross is represented with his legs crossed and his feet pierced by only one nail (as it happens, an impossible posture). This contrasts with representations of the crucifix before 1200 showing a generally impassive and regal figure, with his feet separately nailed.

It would not be wise to consider such religious enthusiasm, of which I have given a necessarily simplified version, as the most typical expression of the age, despite the prominence in our eyes of much religious writing. It was the product of high sensibilities of a particular kind. There were others less exalted. To judge from the general run of reports of daily life, more common was a sort of natural but conventional religious conviction. Something of its quality and its ubiquity is suggested by Eamon Duffy's *Stripping of the Altars* (Yale, 1992). Humanity was still much involved with the earth, the seasons, under the eyes of the sky. It was virtually impossible to imagine being an atheist. Chaucer's Physician in *The General Prologue* comes nearest, but as a good scientist he knew his astrology, and astrology had strong if ambivalent religious connections. Religious feeling could be genuine, unspiritual, and casually unreflective for many people, as perhaps for Holland, while a minority of others, in their monasteries and reclusive cells, experienced a genuine ascetic mystical illumination, which had its own intense joy.

The new spirituality was part of a more general cultural movement which encouraged pity. Pity is the key emotion in this kind of devotional literature, as it is in Chaucer's writing on love. Langland too in a less sentimental self-regarding way is remarkable for the pity he expresses for the poor, absent in Chaucer and Gower. But Langland's account of the Crucifixion is notably unsensational and brief, while Chaucer himself is so far from physical self-mortification that he remarks several times on his own plumpness and also that his 'abstynence is lyte' (*The House of Fame*, 666). Chaucer's affinity with many Lollard attitudes, which repudiated the extreme self-punishment of the ascetism of the 'humanisation of Christ' reinforces our sense that he is just as detached from this kind of religious enthusiasm as he is from other secular enthusiasms of his age, like hunting, jousting, feasting and politics. He is scornful of the Pardoner who exploits simple-minded rustic piety, and of his bogus relics. Chaucer was to some extent associated with the Lollard knights, as will be noted later, and Lollardy was opposed to or unaffected by extreme ascetism, radical in this as in many other ways.

THE PERSONAL RELIGION OF EDWARD III

Edward III is a leading example of conventional courtly Christianity. He believed devoutly, attended mass frequently, gave large benefactions to religious houses. He had a wonderfully large collection of sacred relics, and believed in all the saints. This did not prevent him from many amorous adventures, despite his undoubted love for his admirable Queen Philippa, nor from slaughtering innocent French civilians in his zest for conquest. He conducted a kind of bartering of relics and benefactions against sins, and hoped thus to lessen his time in purgatory. He was extravagant and self-indulgent but a very successful and popular king for most of his long reign. It must be remembered that Church and State were closely intertwined. The king was divinely ordained by God through anointing by the Archbishop. This did not prevent Edward strongly resisting the Pope and doing his best to purloin church revenues.[1]

LEISURE AND CULTURE IN THE COURT

The king had a number of palaces, and his court, comprising not only his intimate household but the larger number of courtier-servants of whom Chaucer became one, the various evolving departments of state, and the large retinue of lower servants, numbered some hundreds. At the beginning of the century the court had no one fixed place of abode. Such large gatherings of people were difficult to feed for long at a time when communications were slow and almost every household had to be self-sufficient. The court had to move about the country so as to spread the burden of its maintenance. This was the case not only for the king's court but for the court of any magnate, or even sometimes for the abbot of a great monastery. This ceaseless moving about was still characteristic of the king's court right to the end of the century. When Froissart paid his last visit to England, in the mid-1390s, he says he stayed in the king's court as long as he pleased, not always in one place, for the king often moved to Eltham, to Leeds, to Kingston, to Sheen, to Chertsey, or to Windsor, all of them in the surroundings of London.

It had been necessary for the king's court to move not only to find provisions, but to govern the country, and all the departments of state moved with him. Even in the late fourteenth century Parliament met in different places, such as Gloucester and Northampton, as well as Westminster. But the important development of the latter part of the century was the increasing fixity of the departments of state at Westminster, and their consequent detachment from the king and his court. They began to have a life of their own, which increased their efficiency, but which also altered both their character and the character of the court. The court itself became rather more a place of entertainment and less a place of business. As a result, it was possible to realise the essential courtly life more fully than in any previous English court. From the time at least of Richard's marriage to Anne of Bohemia in 1382 a great court existed for the first time in England, taking much of its inspiration from the papal court of Avignon and the French court at Paris. It was leisured though still basically functional; it had many people (far too many, in the opinion of Parliament); most of these people were on a footing of general equality. How many ladies there were is an interesting problem. Chaucer's poems imply the presence of a goodly number: the records give details of far fewer. Presumably there were a number of hangers-on, 'unofficial' ladies of various kinds. But the grandest ladies, such as Joan of Kent, wife then widow of the Black Prince, and Blanche, John of Gaunt's wife, must have had considerable influence.

New demands for luxuries imported from the South, new feelings about the way life should be lived, new feelings about literature, paintings, music, were all seeping in from the southern courts, to settle in the poetry of Chaucer, based so largely on French and Italian poets of the new movements, like Machaut and Boccaccio. If one major influence which Chaucer felt and recorded was the new mixture of devoutness and scepticism, mathematics and morality, deriving from the city, the other major influence was the new decorativeness, the new sensibility, which characterise the court culture of his time, the new international Gothic Style.

A suggestion of the elaborate organisation and multifarious activities of a great medieval court can very well be gained from a few extracts from the registers of the Black Prince, who in his day was the flower of princes. These records of payment, administrative decisions and the like, open up many windows on the times. Thus, there is a long list of payments made on 5 September 1355. The sums paid are not important, but the totals of which they are part show how a medieval prince valued what he thought important or desirable. An embroiderer of Brussels is owed the almost incredibly vast sum of £1436 8s. 4d.; Martin Parde of Pistoia, a jewel merchant, is owed £3133 13s. 4d.; a London goldsmith £574 3s. 8d.; another embroiderer

£295 4s. 10d.; yet another of Cologne £97 15s. 11d.; Hugh le
Peyntour of London is paid for painting £82 13s.; Lambkeyn, a
saddler of Germany, is given an advance of £1368 for saddlery for
a forthcoming campaign. Various knights also receive payments.
Here is evidence, like that of Chaucer's poems, for the international
quality of the court culture of the day, as well as its extravagant
splendour. Another long list of payments was made on 7 July 1361.
Several knights received instalments of sums of £100 or more which
the Prince had promised them for their services at the battle of
Poitiers. It is easy to see here the 'magnificence' which men ex-
pected of a prince; and also the efficient administration which main-
tained the courts of magnates and the king. Such payments are not
quite typical of the register as a whole; the entries are almost daily,
and the Prince did not spend hundreds of pounds daily on jewellery;
the usual run of entries refers to the continual stream of minor
decisions, judgements and payments connected with the running of a
great estate, and though the Prince himself often ordered them, high
officials, trusted knights of his household, did most of the administra-
tion, or advised the Prince. Chaucer eventually became a minor
figure among such as these, in the king's court.

   Idleness, or at any rate leisure, is necessary to the attainment of
any way of life that is not governed by mere brute necessity. Yet
much of the apparently merely decorative part of court life served
practical purposes, even political purposes, while the performance of
practical necessities was enlivened by turning them into occasions for
ceremony and enjoyment. Some feeling of this underlay the justifica-
tion of such a life. Why should lords and prelates be allowed more
delicate foods, clothes, etc., than ordinary men, asks the monk and
scholar, Uthred of Boldon, and immediately proceeds to answer him-
self: because, according to Aristotle, superiors are occupied with the
mental and spiritual work of government, while others are occupied
with less demanding bodily work; and superiors are more discreet
in avoiding excess, and so may be allowed more subtle food and
so on, while subjects are less able to restrain themselves. But illicit
self-indulgence is even less lawful for superiors than for inferiors.
It is very hard for us modern liberal democrats to take such hier-
archical attitudes for granted, and some in the fourteenth century, not
yet democrats, were beginning it find it hard. But of course similar
discrepancies still exist in the modern world on the international
scene, and we accept them. Natural self-interest, custom, the dif-
ficulty of change, all have their effect. People were not in general
hypocritical or cynical, or at least, not more so than we are.

The working of such feelings of justification in practice are seen in the case of King John of France who had been captured by the Black Prince at the English victory of Poitiers in 1356. He spent years in England, living in a sumptuously courtly style, waiting for a huge ransom to be collected from his subjects. He was allowed to return to France, leaving hostages, including his son, for his ransom; these hostages broke their parole and returned to France. Deeply humiliated, the King insisted on returning to prison in England, against all the advice of his nobles. Here was a fine sense of that truth and honour which for Chaucer distinguish the Knight, besides the generosity and courtesy which are equally a part of the ideal, and which John had also amply shown. The justification for such a life lies in the ideal of chivalry, an ideal which Richard himself, at the end of his life, claimed he had always followed.

CHIVALRY AND ITS IDEALS

The Golden Age of chivalry was always in the past. The present always sees how miserably the ideal is now betrayed in ordinary daily life. Yet the ideal was real in itself and all knights at least paid it lip-service and often it must have softened and ennobled lives otherwise thoughtless and harsh.[2] And furthermore, though envisaged in the past, it was really creative of the future. Chivalry eventually produced in England one of the most potent ideals of social behaviour that the world has drawn from the West – the ideal of the gentleman. Probably we are seeing, or have already seen, the last age of this ideal, but it still deserves honour. In the fourteenth century it was still maturing, but yet Chaucer conveys much of its essence in his portrait of the Knight in *The General Prologue* to *The Canterbury Tales*.

Chivalry was the code of the knighthood, the armed retainers of great lords, the most important fighting men, who were drawn from the upper classes of society. Since the prime need for any society is to maintain itself, and this can ultimately be done only by force, in the days when force depended largely on personal strength the chief persons in society were those best able to fight by force of arms. In an age of primitive technology the mounted horseman was supreme. Chivalry began in the eleventh century when these rough and violent chieftains and their followers began to be brought to recognise some of the medieval Christian ideals. It developed with the polishing of manners which a slowly improving civilisation made possible, and which borrowed much from the superior civilisation of the

Arabs, with whom the West fought so long, especially in Spain. The improvement in manners led to a special conception of love which is the tap-root of our whole idea of romantic love. Personal bravery, Christian faith, polished manners, love: these are the elements of the chivalric ideal – an ideal confined to the knightly class, inappropriate to clerics and peasants.

In the life of the Black Prince, written by his own follower and admirer, Chandos Herald, the two chivalric virtues which are emphasised are bravery and loyalty; and with them go *franchise*, generosity, and pity. In *Sir Gawain and the Green Knight* the virtues of the hero, Gawain, are *franchise*, fellowship, chastity, courtesy and pity. The bravery that men admired was, in our eyes, sometimes a foolhardy recklessness. Sir Ralph Hastings did not value death at two cherries, says Chandos Herald, and Sir William Felton 'the valiant, very boldly and bravely charged among the enemy like a man devoid of sense and discretion'.

The loyalty was usually conceived on an intensely personal level. It might be loyalty to one's lord, though the lower ranks of the people seem to have felt this more than the upper. It might be loyalty to one's friend. We have almost lost the concept of the passionate friendship between men that is part of the basis of *The Knight's Tale*, and which was quite free from perversion. It is said that when Sir John Clanvowe died near Constantinople in 1391, his friend Sir William Neville, another of the Lollard knights, died within two days of grief. Machaut in his *Prise d'Alexandrie* describes how a squire fought over the body of his friend and cousin, for they loved each other and were companions in arms (ll. 5131–3). Such comradeship was fully recognised during the First World War and even in the Second World War – I saw it myself. It is generally recognised that comradeship is the strongest support for men under stress. The old-fashioned adventure novels of writers such as John Buchan and Rider Haggard evoke it easily and unsentimentally. J. R. R. Tolkien's *The Lord of the Rings*, which has been so deservedly popular, is of the same kind as these other authors, mingled with influences from William Morris and others. The success of *The Lord of the Rings* suggests that comradeship between men is still easily enough recognised by the ordinary reader.

Chaucer as it happens is not much interested in such comradeship, which is essentially connected with fighting, in which he was also not much interested. The comradeship between Palamon and Arcite in *The Knight's Tale* is soon shattered when they both fall in love with Emily, though its previous existence is a vital element in

the poignancy of their rivalry. Chaucer is far more interested in that
other kind of loyalty, which has also rather dated in modern times,
the personal loyalty that a knight feels for the lady he loves, and
which he maintains till death.

Franchise is to some extent still described by its modern relation
frankness. It means openness, generosity, friendliness, and a natural,
easy, well-loved manner. It implies self-confidence, and therefore a
frank and easy approach to other people. Pity is a virtue obvious in
itself; Chandos Herald says that the Black Prince undertook the
Spanish campaign out of pity and friendship for the exiled King
Peter. One of Chaucer's favourite lines (which he took from Italian
poetry) is

For pitee renneth soone in gentil herte   *runs; noble*
(*The Knight's Tale*, CT, I, l. 1761, *The Merchant's Tale*,
CT, IV, l. 1986, *The Squire's Tale*, CT, V, l. 479,
Prologue F, *The Legend of Good Women*, l. 503;
cf. *The Man of Law's Tale*, CT, II, l. 660)

Pity is the virtuous feeling that Chaucer most often expresses. It had
its limitations; Chandos Herald does not tell us, but Froissart does, of
the sack of Limoges, when the Black Prince looked on unmoved as
men, women and children were slaughtered on their knees as they
besought mercy from the English soldiers. His stern heart was at last
melted when he saw three Frenchmen gallantly and desperately
defending themselves against a greater number of Englishmen. These
fighters he spared.

Generosity again is a self-explanatory virtue, yet even so it had
somewhat different aspects. A knight was expected to be without
regard for money and possessions:

Fy on possessioun   *Fie*
But if a man be vertuous withal!   *Unless*
(CT, V, ll. 686–7)

says Chaucer's Franklin. Generosity was especially the virtue of a
prince, and Edward III and the Black Prince were both models of
knighthood in the prodigal way in which they scattered rich gifts
among their retainers and friends. Men loved the prince to be mag-
nificent and if he had not been he would have lost their regard. As
a result, the treasuries of medieval kings were continually in trouble;
Edward bankrupted several great Italian banking houses by not pay-
ing what he owed them, and though the Black Prince had enormous

revenues he died heavily in debt. (On the other side of the picture it
was becoming increasingly possible to make one's fortune at court,
and men like Clanvowe, Burley, Sturry, and Chaucer expected per-
sonal gain.)

The last virtue was courtesy. In this had once been included all
the others, but by the end of the fourteenth century its chief mean-
ing was 'good manners' of the kind that was encouraged by the
courtesy books already current. Perhaps the extreme example of
the new delicacy of manners that was being slowly developed was
Richard's almost unique use of the handkerchief. An earlier example
is the Black Prince's insistence on serving King John as a squire after
the King had been captured at Poitiers. Courtesy was conceived very
much in terms of speech. The knightly and learned educations both
emphasised the 'art of speech', which Chaucer refers to, for example,
in *The Squire's Tale*. Ability to speak convincingly was continually
needed in the courts of law, in diplomacy, in university disputations,
in the King's court: it was still a largely oral culture, as much English
law still is. Words were felt to have more authenticity as spoken than
as written, and a speaker can be questioned on what he has said. As
well as usefulness a grace was sought. Thus, when Sir Gawain, hero
of the late-fourteenth-century poem, *Sir Gawain and the Green Knight*,
reaches a castle, and people learn that he is the Gawain of Arthur's
court who is famed for his courtesy – 'Lo, Gawain with his olde
courtesie' as Chaucer elsewhere describes him – they rejoice that he
will be able to instruct them in the 'stainless terms of noble speech'.
Chaucer's perfect knight

| nevere yet no vileynye ne sayde | *rudeness* |
| In all his lyf unto no maner wight | *to any kind of person* |

And in *The Book of the Duchess* the Black Knight does not fail to
praise the *eloquence* of his lady.

The chivalric ideal was not staid. Time and again there is emphasis
on joy as one of the supreme qualities or even virtues of courtly
knights and ladies. Joy is not so appropriate on the battlefield, though
most knights loved fighting. The traditional praise is 'like a lion on
the field', but it goes on, 'like a lamb in the hall'. Joy was especially
the virtue and the reward of lovers. Chaucer says at the end of the
third book of the *Troilus* that he has 'said fully in his song'

| Th'effect and joie of Troilus servise. | *love* |
| | (III, 1815) |

In the portrait of the lady in *The Book of the Duchess*, which is almost wholly taken from French sources, the lady's joyfulness is everywhere praised and, though care is taken not to make her appear light-minded, 'dulnesse was of hir adrad'. Nothing is more typical of the courtly ideal than the praise of joy; life was so often nasty, brutish and short; youth passed soon; religion was often gloomy and repressive, but even if, as in one of Chaucer's favourite phrases, 'ever the latter end of joy is woe', then at least let joy be gathered while it flowers.

The chivalric and courtly view of life is entirely accepted by Chaucer. He deepens and ennobles the ideal, though he appears not to be much interested in some of the more superficial and popular parts of it, in hunting and sport generally, for example. (In this he shows himself rather similar to Richard, and different from the majority of English people.) But he has no reservations about chivalry. In the *General Prologue* the knightly ideal is split up between two characters, the Knight and the Squire, his son. The Squire represents the more obviously youthful parts of the ideal, the gaiety and fashionableness of courtly life, the bright clothes, the music and poetry, and the interest in love. The Knight represents the deeper moral qualities of the ideal, which the Squire has yet to grow into. The Knight

> loved chivalrie,
> Trouthe and honour, fredom and curteisie.
>
> (*CT*, I, 55–6)

'Truth' is one rendering for loyalty, but goes beyond this. It is the supreme virtue of Troilus, Chaucer's own great hero, and implies not only loyalty but a strong personal integrity.

A few modern critics have found it impossible to believe in such virtue and argue that Chaucer is speaking ironically. But too many different authors of many different works have testified to the ideal for it to be regarded as ironical, and no competent scholar now accepts this cynical view.

THE LOVE OF LADIES

Romantic love is the abiding interest of medieval secular literature, finding many different forms, and altering the sentiments first of Europe and eventually almost the whole free world down to our own day. In literature a knight is always braver for being in love, though there is very little in the chronicles even of Froissart, and nothing in less gossipy records, to suggest that in actual warfare much account was made of being in love. Yet at least in literature, and eventually perhaps in life, an exalted feminine ideal of the beloved was created, which is beautiful and refreshing. It created the concept of 'the lady', who appears so frequently embodied in Chaucer's heroines, from Blanche the Duchess onwards, and who was surely a potent image in his mind, created by, or for, the ideal of the court. The lady is beautiful, honourable, chaste, educated, eloquent at need, kind and merciful. She still lives in what is entirely a man's world and most of her virtues are seen as adaptations of those of the knight. Bravery alone is not required of her. She is passive, not expected to love except after long wooing, and then it is not her love she grants, but her 'pity', her 'mercy'. Rarely is there any sense of equality. The lady is either superior, as in love, or inferior, as in marriage. The ideal of pre-marital chaste romantic love is presented on the man's part therefore, since the lady is superior, as 'service', obedience, humility. These are the 'gifts' he offers to the beloved, and their exercise is a sort of rite of passage, a test. If the gifts are accepted, the test passed, the lady reciprocates with the gift of herself, her honour, i.e. her chastity, always saved. The lady's qualified, temporary, and idealised superiority must surely have affected the rough military society and softened and subtilised it. In Chaucer's poems the reward of successful love is equality between the two – each serves the other, does what the other wishes.

Many of Chaucer's remarks in his poems show that he was conscious of the ladies in his audience, and no doubt their presence encouraged his interest in the personal and private aspects of life, as a female audience used to: witness the history of the novel, which has always relied on women readers for its steady audience. The typically public and impersonal subjects of literature have until recently interested mainly masculine audiences, and where Chaucer deals with such serious subjects directly and explicitly, as in his writings on philosophy, astronomy and religion, his audience is not essentially courtly.

The ideal of the courtly life was joyous, young, passionate and colourful. Tournaments, dancing, feasts, these are the joys of the court, to which one must add, as is clear from the poetry, hunting, May games, indoor games and poetry itself.

THE TOURNAMENT

The tournament had all the glamour, excitement and popularity of its modern equivalents of football matches and baseball games. It mirrored the complexities, contradictions and colourfulness of courtly life. As armed conflict it represented the ultimate origin of the court and society as a fighting unit, of which male prowess and bravery were the foundation, and the source of most prestige. It was intensely competitive by nature. At the same time the tournament by the fourteenth century also represented the class ideal of chivalric conduct, the adherence to rules, the acceptance by all of the general ethos of honour and was a force for unifying the knightly and therefore governing class. Edward III's natural passion for this chivalric sport had excellent political sense, which was shown by his creation of the Order of the Garter in 1348, for the élite of the élite, with its Arthurian and patriotic colouring.

The development of the tournament from a general mêlée throughout the countryside, real training for war, to a more stylised conflict within lists, and the presence of ladies to adorn, admire and be admired, made the tournament a still more social and representative activity. After the fighting came the feasting and the dancing. The king made sure that he, and not disaffected barons, organised it, and it retained political significance. The Church, at first opposed, came to accept it. Heralds regulated it and helped to reinforce its glamour. For such as Froissart it became virtually the icon of courtly life. Even Richard II used the tournament, and the grandest tournament of Chaucer's lifetime was probably that held in Smithfield in London in 1390, rich in practical symbolism, which Froissart describes in glowing and extensive detail.

It is unintentionally symbolic of Chaucer's participation in this affair that he, as then Clerk of the Works, an unglamorous if courtly post, was responsible (not directly, of course) for erecting the scaffolding which held the spectators, and it did not, as sometimes happened, collapse. He left no description of the event.

Once again we have to note Chaucer's blend of participation in yet detachment from some of the main streams of the culture of his day. He does not mock chivalry, though in *Sir Thopas* he jokes at lower-class effeminate and probably Flemish would-be practitioners. The hot-blooded young men in *The Knight's Tale* are gently mocked. It is now generally accepted by scholars once again that the portrait of the Knight in *The General Prologue* to *The Canterbury Tales* presents a noble ideal of chivalry, as it has been accepted, until recently questioned, for 600 years. In *The Knight's Tale* the glamour of the tournament is fully realised, though presented with some extravagance as a pagan event. But the actual tournament is more like the old-fashioned mêlée and the reason for the tournament is not mere sport but to decide which of the lovers shall win the beloved lady. Moreover, Chaucer gives us an unparalleled glimpse of the practical activity and bustle, not only of knights and squires but of the more humble people, for example the armourers, and the lower-class spectators. No sporting enthusiast, he was interested in human society.

MUSIC IN COURT

The court was a place of music and Chaucer's poetry is not just musical in itself but full of references to music. From the time that Chaucer became a page he would have had occasion to hear, and probably sing, certainly to write, songs to entertain the company. Music for Chaucer is 'heavenly'.

All educated people seem to have had some ability at music, though medieval music was so difficult to read that they must always have played and sung by ear alone. There are frequent references in Chaucer's poetry to ladies playing music, while the Squire was singing or playing the flute all day. Not only was the Squire a beautifully dressed young man, and a good soldier and jouster; not only could he write and draw; he could also compose poetry and write the music to it. This was the normal courtly ideal, as we see from several knights and squires in Chaucer's poetry, and also from what we know of such a man as the third Earl of Salisbury. Richard II himself wrote songs, though none of them has survived. That great soldier and courtier, Henry of Lancaster, says that from his lips have come many love-songs which have often drawn him and others to sin. Chaucer makes the same confession at the end of *The Canterbury Tales*. One of the noticeable things about *The General Prologue* is the number of times music and especially singing are mentioned.

In Chaucer's works, and as we may suppose was also largely true of the court, music is mainly festive and social, associated with warm feelings, especially love and joy. The great music of the time was religious, and the greatest European musician was none other than Machaut, but the English court seems not much interested in religious music and no great musicians are found in England until the fifteenth century.

FEASTING

The glamour of courtly life was embodied in many other forms. Feasting in company often provided the focus, because food and drink may not only be delicious in themselves but also symbolise loving fellowship, common interests, stability. Feasts at great religious festivals emphasise spiritual truths. Feasts mark the passage of the seasons. By ingesting food and drink we symbolically absorb and control the world. Order and happiness are seen and felt to prevail.

Feasts were accompanied by music from minstrel bands, playing wind and stringed instruments and various kinds of drums. Entertainments like masques (sometimes called 'mummings' or 'interludes') were played, with fancy dress and sometimes with very elaborate scenery. The food was in vast quantities and very elaborately dressed, often with ornate if ephemeral table decorations made of paper painted by talented artists and adorned with verses, called 'subtleties'. After the feasts came more music and much dancing, where saucy or loving looks were interchanged between knights and ladies. Chaucer, the practised courtier, often mentions feasts, but also dismisses them briefly, in a somewhat *blasé* fashion saying, for example, that everyone knows very well that there is plenty to eat at a king's feast and no detailed description is needed, in *The Squire's Tale* (*CT*, VI, 298–301).

LITERATURE

Somewhere among all this, or more likely scattered everywhere, was what we call 'literature'. The word gives too formal a notion. There were songs in plenty on all sorts of occasions as already noted. The 'interludes' and 'mummings' had speeches (Chaucer's follower, the monk and author Lydgate, wrote a 'Mumming'). Minstrels may have told romances to small groups, for some romances represent themselves, truly or not, as being told by a minstrel to a listening group. As will be noted later, squires were expected to 'occupy the court' with stories or readings from chronicles. Small groups of ladies were probably read to as they sewed, and in *Troilus* Book II Chaucer shows Criseyde and her ladies being read to in her parlour. The famous frontispiece to the Corpus Christi Manuscript of *Troilus* shows Chaucer himself reading from a pulpit in a garden to the young king and queen and a group of brightly clad courtiers. This is probably an idealised view of the past, since it was painted soon after 1400, some 20 years after the poem was written, but it gives something that is genuinely in the 'feel' of the poem as written for and perhaps delivered to an interested group of courtiers, young knights and ladies, including the young king and queen, older men, scholars and lawyers, representing many different kinds of interests but united in loyalty to courtly ideals.

OUT-OF-DOORS

Most courtiers spent much of their time out-of-doors. Although the tournament represents the out-of-doors quintessence of the courtly life, an even more frequent activity, passionately pursued by most men, was hunting.[3] Even ladies might go hunting with hawks.

For men were reserved the even more exhilarating joys of the chase after fox and deer, and after the more dangerous boar, which had to be killed by the thrust of a spear at close quarters. Beyond the intrinsic physical pleasure of exercise, hunting, like eating, is a way of symbolically and actually controlling the world while being a part of it. The royal passion for hunting caused great forests to be turned into game reserves. The laws protecting the king's forests inflicted cruel punishments on those who infringed them. The paradoxical sympathy between hunter and hunted has often been noted – they share the same carnal nature. The delights of the hunt are vividly portrayed in the contemporary poem *Sir Gawain and the Green Knight*, but Chaucer himself shows little interest in the hunt. In what seems to be the earliest of his poems that we have, *The Book of the Duchess*, he represents himself going off to join the hunt, but he soon wanders away on his own, eventually to find the Man in Black in the depths of the forest lamenting the death of his beloved.

CHAUCER'S REPRESENTATION OF COURTLY LIFE

Though Chaucer vividly represents the lively surface of life, he soon turns, especially in his earlier poems, to the inner life of feeling and personal relationships. He was not entirely typical – what great poet could be? – of the general traits and interests of the ordinary run of people, for all his capacity for sympathising with them. Nevertheless, since he was orthodox rather than rebellious, wise as well as cynical, he makes an extraordinarily good spokesman for the court culture of the second half of the fourteenth century, and for chivalry as it was then understood. To anticipate for a moment his later life, we may say that the whole body of his work, but above all *The Knight's Tale*, is the greatest document of courtly and knightly values in this period. In *The Knight's Tale* we find the court as the centre of the kingdom, with its concerns for war and justice, but also its leisure, its delight in hunting and tournament. The younger people are chiefly concerned with love and war, but Theseus, the wise king, and his father, Egeus, can make a sober assessment of the whole of life. Religion, philosophy and science find a place in controlling and interpreting the harsh chances of life. For all the splendours of the court, the raptures of love, and the glories of martial success, much, perhaps most of life, is hard, and there is plenty of suffering. *The Knight's Tale* is a sympathetic poem, but it contains also a note of stern resignation, and a resolute will 'to make a virtue of necessity' as Theseus says. It also occasionally sounds a note of flippant hardness which is one of Chaucer's most constant though intermittent features, and which is very difficult to describe in modern terms, because it lies alongside, yet does not, as one might have thought, cancel out, the positive ideals, values and sympathies. Even when we have made allowance for Chaucer's remarkable genius, we must agree that the court culture which could help to produce such a body of writings which so variously blend love and loyalty and gaiety, bravery and pity, *franchise*, generosity, courtesy, and religion with philosophical thought and worldly wit and wisdom, was one of the great achievements in the history of English culture.

CHAUCER'S EXPERIENCE OF WAR

The sober hardness and stoic acceptance of pain that underlie *The Knight's Tale* also recall us to the facts of Chaucer's own experience of courtly life. We see him as a page in 1357. In 1359–60 he was taking part in a military campaign. Men usually 'took arms' about the age of 20 or 21, and Chaucer in later life gave evidence in the Scrope–Grosvenor lawsuit that it was in this campaign that himself took arms, so we may suppose him to have been about 20 in 1359–60. He went as a *valettus* or 'yeoman', probably in the contingent led by Lionel, husband of Chaucer's 'lady', the Countess Elizabeth of Ulster, and was paid sixpence a day.

The campaign was rather miserable. It began in autumn 1359 and various delays caused trouble with mercenaries over rations. The vast army moved slowly and the rain was almost continuous. The army reached Rheims by 4 December and besieged but could not take the town. At some stage after 11 January Chaucer was captured by the enemy. In the negotiations after the end of the campaign, in March 1360, Chaucer was ransomed by the king – in actual fact, of course, through the office of the king's court, not by personal intervention – for £16. Various other *valetti* were ransomed for £10, a chaplain for £8. Sir John Burley received for his horse £20, and Robert de Clynton £16 14s. for his. Later in the year Chaucer was still in Duke Lionel's service, as can be told from the Duke's expense book; and during the peace negotiations he went back to France, on his return carrying letters from Calais to England. This was perhaps

the first of his many journeys in a position of trust, or he may simply
have acted as a courier.

1360 marks a stage in Chaucer's career. He had entered the court
and seen something of its glamour. He had been blooded and seen
something of the splendour, horror and boredom of war. He was
about to become a working courtier and he was surely known as a
promising poet. Before turning to his more specifically literary back-
ground we may well sum up what sort of person he was by quoting
his own description of the Squire in *The Canterbury Tales*. Of course,
Chaucer was not the son of a knight. But he was certainly page and
perhaps squire in one of the greatest households of England. He had
been in 'chivachye' in Flanders, Artois and Picardy; he certainly
was a rhymer; and many young men of his age have been in
love. Chaucer's picture of the Squire is an idealised one and not
consciously a self-portrait. But it describes the type of young man
superbly well and Chaucer must have been such another. We are
hardly likely to get nearer to a description of the young Chaucer
than this, and all the most attractive elements of the secular aspects of
his culture are noted, its grace and good manners, appropriate defer-
ence, bravery, beauty, art:

a yong Squier,

A lovyere and a lusty bacheler,	*young knight*
With lokkes crulle as they were leyd in presse.	*curled*
Of twenty yeer of age he was, I gesse.	
Of his stature he was of evene lengthe,	
And wonderly delyvere, and of greet strengthe.	*nimble*
And he hadde been somtyme in chyvachie	
In Flaundres, in Artoys, and Pycardie,	
And born hym weel, as of so litel space,	
In hope to stonden in his lady grace.	
Embrouded was he, as it were a meede	*embroidered; meadow*
Al ful of fresshe floures, whyte and reede.	
Syngynge he was, or floytynge, al the day;	
He was as fressh as is the month of May.	
Short was his gowne, with sleves longe and wyde.	
Wel koude he sitte on hors and faire ryde.	
He koude songes make and wel endite,	*write*
Juste and eek daunce, and weel purtreye and write.	*joust; draw*
So hoote he lovede that by nyghtertale	*night-time*
He sleep namoore than dooth a nyghtyngale.	
Curteis he was, lowely, and servysable,	
And carf biforn his fader at the table.	

(*The General Prologue, CT*, I, 79–100)

That most young men, and ordinary life, even at court, can hardly have been so perfect, must be taken for granted. Ideals are by definition hard to be achieved. But that the age, and Chaucer himself, could image themselves in such high romantic and beautiful terms is itself significant of attitudes and hopes that really existed.

NOTES

1. W. M. Ormrod, 'The Personal Religion of Edward III', *Speculum* 64 (1989), 849–77.
2. On the development of chivalry see Richard Barber, *The Knight and Chivalry*, revised edition (Woodbridge, 1995); and *Age of Chivalry*, edited by Jonathan Alexander and Paul Binski (Royal Academy of Arts, London, 1987).
3. Anne Rooney, *Hunting in Middle English Literature* (Cambridge, 1993).

Chapter 4

The English and European Literary Traditions

EARLY READING

What had Chaucer been reading as a boy and young man? Youthful reading is the seedsowing time of the mind and Chaucer was obviously an avid reader. The reading which made the deepest impression on him, most attracted his imagination, and formed his intellectual habits, can be traced partly from its effects and partly from his own references. Everywhere he seems driven on by continuous curiosity, intellectual seeking, imaginative enjoyment. He had a powerful yet unstrained vitality, a wonderful sense of participation, and also a sharply critical response. He was always going beyond what he received. Without animus or reforming zeal, he both accepted and left behind what he experienced. There is no rebellious bitterness, yet no complacent conservatism.

THE ENGLISH ROMANCES

The earliest impression was that made by English romances. We can detect their influence in Chaucer's earliest datable poem, *The Book of the Duchess*, at the least conscious level, the minor points of style. The first 15 lines of that poem are translated from a poem by Froissart. The style is that of oral delivery, real or imitated. It buttonholes the reader with its direct, informal intimacy, its conversational, personal ease. At once a relationship is created between poet and audience or reader. It is in one sense a climax of the earlier minstrel style, but here the minstrel is the poet himself.

It is notable that these poems, and the lyrics to be mentioned in a moment, were in English. The establishment of the English language as that of the whole people at all cultural levels is proved by Chaucer's own poetry, but clearly took place independent of him earlier in the fourteenth century. English is his mother tongue, and the mother tongue of Court and City.

We may imagine Chaucer listening when younger to narrative poems, perhaps read to the family at home from such a book as the large Auchinleck manuscript (now in the National Library of Scotland), which among over 50 separate items, almost all in English, contains 18 romances. These account for three-quarters of the surviving bulk of the manuscript (and what has been lost is mostly texts of romance). This big book, produced around 1330–40 by a London bookshop, for just such an audience as wealthy merchants, contains many other items of a kind which influenced Chaucer; the four saints' lives, the 15 varied religious and didactic pieces, and the five humorous or satiric pieces. It has been argued that Chaucer knew this very volume. Whether he did or not, it is a true 'Gothic' miscellany of the very type of *The Canterbury Tales*.

The English romances are usually written in tail-rhyme: that is, of stanzas of around 12 four-stress, eight-syllabled lines, rhyming, and each stanza concluding with a two-syllable, one-stress phrase, the tail-rhyme itself. They tell stirring stories of virtuous, often patriotic, heroes who fight evil and win a bride and a kingdom. The stories are essentially folktales, to be associated with fairytales. The clear favourite is *Guy of Warwick*, which has versions in short couplets (like *The Book of the Duchess*) as well as in tail-rhyme. A very typical shorter example is the tale of *Sir Degaré*, where the hero, abandoned in childhood, almost marries his unknown mother, and has to discover his father.[1] Romances such as these were popular until the seventeenth century. Shakespeare knew *Guy of Warwick*.

These archetypal stories, often slackly written, came to seem as ridiculous to Chaucer as they do to most moderns. As usual he was *avant-garde* for his age and untypical in some of his tastes. He mocked them cruelly in *The Canterbury Tales* by the comic parody *Sir Thopas*, but it is quite significant that he attributes *Sir Thopas* to himself as one of the pilgrims. The self-mockery has a real basis in his actual origins, as well as in his poetic character.

ENGLISH LYRICS

At the same time we may be sure that Chaucer knew a large number of English lyrics. Many such lyrics survive from the thirteenth century onwards and are of great charm. There is a great anthology of them recorded in what is now British Library Harley 2253. This manuscript of the early fourteenth century is a miscellany of French, medieval Latin and English poetry which thus illustrates not only English writing but the trilingual culture of the time. It was probably written somewhere in the West Midlands but the poems have place-names which refer as far afield as Lincoln. The famous lyric 'Blow Northern Wind' is among them. All England is represented in these English poems now known as 'The Harley Lyrics'. Many are love-songs, influenced by the French tradition and written in a variety of iambic metres, though with some alliteration.

Bytuene Mersh and Aueril	
When spray biginneth to spring	*leaves: grow*
The lutel foul hath hire wyl	*little bird*
On hyre lud to synge.	*song*
Ich libbe in loue-longinge	*I live*
For semlokest of alle thynge;	*loveliest*
He may me blisse bringe	*She*
Icham in hire baundone	*I am: power*
An hendy hap ichabbe yhent	*a gracious fortune I have received*
Ichot from heune it is me sent	*I know: heaven*
And lyht on Alysoun	

All the notes of spring and aching young love are here, the song of birds, the pain of the lover, the bliss he hopes for, the beauty of the lady, the sense that love is divine. It will all be repeated in a different style in *The Book of the Duchess*, as it had already a thousand times before, and will be millions of times later, down to the latest pop-songs, different as their tone is. Chaucer's Chantecleer sings a snatch of one of them, not otherwise recorded, 'My lief is faren in londe' (*CT*, VII, 2879) 'My love has gone away'. In Gower's poem *Confessio Amantis* written about 1390, he causes Venus, goddess of love, to say to himself in the poem:

And gret wel Chaucer when ye mete	*greet*
As mi disciple and mi poete,	
For in the floures of his youthe	*flower*
In sondri wise, as he wel couthe	*knew*
Of dities and of songes glade	*ditties*
The whiche he for mi sake made	
The lond fulfild is oueral.	

(*Confessio Amantis* (first version), VIII, 2941–7)

Chaucer explored the feelings of love more deeply than any pre-vious English poet, continuing the line of the romances and lyrics, but just as he developed from the style of the romances, so he did even further from that of the lyrics. The style of the Harley Lyrics is provincial and old-fashioned by Chaucer's standards. He never seeks their fresh and unsophisticated response to spring and love, and in *The Miller's Tale* mocks such old-fashioned words as 'hende' (courteous) and provincial low-class names like 'Alison', which is also the name of the Wife of Bath. Chaucer, like his Monk, 'holds with the newe world the space'. His lyrics become philosophical, or witty in a courtly style. Yet the English lyric, whose beauties and variety cannot be explored here, and which also had a rich religious content, is where he started from. Of other earlier English verse, equal in wit and feeling to his own, he shows no knowledge.[2] It would perhaps be too much to say that Chaucer rebelled against his earliest English origins, or was ashamed of them, but he developed beyond them and mocked them, very much the English courtier who enriched English court culture by grounding the International Gothic Style in English life. Chaucer grew and developed from the English romances and lyrics under other powerful influences. At some depth was the complex of underlying new sensibilities like those related to the study of arithmetic, as already described, but more obvious, and more immediately useful, was his knowledge of French poetry – poetry of Paris.

There are two main sources which strike us particularly when considering Chaucer's early reading. The first is *Le Roman de la Rose*, and the second is the poems by Machaut. Other poems and poets there were, like the love-visions which derive from *Le Roman de la Rose*, and the poems of his contemporaries Froissart and Deschamps, who followed Machaut. There were manuscript anthologies of French poetry which must have been known to him. It has been argued that his own earliest poems were written in French, and there is a collection of poems in French by 'Ch' which could be attributed to him. Other English courtiers and Gower, as already noted, wrote poetry in French. But the only early poems which are certainly by Chaucer are imitations of the French, like *The Complaint unto Pity*, and such translations as *The Romaunt of the Rose* and *An ABC*.

LE ROMAN DE LA ROSE

The English *Romaunt of the Rose*, which survives in only one manuscript, is a fragment of some 7500 octosyllabic lines, of which probably only the first 1705 lines are Chaucer's. This English *Romaunt* is a translation of parts of the French *Le Roman de la Rose*, one of the great formative books of the Middle Ages. More than 200 French manuscripts of the *Roman*, besides translations into other European languages, and 21 early printed editions, bear witness to its enormous popularity. It was at the well-head of the tradition in which Machaut, Deschamps and Froissart wrote. And although Chaucer actually translated very little of its more than 20 000 lines, he knew the whole poem extremely well. It permeated his thought so deeply that his later works reveal its influence even more profoundly than his early poems.

The *Roman* was written by two authors as different as chalk from cheese. Guillaume de Lorris wrote the delightful first part of some 4000 lines, about the year 1225. The poem tells how the narrator fell asleep and dreamed it was the sweetest of May mornings. Wandering by a clear river, he came to a beautiful Garden 'from whose walls sorrow flies far', whose gate was kept by Idleness, and whose lord was Mirth, and from which everything old, ugly, poor and vicious was excluded. Within this garden of youthful delights the Dreamer eventually saw the Rose, and as he looked, the arrows of Cupid, the god of love, struck him again and again. But the Rose (a lady's love) was defended by thorns, by guardians such as Modesty and Rebuff (*Daunger*). Furthermore, the Lady Reason, who had been created in Paradise by God himself, attempted to dissuade the Dreamer from trying to win the Rose at all.

Guillaume did not finish his poem. It was finished some 50 years later by Jean de Meun, whose nickname, 'Le Clopinel', the Hobbler, not unaptly suggests his difference from Guillaume. Jean took over the machinery of the poem to convey a great quantity of very various matter: philosophy, science, nature poetry, controversy and satire of all kinds, but especially of women. It was this huge addition of Jean's that caused the *Roman* to be sometimes cited in the fourteenth century as a satire against love, notwithstanding its beginning.

The whole poem is a Gothic poetic encyclopedia. It set or reinforced the fashion for several important literary traditions. The device of the dream, the artificially bright May morning, the lovely Garden representing the youthful view of the joyous world, the allegorical framework, as well as many individual types and comments, from Guillaume's first part, all appear again and again in later poetry. Guillaume's poem sets out the 'law of love'. His god of love is the medieval Cupid: no fat, blind, naked infant, but a princely youth who hunts men. The lover receives his code from the god and learns that nobility must derive from virtue, not from lineage; that he must always be faithful; always fashionable though not extravagant in dress; accomplished in both manly and artistic exercises. In a word, he must be a gentleman in every respect, with his teeth as unstained as his honour. For the practice of these virtues the lover is promised the highest joys and bitterest sorrows that life can offer.

Even in Guillaume, however, love has an antagonist, the Lady Reason, who descends from her tower to defend Chastity and to argue against the dictates of Cupid. Guillaume makes her arguments seem cold and merely prudential, and we sympathise with the lover's rejection of them. But the conflict is deep at the heart of love as seen by the medieval poets, and it is by no means certain that Guillaume himself would have been finally on Cupid's side. The antithesis between the service of love and the service of God was clear, and always profoundly felt. There is no doubt that Chaucer also felt it.

Jean de Meun's addition, swollen and inconsistent as it is, contributed as much or more to the poem's reputation as Guillaume's beginning. In both parts the ideal of love is less intense than the feudal aristocratic tradition of Provence from which it derives, in which the lady was worshipped almost as a goddess. But it was perhaps largely due to Jean that later poets felt there was nothing strange in using the device of a love story to treat all kinds of philosophical and scientific matter in poetry. The habit of mind by which all subjects may be gathered in under one heading of love is aptly summed up in the words of Thomas Middleton as late as 1623:

> Love has an intellect that runs through all
> The scrutinous sciences, and like a cunning poet
> Catches a quantity of every knowledge
> Yet brings all home into one mystery,
> Into one secret, that he proceeds in.
>
> (*The Changeling*, Act III, Sc. 3)

The scientific and philosophical aspects of Jean's addition were well calculated to stimulate Chaucer's already awakened interest and new sensibility towards intellectual questions. The new urban spirit breathes through this work from Paris.

Jean's work includes much more in its Gothic miscellaneity, some of it highly traditional. There is the clerical satire of women, which goes back for many centuries, and also the more rollicking rough derision of women found in popular folktale, which probably goes back to the beginning of the human race.

Parts of Boethius's *Consolation of Philosophy*, and Ovid's story of Pygmalion, are translated in the *Roman*. Jean also partly translates the twelfth-century Latin *Complaint of Nature* to create an image of fecund Nature, a goddess who urges both sexes to vigorous promiscuity in order to people the world. She has something of the power of myth. Jean's bold sophistry brings the whole poem to a remarkable ending in which he allegorically portrays, with a touch of humour, and without much concealment, the climax of sexual intercourse.

MACHAUT

The tradition of European love-poetry became exceedingly rich and varied by the fourteenth century. It was not so much a river as a whole series of rivers flowing in the same direction but each with a somewhat different course and character. Medieval romantic love certainly cannot be summed up as always adulterous, courteous, parodic of religion, joyous. It was all these things at times. It was also tender, pious, violent, tragic. Much of its charm lies in the different forms of story and song that it takes at different periods with different authors. It should not be called 'courtly love', a term invented by nineteenth-century scholars. We should rather call it romantic love, or use the term often mentioned in its own day, *fine amour*, 'refined love', which hits off its essential element and distinguishes it from simple sexual passion.

Machaut (*c.* 1300–77) who was the leading musician of his day was also the leading poet of France (which was at that time made up of several kingdoms) and a major influence on Chaucer. He was nominally a cleric, yet he led the adventurous, amorous, much-travelled life of a courtier, indebted to various kings for patronage and for the conferment of well-paid benefices of which he was an absentee incumbent. He wrote many poems developing the tradition of love, and two debate-poems, the *Jugement du Roi de Behaigne* and the *Jugement du Roi de Navarre* which much influenced Chaucer. *Behaigne* presents a debate between a sorrowful knight and an equally sorrowful lady, who meet by accident in a forest. The lady's own knight is dead; while the lady of the knight in the forest has betrayed him. They debate as to whose plight is worse, and go to Jean of Luxembourg, King of Bohemia (Machaut's current patron) for a decision. He decides that the knight suffers more. Although the situation is set up artificially, the human problems are real and painful. The artificiality distances but does not trivialise them. Machaut has some delicacy of perception and an extraordinarily copious style. This may make him seem tedious now; it must have been a wonderful stimulus to the imagination of one brought up on the much barer style of English lyrics, or the colloquial clichés of the English romances. Close but not slavish imitation of *Behaigne* gave Chaucer the basic structure and much of the very phraseology for his much subtler *Book of the Duchess*. Both poems indicate by their fictional characters real people without being allegorical in any strict sense.

The other poem by Machaut, *Le Jugement du Roi de Navarre*, is notable for its prologue of 458 lines in which the poet tells of the horror he felt, shut up for safety in his own room, during the plague at Rheims, where he was a canon, and where he resided during Edward III's siege of 1359–60, when Chaucer was outside the walls. Most fourteenth-century European poets introduce themselves into some of their own poems. Guillaume virtually does so in *Le Roman de la Rose*; Dante is the most famous example; Machaut, Deschamps, Froissart follow suit, and all the major English poets, Langland, Gower, the *Pearl*-poet, and some minor poets, like Lydgate and Hoccleve, do the same. The poet-in-the-poem may be said to be a characteristically Gothic frame-breaking device, for he is both in and out of the picture. In the poem he is not quite literally his entire 'real' self, yet he is not entirely fictional. Such a personage is sometimes called the 'Narrator', and so he is, but the term is misleading if it implies a character entirely 'inside' the poem, unrelated to a genuine autobiographical 'outside' reality. Machaut illustrates this in *Navarre*. He was really in Rheims, as he writes in the poem, but when he describes himself going into the forest and having a dispute with a lady called 'Happiness' (*Bonneurté*), he slides into fiction. Yet the fiction was probably based on real situations and debates, for the lady in the poem accuses the judgement in the previous poem, *Behaigne*, of being unfair to woman. She probably represents actual criticisms made to Machaut in real life. Chaucer was influenced by this characteristically Gothic shifting viewpoint created by the poet's variable *persona* in the poem. He developed the device of the *persona* in his own way very elaborately and fluidly.

OTHER READING AND INFLUENCES

Chaucer's earliest work might almost be described in horse-breeding terms as by Machaut out of the English romances, but that would weaken the sense of other greatly varied resources acquired and poured into the prepared mould of English language and literature. We have so far concentrated on those literary influences which came to him through living how and when he did, in an English upper-class family and in an Anglo-French court culture. Not to be forgotten are the formally learned Latin school-texts, which made him not only an educated man but a poet. Virgil may have given him some sense of the dignity and gravity which great poetry could aspire to, and which he mentions at the end of *Troilus*, where he places himself quite consciously in the great line of

Virgile, Ovide, Omer, Lucan and Stace.

(V, 1792)

Of the poets mentioned besides Virgil, he could only have read Homer in a brief poor Latin summary, and he was relying rather on his great reputation, than on direct knowledge. Lucan and Statius were well-known Silver Latin poets of elaborately rich style with valuable material. Ovid was the favourite, as he was of almost everybody, read at school and cherished throughout life. Ovid, though a classical writer, enshrines a very medieval ideal of writing. He is full of matter, mythological, historical, amorous, personal, comic, pathetic. His style is richly rhetorical. He can be ironical, and in his *Ars Amatoria* is sexually very explicit. He also condemns love in his *Remedia Amoris*. Lively and various, he provides something for everyone. In his *Heroides*, a series of poems purporting to be letters from ladies betrayed by their lovers, wittily written but full of genuine pathos and sympathy for women, he touched a note which Chaucer responded to in various ways from *The Book of the Duchess* through *Troilus* to *The Legend of Good Women*, many of whose heroines are based on Ovid's poems. The sadness of betrayal in personal relationships, and of death, which is the greatest betrayal, imaged in these stories, corresponds to some deep sense of loss in Chaucer himself, which he managed at last to express and purge only in middle life.

Finally, we must recall the devotionally religious element in the early influences on Chaucer. On the basis of all those prayers learned at school and home was built a series of devotional works, saint's lives and sermons, which found incidental expression in many poems, and more explicitly in such major Canterbury tales as *The Man of Law's Tale of Constance*, *The Clerk's Tale of Patient Griselda*, *The Second Nun's Tale of Cecilia*, *The Prioress's Tale*, and the moralising prose tracts *Melibeus* and *The Parson's Tale*. At this early stage in Chaucer's life the vein of devotion is represented by the translation from French, *An ABC*, a devout poem to the Virgin Mary, elaborate, pious, sentimental, metrically very adept. Probably he also tried his hand at prose, but no early prose survives. It would have been practical utilitarian devotional or scientific prose. English prose was becoming an instrument for fictional entertainment during Chaucer's own lifetime in the *Travels* of Sir John Mandeville, but this was an historical spoof of a kind which somehow seems quite alien to Chaucer. Chaucer's own prose is all serious, and at this point we may note that Chaucer shows, for a layman, such unusually wide knowledge of the Bible, which he would have taken as literal, historical, as well as divinely inspired, truth, that he must have had a copy of his own, read in private. It would have been in Latin.

While all this reading was going on, Chaucer was also living a full life as a young courtier and, for a brief interlude, a sort of soldier. He was travelling a great deal, in England, France and Spain. All this activity must have stimulated his extraordinarily vital imagination. Physically, intellectually and spiritually he was experiencing, exploring, seeking.

NOTES

1. For a discussion of these, related tales, and Chaucer's reaction, see Derek Brewer, *Symbolic Stories* (Cambridge, 1980).
2. For an introductory essay see Derek Brewer, *English Gothic Literature* (London, 1983), 30–69. For an account of the romances in rhyme, see *ibid.*, 70–88.

Chapter 5

Courtier and Soldier

A SIX-YEAR GAP IN THE RECORDS

In October 1360 Chaucer had been paid by Lionel, Earl of Ulster, for bringing letters from Calais to England, The next record is for 22 February 1366. It is a safe-conduct (i.e. a kind of passport) for Chaucer and three companions to travel in the kingdom of Navarre, the Basque country, which lay over the Pyrenees between Aquitaine, held by the English, and the Spanish kingdoms of Castile and Aragon. During these six years Chaucer presumably continued at least at first in Lionel's court. He was reading widely, and probably writing. At some time he started translating *Le Roman de la Rose*, and may have written a number of love-lyrics for which he became well known, but which are lost. What else did he do?

CONTINUING EDUCATION

For long it has been suggested, as in the earlier version of this book, that Chaucer may have spent some time as a part-time mature student in attendance at a law-school in the Inner Temple, one of the so-called Inns of Court. This was based on a remark by Speght, Chaucer's first serious editor and biographer, in his edition of Chaucer's works (and a good deal more) of 1598. Speght said that 'Master Buckley' had seen a record that Chaucer was fined two shillings at the Inner Temple for beating a friar in Fleet Street. The record does not exist, and now it has been shown that nor did the Inner Temple until after 1381, far too late anyway for the young Chaucer. In short the story, and the education proposed, are without foundation. It took root because it suited sixteenth-century Protestant assumptions and twentieth-century educational assumptions.[1]

It is now clear that the only place at which Chaucer, granted his genius, could have acquired his education, after a presumed first schooling, was in a royal court. We have seen him placed as a page, perhaps through his father's influence, and probably moved to Lionel's court. My own guess, seeing that he was passing through Navarre in 1366, is that he spent some of the intervening years at the Black Prince's court in Aquitaine, (see below, p. 69). Then he moved up, or back, to the king's household in 1367. This would indicate that he had received some training and was considered a useful man.

The great historian of fourteenth-century government administration, T. F. Tout, thought that service in a great or royal household, requiring three languages, English, French and Latin, must also have included instruction in official forms of service, acquaintance with several different kinds of law and knowledge of customary duties. A young 'civil servant' became a sort of apprentice either in the royal household or in some more specialised government office under a senior officer. The education was technical, 'hands on', rather than humanistic. It was learning by doing, under supervision. Moreover, court life was still an 'archaic' rather undifferentiated mixture of official, ceremonial, social and personal activities, with much waiting about that might provide private leisure time, unless a man became one of the great administrative officers of state, which Chaucer never did. There were a number of well-educated men about the court. So informal a system would have allowed time for an eager mind to pick up many kinds of knowledge other than administrative. There were skilled writers who spent much of their time in composition.[2] Froissart is the obvious example. There were noblemen like the Earl of Salisbury who had reputations as good lyric poets. The anonymous herald of Sir John Chandos wrote a life of the Black Prince (not yet so named) in French verse. There were the chronicler Geoffrey Baker, the cleric Laurence Minot who wrote jingoistic war songs in English, the friar Richard Maidstone, confessor to Richard II, who recorded Richard's entry into London in 1392 in a Latin poem. Chaucer's contemporary Oton de Graunson, a Savoyard knight who spent much time in the English court celebrated, as did Chaucer, St Valentine's Day, though in French verse. Three other poems of his were transposed with alterations into English verse by Chaucer as *The Complaint of Venus*. Chaucer's friend and poetic disciple, Sir John Clanvowe, composed the elegant courtly poem, *The Boke of Cupide*, and the Lollard-flavoured religious tract *The Two Ways*. And we should remember that the Squire described in *The General Prologue* to *The Canterbury Tales* could not only sing and play an instrument but draw and also write (poetry, I suppose).

All these various people mingled at court with the fighting men who were still active in war or who had become administrators, with university-trained clerics, with lawyers, and with a number of ladies. Although clerics still dominated the 'civil service' a number of the type of men just referred to were laymen, who were beginning to make their way into administrative, or as we might now rather say, managerial positions. The laymen may not have differed greatly in general views from the clerics, but there was a very significant economic difference. Clerics who were employed even in the lay administration of the court could be rewarded with church benefices of various kinds, and the major administrative officers were usually handsomely rewarded by bishoprics or even archbishoprics. The emerging class of literate laymen, of whom Chaucer is so outstanding but by no means the only example, could not be so rewarded. Some of them, like Chaucer's own father, or Chaucer's contemporaries, the great merchants, might make great commercial fortunes, like the grocer Sir Nicholas Brembre (who eventually paid for his success, and for backing the wrong party, with his head). But Chaucer and others like him were more deeply enmeshed at a lower level of administration. For their principal income they had to rely on court favour both for 'jobs' and for the grants and pensions that went with them. The complication here was the power struggle that usually went on in the court, which determined who would get the jobs, rather as in the United States of America today, where much of the administrative personnel depends on which political party is in power. On the other hand, at Chaucer's level, it would seem that most officials were content to act, if they could, for whomever was in power, like the later English Civil Service. Personal loyalty or enmity were only occasionally significant (though we must remember that Chaucer's friend and follower, Thomas Usk, who wrote the English prose work *The Testament of Love*, was executed in the internecine political disputes in the City of London. Not only the court was dangerous to the politically adventurous.) At the very end of his life Chaucer, like the vast majority of officials and the English people as a whole, seems easily to have acquiesced in Henry IV's accession to, which some later enemies said was usurpation of, Richard's throne. Henry IV was after all the son of John of Gaunt and Blanche the Duchess, and both Chaucer and his wife kept within the Lancastrian circle all their lives.

Yet Chaucer seems rarely if ever to have received reward as a poet, or to have written for a patron. (Possible exceptions are *The Book of the Duchess* and *The Legend of Good Women*.) Those grants and gifts that he received must have been in at least the overwhelming majority of cases pay for the work he did as a 'civil servant'. His official career can be paralleled by that of others of whom only the name is now known, as for example Geoffrey Stukeley. If Chaucer had not written great poetry his name too would have been only one of the thousands that recur with some frequency in the records, then disappear leaving not a wrack behind. They are important for the trace they have left of the development of English governance. T. F. Tout sums up the position thus:

> There was an increasing tendency towards the building up of a homogeneous civil service within which circulation was unrestricted, and whereby a permanent career was more easily obtainable in the service of the state. Particularly noticeable was the tendency towards making the posts of the [royal] household the training ground of professional politicians. Even when dwelling in the king's court, these men were more than courtiers, and, on obtaining political charges, they showed that it was possible to combine their duty to the crown with general sympathy with the episcopal and baronial tradition of independent watchfulness of royal action. When the court officers did not rise to this higher level, they remained personally insignificant, and left little mark on history. Though anticlericalism as a principle was no longer prominent, there remained a career for lay as well as for clerical talent. This was the inevitable result of the extension of education to circles outside the clerical sphere. There was the education of the court, which made the *miles literatus*, the knight who knew Latin, no longer a rare or an extraordinary phenomenon, as he had been in the reign of Henry III. How far a court training could under Edward III give a thorough culture to men, originating in the middle class of townsmen, and so remote from the clerical profession that the university had nothing to say to them, can well be illustrated by the career of that eminent civil servant, Geoffrey Chaucer.
>
> (T. F. Tout, *Chapters in the Administrative History of Medieval England* (Longmans, 1928) vol. iii, 201–2)

Although lawyers did not occupy the position they later came to occupy in the bureaucracy, legal matters of various kinds came within the range of activity of working courtiers like Chaucer. In his official career he was briefly appointed in 1386 a Justice of the Peace (i.e. a sort of unpaid magistrate, one of ten), for the county of Kent, and in the same year Member of Parliament for Kent to serve in the contentious parliament later that year, perhaps to support the king's interest. (If so he kept his head down.) At other times he was appointed to various legal or quasi-legal commissions of inquiry which were part of the normal system of government. When he became Controller of the Wool Customs he must have acquired a working knowledge of the relevant 'law merchant' as it was called.

Later in his personal life he had various occasions to deal with aspects of the law, sometimes as 'mainpernor' or guarantor of others, and not least as defendant against the charge of *raptus* by Cecily Champain (see below, p. 118). As fourteenth-century England had no police force and was by modern English standards extremely disorderly, the only remedy against ill-treatment or injustice was litigation. There were many different kinds of court and law, and it was a litigious society. So it is not surprising that references to legal procedures are scattered throughout Chaucer's works, revealing accurate knowledge. None of this required training as a lawyer.

For Chaucer's education we can assume some early schooling, wide experience in a royal court, and then the continuous education acquired by a constantly enquiring mind, rich in experience of court life, travel, people of all ranks and, above all, of books of science, poetry, history, religion, and not least the Bible.

CHAUCER WAS PROBABLY IN AQUITAINE

The safe-conduct through the kingdom of Navarre in 1366 does nevertheless raise most interesting possibilities of experience for Chaucer much closer to knighthood than any legal Inn of Court. The reason why he was travelling through Navarre is not given. That he had three unnamed companions suggests that he was the senior. Such a group was more likely to be on some diplomatic mission than on a pilgrimage. There is no record of his being sent from any English court, but there was no need for him to be, since there was a major and magnificent English court at Bordeaux: that of the Black Prince, no less. The Prince was continuously in Aquitaine in the 1360s, conducting intermittent warfare with the French, who claimed the sovereignty of Aquitaine. The English had a particular interest in the kingdom of Castile, which bordered Navarre. If Castile were allied with France it could send its highly efficient navy to harry English shipping in the Channel and attack English south-coast towns. The king of Castile from 1350 to 1369 was Don Pedro. He was known to his enemies as Pedro the Cruel, but Chaucer calls him the noble, worthy Pedro, glory of Spain (*Monk's Tale*, CT, VII, 2375). He favoured the English, so they supported him. In 1367 he was dethroned by his half-brother Henry of Trastamara, supported by the French. The Black Prince therefore in the same year invaded Spain with a large army and won the great battle of Najera, which enabled Pedro to regain his throne. He was murdered two years later.

Chaucer would have missed Najera because by 1367 he had become a *valectus* of King Edward III in London, but he could well have been previously a member of the Black Prince's household in Bordeaux, for his earlier lady, the Countess of Ulster, had died in 1363. Several of Chaucer's later friends and associates, especially among the Lollard knights (to be mentioned later) had been knights of the Black Prince and had seen action in Aquitaine and Spain. Most prominent of these was Sir Lewis Clifford, a very distinguished man, a friend of Chaucer's, who once carried a poem from the French poet Deschamps to Chaucer complimenting him on being noble, learned, wise and a great translator. Another was Sir Thomas Latimer, and another was Sir William Beauchamp who became Captain of Calais. Chaucer may have first come across these men when serving with them in Aquitaine. Moreover, Chaucer was married by 1366 to Philippa, who was the daughter of Sir Giles (otherwise Payne) Roet, who was a herald and King of Arms for Aquitaine. If he was part of this circle then he must also have been known to the wife of the Black Prince, Joan of Kent, who while the Black Prince lived, and as the widowed mother of the boy-king Richard II from 1377, seems to have had some beneficial political and cultural influence. Perhaps some of the imperious ladies in the later poetry owe something to her.

It would seem a fair guess that between 1360 and 1366 Chaucer passed a year or years, in Aquitaine, associated with the Black Prince's household, and that in February 1366, when he was certainly in Navarre, he was engaged on some diplomatic mission, probably between the courts of the Black Prince and Pedro of Castile. He made many such diplomatic journeys in later life.

CHAUCER'S WIFE PHILIPPA

Philippa Chaucer is first recorded as receiving an annual salary of ten marks (£6 13s. 4d.), for being one of the Queen's ladies-in-waiting, on 12 September 1366. The date of Chaucer's marriage to Philippa is not known. She was herself a working court-lady. When Edward III's Queen Philippa died in 1369 Chaucer's wife became lady-in-waiting to John of Gaunt's second wife, Constance, who was daughter of Pedro of Castile, and who after his death claimed his throne. Philippa's younger sister Katharine, widow of Sir Hugh Swynford since 1372, was also a lady-in-waiting to Constance, and became John of Gaunt's acknowledged mistress, for his second marriage was purely political. She bore him several children and on Constance's death in 1396 married him, thus scandalising the great ladies of court. They did not object to his having a mistress, but they did object to the social implications of his marrying his concubine, daughter of a plain knight. These subtleties of conventional morality are worth bearing in mind when we read the love-affairs in Chaucer's poems. The poems' own morality is not simple.

Philippa, besides her salary, received various gifts from Gaunt, such as his New Year gifts in 1380, 1381, 1382, of a silver cup. She received her last payment on 18 June 1387 and probably died soon after this. Nothing is known of the family life of Geoffrey and Philippa, except that they were often necessarily separated by their work. Chaucer tends to make jokes about marriage and in the late poem to Bukton refers jestingly to his own freedom – his wife being dead. He may well have been a trying husband, with his love-poetry and all. We do not know. His marriage was long-lasting, and jokes at the expense of wives and marriage are traditional and popular among men. Thomas Chaucer, who became wealthy and distinguished in the fifteenth century, was one of their sons. 'Little Lewis' for whom Chaucer wrote his *Treatise on the Astrolabe* was presumably another, but has left no further trace. No other children are known. The gifts received by Philippa, and others that Chaucer received from Gaunt either jointly with her, or separately, are no evidence of special favour from him. They were part of the general system of normal remuneration, where wages were still partly in kind, in the form of food, drink, clothes and valuables.

WORKING IN THE KING'S COURT

From 1367 to 1369 both Chaucer and his wife were occupied in the royal household, with a modest but sufficient income. By 1368 Chaucer had become an Esquire of the King's Household. It was an age before personal service had come to be thought degrading, and his occupations varied between making beds and going on important ambassadorial messages. He remained an Esquire at least till 1378, perhaps later, and doubtless there was more bedmaking in the first year of his appointment than in the last. But it was not a job which the well-born despised. We get most of our information about it from Edward IV's fifteenth-century Household Book which was based on earlier ordinances. There were four 'valecti' or 'Yeoman of Chambre', and they had to

make beddis, to beare or hold torches, to sett boardis, to apparell all
Chambers, and such othir seruices as the Chamberlaine, or Vshers of
Chambre, comaunde or assigne; to attend the Chambre; to watche the
King by course; to goe in messages, etc.

They were to eat in the king's chamber, or in the hall.

Of Squires of the Household there were to be 40, or more if the
king so pleased, with the advice of his high council, 'chosen men of
worship' (i.e. honour) and of great worth. It was a high-class occu-
pation, more than a simple paid 'job', and menial service at such a
level was not degrading. Chaucer would have been expected to keep
up a fashionable honourable appearance as personal servant and aide
to the king, taking his part in a well-run (for the times) administrat-
ive machine. With 20 squires on duty and 20 off, his tasks cannot
have been heavy. The Household Book notes that:

> These Esquires of household of old be accustomed, winter and summer,
> in afternoones and in eueninges, to drawe to Lordes Chambres within
> Court, there to keep honest company after there Cunninge, in talking of
> Cronicles of Kinges, and of others Pollicies, or in pipeing or harpeing,
> synginges, or other actes marcealls, to help to occupie the Court, and
> accompanie estraingers, till the time require of departing.

We may imagine these gatherings, splendid as the frontispiece to the
copy of *Troilus*, in Corpus Christi College Library, Cambridge, when
the great lords and ladies, as well as the less noble ranks, talked of
arms and love, gossiped about the political news, heard songs and
stories. Here the youthful Chaucer, in splendid livery, perhaps sang
those lyrics, now lost, which have already been referred to. These
splendid, sophisticated courtly gatherings were perhaps the primary
audience Chaucer had in mind for his love-poems, his popular comic
tales, his sermons.

Chaucer was now at the centre of the mainstream of English
culture. In himself he draws many of the multiple threads of the
secular culture of the nation together: the English, the popular, the
learned and intellectual, the pious and devout, the chivalric and
military, the administrative, the courtly. Some of these strands did
not easily interweave with others, but the acceptance of this mixture
of partly incompatible elements is very characteristic of the medieval
Gothic amalgam, and of some self-questioning.

Not even Chaucer could bring everything together. His two great
contemporary poets, Langland and the *Gawain*-poet, though not quite

so inclusive, have a broad range which includes other elements not found in Chaucer's work. Langland represents the more anguished depth of religious feeling as it contemplates suffering and evil. Langland lived in London and wrote in a mainly London dialect. His work could have been known to Chaucer and would have been perfectly comprehensible to him, though written in the alliterative form which Langland brought with him from the West Midlands. The *Gawain*-poet moves in a world of romance and myth, of heavenly vision, public cataclysm and personal grief, of resolute endurance. Langland sees the countryside's labour and poverty, the London of low-class pubs. The *Gawain*-poet sees the world of the Northern hills and the jewelled brightness of the Heavenly Jerusalem. He wrote in a north Midlands poetic diction which would have been very difficult to Chaucer, and in alliterative verse which Chaucer associated with warfare. These are the areas which Chaucer only glimpses. But no man can do, or see, everything, and the inclusiveness of Chaucer still exceeds that of any other writer of his time or later, including Shakespeare. The centrality of the king's court, with all its multiple relationships with, and travelling about, in England gave him a position unique for an English poet. His own responsibilities were serious and they forced upon him travel, knowledge of men and affairs, a sense of the world.

KING EDWARD III AND THE HUNDRED YEARS WAR

King Edward III, who dominated his court, came to the throne in 1327 at the age of 14, when his father, Edward II, was foully murdered at the instance of Mortimer, who then ruled with Edward's mother, Isabella. At 15 Edward was married to Philippa of Hainault. At 17 he displaced Mortimer and, in spite of Isabella's pleading, had him hanged. Almost immediately he was engaged in an ill-advised war with the Scots, as he was frequently to be throughout his reign. While he was engaged in winning fruitless victories in Scotland, the French king, Scotland's ally, was stirring up trouble in Aquitaine, the great area in south-western France of which Bordeaux was the chief town, and which at that time owed obedience to the English king. There were also conflicts of trading interests between France and England in the Low Countries, and English and French traders were killing each other on the seas. But, with all the other reasons for English enmity to France, no doubt Froissart has much of the truth of it when he says,

The English will never love or honour their king, unless he be victorious and a lover of arms and war against their neighbours and especially such as are greater and richer than themselves. Their land is more fulfilled of riches and all manner of goods when they are at war than in times of peace. They take delight and solace in battles and slaughter: covetous and envious are they above measure of other men's wealth . . . The King of England must needs obey his people and do their will.

Edward was warlike and successful. In 1337, two or three years before Chaucer's birth, he declared war on France and began the so-called Hundred Years War, an intermittent affair which lasted throughout Chaucer's life. Apart from French raids on English south-coast towns the fighting was in France, a dismal record of pillage and plunder. The great English victories against superior French numbers and old-fashioned tactics at Crècy (1346) and Poitiers (1356) could not offset the long English retreat from their French possessions, but made the war in its earlier stages appear profitable and glorious. Edward celebrated the victory of Crècy and the capture of Calais by instituting in 1347 the Order of the Garter, based on the idea of King Arthur and the Knights of the Round Table. The institution of such orders was popular with the nobility of the time, but few such orders have lasted, like the Garter, to the present day. Several of Chaucer's friends, for example Sir Lewis Clifford, were Knights of the Garter.

THE BLACK DEATH

The second half of the fourteenth century, covering the whole of Chaucer's lifetime, was a period of great stress and rapid development, including the great calamity of the Black Death, 1348–9, and what seemed to some at the time the equally great calamity of the Peasants' Revolt of 1381. It may be useful to remember these as a backdrop to our view of Chaucer's own life, especially as we come to 1368, which is now usually thought to be the date of *The Book of the Duchess*. The poem is an elegy for John of Gaunt's first wife Blanche, daughter of Henry of Lancaster, through whom Gaunt inherited the vast Lancastrian estates. The marriage had been a political match for this second of Edward III's sons, but there is little doubt that it was also a love-match. The death of Blanche reminds us of the death and grief which always threatens the pride of life.

The first of the great national calamities of Chaucer's lifetime was the great visitation of the plague which swept Europe, and which devastated England in 1348–9. Known as the Black Death, it is thought that about a third of the population died. Apart from the terror of such widespread death, the disease was in itself horrible. Hard lumps arose in the groin and armpit which were exceptionally painful and could not be lanced. Swellings, carbuncles, vomiting, spitting blood, were among the other symptoms. Sometimes the victims flung themselves out of their beds from pain and delirium. The mortality was so great that in some places whole villages and tracts of land lay waste and uninhabited; but the towns suffered most with their crowded and insanitary conditions.

The fearful mortality hastened many changes which were bringing a new world with so many birth-pangs out of the old, but the immediate results were misery, derangement and loss. The progress of the arts and sciences was hindered. The University of Oxford almost ceased to function for two or three years after the Black Death. The economic results were a great rise in prices and a great shortage of labour, and paradoxically for a while greater prosperity. This led to rising expectations. Special statutes were enacted to keep wages down but this produced great tension since for the poor the potential value of their labour became quite disproportionate to its legal reward. Parliament tried to enforce the Statutes of Labourers, to keep wages down. The great nobles who paid lip-service and more to the ideal of chivalry were the actual leaders of the country, and their government in this long crisis was bad. The Black Prince, the embodiment of fourteenth-century chivalry, great in tournaments, great in war, devout in religion, was also selfishly extravagant, and coldly indifferent to the sufferings of his people.

Yet the pessimism caused by the Black Death in England can be exaggerated. Certainly the chroniclers express their horror, and there was great dislocation and social discontent. But the plague was a dreadful intensification of the normally difficult conditions of life rather than a total change in the quality of disaster. Much of normal life continued. Building was not totally stopped. Perhaps the morbidity and sentimentality of much specifically religious writing, such as sermons, in the fifteenth century, were an indirect result of continuous later visitations of plague, which if not as bad as the Black Death were bad enough. But fourteenth-century English literature, which expresses something of the mind of the national culture, is by no means mainly pessimistic. It may be stoically grim, but it has none of the nihilism, *ennui*, *angst*, and horror of life often found in late twentieth-century literature.

NOTES

1. C. F. E. Spurgeon, *Five Hundred Years of Chaucer Criticism and Allusion, 1357–1900* (Cambridge, 1925); *Chaucer: The Critical Heritage, 1385–1837*, edited by Derek Brewer (1978), 9, 34; J. A. Hornsby, *Chaucer and the Law* (Norman, Oklahoma, 1988), 7–20.
2. T. F. Tout, 'Literature and Learning in the English Court', *Speculum* 4 (1929), 365–89.

Chapter 6

The Book of the Duchess I: Quest and Commemoration

Throughout this long period through which we have sought the formative elements of Chaucer's genius he too must have been seeking answers to questions hard to formulate, and surely also enjoying himself on his pilgrimage-quest, as later, and in as varied ways, did the pilgrims he immortalised.

His own and Gower's testimonies suggest that he successfully wrote many lyrics. He developed great skill in rhyming and various verse forms, all in the French tradition. The traditional English alliterative 'rum, ram, ruf' (*CT*, XII, 43), with its Western and Northern associations, he only rarely touched on much later out of virtuosity.

Apart from lyrics Chaucer's earliest attempt at sustained narrative, we might guess, was his beginning to translate *Le Roman de la Rose*. As this is more than 20 000 lines long, the attempt was over-ambitious and prudently abandoned after 1705 lines. Its style is close to that of *The Book of the Duchess*, to be discussed in a moment, and it is well worth reading for its cheerful vigour, as the whole poem is worth reading for what it tells us of the life and thought of the period. Perhaps sometime too Chaucer tried out his hand at translating, with Machaut's help, part of the classical Latin author Ovid's story of Ceyx and Alcyone, one of the rare accounts of devoted married love in the whole of the *Metamorphoses*. Ovid tells of the death of Ceyx. The contrast of happy married love with early death, the mixture of joyous love and pathos, always affected Chaucer. It is part of the mystery of life. If Chaucer did translate this poem early in his writing career, it was to prove useful.

GRAND TRANSLATEUR

At this point the significance of translation in Chaucer's work must be emphasised, though only a brief comment can be spared on a large topic which has recently received much attention.[1] Translation was 'in the air' in England in the second half of the fourteenth century, connected with the desire to have notable works in English. The Lollards were pressing for the Bible in English; the common people demanding political documents in English.[2] The Lord in John of Trevisa's *Dialogue Between a Lord and a Clerk* claims that English is as good as any other language, and the *Dialogue* is the preface to Trevisa's translation of Ranulph Higden's history, *Polychronicon*. There was little sense of linguistic nationalism but a strong sense of the present appropriateness of English for important material. Chaucer's travelling curiosity led him not only to French, Latin and Italian but returned him to English, with no sense of the inferiority of English (except in 'scarcity of rhyme', *Complaint of Venus*, 80), but with an eager appropriation of further subject-matter. He moved easily between English and Continental French. It was natural for him to write in English, while Anglo-French, to judge from his rather snooty comment on the Prioress's French of the 'school of Stratford-atte-Bowe' (a London suburb) (*CT*, I, 122), seemed provincial and naïve.

Though Chaucer's work has been longer continuously commented on by his own countrymen than that of any other European poet in the vernacular, it was a Frenchman (who spoke 'the French of Paris' (*CT*, I, 126), Eustache Deschamps (*c.* 1340–*c.* 1406), who first commended his poetry. He sent a poem to Chaucer by the hand of a mutual friend, the great soldier Sir Lewis Clifford, complimenting Chaucer on being the English Socrates, Seneca, Ovid, etc., and above all the translator of *Le Roman de la Rose*. The four stanzas of the Balade each concludes with the line

Grand translateur, noble Geoffroy Chaucier[3]

There seems nothing patronising in Deschamps' attitude to Chaucer's poetry, and the French poet is graciously and extravagantly modest about his own achievements, which were, or became, very extensive.

Translation might be 'word for word' or 'sense for sense'. There was often a feeling that the intrinsic meaning was the same, whatever the language, which reflects the underlying unity both in time and space felt by medieval culture. Chaucer's translation of the first 1705 lines of *Le Roman de la Rose* seems early partly because of the style, reminiscent of the English metrical romances, and the closely literal sense. Soon after Chaucer took more freedom, sometimes translating closely, sometimes freely embroidering, sometimes inventing quite new material. The degree to which he does this is part of the fascination of his later works. There is nothing unusual in itself about his easy use of French, Italian or Latin material. All traditional writers, up to and including Shakespeare, adopt and adapt pre-existing material. Novelty in subject-matter was not felt to be of first importance, though an author naturally updated his material in order to appeal to his current audience or readers.

In Chaucer's case they were probably both. At all events he plays with the notions of both hearer and reader within his poems up to *The Canterbury Tales*, near the end of his life. In his earlier poetry the idea of the audience seems more prominent, and he uses an 'oral' style, but nevertheless he employs, and translates, written material, adapting it, closely or loosely, for his own novel purposes. Such was the case with the remarkable poem, on the death of the Duchess Blanche, wife of John of Gaunt, which is his earliest datable poem.

THE DEATH OF BLANCHE, THE DUCHESS

It is so interesting and unusual a poem, and introduces so many topics and themes that will echo through so much of Chaucer's later poetry that the poem deserves much fuller study than it is usually given. *The Book of the Duchess* is the prototype of Chaucer's poetry at least up to *The Canterbury Tales*. It gives the prime concrete examples which will hold for much of his later writing. Even its weakness – a certain verbosity – provides fascinating material. It is never vapid. Unfortunately much interesting detail will have to be passed over.[4]

Although we come fresh to the poem, there is an essential piece of preliminary knowledge we must share with the first audience or readers. It was written in the knowledge of a death. Blanche, wife of John of Gaunt, one of the most powerful men in the kingdom, the fourth son of King Edward III, was married aged 19 in 1359, had five children, and died in September 1368 aged 28. Although the marriage had been convenient, for Blanche inherited the vast lands and wealth of her father the great Henry Duke of Lancaster, and although the 19-year-old Gaunt had had an early affair which had produced a daughter,[5] there seems no doubt that her death was a bitter blow to her husband. He and she and Chaucer were all much of an age, and must have known each other for some ten years.

It could well be that the poem had been called for and written in haste. Blanche certainly died in September 1368 and there were already suggestions in November 1368 that Gaunt should marry the daughter of the Count of Flanders, though this came to nothing.[6] Political arrangements would not wait on personal feelings. And personal feelings, though natural and intense, are often, in such a vulnerable traditional society, felt for a shorter period, perhaps because they are so intense, and life is brief and changeable. Chaucer may have put the poem together, perhaps using an already composed 'Ceyx and Alcyone' as part of it, between 12 September and early November 1368.

The poem has a sense of trouble, and a pretence of ignorance of its cause, which makes us feel that it was composed soon after Blanche's death. Our most likely imagination is that it was read on some courtly occasion to a group including John of Gaunt. As only three manuscripts survive, with a fourth implied by the different text printed by W. Thynne in 1532, it can never have had wide distribution. A personalised partly domestic occasion seems the likeliest, and adds poignancy of our reading. To suppose it read at one of the annual commemorations of Blanche's death, at which Gaunt was not present till 1374, implies an artificiality of context that seems wrong. In 1374 a magnificent alabaster tomb for Blanche was set up in Old St Paul's in which her effigy was accompanied by his, for when he should die and be laid beside her, although in 1372 he had married Constance of Castile. Chaucer's poem might have been another monument. But the poem has an immediacy, despite a certain flippancy, to be discussed later, which encourages a belief that it was written in the immediate context of Blanche's death.

To some extent the poem creates its own context of a private colloquy reported to a very small audience, and this should guide our response – discreet, sympathetic, close but not closely intimate, sharing the knowledge of the sad recent death of a beautiful beloved lady whom we had known and at a distance revered.

THE STORY AND STYLE OF THE POEM

We can therefore join in imagination some relatively small group of the highest in the land, in some degree of social intimacy, perhaps to console a great man, certainly to commemorate a great lady. This group is the core of all Chaucer's listeners and readers for most of his life: the royal court, royal patronage, lords and their ladies, with attendant knights and ladies. It is a remarkable beginning for a young English poet.

At this level of society they mostly knew French, but English was normal except perhaps for the old King Edward III (56 in 1368) though even he could at least swear and pray in English. They were familiar with contemporary or slightly earlier French poets like Machaut and Froissart. They were also familiar, with the less artistically sophisticated English metrical romances, as listed in Chaucer's later parody, *Sir Thopas* (*CT*, VII, 897–918), and as revealed in the very style of the opening of *The Book of the Duchess*.[7] So there is a mixture of familiarity and novelty to be found in these opening lines

> I have great wonder, *be this lyght*
> How that I lyve, *for day ne nyght*
> I may not slepe *wel nygh noght*,
> I have so many an ydel thoght
> *Purely* for defaute of slep
> That *by my trouthe* I take no kep
> Of nothing, how hyt *cometh or gooth*,
> Ne me nys nothyng *leef nor looth*
>
> (1–8)

These are the four-stress lines (final -*e* being sounded where necessary), the jog-trot rhythm, the colloquial familiar style, of the vernacular English romances. I have emphasised the typical romance phrases. Chaucer must have been brought up on them. Yet there is a real difference. It is an historic moment for English poetry because never before had an English poet put his personal feeling so blatantly to the fore. Nevertheless, Chaucer is actually paraphrasing, in *English* style, the opening lines by the *French* poet and chronicler Froissart of his *Paradys d'Amour*, and the audience would have recognised the familiar French topic. Although English verse had long been indebted to French for the material of the metrical romances, this particular blend of personal feeling, perhaps helped by the practice of lyric, had not been heard before so far as our evidence goes. Chaucer, using English and French tranditions, has already struck a characteristically personal note, a blend of the serious and the flippant that often recurs in much of his later verse. It makes his work intriguingly enigmatic, open to a variety of responses.

The poet declares that the sleeplessness he is suffering could be fatal. Someone may ask, he says, why he suffers so – he cannot tell. But he has suffered this sickness for eight years with no hope of cure, for there is only one physician may heal him. Eight years is too long for this to refer to the death of Blanche. Moreover such a reference to so great a lady would be an impertinence of the kind that Chaucer, for all his occasional flippancy, would never commit.

Froissart in his original makes it clear that he is suffering from the sickness of unrequited love. Frank though Chaucer seems to be about his state of mind he nevertheless maintains an ultimate reserve, and leaves the question open for the readers, then or now, to come to their own conclusion.

Nevertheless the oblique reference does seem most likely to refer to an uncured, incurable, love-sickness. It is highly conventional, and to that extent fictional (and Chaucer had been married for at least two years). This does not mean that the speaker is presented as if he were a purely dramatic figure *within* the poem, bearing no relationship to the real-life man outside. To believe this deprives our reading of a richness, a tang, removes a stimulating obscurity or puzzle about the relationship between the real poet and his presentation of himself in the poem, cutting the poem off from actual life and death in the fourteenth century, and from our own full response in the twentieth. Here I simply use the word 'poet' to indicate my sense of the author as revealed in his work. The author's – any author's – presentation of themselves in words, to an audience or readership, must inevitably be in part like a script for an actor; must have a certain (or rather, uncertain) fictional element. Language itself, verbal expression, being a selection of what *could* be said, has inevitably a fictional element, however much it sets out to tell the truth.

The poet presents himself as sleepless from sorrow, as if implicitly to remind John of Gaunt that there are other griefs, and that grief if persisted in will lead to death, as lack of sleep would. The conventional pose of the sleepless lover distances the poet from the real grief in his audience and removes any ponderous intrusiveness. We are led indirectly into the central subject of the poem. This beginning is original to the point of genius and oddity.

As often in Chaucer it is hard to be quite certain of the intended tone of the extravagantly emotional introduction quoted above. Its feeling goes beyond the tone of the passage in Froissart on which it is based. Is it just an unintentional naïve vulgarity on Chaucer's part, derived from the similar exclamatory style of the English romances? Does Chaucer intend, by the exaggeration, to give a hint of self-parody? How serious is his feeling of deprivation, his desperation? It is an attitude he will often strike in the future, at once putting himself forward, yet protesting his exclusion, his ignorance, his sense of loss.

The 'mased thing' he describes himself as being

Alway in poynt to falle adoun

(13)

strikes no stoical, self-restrained note. Suffering is intrinsic to love, and the lover is timid. The lady is different and, as part of her attraction, *in*different. But all this is only hinted.

Soon after this mysterious and only half-relevant reference to the cause of his own distress the poet shifts his tone. There are rapid changes of mood in much of Chaucer's poetry. The tone now becomes more resolute, the interest is turned outward, the style of address equally confidential, but also lighter in spirit.

> So whan I saw I might not slepe
> Til now late this other night,
> Upon my bed I sat upright
> And bad oon reche me a book,
> A romaunce, and he it me tok
> To rede and drive the night away;
> For me thoughte it better play
> Then playe either at ches or tables ...
>
> *backgammon*
> (44–51)

The poet has a servant at his call even at night-time. He must also have had one or two candles brought, and he has books nearby. Here he constructs a well-to-do courtly domestic situation.

The passion for the imaginative experience of reading, and particularly the passion for stories, and therefore people, is again personal and heavily emphasised. It raises one of the eternal paradoxes of reading for pleasure – that it may make one miserable, yet satisfy an imaginative need. After reading the book he had sent for, the poet says the sorrow which the heroine of the story feels at the death of her husband affected him so deeply that

> I ferde the worse al the morwe.
>
> (99)

All serious readers know that feeling. And we have our minds implicitly turned to thoughts of that other marital bereavement, not yet mentioned, which we know to be the poem's *raison d'être*, and which has recently taken place.

The story the poet reads is the legend of King Ceyx and his Queen Alcyone, told by Ovid, *Metamorphoses*, 11, 410–749, though a number of minor details are interestingly altered. Chaucer probably knew the not-too-easy Latin, but also may have used French versions.

The story in Chaucer's account tells how Ceyx the king is drowned. His wife, Alcyone, not knowing this, fears his loss. The goddess Juno causes the drowned corpse of Ceyx to be briefly animated so as to appear to Alcyone and tell her of his death. She then dies of grief. Ovid concludes and softens this grim little narrative with the metamorphosis of Ceyx and Alcyone into birds, as some of

Chaucer's educated readers may well have known, but the poet leaves it out. He will have no absurd consolation. But he inserts an extensive and entertaining passage of how Juno sends a messenger to Morpheus the god of sleep to tell him to animate the dead body of Ceyx and bring it before Alcyone. There is lively colloquial dialogue, even a touch of farce, which makes a strange compound with the pathos of the story. Flippancy and sadness go hand in hand. After reading the poet makes a confessedly comic vow to Morpheus, the god of sleep, with a jesting reference to his own religious belief. To make sure we know he is jesting he adds, a little apologetically,

> And in my game I sayde anoon . . .
>
> (238)

Having made the deliberately facetious vow of dedicating feather-bed, sheets, pillows, etc. to Morpheus, he falls asleep and has a remarkable dream.

He dreams he is awakened at dawn on a bright May morning by a beautiful dawn chorus of birds. He is in a lovely chamber, the sun shining through windows of stained glass that tell the whole story of Troy. The walls are beautifully painted with the text of the whole immense French poem *Le Roman de la Rose*, and its commentary. Plainly this is dream impressionism of space, quite unrealistic yet in dream convincing. The narrative goes on with the same dream-like abrupt transitions, and omissions, yet bright salient details. The poet hears outside the noise of the beginning of a hunt. At once he is out of his room on a horse to follow them. The huntsmen lose the scent and, the horse forgotten, the poet is then walking in a wood, led away by a little dog, in its turn immediately forgotten. In the flowery ways of this great wood, full of wild creatures, he comes upon a man in black, a young knight 24 years old (Gaunt was 29 but people's ages were vague (no birth certificates) and more approximately treated). He speaks aloud a poem which laments the death of his lady.

There follows a beautifully courteous exchange, in which it is clear that the man in black is the superior, because the poet speaks to him so deferentially, using the polite second-person plural form 'you', while the man in black uses the more condescending second person singular 'thou'. The poet, disregarding or forgetting the earlier poetic complaint about death, gently asks the man in black the cause of his sorrow. Although this has already been stated, Chaucer has to make clear to his audience without question what the true issue is. In this kind of poetry the audience, as in Shakespeare, is always put in possession of all the knowledge it needs, which normally exceeds that of the characters within the poem. The dream-like atmosphere, and the poet's deferential presentation of himself as a simple-minded, literalistic, but sympathetic person, allow us to accept the situation without question, and though we realise the essence of the matter we are eager to follow the poet's gentle questioning in order to hear the account of the man in black, and how he came to this plight. He describes himself metaphorically as in conflict with Fortune. He has fallen in love with a bright lady, described as all medieval heroines are, with golden hair, fair face, long slender neck and arms, joyous and eloquent in speech, good, rational and gentle of nature. The long description of her beauty and goodness is conventional, but still a touching evocation.[8] The poet's simple questioning prompts an account of how eventually the lady came to love the man in black after his long and faithful service. The poet represents himself as unable to understand metaphors of death, and the man in black is forced to undertake his own self-expressive therapy, to accept cruel reality for himself, by saying literally, 'She is dead.' The poet utters a brief exclamation of surprise and pity that is almost banal

> Is that youre los? Be God, hyt ys routhe. *pity*
>
> (1310)

The whole presupposition of the poem is a respectful pity, and the only surprise here is the surprise that the poet-dreamer expresses. The abruptness, we can see, once it is expressed, is the *only* way to conclude. It is far the best way to avoid anticlimax and show respect.

The poem is rapidly concluded. The hart-hunting is done, the king goes home to a place nearby. The king must be the 'emperror Octovyen' to whom it was earlier said the hunt belonged. The reference is perhaps an evocation of the Roman Emperor Augustus, with whom was associated the Golden Age of Rome, but equally there is an oblique reference perhaps to the real King Edward III, or even to Gaunt, for the home is

> A long castel with walles white
> Be seynt Johan, on a ryche hil
>
> (1318–19)

which is a series of non-comic puns on the names of *John* of Gaunt, otherwise *Lancaster* (= long castle), and his castle at *Richmond*, then called *Rychemont*, or 'rich hill', in Yorkshire. It belonged to Gaunt until 1372, which itself suggests an earlier date for the poem.

These references, along with the earlier reference to the now dead lady's name as 'White' (914), the English for Blanche, fixes the poem firmly to her, and to John of Gaunt as the man in black, the colour of mourning.

THE STRENGTH OF AN ENDING

The effect has been to express mourning, but also recreate and commemorate a beauty and joy that had really been, and as recalled by memory and poetry, still is. Now we have mourned enough. It is commonly recognised that intense mourning for a short period is probably the best way of coming to terms with the death of a loved person. Sorrow has been re-enacted and so absorbed, an elegy turned into praise-poetry. It is a kind of consolation, a kind of monument. It is hard to think of all this as written and probably first spoken very long after Blanche's death in a culture where early death was so frequent, rapid remarriage common. Throughout his poetry Chaucer is both sympathetic and unsentimental on the subject of death.

Endings of narratives (closure) are important. A medieval rhetorical rule was that 'the ende is every tales strengthe' as Chaucer makes Pandarus, an accomplished rhetorician, say (*Troilus and Criseyde*, II, 260). Medieval men believed in a strong apocalyptic ending to the world, the Day of Judgement, when the dead should arise, and divine Justice at last be done. Something of the division between just and unjust in Chaucer's own work occurs right at the end of *The Canterbury Tales*, when he condemns all his secular writing, including *The Book of the Duchess* among most of the rest of his finest work. Here, in this poem, the end is certainly strong. But it is an end without finality. There is also in Chaucer a resistance to closure, perhaps a constitutional reluctance to come to a final conclusion, the product both of scepticism and the consciousness of many different possible opinions about the same thing. (One of Chaucer's favourite remarks is to the effect that 'Diverse folk diversely they seyde,' repeated in similar words in contexts as different as *The Reeve's Tale CT*, I, 3857; *The Man of Law's Tale*, *CT*, II, 211; *The Merchant's Tale*, *CT*, IV, 1469; *The Squire's Tale*, *CT*, V, 202. There are other related remarks elsewhere in his works.

CENTRE AND MARGIN

So Chaucer from the very first confronts death and suffering at the heart of courtly glamour and joy. The only consolation offered is to have known beauty and joy in a beloved person. Symbolically, in the heart of the wood, Chaucer goes to the heart of the matter, leaving aside for a while the pleasant superficial bustle of the world, yet returning to it with resolution and relief.

The centrality of Chaucer's position in life is complemented by the urgent necessity he obviously feels also to go to the depths and margins of experience, to the extremes, for it is there, paradoxically, that the central issues of life and death show most clearly. Margins and borders of experience, and transitions, the crossing over from one sort of life to another, of which the most startling example is death, continually draw his attention. Although he refuses to cross borders, restless curiosity possesses him, to find the hunt, to wander in the wood, to ask the man the cause of his grief; all his life he seeks, through philosophy and science and religion, through love and marriage, through the texture of ordinary life, for further meanings, as he explores experience from the new reading of both familiar and unfamiliar texts. He has a restlessly creative mind, not disdaining the old, but feeding on it and continuously transforming it.

The poem is beautifully easy to follow, like all Chaucer's poetry. It was not intended to be difficult, partly because Chaucer often appears to have an *audience* in mind, and his purpose is entertainment, however serious the ultimate message may be. Perhaps the desire to entertain is one of the sources of his irrepressible jesting which crops up everywhere. Too keen a sense of humour can lead to breaches of decorum, as may be thought to happen in *The Book of the Duchess*. This raises some interesting problems which add to the fascination of so much of Chaucer's work. Diversity is uncertainty, and is also inconsistency. We must recognise the uncertainties and contradictions present in all cultures and works of art, and notably in Chaucer's. Decorum and unity of tone are requirements of the eighteenth century, not of the fourteenth century. Recognition of apparent contradictions often leads to deeper understanding, as if we look through some cleft in a surface to the more fundamental, but mysterious, substances below that provoke our wonder. This 'fractured', sometimes extravagant, or inconsistent surface quality is more typical of Chaucer's achievement of poetic resonance than the more superficial mysteriousness or vagueness or association of much and later Romantic poetry.

QUEST AND QUESTIONING

The poet seeks the mystery of death and the poem in part proceeds by questioning. Why, since the poet-dreamer has heard the young mourning knight say quite clearly that his lady is dead, does the dreamer ask the reason for the knight's sorrow? A partial answer has already been suggested in the non-realistic nature of such public, primarily oral poetry, which has to make its point explicitly whatever the psychological or rational improbability. We often need an answer to be stated several times before we can fully take it in.

A different kind of answer attributes a psychological subtlety to the poet-dreamer, namely that by presenting himself as a rather stupid enquirer he wishes to draw out from the man in black an explicit account of his sorrow – in other words, employing the twentieth-century psychoanalytical 'talking cure'. But this implies a modern subtlety of characterisation based on novelistic assumptions about naturalism, consistency, unity in literature, which do not usually apply to medieval literature.

Again, it is almost universally accepted that 'hunting the hart' is an analogy, or symbolic expression, for 'hunting the heart', expressing the effect of the poet-dreamer's questioning of the man in black. This seems to me a misunderstanding. Certainly both 'hart' and 'heart' are spelt by Chaucer 'herte'. Chaucer does use some puns very obviously and a number of metaphorical expressions are found in his poetry describing the human heart.[9] The animal hart is the male stag. We are not told whether or not the hart was killed but simply that

> al was doon
> For that tyme, the hart huntyng.
>
> (1312–13)

In what sense can either the delicate questioning by the poet-as-dreamer, or the unrestrained outpouring of the mourner, be thought of as 'hunting a feeling'?

Nor is there any reference to the quite different 'hunt of love' found in some Continental literature. In no sense is love hunted, or hunts, here. We should take the text as adequate in its own obvious meaning, for Chaucer several times expresses his preference for the 'naked text' without 'glose': that is, without allegorical interpretation, for example *Prologue G*, 86, to *The Legend of Good Women*.

ARITHMETIC AND NUMEROLOGY

But it is possible there is a further pattern of meaning suggested by the reference to 'Argus' (435), who invented Arabic numerals. Numerology has been briefly noted above (p. 18). It has been noted[10] that there are three clearly marked sections in the poem, 62–214, 290–442, 1145–1297, each of 153 lines, traditionally the Number of Salvation. The 'song' of the man in black is 11 lines long (line 480 does not exist – it arose from scribal error). Eleven lines is odd in a poem of rhyming couplets but the number 11 is traditionally the number of death. The message would be of death but salvation. The total number of lines of the poem is 1333, or in Roman numerals MCCCXXXIII which, with its emphasis on threes, might signify the Trinity.

This is tantalising. The numbers seem more than coincidental. We note that in *The Parliament of Fowls*, the seven-line stanzas, the date of St Valentine's day – twice seven, the total number of lines, 699, multiplying threes – may have numerological significance. If so it marks a deeper layer of meaning. But no pattern is as complete and satisfying as (once it is noticed) in *Pearl*. Maybe they are early partial experiments. They do not seem to be characteristic of the later Chaucer. And why should Argus, inventor of Arabic numerals, thus arithmetic, be mentioned?

NOTES

1. For an example see the essays in *The Medieval Translator*, edited by Roger Ellis *et al.* (Cambridge, 1989).
2. Stephen Justice, *Writing and Rebellion: England in 1381* (Berkeley, 1994).
3. For the full text and translation see Derek Brewer, *Chaucer, The Critical Heritage* (London, 1978), vol. I, 39–42.
4. There is an excellent separate edition by Helen Phillips, *The Book of the Duchess* (Durham Medieval Texts, 3rd edn 1997).
5. He had had an affair with Marie de St Hilaire: Chris Given-Wilson and Alice Curteis, *The Royal Bastards* (London, 1984), 147.
6. J. N. Palmer, 'The Historical Context of *The Book of the Duchess*', *The Chaucer Review* 8 (1974), 253–61.
7. Derek Brewer, 'The Relationship of Chaucer to the English and European Traditions', in *Chaucer: the Poet as Storyteller* (London, 1984), 8–36.
8. Derek Brewer, 'The Ideal of Feminine Beauty in Medieval Literature', in *Tradition and Innovation in Chaucer* (London, 1982), 30–45.
9. Derek Brewer, 'Chaucer's Poetic Style', *The Cambridge Chaucer Companion*, edited by P. Boitani and J. Mann (Cambridge, 1986), 237–8.
10. T. A. Shippey, 'Chaucer's Arithmetic', *The Chaucer Review* 31 (1996), 184–200.

Chapter 7

The Book of the Duchess II: Dreaming the Spoken and Written Self

DREAM POETRY

Chaucer chose the form of a dream because it suits his questioning purposes so well. Dream poetry was fashionable and allows a great fluidity of narration. He does not have to give tedious details of how he got up, dressed, went outside to the stable, got his horse, etc. Dreams actually happen, as we all know, as a mixture of realism and fantasy, told through a single individual whose word we must accept. Nothing in dreams can be proven and they usually have a certain mysterious remoteness.

Dream poetry is a whole genre, even a collection of genres, in medieval European poetry, of great wealth, as A. C. Spearing has shown.[1] It was the essential vehicle of the love-vision, and *Le Roman de la Rose* had set the fashion. A dream is so internal and unverifiable, yet so authentically personal; so vivid, yet so free from everyday limitations of cause and effect; obviously symbolic, yet obviously attached to life. All this makes it the perfect vehicle for poetry like Chaucer's which has one foot in the real world, one foot in fantasy. It has the necessary non-responsibility of art, yet dreams from Biblical times onwards have been claimed to reveal religious and other truth. By Chaucer's time an elaborate classification of dreams had developed with its roots in late-Classical Latin literature. Chaucer fully avails himself of the variety, charm, touches of realism, apparently arbitrary sequences of event and symbolic possibilities of the form.

The dream-setting softens the harsh fact of death and puts contemporary affairs at a distance. It allows for varieties of mood, an abrupt switching of the scene. All is held together by the poet's narrating voice, not by his 'character', but simply by the assertion of what has happened to him. The three-fold structure of *The Book of the Duchess* is thematically connected, begins with the present everyday world, and ends with it. There is no need to press for a consistency greater than this, nor any feeling that discontinuity is disruptive. The poem is held together by the poet's authenticating voice.

DREAM AND REALITY

One of the marvels of the poem is that it is both in and out of history, as the dream allows. The death is historical, but the hunt is led by the 'emperour Octovyen' (368), partly a figure from the English romances, partly a remote evocation of the Roman emperor Augustus. The details of the hunt are realistic, though the poet shows no interest in it. The Lady and the man in black are presented in idealised literary terms; they also correspond to real people.

These people, John of Gaunt in particular, were of the highest social, political and economic rank. The court was that of Edward III. Though it is a poem for a court and accepts the glamour and order of an ideal court, courts in medieval literature are normally represented, doubtless correctly, as hotbeds of envy, jealousy, flattery, immorality, as well as places of colour, festivity and power. Chaucer, fully a courtier, is never fully committed to the court as a way of life. In the poem he withdraws from it to question a more personal joy and grief. In later poems royal courts can be criticised, as even Queen Alceste does (*Legend of Good Women, Prologue* F, 352–9).

Chaucer always shows a certain detachment from the court, whether Edward's or more particularly Richard's.[2] For some critics this implies on Chaucer's part the anxiety or social unease of the upwardly socially mobile bourgeois among the aristocracy. That is an anachronistic judgement. Condemnation of the court is absolutely standard among authors (a touchy group) from Walter Map to Pope and later. But a love–hate relationship is apparent. In Chaucer's case throughout his life he is a courtier writing for courtiers and gentry. He is gentry, like others in similar positions in the court. He is close to men and women at the very centre. Later in life he is ready to exhort Richard II to be 'honourable', and also 'Shew forth thy sword of castigacioun' (*Lak of Stedfastnesse*, 22, 26), so he is not lacking in confidence and is on the side of authority. He petitions for reward. But he also has a personal reserve which seems strong and independent. It is not a feeling of inferiority before his social superiors. The symbolic structure of *The Book of the Duchess* shows him more interested in the emotions of the heart than in the courtly activities of hunting or festivity or elaborate public mourning.

THE CONSTRUCTION OF THE SELF

The dream-poem allows the play of the poet's 'I' and 'not-I'. It reveals the compulsion that Chaucer seems to feel here, and in his later poetry, to present himself with a kind of egoism, yet also to conceal himself, to keep his own secrets. He acts himself; but all acting is impersonation of one person by another. The divided self is more a modern than an ancient phenomenon, but the development of individualism in fourteenth-century poets leads them towards this kind of self-consciousness, which some critics call a subjective reflexivity.

Such self-awareness, even self-promotion, comes and goes in the European tradition. Classical Latin poetry has it in Ovid among others. St Paul's letters in the New Testament touch on the paradox of the divided self. The rise of the lyric in late Latin and in the medieval vernaculars encouraged consciousness of the individual self. For Chaucer the ultimate model of his poetry, combining dream-poem and the presentation of the self, is *Le Roman de la Rose*. When Chaucer translated the first 1705 lines at the beginning of *The Romaunt of the Rose*, he fell into the same perky style as the beginning of *The Book of the Duchess*, with the poet talking of himself, of love, and of his dream five years ago when he was 20, except that his subject is joy not sorrow. Fourteenth-century European poets regularly introduced themselves into their poems. Chaucer's English contemporaries, William Langland in his *Piers Plowman*, the *Gawain*-poet in *Pearl*, Gower in his *Confessio Amantis*, all in their very different ways presented aspects of themselves in their poems in ways that are clearly not entirely fictional.

In *The Book of the Duchess* Chaucer puts himself forward at first as one who is unsuccessful in love, suffering deprivation. Then, with a certain social confidence, follows the account of how he lay sleepless in bed. He calls a servant for a book. He does not tell us what language the book is in but it can be assumed to be French – he calls it a *romaunce* (48), which implies a story in that language. As a reader he is moved by the pathos of the story, but remains cheerful enough to make a jesting vow to the non-existent god of sleep. Early in the course of his dream he speaks with casual social superiority to one of the hunt-servants.

Say, felowe, who shal hunte here?

(366)

The servant politely calls him 'sir', and the dreamer joins the hunt of the Emperor Octovyan as one entitled to. In other words he moves in an assured manner in the best courtly circles. When he speaks to the man in black it is in an equally assured manner but this time to an acknowledged superior. It is a hierarchical society where everyone knows their place. The poet knows his. He has no social or gender-based 'male anxiety status' any more than has the hunt-servant or the young knight he addresses.

The hierarchy of degree from low to high is as natural to them as the air they breathe. 'The rich man in his castle, the poor man at his gate', as the old hymn sings, are for all of them part of the natural order of things. The poet's deference is not servile. The nature of his questioning shows that he is part of the social group which understands the refined feelings and sufferings of a love which is not mere lust. But love itself, which can no more be separated from suffering than from joy, also isolates and thus individualises the lover. The poet goes alone into the forest and finds the knight in solitude, reflecting on his own sadness. Although we are still dealing in stereotypes, they are stereotypes of individual feeling – for by definition this kind of love is exclusive and particularised. Although the description of White is the evocation of an ideal of beauty standard in the West for over a thousand years, yet she has a name and to her is attributed singular power.

To our egalitarian, highly individualised, fragmented culture these attitudes seem strange. But it is we who are strange, compared with the long course of human history. Our attitudes are relatively recent. Yet the seeds of our attitudes are already sown by Chaucer's time, and our own actual practices may have more of hierarchy and group feeling than we are always aware. It was not only medieval people who sometimes lacked self-awareness.

In the poem as a whole there are three 'I' persons, the first two closely connected. They are first, the 'I' of the introductory poet, second, the same 'I' as a dreamer, and third, the 'I' of the man in black's narrative of his love and loss. They represent two clearly defined people. But they also mirror each other, just as the narrative of Ceyx and Alcyone mirrors the love and loss of the man in black. The poem reaches out to the man in black without so breaching decorum as to offer direct consolation.

There is a sense, too, in which all narratives present aspects of the mind of the author, who creates the whole, including others and the representation of himself as himself, yet not all himself. The whole work represents the whole mind of the author as it divides itself up into its component attitudes. The man in black, different as he is, also represents the poet's feelings and attitudes, as well as those not his. To this extent Chaucer constructs a self of great complexity, and some incompatibilities, reflecting the trends of his complex culture, with its developing individualism, secularism, its new tenderness, also its hard-boiled acceptance of both life and death, and a resolute will to get on with life. Despite the ravages of the Black Death 20 years before, and various national troubles, there is no pessimism nor undue anxiety here. Chaucer is *not* our contemporary. Modern characteristics of egalitarianism, utilitarianism, relativism, altruism, are not apparent.[3]

IS THERE A NARRATOR SEPARATE FROM THE POET?

The poet's presentation of himself as recounting his own experiences, familiar in fourteenth-century poetry, has given great impetus to the modern critical concept of the Narrator. It had long been realised that the poet-in-life was or is not quite the same thing as the poet-as-expressed-in-the-work, but nineteenth-century criticism had brought the two aspects perilously close together. Romantic notions that 'sincerity' should be a key factor in poetry, and that literature should be a true expression not only of the writer's feelings at one time but of the actual circumstances of the writer's life, came to be accepted in the nineteenth century. Chaucer's realism was taken not as a literary device but as expressions of fact, by F. J. Furnivall in the mid-century, for example. For Chaucer it has some truth. How can it not? There is 'true' feeling in the greatest poetry, and in such a fine poem written in England in the twentieth century as T. S. Eliot's *Little Gidding*, there is clear 'self-expression', clear reference to such contemporary circumstances as air-raids and to the poet's personal experience as air-raid warden, which merge into his encounter with a phantasmal Dante and a personal confession.

We also know nowadays from other contemporary sources very much – all too much – about the personal lives and attitudes of our own good contemporary poets, and may well find them inferior in quality to their writing. W. B. Yeats referred to the poet's choice between 'perfection of the life' and 'perfection of the work' and the choice often goes to the work. What is the relation between 'work' and 'life'?

The writing of a general book such as this on both the life and work of Chaucer must be haunted by such questions. The relations between life, works, general culture, are very complicated.

In consequence we see that the nineteenth-century view, though attractive and not without truth, is too simple. The most obvious development in a more subtle criticism began with the New Criticism, a critical movement in the United States, beginning in the 1930s and dominant until the late 1980s.[4] It cut the living authors clear from the poetry they wrote.

The core ideas of the New Criticism were that only 'the words on the page' count, and that the essence of poetry is irony. It was very much an unconscious product of print culture and very consciously a reaction against poetry seen as 'life', against notions of poetic literalism, and against that belief in 'sincerity' as a quality of poetry which indicates a simple relationship between literature and what used to be called the historical 'background'. That these old-fashioned views were not totally wrong is born witness to by the classic work of G. L. Kittredge on Chaucer, first published in 1915, representing a line in which this present book on Chaucer is a modest though developed successor. The New Criticism, with a conscious emphasis on style as a chosen quality, came to Chaucer criticism with Charles Muscatine's percipient book *Chaucer and the French Tradition*, 1957, and the essays of E. Talbot Donaldson of the same period, gathered together in *Speaking of Chaucer* (1970).

The New Criticism in the hands of brilliant critics like Donaldson and Muscatine gave a great impulse to Chaucer studies, matching Chaucer's subtlety with their own. They have made a permanent advance in understanding. But they also make sharp a division between the poet and what may be summed up as the 'subject in history'. In particular the nature of poetry conditioned by oral tradition was neglected. Such poetry is characterised in part by repetition (with variation), hyperbole, sententiousness (the repetition of accepted human truths, use of proverbs and commonplaces) and wordplay (conscious art and artfulness). The New Criticism regarded such characteristics as pompous, pretentious or vapid. Since Chaucer is known to be a great poet, in order to excuse him from such faults, the concept of irony was invoked – he didn't really mean it. Since Chaucer is obviously at times humorous, it was thought that he must be joking if his poetry is sententious, or hyperbolical, or elaborate. His real intention must be different. He must be mocking somebody or something, usually the topic he is writing about, love, or chivalry, or some ideal. But then who is speaking the surface or literal meaning if it is different from the poet's assumed real, ironically conveyed meaning? It must be some stupid ventriloquist's dummy – the Narrator. There are two voices: the unheard one conveying the real meaning, and the one we hear, whose meaning is always silly, uncomprehending, wrong.

This idea, not taken quite so far, has some use in reading *The Book of the Duchess*. The poet-dreamer can be thought of as uncomprehending. But we lose the subtlety of the presentation, we cut off other openings, if we separate him completely from the poet. The poet himself is genuinely in the poem as an authenticating voice in a situation with clear historical conditions.

The idea of the Narrator as a totally different person from the poet cannot be sustained in *The Book of the Duchess* nor in later poems into which the poet introduces himself with clear reference to his own historical existence and poetry. It becomes absurd when in order to divide the style and to condemn Criseyde, the assumption is made that in *Troilus and Criseyde* there is another dramatic character, unnamed, never noticed by the main characters, but fully within the fiction, called by critics the Narrator. This is currently the most popular critical notion and is extremely widespread. It suits modern ideas, but I cannot share it. The Narrator is invoked when the critic wishes to discount the literal meaning of what the poem says, or to account for what seems dull or platitudinous in the poem, as if the poet were intentionally writing poorly as a joke.

Some of the confusion of judgement arises from a failure to respond to the mixture of the spoken and the written (and we should remember it was not *printed*) in Chaucer's poetry – the mixture of orality and literacy, and literacy's relation to the literalistic.

ORALITY AND LITERACY

The Book of the Duchess is very much at bottom a written, partially translated, poem – all the more so if it incorporates numerological patterns which must be counted on the page and can never be heard. But the small number of manuscripts suggests that it was perhaps originally also written to be spoken, and the rather discursive style of the poem challenges us to use our imagination in recreating oral conditions. There is no doubt that at the very least, from the very beginning of the poem, Chaucer *imitates* oral delivery, and we shall find that to be the case throughout his poetry. He says of the message delivered by Juno's messenger:

> And tolde hym what he shulde doon
> As I have told yow here-to-fore,
> Hyt ys no nede reherse hyt more.

(188–90)

The poet repeats the same kind of phrase 'as I have told hyt yow' (271). He is anxious not to bore his audience – a note frequent in his later poetry – and intends

> To telle shortly, att oo word   *one*
> (306)

Chaucer builds his audience as it were into his very poem and, to some extent, thus creates his audience once we have learned his language. Even we modern readers are partly for this reason, and partly because of his self-presentation, enabled in turn to create for ourselves our sense of the poem 'speaking' to us. There is a paradox here. The poet addresses the 'audience' in an oral style, typically formulaic, repetitious, sententious, hyperbolical, aggregative. Yet he also manages the effectiveness of writing or print, which has to build context and tone into the very text. The modern solitary silent readers are enabled to imagine themselves as part of the listening, participating and even conditioning audience, as the poet appeals to the readers and invites them to imagine for themselves and lessen or intensify the power of the meaning.[5]

The Book of the Duchess is full of Chaucer's book-learning, and much of it is translated so closely than he must have had Machaut's poems in a book on his desk beside him as he wrote. In a sense he had written a script for himself to act. This need imply no falseness of feeling, but often tempts a person to make self-depreciatory humorous remarks. Writing is deliberate and calculated. It allows Chaucer to use a more elaborate, learned diction than he might have done in a purely oral performance. As an example, he is the first writer recorded in English to use the word 'imagination' in that sense (14) though it comes at the end of a notably 'oral' introduction. Writing extends the vocabulary and allows for a more complicated sentence structure, more complicated thought. It releases speech from the pressures of the immediate social context. Print, of course, carries this effect even further but print in England was still a hundred years away, and writing is as it were half way between speech and print.

Writing therefore, in freeing the poem from its 'warm' oral context needs to be more dense, richer in content, with more clues to the reader. Of Chaucer's literacy there can be no doubt, nor that he was often ready to recycle it back into at least the pretence of oral delivery for the sake of extra liveliness, creating, if only in imagination, an audience. One aspect of his exceptional literacy is a vein of literalism. This deserves a few words as a topic on its own, not least because it is a noticeable characteristic, even a poetic and narrative device, in *The Book of the Duchess*.

LITERALISM

Literalism is restriction to the primary meaning of a word without any figurative, metaphorical, allegorical or ironical implication. It asserts a close correspondence between 'word' and 'thing' or 'idea'. The poet in *The Book of the Duchess* represents himself as very literal-minded when he cannot understand the man in black's metaphor about losing his queen in the game of chess with Fortune, meaning the death of his lady.

Medieval thought in general regarded the literal meaning of words as only the beginning. In discussing the Biblical text in particular it was accepted that while the literal meaning was primary, other levels of allegorical or symbolic meaning might well be more important. In secular rhetoric 'similitudes' and irony were well understood. Mere literalism was often the subject of humour. There was, for example, a well-known joke about an old woman who wished for a favourable outcome from a lawsuit. She was told she would have to 'grease the judge's palm', meaning 'to bribe' the judge. So she brought some pork fat to court and smeared it on his hand while everyone was watching, to their great amusement. As it happens the judge was so embarrassed, says the story, that he gave judgement in her favour. The action was ludicrously literal – but there is a further perhaps unintentional irony in the story, in that the absurdly material literalism did in fact work. Literalism is very powerful.

Another widely known story concerns literalistic intention. A version of it is given in Chaucer's *Friar's Tale* (*CT*, III, 1301–664). The point is that a curse may or may not be literally meant, 'from the heart', and if not meant literally is of no effect. In such cases a superior person, often an oppressive church official, who does not understand the difference, is mocked and carried off to hell. Intention, not the literal sense on its own, decides the true meaning, though again the literal sense is shown to have material power. The association of literalism with destructive yet comic power in the Middle Ages is most vividly illustrated by the stories (many derived from earlier centuries) associated with the German or Netherlandish trickster-figure Till Eulenspiegel, but very popular in sixteenth-century England.[6]

It is a question of how far the literalistic incomprehension of the poet-dreamer in *The Book of the Duchess* is meant to be comic – part of the general question of humour in this remarkable poem. The poet-figure's failure to understand the metaphorical expression of loss by the man in black is a usefully deferential device for allowing the man in black, or forcing him, first to tell his own story without egotism, and second to be explicit, and thus face the harsh material reality of his loss. Thus, the dreamer's literalism makes the dreamer seem less intelligent, which is a sort of compliment and an apology to the man in black. The literalism then forced upon the man in black becomes an instrument of clarity and secular power.

The close connection of literalism with materialism thus leads not only to comedy, but to death. All things must perish. The material body is both absurd and doomed. In the end, the man in black's metaphors of death, his hyperbolical praise of the lady, have to be resolved when the literalism of the poet-in-the-poem forces the plain literalistic explanation, 'She ys ded' (1309). This is met with the poet's banal response 'By God, hyt ys routhe' (1310). Yet what more could be said? Then the bustle of the hunt is briefly resumed to be dismissed to its home, and the punning, therefore non-literalistic, identification with what is nevertheless a materially real person and castle is made. The poet promises to put his strange dream into rhyme. We are back in the everyday world.

Literalism has been used in *The Book of the Duchess* as an instrument not to destroy hyperbole and idealisation but to give them a grounding, a foundation. Chaucer's later poetry has a strong vein of literalism. Its materialism is closely associated with realism in literature, and Chaucer is often very realistic both for comic and serious purposes. Literalism embodies a kind of secular reality principle – the principle that ultimate reality is to be found in the visible material world. This was the opposite of the dominant official, clerical and learned view in the Middle Ages, which was that reality existed beneath (or above) the world of appearances. The unofficial pragmatic view is more likely to be held by lay people, and Chaucer, well-read but not clerical, is a layman, one of a new generation of educated lay people. Yet even for the clerisy things were changing in the fourteenth century.

Interest in the literal meaning of the Bible was growing. There was an increasingly empirical attitude in theological debate, associated with the Oxford theologian William Ockham (d. 1349). The Lollard movement especially, inspired by another Oxford theologian, John Wycliffe (d. 1382) but representing a wider lay movement, was essentially literalistic. In the debate on the true presence of Christ in the bread and wine of the Eucharist when they are consecrated by the 'magic' words of the priest, Lollards denied that words could change the material substance of the elements. Chaucer was associated with a number of prominent Lollard knights. In the fifteenth and sixteenth century men and women were burned to death for their beliefs in one side or other of this question. The relation of 'words' to 'things' is not a light question.[7]

The close relationship of 'words' to 'things' only became insisted on as desirable in the seventeenth century. It reflected a shift towards a basically materialist view of reality, with a distrust of the slipperiness of the meaning of words. At first sight to modern minds that words should correspond to things seems to be a commonsense view of the world. It was associated with the increasing success of experimental science. It led to the preference of 'concrete' over 'abstract' words still often taught as desirable in English schools. No informed person now takes such a simple view of the relation of words to whatever it is they mean, but the power of literalism is not to be underrated.[8]

NOTES

1. A. C. Spearing, *Medieval Dream Poetry* (Cambridge, 1976).
2. Derek Brewer, 'Chaucer's Anti-Ricardian Poetry', in *The Living Middle Ages: A Festschrift for Karl Heinz Göller*, edited by V. Böker, M. Markus and R. Schöwerling (Stuttgart and Regensburg, 1989), 115–28.
3. Charles Taylor, *Sources of the Self: the Making of the Modern Identity* (Cambridge, 1989) well describes these leading characteristics of the modern conception of the self.
4. It has been very perceptively analysed by Lee Patterson, *Negotiating the Past* (Madison, 1987).
5. A much more extended discussion on which the above is based will be found in Derek Brewer, 'Orality and Literacy in Chaucer', in *Mundlichkeit und Schrifthlichkeit im englishen Mittelalter, ScriptOralia 5*, herausg. W. Erzgräber and Sabine Volk (Tübingen, 1988), 85–120. A shorter account discussing orality in similar terms is Derek Brewer, 'Chaucer's Poetic Style', in *The Cambridge Chaucer Companion*, edited by P. Boitani and J. Mann (Cambridge, 1986), 227–42.
6. Some of these stories may be found in modern translation in *Medieval Comic Tales*, edited and with introduction by Derek Brewer (Cambridge, 1996), 95, 121–3, 166, 169.
7. Beryl Smalley, *The Study of the Bible in the Middle Ages* (Oxford, c. 1983); K. B. McFarlane, *Lancastrian Kings and Lollard Knights* (Oxford and New York, 1972); Derek Brewer, *Chaucer and his World*, 2nd edn (Cambridge, 1992), 144–5.
8. For an admirable and accessible modern survey see Steven Pinker, *The Language Instinct* (Harmondsworth, 1994). See also Derek Brewer, 'Some Observations on the Development of Literalism and Verbal Criticism', *Poetica* (2) 1974, 71–95.

Chapter 8

The Book of the Duchess III: Death, Laughter, Repetition and Comfort

DEATH AND LAUGHTER

Some drastic modern criticism maintains that all stories are, at bottom, as it were allegories about progress towards death, but also a postponement, because they have to offer a start in life.[1] That is a modern view which opens up a stimulating vista of many plots, but does not always fit the medieval plot. For one thing, in the medieval period, despite a natural and widespread horror of death as physical decay (which must have been a familiar sight but which Chaucer never writes about) there was also a general belief in life after death, followed by a general Judgement – though that in itself offered complete finality: Doomsday. Historically speaking, belief in life after death has been far more frequently found in human cultures than the general modern Western belief that we are mere accidental and transitory fragments of an arbitrary and valueless evolution. So death had different terrors for many. But Chaucer's quest is for life, not death. He dismisses mourning at the end of *Troilus* and is flippant about it in *The Knight's Tale* and elsewhere. Yet he cannot ignore death nor its pain. Life must mean death in some way.

In so far as they have a beginning and an end stories must metaphorically echo the span of life. If they reach firm closure the analogy with death is closer. But often the story is more open-ended, or it ends happily. Why should not such happy or inconclusive endings be equally possible models of life and death? In traditional societies, which normally believe in some kind of extra dimension beyond personal decease, such stories may be a truer model of the culture. That could well be for Chaucer, with the mixture of closure and openness in *The Book of the Duchess* and many of his later poems. *Troilus and Criseyde* gives us a glimpse of the dead hero laughing at the folly of the world, at the 'blind pleasure', in which he himself had taken, while alive, such an eager part in both joy and pain.

In medieval literature death is surprisingly often mingled with laughter. In *The Book of the Duchess* Chaucer is unable to keep humour at bay. The mixture of humour and pathos in *The Book of the Duchess* at a superficial level contributes to the variety and interest of the poem. Literalism as already noticed may be a source of humour. Chaucer is self-conscious about his own humour when he refers to 'his game' (238) but adds in the very next line

> And yet me lyst ryght evel to pleye.
>
> (239)

All humour has complex origins in the juxtaposition of conflicting feelings. The fear of death is a strong feeling which may even set off a kind of opposite feeling, or at least create tension. Charles Lamb said he could never see a funeral without bursting into uncontrollable laughter. Soldiers going up to the line of battle will laugh and joke out of sheer nervousness, while one or more may break down screaming. Such is a common human characteristic. Medieval culture, surrounded by visible death, often blends the serious with the comic and grotesque, seen especially in the representation of comic devils in comic stories and in miracle plays. In *The Book of the Duchess* Chaucer does not go so far as the grotesque, except possibly in his vow of soft bedding, etc. to Morpheus.

The mixture of the comic with the serious in medieval writing has been famously, if rather exaggeratedly, celebrated by M. Bakhtin as the 'carnivalesque', popular, non-clerical element in medieval culture, which asserts the physical, materialist, jovial aspects of life. Chaucer's humour is not quite of this kind, nor does he indulge in 'the comedy of corpses'.[2] Chaucer's humour in *The Book of the Duchess* is rather the product of internal tension, relief in the face of sorrow. It is not mockery of sorrow, nor simply the bad taste of as it were joking in church (which some medieval preachers did), and which it may easily seem now. To the modern reader Chaucer seems to have an irrepressible urge towards humour, especially in the presence of death (as, for example, the death of Arcite in *The Knight's Tale* (*CT*, I, 2809–15)). Such humour is blended with, rather than denying, the sadness of death, in an archaic holistic structure sometimes difficult for our fragmented yet shielded modern Western minds, in peaceful times, to grasp. The funeral wake, as occasionally still practised in modern rural Ireland, and as reported in fourteenth-century England, with its first night of deep mourning after a death, its second of uproarious festivity, with pagan undertones, is perhaps the best representation of contradictory emotions and attitudes concerning death firmly blended together.

LOVE AND GENDER ROLES

The story of Ceyx and Alcyone is one of happy married love, and in Ovid's account though death intervenes the pair are reunited as faithful loving birds in their transformation. There seems to be a clear reflection here of the marriage of John of Gaunt and Blanche which it would be impertinent of the poet to praise openly, and which death has now ended.

The man in black records the history of his love of 'White'. He sketches out the conventional ideal very plainly. He says nature taught him to love before ever he saw any lady to love (759–84). Despite the conventionality it is the case that most boys and young men are prone by nature to love women in any culture at any period. It is equally obvious that all cultures impose some patterns on nature – we are all formed by a mixture of biological and social forces – and the man in black tells how he 'chose love to his first craft' (791). He chose a certain kind of behaviour. We are to think of him at the age of many a young courtier, like Chaucer himself perhaps, a page in the household of the Countess of Ulster in 1357, around the age of 15 to 17. The poem enables us to make a fuller analysis of love.

When the young knight saw the lady whom he fell in love with he behaved like many a love-stricken youth in his 'yonge, childly wyt' (1095) and did his best 'to do her worship' (1108): pay her honour, reverence and service. The feeling of reverence and the readiness to do anything for her are natural enough at least for some youths, but medieval literary culture encouraged such natural feelings, emphasising the service of love, the humility of the lover. Such behaviour can be seen as 'self-humiliation' made as a bid for love, and some have even seen it as a 'feminisation' of the youth, on the grounds that humiliation is gendered as feminine. 'Courtship and humiliating oneself seem to be intimately associated.'[3]

Such 'humiliation' is better called 'humility', a traditional Christian virtue, and is part of the socialisation of what is admittedly, and necessarily, the fundamentally aggressive or at least active nature of male sexual desire. The practice of humility is a sort of 'rite of passage'. At the same time it develops and codifies the equally natural uncertainty, insecurity, self-distrust and modesty of many an adolescent male.

The convention of romantic noble love also encouraged artistic expression and self-expression. Young lovers make songs (the Squire in *The General Prologue* to *The Canterbury Tales* could also draw and paint). Such love encourages the development of individuality, albeit on recognised lines, and it also builds the sexual urge into a whole, more self-aware, gentle personality. Sexuality becomes personalised, civilised, and associated with stability of personality, with loyalty.

Love then becomes part of that social reciprocity which all societies recognise because it is the essence of society. Eventually, the young knight with modesty and embarrassment makes known his pain and desire to his lady, who is not at all embarrassed and rejects him out of hand. He asks for her 'mercy', appealing not to her own sexual or social desire but to her womanly virtue of pity for his suffering. She naturally tests the strength of his loyalty and devotion, by at first rejecting him, but if he remains loyal she may eventually accord him 'the noble gift of her mercy' (1270), 'saving her worship' (1271), that is, preserving her chastity, which is the essential honour of women, as bravery is of men. And then they live in harmony and equal love for many years. Chaucer emphasises the equality of love here (1289–97). Until then the lady is repeatedly described by the young man as superior. He can only be described as 'feminized' if it is assumed that all men are by nature boorishly aggressive and domineering at all times. While many youths undoubtedly are, such behaviour depends to a considerable extent on the social ideals set before them, and the shyness and gentleness of the young man in love are in Chaucer's poetry incorporated in the masculine ideal. Part of this ideal will be later shown, in *Troilus and Criseyde* and *The Canterbury Tales*, to include fierce fighting against the enemy. The ideal knight for many centuries was conceived of as 'a lion on the field, a lamb in the hall'. Gentleness and self-control were part of the courtly ideal of manhood. In *The Book of the Duchess* there is no call for the knight to prove his prowess, nor any reflection on his manhood because he is shy.

In this high romantic ideal of love, in which the lover both abases and civilises himself, the natural progress is towards mutual and equal love. Part of many a declaration of love on the part of the man is the statement that the lady *ought* to love him, because he loves her. Thus, he invokes the implicit but powerful rule of social reciprocity – the giving of a gift requires the return of a gift of equal value in almost all societies.[4] Giving gifts is therefore an attempt to assert power over the recipient, but it is notable here that in this convention of love the lady has the power to refuse to accept the gift of the lover, which refusal is the assertion of another kind of power.

In marriage, by contrast, Scripture, through St Paul, clearly asserts the headship of the husband over the wife. Chaucer later in his poetry confronts the problem of the changing relationship of lover to husband at the beginning of *The Franklin's Tale*. In *The Book of the Duchess* it does not arise. Chaucer restricts himself to the stylised love-convention which did not necessarily include marriage. Happy domesticity is not his interest.

The superiority of the lady in love may sometimes seem to lead to a strangely filial, not to say childish, attitude on the part of the lover. It is as if the lady becomes a substitute for the mother, and the knight regresses, becomes, as some modern critics argue, 'infantilised'. Chaucer sees this element and mocks it in *The Miller's Tale*. The whole of that particular poem mocks the provincial lower classes aping the manners and language of their betters, straightforward village lust pretending to be the romantic love of the court. So Chaucer makes Absalom, the lovelorn village barber and parish clerk (a sharp dresser and squeamish in manners), say to the carpenter's pretty young wife, whom he is trying to seduce, when pleading for her love

I morne as dooth the lamb after the tete.   *teat*

(*CT*, I, 3704)

But the man in black, like Chaucer's other manly and courtly young lovers, achieves an equal relationship with his beloved. His love, even before accepted, strengthens his sense of individuality.

There is more to be said about the superiority attributed to the lady in romantic love, with its corresponding overtones of the honour orginally due to a feudal lord, the manly loyalty to a man, but which shades into the supplicatory and the desire for apparently maternal love and protection. In *The Book of the Duchess* and other serious secular love-poems the lady, while remaining an object of veneration, never takes on the status of protective mother. It is she, in the end, who needs protection, or who is so vulnerable as to have her fate decided by men other than her lover. The beloved lady as a maternal figure in Chaucer's work is better discussed in a religious context.

It has seemed to some modern feminist critics that all this fuss about the lady's superiority is a con-trick on the part of men. The lady (the term is deliberately used here instead of 'woman' or 'girl') is seen by such critics as passive, as an icon who merely focuses, or represents, male desires: her own personality and wishes are disregarded. Feminist critics have argued that the poem, in pretending to praise and commemorate, actually excludes Blanche, 'whitens' her out.[5] This is surprising in view of the hundreds of lines devoted to evoking Blanche's idealised image, the deference paid to her by the youthful lover, and the extreme misery caused by her loss. It is of course true that the poet is a man, and the discussion of Blanche is by two men – she is indeed absent. It is her very absence from life that causes her presence in the poem. Truly, had she been present, not dead, the poem would be absent, having no cause to exist, but this is mere playing with words. There is no hidden satisfaction at her death. It may be argued that to exalt her to her idealised status is to exclude her from the world, but first the literary convention and then the sad actuality of death have done that already, and death is bitter.

Another modern critical notion is to take the act of using a pen on paper as analogous to a man's rape of a woman. So the poet is 'raping' Blanche in writing her praise. Or because the woman is called 'White' and ink is black, the description of Blanche writes, and 'whites', her out. These strained analogies have nothing to do with any normal or historical experience of the poem.

Our experience as readers of the word is quite opposite. What do we know of 'White' without the text? It is true that men uphold the text. They have made the woman a pleasing object of worship. While this may be idolatry, as Chaucer presumably thought when he wrote his *Retraction* at the end of *The Canterbury Tales* and of his life, and condemned the poem as worldly vanity, it is not denial of woman's, or especially of that particular woman's, nature.

Generally speaking it is true that by and large men were dominant in practical life in fourteenth-century England. The reasons are those common to almost all pre-industrial agrarian societies with primitive technology. Women are less muscular than men, and it is they who have the appalling strain of bearing children: a most dangerous process in such a society. Even today, in Sub-Saharan Africa one woman in 13 dies in childbirth. The medieval European situation must have been similar or worse. In Western Europe and the USA of the present day, one woman in just over 3000 dies in childbirth, according to the report, *Progress of Nations* (1996) by the United Nations Children's Fund.[6] Blanche had had five children in nine years, and there were plenty of diseases, including plague, to wipe out the weak or unlucky. (At least she, like her husband and Chaucer, all of much the same age, had escaped the Black Death of 1348–9 which wiped out a third of the population.) Nevertheless, women were particularly vulnerable.

England, like many societies with primitive technology, had an elaborate social structure. Since it was largely hierarchical, women of a high class were accorded a high position. There is no doubt of the importance of the Queen, or the duchess, even or especially because they were women in that social position. They were the more precious because the more likely to die young.

The poem is presenting a necessarily stylised account of a human history and situation that could never be quite so smooth as the memorial, just as the effigy on Blanche's tomb must have presented a stylised image of her living beauty. That is a convention easy enough to accept, though a modern reader might, conceivably, have wished for a realistic image 'warts and all'. That would not necessarily have been nearer the general human truth. Anyone who has contemplated those calm alabaster effigies of the knight and his lady, often hand in hand, on fourteenth- and fifteenth-century tombs in many a village church (that of Tong in Staffordshire is famous) must appreciate the idealised yet not unrealistic beauty of these human memorials. It was just such a double memorial monument that John of Gaunt caused to be made; it was destroyed, alas, in the Great Fire of London.

REPETITION AND COMMEMORATION

It has been argued that the aim of all narrative is the 'recovery of the past'[7] and *The Book of the Duchess* is pre-eminently that. In doing so it turns loss into commemoration, elegy into celebration. Recovery of the past is repetition of the past, though in literature always repetition with variation, with difference. *The Book of the Duchess* is repetitious not only in this fundamental way, but in its very structure. The poet begins with his grief at his own 'lack', appropriately short and light. He then tells another story of loss, longer and more serious, the story of Ceyx and Alcyone, which repeats and varies the pattern. Then the third section repeats the same story in nearly literal truth at much greater length. This repetition of a basic pattern is used later by Chaucer in *The Parliament of Fowls* and more extensively still in telling 'the double story' of Troilus.

Repetition of a different kind is equally powerful in all the stories of *The Canterbury Tales*, whether comic or serious. In every case the effect of repetition with variation is recovery, reinforcement and extension. By going back, so to speak, we go forward. This pattern of repetition with variation is not limited to structure. As already noted it is the essence of the style itself. One of the main characteristics of a traditional poetic style, derived from oral origins even when written, is advance by repetition with variation.

In the case of *The Book of the Duchess* repetition is the effective instrument of specific commemoration. Commemoration, as in the Eucharist, or Last Supper, is, as we rightly say, 'celebrated' in the Mass, the dual mourning and glorification of a death which recreated life. In liturgical matters repetition is of the essence. So it is in literature and life. When repetition ceases then we are truly dead.[8]

The repetition of experience as literature is thus also its transformation, interpretation and commemoration. But the actual nature of the experience and the way it is represented varies enormously from poem to poem, and this is well seen in the early poem, *An ABC*, which it is convenient to read alongside *The Book of the Duchess*. At first sight it is very different, and certainly it is much slighter, but it shows another important and continuing element in Chaucer's poetry. It offers another image of the lady. We might put the central images of the two poems side by side, like the two panels of the Wilton Diptych in the National Gallery, which has the idealised picture of Richard II on the left and an equally idealised picture of the Virgin on the right. But in our imagined diptych each panel shows the ideal lady, one secular, one religious.

An ABC is a warmly expressed devotional poem to the Blessed Virgin, the Mother of God. It has 23 eight-line stanzas with five stresses in each line. It may be the first poem written in English in such stanzas and lines if it is indeed one of Chaucer's earliest poems, as the closeness of translation suggests. Each stanza begins with the appropriate letter of the alphabet in sequence, as its title tells us, omitting 'j', 'u' and 'w', as they did not then have independent existence. The whole poem is a translation of a prayer in Guillaume de Deguilleville's popular fourteenth-century Continental French poem *La Pélerinage de la vie humaine*.

While Chaucer's ideal of translation was at this stage fairly close, changes were partly forced on him, partly chosen. There is a different tone, a larger visual element, an additional flavour of legal language. Although the form forces some artificial turns, the skill of versification is great, the style forthright, the terms conventional. She is

> Glorious mayde and mooder, which that nevere
> Were bitter, neither in erthe nor in see.
>
> (49–50)

She is 'Queen of comfort', 'Temple devout', 'Virgine that art so noble of apparaile'. The poem, in strong clear stanzas, owes its origin and its primary imagery to the French poem, but is nevertheless authentically Chaucerian, ending

> Zacharie yow clepeth the open welle
> To wasshe sinful soul out of his gilt.
> Therfore this lessoun ought I wel to telle
> That nere thi tender herte, we were spilt.   *were not; destroyed*
> Now ladi bryghte, sith thou canst and wilt
> Ben to the seed of Adam merciable,
> Bring us to that palais that is bilt
> To penitentes that ben to merci able. Amen.

(177–84)

This is orthodox fourteenth-century Christian thought and feeling. The attribution of royalty and noble dress to the mother of the carpenter's son, himself a carpenter, a skilled artisan; the emphasis on the human Mother of God and her redeeming mercy; the sense of sin; the hope of heaven for those who repent; all are a fundamental part of Chaucer's whole sensibility and mentality, on which he relied at the end of his life. They go alongside many other and diverse interests, of some of which, as the *Retractation* to *The Canterbury Tales* testifies, he repented at the end of his life. The devoutness which seems minor at this earlier period of his life becomes major at the end. The poem is a clear example of repetition with variation, each repetition building up more of the general image, creating as it recovers the past, present and future power of the Virgin – Mother of God.

An ABC relates in a way to *The Book of the Duchess*, although it is more formal, less personalised. There is no reason to think it less deeply felt. Both poems are concerned with an idealised female figure, each woman having had a real earthly existence, even if with a gap of nearly fourteen hundred years. The description of Blanche is as it were the incarnation as also the memorial of youthful feminine beauty, goodness and joy: the other is the incarnation of the protective suffering maternal figure which young women become. The profoundly paradoxical concept of the Virgin-Mother links the two. In each case the male-dominated patriarchal society worships, in secular or religious manner, the elected, morally supreme, dominant Lady. The Father is so awesome and severe that he cannot be approached. The poet says of him to the Virgin-Mother

> Spek thou, for I ne dar not him ysee.

(53)

To many devout minds in the fourteenth century Christ the Redeemer had become so assimilated, as Trinitarian doctrine required, to God the Creator, the Father, and the Judge, that redemption, pity, mercy were lost in justice. In popular devotion Mary, the protective, nourishing, suffering Mother, displaced what were felt to be the harsher masculine aspects of deity. It is said that even in the twentieth century, as young soldiers die, they call for their mothers, or sometimes, if Roman Catholic, for the Blessed Virgin Mary. Even in the fourteenth century this displacement did not always happen, and scholastic theology was another matter, but Chaucer and popular, including courtly, devotion were not scholastic. Another vein in fourteenth-century thought, as expressed by Chaucer's contemporary, the woman mystic, Julian of Norwich, worshipped *Jesus* as mother. Chaucer shows no knowledge of Julian, or of this mode of devotion, but it illustrates the importance of the image of the maternal in Christian worship of the time, and it is a type of devotion to which Chaucer was clearly sympathetic. No critic has so far thought of the sentiments expressed in *An ABC* as those of a narrator, stupid or otherwise, and we may sensibly take them, though translated, or even because translated, and so deliberately appropriated, as expressing Chaucer's own feelings and ideas. That does not mean that he always felt in such a way, or that there were not many other aspects of his mind. If one thing is clear about Chaucer and his culture it is that it was multifaceted, and that a number of its aspects were inconsistent with others.

There is no doubt, however, of a strongly feminine or feminist element in Chaucer's poetry despite the predominantly masculine values of his society, and that this feminine element is found elsewhere in the religious artistic culture of fourteenth-century Europe. France and Italy, which were all part of the same mental world, have many clear examples – we need go no further than the Cathedral at Reims covered in religious feminine images. Chaucer's heroines like Constance in *The Man of Law's Tale* and Griselda in *The Clerk's Tale* achieve a kind of power which is related to the attributes of the Virgin Mother of God: love, steadfastness, forgiveness, courage, loyalty. Both are mothers. Many of the popular medieval female saints – Catherine, Margaret, Mary of Egypt, and scores of others, whether mothers or virgins – exemplify the same virtues. Many are notable for their defiance of male tyrants. In Chaucer's comic poetry even those wives who cannot claim to be virtuous, such as the pretty Alison in *The Miller's Tale*, are gently treated. The Wife of Bath herself, constructed out of traditional misogynistic materials, and despite her five husbands and other company in youth never a mother, achieves our sympathy. Even Criseyde, famously unfaithful, is shown as more to be pitied than blamed. The Mother of God may be said to cast her protective cloak over them all. Chaucer reserves his contempt for men.

Although respect and reverence for women is genuinely deep in medieval culture, Chaucer is exceptional in the tenderness with which he treats women. The general run of medieval culture, especially of the official clerical culture, is much more misogynistic, some of it violently so. But Chaucer was that new type of man: the literate layman.

So *An ABC*, like some fourteenth-century picture of the Madonna and Child, ornate and hieratic as it is, deservedly goes alongside *The Book of the Duchess* as a basis for the sympathetic understanding of Chaucer's view of some parts of life, and the early quality of his poetry. But there is much more variety to come, wider in range, and more down-to-earth.

NOTES

1. See the stimulating and subtle discussion by Peter Brooks, *Reading for the Plot: Design and Intention in Narrative*, New York, 1984, Vintage Books, 1995, e.g. p. 103.
2. M. Bakhtin, *Rabelais and his World*, translated by H. Iswolsky (Cambridge, Mass and London, 1996); Aaron Gurevich, 'Heroes, gods and laughter in Germanic Poetry', in *Historical Anthropology in the Middle Ages*, edited by Jana Howlett (Oxford, 1992), 122–76; for comic tales about corpses (among other matters) see *Medieval Comic Tales*, edited by Derek Brewer (Cambridge, 1996) Introduction, xvii, xxxi, and a number of individual tales translated from different languages. Death figures quite often in the working out of the comedy.
3. William Ian Miller, *Humiliation* (Chicago, 1993), 169.
4. On this complicated and vital social principle the fundamental work is M. Mauss, *The Gift*, translated by Ian Cunnison. See also W. I. Miller, *Humiliation*, above.
5. For vigorous assertion of this see Maud Ellmann, 'Blanche' in *Criticism and Critical Theory*, edited by Jeremy Hawthorn (London, 1984), 99–110, and Elaine Tuttle Hanson, *Chaucer and the Fictions of Gender* (Berkeley and Los Angeles, 1992). For a general feminist treatment see Carolyn Dinshaw, *Chaucer's Sexual Poetics* (Madison, Wis., 1989).
6. *The Daily Telegraph*, 12 June 1996, 16.
7. Peter Brooks, *Reading for the Plot* (London, 1995), 311.
8. On repetition, beside Brooks, *op.cit.*, see Derek Brewer, 'Retellings', in *Re-telling Tales*, edited by T. Hahn and A. Lupack (Cambridge, 1997).

Chapter 9

Diplomat and Civil Servant: Private and Public Trouble

The mingled flow of business and ceremony – whose differences were hard to distinguish in the fourteenth century – continued uninterrupted after the death of Blanche. Christmas was celebrated in 1368 with customary splendour. Cloth and robes were duly issued to all at court, including Geoffrey and Philippa Chaucer, whose work was often thus paid in kind. From now on there is a steady flow of documents recording such issues, other gifts, and the payments of annuities, to both Geoffrey and Philippa. Through them we are able to trace the outline of their lives.

THE ITALIAN JOURNEY

For several years Chaucer remained with the Court, though he made a short trip abroad in the summer and autumn of 1370. Then on 1 December 1372 he left London on his first visit to Italy.

This Italian journey was of the utmost significance to Chaucer's imaginative life if only because it must have been when engaged upon it that he bought some books in Italian and read them. The books were Boccaccio's *Teseida*, Dante's *Divina Commedia*, and one that contained at least one sonnet by Petrarch. He also came to know Petrarch's reputation as 'the lauriate poete'

> whos rethorike sweete
> Enlumyned al Ytaille of poetrie
> As Lynyan dide of philosophie
> Or lawe, or oother art particuleer.
>
> (*CT*, IV, 32–5)

The conjunction of poetry with philosophy, law and other art is characteristic of Chaucer and perhaps of medieval European culture generally. Petrarch had had a European reputation since 1340 and died in 1374. He recorded much of his daily life and never mentions

Chaucer even as an anonymous passing Englishman. It is unlikely they ever met. Linyan was Giovanni di Lignano, principally known in England as a political and theological lawyer. When Chaucer wrote this particular passage as prologue to *The Clerk's Tale* he laments that both great men are dead. The passage illustrates to some extent how his Italian journey had broadened Chaucer's outlook and extended his knowledge. The influence of Dante appears at once in his next poem, *The House of Fame*, but we should pause to consider what the nature of Chaucer's Italian experience might have been, remembering always that other Englishmen knew Italy, even if very few knew Italian, and it was Chaucer's special genius that made his encounter with Italy so remarkable.

Chaucer was one of three commissioners who were sent to negotiate a trade agreement with Genoa. Often one of such a group of commissioners was legally trained, but we now know that Chaucer had not had such a training. But perhaps he already knew Italian. At any rate a special position of trust and responsibility seems to have been his, for he was detached on a secret mission to Florence, perhaps to negotiate a private loan for the king. He was back in London by 23 May 1373, so that, allowing for travelling time, he spent two or three months in Italy, in winter and early spring. A few years later, in 1378, he spent July in Milan, on another diplomatic mission. His first visit in particular was of the greatest importance for the development of his poetry.

FOURTEENTH-CENTURY ITALIAN CULTURE

Italy was already rich in the visual arts, though the contrast with England in the fourteenth century was not so great as might be thought. England was almost as rich as Italy in decorated churches, in coloured statues plated with gold and silver, in tapestried and frescoed chambers. The great efflorescence of Italian Renaissance art had barely begun.

But Italian towns were much richer. Even small towns had from the thirteenth century been built in stone and contained magnificent public buildings and private palaces. There were far more schools, far better shops. Science was more advanced. Modern arithmetic at the service not only of merchants but of painters was well advanced, with all that that implies. Clockwork, the associated science, which measures time neutrally and regularly, was well developed. The best medicine, the best architecture, much of the best metalwork, in the fourteenth century, were all Italian.

Chaucer would have had a Londoner's kinship with the city of Florence, and would have been able to appreciate Florence's more advanced civilisation. Florence was the chief industrial and financial city of Europe, holding a position comparable with London's in the early twentieth century. It was at least twice the size of the London of Chaucer. Florentines were the principal bankers of Europe (Edward III had borrowed very much money from them) and they had agents and correspondents everywhere. A relic of their importance in London still survives in the name Lombard Street.

Florence was far ahead of London in the production of books. In the manufacture of paper, slowly beginning to supplement and eventually to supplant parchment, Italy had almost a monopoly. England had not one paper mill until 1490. And in Florence Dante was venerated, and Petrarch and Boccaccio were still alive. A few months after Chaucer's first visit, Boccaccio was lecturing on Dante. In Italy certainly, and Florence probably, Chaucer first became acquainted with some of the Latin and Italian works of these great writers. It is probable that here too he extended his own library. Chaucer seems to have had an astonishing number of books for a private Englishman of his time. He must have greatly extended his reading and bought copies of the Italian works of Dante and Boccaccio, something of Petrarch, an Italian translation of Ovid, etc. Even here, however, the limited distribution of all books must have made his acquisitions to some extent casual and fortuitous. Manuscripts have no title-pages, and rarely tell the authors' names. Many miscellaneous items might be bound up in one volume, and it was next to impossible to collect an author's works, because the author himself was largely ignored. One of the curiosities of literary history which illustrates these matters is Petrarch's ignorance of the *Decameron* until a year or two before his death, although he and Boccaccio had been intimate for many years, and the *Decameron* a popular work. But Boccaccio in his later life was prouder of his Latin works, and even after Dante's great example of vernacular poetry in *La Divina Commedia* Latin had in general more prestige than the vernacular.

There is no evidence that Chaucer met Petrarch or Boccaccio and he apparently remained in ignorance of the latter's very name, but he read some of their Italian works with the greatest eagerness. Boccaccio's poems and Dante he read and re-read, and the result was a continual enrichment and strengthening of his poetic powers throughout the rest of his life.

WHAT CHAUCER LEARNED FROM ITALIAN LITERATURE

Chaucer learned from the Italians new subjects, a new magnificence and control of diction, a new clarity, a new sense of the dignity of poetry. More profoundly, he seems to have responded to the new sense of the world found in Italian city culture and reflected in the poetry of Dante and even that of Boccaccio. In these writers ordinary everyday reality comes through, even when Dante is reporting on Hell and Heaven, and Boccaccio is trying to write (with his own modern annotation) an ancient epic.

Not least important was the sense especially strong in Italian literary culture, but already present in French, of the conception of the 'poet', implying the ambition of the modern vernacular writer to achieve the status of the ancient classical poet, as Chaucer remarks later of Petrarch 'lauriat poete' (*CT*, IV, 31) and Dante 'the grete poete of Ytaille' (*CT*, VII, 2460).

We must not make too much of this. Chaucer did not become a Dante. He retained much that is Gothic, and he was firmly set in a rather different popular and even humorous tradition. His Italian experience broadened his perspectives, warmed his imagination, enriched his knowledge, increasing the effectiveness of what was already present in actuality or potentiality.

COMPTROLLER OF CUSTOMS

Chaucer returned from Italy in May 1373, and probably his wife had to go almost immediately to Tutbury Castle in Staffordshire with Gaunt's second wife, Queen Constance of Castile, to whom she was lady-in-waiting. Since Chaucer personally received payments at Westminster in the following November and February, they were presumably separated a good deal. If they were a devoted couple they were unlucky, though many other esquires and ladies-in-waiting were in a similar position.

In the spring things improved rapidly. On 23 April 1374, during the Garter feast of St George, Chaucer was granted a pitcher of wine daily (later commuted to an annual grant of 20 marks – £13 6s. 8d., a considerable sum). A fortnight later (10 May 1374) he obtained the dwelling-house, or what we would now call a flat or apartment, above the city gate of Aldgate, for no rent, though he had to keep it in repair. Such a dwelling was pleasant and convenient and Chaucer was lucky to get it. It must have been obtained by influence with the

City, though we do not know whose. The house was obviously taken to prepare for his new appointment, which came four weeks later. On 8 June 1374, Chaucer was appointed Comptroller of the Customs and Subsidy of wools, skins, and tanned hides in the Port of London, with the usual fees. His place of business was about ten minutes' walk from his new house. Five days later (13 June) he and his wife received an annuity of £10 for life from Gaunt, which was presumably a recognition of Philippa's services now that she was leaving to set up house for the first time.

Chaucer's new appointment was not completely a sinecure. He was to write out the rolls of his office with his own hand, and perform his duties personally. These were mainly to act as check on the two collectors, who were such men of substance as Nicholas Brembre, William Walworth (the lord mayor who struck down Wat Tyler) and John Philipot. They were important businessmen in the City. Chaucer's income was £10 a year, probably a good deal increased by fees and, once at least, by £71 4s. 6d., being the fine of a merchant whom Chaucer detected shipping wool without paying duty. The house at Aldgate and his work at the Customs were Chaucer's main concerns until 1385 or 1386. During his time here at least two sons, Lewis and Thomas, were born, and he composed *The House of Fame*, *The Parliament of Fowls*, *Troilus and Criseyde*, and several minor poems, besides translating Boethius's *Consolation of Philosophy*. He may have thought of *The Canterbury Tales* here, and even written some of them. It is an astonishingly productive period. There is an amusing and interesting passage in *The House of Fame* referring to this time where he represents himself as being reproached (by an Eagle) for his dullness, because being chained to the office desk all day, and reading half the night, he sees nothing of his very neighbours. There is surely an underlying suggestion here (not necessarily conscious) both of his impatience at his office drudgery, and his escape from it into imaginative flights of the mind, into the imaginative world of books, as symbolised by his flight with the Eagle. Jupiter has considered, the Eagle says, how dutifully Chaucer has laboured in writing songs of love, without any reward, and also,

> beau sir, other thynges;   *good sir*
> That is, that thou hast no tydynges
> Of Loves folk yf they be glade,
> Ne of noght elles that God made;
> And noght oonly fro fer contree
> That ther no tydynge cometh to thee,

But of thy verray neyghebores,
That duellen almost at thy dores,   *dwell*
Thou herist neyther that ne this;
For when thy labour doon al ys,
And hast mad alle thy rekenynges,
In stede of reste and newe thynges,
Thou goost hom to thy hous anoon;
And, also domb as any stoon,
Thou sittest at another book
Tyl fully daswed ys thy look,   *dazed*
And lyvest thus as an heremyte,
Although thyn abstynence ys lyte.   *little*
    And therfore Joves, thorgh hys grace,
Wol that I bere the to a place   *thee*
Which that hight the Hous of Fame,   *was called*
To do the som disport and game.

(*HF*, 643–64)

It was remarkable at that time for a man to read silently, and that
Chaucer could shows the advanced state of his literacy. Most people
in reading murmured the words to themselves, as inexpert readers
still do. Chaucer had much internalised the reading process.

The reference to his 'reckonings', his arithmetical calculations, his
lists of tariffs and customs duties, indicates his arithmetical training,
and also suggests that though it was influential it was in tension with
the desire for personal and imaginative experience, the longing to
meet people, to know love, to hear stories, to know what is going
on in the world.

Chaucer's daily duties cannot have been too rigidly enforced,
notwithstanding his complaints, for he was sent abroad several times
on commissions handling delicate negotiations to stop the war with
France, and trying to arrange the marriage of the ten-year-old Prince
Richard with Marie of France. (Neither object was achieved.) In
December 1376 he was associated with Sir John Burley, Captain of
Calais, on a secret mission: from February to March 1377, he went on
a mission to Paris, Montreuil and elsewhere, with Sir Thomas Percy
(later Earl of Worcester). He was away again 30 April to 26 June
1377. He seems to have been associated with Sir Guiscard d'Angle
(one of Richard's tutors) and Sir Richard Sturry, in the marriage
negotiations. Sturry was known for his Lollard sympathies. There is
every reason to suppose Chaucer high in favour at court, and re-
garded as an accomplished courtier, diplomat and administrator.

On 26 June 1377 Edward III, for some years failing, at last died, and the child Richard succeeded to the throne. All Chaucer's posts and emoluments were formally renewed, and in January 1378 he was again abroad negotiating on the same delicate matters. From 28 May to 19 September 1378 he was again in Italy, in Milan, negotiating with Bernabò Visconti, and the famous English *condottiere*, Sir John Hawkwood. During this latter absence he granted the poet John Gower powers of attorney to act for him, so they were evidently good friends. This was the last time Chaucer went abroad on the king's business.

CHAUCER'S RELEASE FROM ACCUSATION OF RAPE: HIS FRIENDS

It was a period of continuing prosperity for him. He and his wife received a steady flow of payments and gifts. There was the fine mentioned earlier, and in November and December 1378 he was granted two lucrative wardships. However, the smooth progress was marred by two incidents: one private, one public. The first is suggested by the deed, dated 1 May 1380, whereby one Cecily Champain released Geoffrey Chaucer Esquire of every sort of action 'both of my rape' (*meo raptu*) 'and of any other matter or cause'. Professor Pearsall in his admirable biography of Chaucer (1992) considers that 'raptus' in this case means rape in the modern sense, but that judging from the curious sequence of documents which surrounds this case Chaucer, while certainly guilty of something, may not have been guilty of violent physical rape. For example, Cecily Champain may have been demanding payment for a love-affair which Chaucer had tired of and which she regretted. At any rate the main document suggests some sordid business, though we shall never quite know what. Professor Pearsall uses the incident as a base for a consideration of Chaucer's attitude to women, in which he points out both Chaucer's quite unusual interest in the nature of women and their rightful claims to fully human independence, and the underlying misogyny of the culture, leading to an uneasiness about allowing women fully human freedom, which Chaucer shared. The incident may also suggest the powerful passions which surged within this remarkable man who seems normally to have maintained a genially self-deprecatory unaggressive appearance, and whose poetry, though often satirical, is so free from personal anger.

In the business of Cecily Champain, Chaucer gathered a formidable collection of witnesses to the release (which, as Pearsall points out, do not necessarily witness to his innocence), rather as Pandarus in *Troilus and Criseyde* seeks to gather influential supporters for Criseyde in the lawsuit he claims is being brought against her. In Chaucer's case some critics have seen the assemblage of witnesses as an example of men ganging up together. But it was a common medieval legal procedure to have such 'compurgators' to witness to one's good character. They were distinguished men, worldly but honourable: Sir William Beauchamp, Chamberlain of the King, and for long one of Chaucer's circle; John de Clanvowe and William de Neville, two serious-minded Lollard knights; John Philipot, grocer, Collector of Customs, and later a lord mayor of London. These were all men of the 'king's party' at court (as were the lawyer Strode, and Gower, to whom *Troilus* is dedicated) and with the two latter give an interesting cross-section of the friends who made up Chaucer's more intimate circle of acquaintances – solid men, courtiers, merchants, men of learning, all closely associated. Personal and political loyalty may not have meant a cynical attitude, and all these men seem to have remained associates and perhaps friends of Chaucer.

The other incident which must have disturbed Chaucer was a disaster of national dimensions – the Peasants' Revolt, when in June 1381 a wild mob stormed the City, and for three days held it under a reign of terror, the objects of their particular hostility being lawyers, collectors of the king's taxes, John of Gaunt and his followers, and the wretched immigrant Flemish weavers. There was some incendiarism and Gaunt's splendid house, the Savoy, in the Strand, was totally destroyed. There were many killings; the aged Archbishop Sudbury, regarded as the representative of oppressive government, being Chancellor, was haled out of the Tower and beheaded; and many Flemish weavers suffered. The rebels were, however, pathetically loyal to the person of the king, and the Revolt was calmed down, as is well known, by Richard's bold meeting with the peasants. He made a promise of general pardon and though the ring-leaders were punished this was generally adhered to. There was no cruel aftermath of punishment of the rebels, though Chaucer's friend Gower (a small landowner in Kent) represents a more hysterical attitude when in his poem *Vox Clamantis* he describes the peasants as domestic beasts gone suddenly and outrageously mad.

CHAUCER'S POLITICAL ATTITUDE

Chaucer kept his views to himself; he was not a man fanatically to espouse one party or another. The orthodoxy, the idealism, the conviction of the world's sinfulness which are the ground-bass of his poetry, lead us to expect nothing else. His summing-up of experience which is the nearest thing we have to a personal expression of emotion about the world may well have been written within a few years of these events. It is to be found in the Balades, *Gentilesse* and *Lak of Stedfastnesse*.

> Trouthe is put doun, resoun is holden fable;
> Vertu hath now no dominacioun;
> Pitee exyled, no man is merciable;
> Through covetyse is blent discrecioun.   *blinded; moderation*
> The world hath mad a permutacioun
> Fro right to wrong, fro trouthe to fikelnesse,
> That al is lost for lak of stedfastnesse.
>
> (*Lak of Stedfastnesse*, 15–21)

Wickedness and misery are seen as springing from 'instability', that is, from lack of loyalty, and the consequent upsetting of the proper order of society. The *envoy* to King Richard in the same poem aligns Chaucer with the usual political theories of his day, in both their punitive and idealistic forms:

> O prince, desyre to be honourable,
> Cherish thy folk and hate extorcioun!
> Suffre nothing that may be reprevable
> To thyn estat don in thy regioun.
> Shew forth thy swerd of castigacioun,   *punishment*
> Dred God, do law, love trouthe and worthinesse,
> And wed thy folk agein to stedfastnesse.
>
> (*Lak of Stedfastnesse*, 22–28)

These sharply expressed traditional commonplaces clearly express an important element in Chaucer's concept of the world, and it could coexist with an acceptance of the human comedy. It suggests acceptance even of vice, rather than reform. It is a kind of cheerful, certainly worldly, pessimism.

Behind and beneath this is the even more fundamental Christian and Boethian combination of resignation to fortune, and contempt of the world. Such an attitude is most clearly found in the stoical pessimism of the poem *Truth*, written when Chaucer was a good deal older. At this earlier and most successful period of his life Chaucer was less inclined to deny the world; nevertheless the doctrine of rejection was at all times an important element in his thought, and it may well be mentioned in connection with this crisis ('trouthe' here means also God):

That thee is sent, receyve in buxumnesse;   *obedience*
The wrastling for this world axeth a fal.   *wrestling; asks for*
Her is non hoom, her nis but wildernesse: *is not*
Forth, pilgrim, forth! Forth, beste, out of thy stal!
Know thy contree, look up, thank God of al;
Hold the heye wey, and lat thy gost thee lede;   *high; spirit*
And trouthe thee shal delivere, it is no drede.   *doubt*

                                                      (*Truth*, 15–21)

Chaucer continued at the Customs House until 1386, apparently
with success. In November 1381 he received ten marks as a reward
for diligence, and in 1382 he was appointed controller of the petty
customs in the port of London. This latter was also probably a
reward, as he was allowed to appoint a permanent deputy.

WITHDRAWAL TO KENT

In February 1385 Chaucer applied to exercise his main controllership
also by permanent deputy. Since in each of the two preceding years
he had been allowed to be away from his post for a month or so
to attend to his private affairs, it seems he was breaking away from
his administrative duties. He was appointed a Justice of the Peace
for Kent in October 1385, and in August 1386 became Knight of
the Shire to attend the Parliament of October. He probably went
to live in Kent some time in 1385. His house over Aldgate was
leased to another man in October 1386, and in December his two
controllerships were granted to two other men. It is possible that he
voluntarily resigned, but he may have lost them for political reasons.
There were three main factions, a 'court' or 'king's party', led by
Sir Simon Burley; a Lancastrian faction, grouped round John of
Gaunt; and a baronial opposition led by the Duke of Gloucester and
the Earl of Warwick, which hated the Lancastrians and was largely
contemptuous of the court. In 1386 the barons, called the Lords
Appellant, struck first at the Lancastrians, who were in uneasy alli-
ance with the court party, and then, even more devastatingly, at the
court party. The barons succeeded, temporarily, in 'capturing' the
king's authority and the royal administration. Chaucer seems to have
been associated principally with the court party, as were most of his
circle. There was a purge of the king's men from administrative
posts. This is perhaps why Chaucer lost his controllerships. It was an
uneasy and dangerous time, and he may have felt himself well out of
it down in Kent.

We do not get the impression from all this that Chaucer was a sycophantic courtier, a placeman greedily sucking up such jobs as would give him wealth and power. At any rate, if he was such a person, he was not very successful. Others did much better. He could have wished to obtain income, and yet be a loyal servant to the Crown, and yet again to have a certain detachment from the court and from more general worldly desires. No doubt, like the rest of us, he was a bundle of conflicting desires.

Chapter 10

From *House of Fame* to *Parliament of Fowls*: Discontent and Search

The years of business at the Customs House were thus extraordinarily full of literary activity, both reading and writing. Chaucer's intellectual interests led him to delight in knowledge for its own sake, and for the sake of understanding the full spectacle of life. In this period he translated the great work of Boethius, *The Consolation of Philosophy*. His interest in astronomy and astrology (the two were almost indistinguishable in his day), based on his command of arithmetic, now clearly appears as an important element in his thought. His interest in the psychology of dreams and in physics is shown in *The House of Fame*. The many references to the natural sciences and to medicine in *The Canterbury Tales* reflect reading of which at least part was done at this period. None of these many subjects can be considered as diverging from, or hostile to, his poetry. They were in part the very material of his poetry; and they helped to focus his view of the world, of human character, of the course of good and ill in human life. The desire for a total view, a *Summa*, of earthly knowledge and experience, is a characteristic of the men of the High and Late Middle Ages, whether they wrote in prose or verse. They are such encyclopedists as Vincent of Beauvais and the Englishmen Alexander Neckham and Bartholomew; the great theologians, St Albertus Magnus and St Thomas Aquinas; and chief among poets, Dante. Chaucer's contemporary Langland and his friend Gower each attempted similar syntheses, and *The Canterbury Tales* is partly to be understood in this light. *The House of Fame* and the *Parliament* are also probably attempts at synthesis, for when a learned and courtly poet wished to gather in the whole created universe, he bound it together with 'the fayre chain of love'.

WHERE DO WE GO FROM HERE? A GOTHIC MISCELLANY

The House of Fame must have been written after the Italian journey, because it is threaded with reminiscences of Dante. On the other hand, it is still written in the old short four-stress English couplets and in the French manner. It must have been written some time in the mid-1370s. Chaucer has still not read the book by Macrobius on Cicero's *Dream of Scipio* because he still thinks, as he did in *The Book of the Duchess*, that Scipio was a king (*HF*, II, 916). The poem is unfinished and of the three books into which it is divided the third has a disproportionate number of the total 2158 lines.

It is an extraordinarily interesting, odd poem. All the elements we have already met in *The Book of the Duchess* are present: the person-alised direct tone, the framing dream-convention, tripartite structure, the wealth of reading, the recycling of bookish material into orality, variability of tone, the reluctance – in this case the failure – to close; altogether, the same mixture of remarkable innovation arising out of traditional material.

Curiosity and search are stronger than in any other of Chaucer's poems. He wanders and wonders in strange lands of the imagination supported at times by a comic version of scientific law. The impul-sion is discontent with his own dull, hardworking life (above, p. 116). The aim (he says) is to learn more about love but he dis-covers about anything but that. He strays through entertainments, historical stories. He sees the unreliability of Fame – he is implicitly ambitious, and characteristically sceptical. But he sturdily asserts his own self-contained independence of other people's opinion (1873–82). What he seeks, he says, is 'news', stories (1884–94), new things, pleasant things – he doesn't know what – if possible about love, none of which he has yet found.

Dissatisfaction, looking for one doesn't know what, quiet self-assertion, do not convey self-regarding Romantic *angst*, introspec-tion, self-posturing. He gently mocks himself. The poet for the first time refers to his own plumpness (574), a joke he is happy to repeat on occasion for the rest of his life. (Whatever scepticism we may have about reading a biography of an actual man out of his poetry there can surely be no doubt that in actual life Chaucer was unromantically fat at least from his middle-thirties onwards.) In this poem too the eagle calls the poet by his veritable name, Geoffrey (729). Of course this authentication does not attribute literal truth to the experiences the poet records: no one thinks he was really carried up into the skies. To this extent 'Geoffrey' is a fiction, or even a 'foolish narrator': he is a projection of the poet's imagination, but closely linked to the poet himself, who is thus both inside the poem, as a genuine fictional character, like the Eagle, and outside, as the creative personal writer. The Eagle may be something of a parody of

Dante or could even be a skit on some learned friend or teacher – we shall never know. And 'the man of great authority' who appears at the very end of the poem and signally fails to deliver, may equally represent a 'real' person, as well as a projection of the poet's imaginative loss of his way.

This most personal of Chaucer's poems, the most self-conscious, is also self-conscious about his art, as in the prologue to Book III, apostrophising Apollo 'god of science and of light', commenting on the poet's own 'art poetical' and the number of syllables in a line, and the occasional lack of one (1098). Syllable counting was new in English verse, which depends fundamentally on stress.

Personal as the poem is, it is driven by intellectual curiosity into the things of this world, on the relation of merit to Fame (none), on the mixture of truth and lies in stories. Contempt for Fame is traditional, as is the desire for it, especially by poets. The desire for stories is traditional, and Chaucer mixes it with an equal desire for knowledge, 'science'. Yet he also proclaims, and displays, his desire to amuse and please. It is the courtier's job to please, with stories, jests and songs, and such is Chaucer's aim. He starts from the minstrel's base in stories but he wants more and better stories, and he has a passion for knowledge which he partly mocks in himself through the figure of the Eagle.

There is a huge pressure of things to say and feel in the poem. It is bursting with fascinating material to such an extent that it loses shape. Of three 'books' into which it is divided the third is disproportionately long. For all the underlying discontent, if such there be, there is huge zest, though nothing is taken seriously. The poet does not quite know where he is going. He does not fully accept authority, or at least he can find nothing authoritative to say. He presents himself as an outsider, or at any rate as marginal, as in all his poetry: his allegiance to the social frame is qualified, it may seem. On the other hand, there is nothing radical, nothing rebellious. The poem, like others of Chaucer's, constantly invites our questioning in presenting his own. Perhaps it owes something of its tone to the fourteenth-century development in England of a kind of empiricism, developed by the influential Oxford philosopher William Ockham (d.*c.* 1349), who divided faith from rational enquiry and emphasised individual 'facts' as against 'universals', abstract names without real content (see also below, p. 151). Whatever Chaucer's empiricism he was also attracted, as was inevitable in his culture, to grand generalisations and principles. Perhaps the clash between these two tendencies is at the root of *The House of Fame*.

Part of the inspiration, yet also one of the destabilising factors, is the influence of Dante's *Divine Comedy*. Chaucer seems to have not surprisingly been more impressed by Dante's great poem than by Boccaccio's poems. He made both more and less use of Dante. He could not master his work, not translate long passages (with the one exception later discussed in *The Monk's Tale*) but he was struck by his power and thought. The beginning of Book II of *The House of Fame* (509ff.) illustrates the curious mixture. It begins in the chirpy style of the English metrical romance, then absorbs a bit of Dante (*O Thought*, 523) and then picks up again with the descent of the eagle, using Dante. Chaucer both uses and resists Dante as a source.

The poem begins as it continues with a serious topic treated lightly. It comments on the classification of dreams, a well-known scientific topic, but flippantly treated. The poet then proceeds to an invocation of the god of sleep in the same light-hearted manner and tells how he fell asleep on the night of 10 December. Why so precise a date, and what meaning to attach to the apparently tiring but only two miles pilgrimage to the holy body of St Leonard which is then referred to, remain unknown. There is a strong sense of a private joke to an inner circle.

The poet dreams he is in the Temple of Venus, made of glass, full of tabernacles and richly adorned images, like a fourteenth-century Gothic church. The portrait of Venus is there, shown naked, floating in the sea, with a rose garland on her head, carrying a comb, accompanied by doves, her son Cupid, and her husband Vulcan, the lame god of smiths, with his brown face. There is a long literary history behind this description, to be described later (p. 157ff.). Here it is enough to say that such a picture of Venus shows her as the goddess of sexual lust and unfaithful love. Doves were thought to be specially amorous birds; red and white roses illustrated sexual passion; Vulcan had caught Venus naked in bed with Mars.

The poet sees written on the walls the story of Virgil's *Aeneid*, ambiguously conveyed both as writing and a series of pictures. Virgil's *gravitas* is abandoned in favour of Ovid's pathos, for the story is mainly focused on the seduction and betrayal of Dido by Aeneas, the son of Venus. The plight of Dido is emphasised by a speech from her after the manner of Ovid's *Heroides*, and reinforced by reference to other deserted heroines.

The poet leaves the temple and finds himself in a barren sandy desert, which is a surprising image for a man who presumably had never seen such a sight. It symbolises, consciously or unconsciously, a spiritual barrenness and uncertainty where to go, what to do. But a shining golden eagle descends and so this first book concludes.

The poem of the Second Book returns to the sportive tone of the Introduction to the First. Chaucer makes a playfully exaggerated claim for the outstanding worth of his dream, and comprehensively invokes Cipris (i.e. Venus), the Muses, and his own Thought. Throughout this passage there are reminiscences of Dante and Boccaccio, sometimes close, but Chaucer has not yet caught their larger manner.

The story of the dream is then lightheartedly continued. The poet dreams he is swept up into the heavens by the eagle. He is stunned with fear and astonishment, for which the Eagle admonishes him pretty sharply, softening enough, however, to explain to him that Jupiter has taken pity on him because he has served blind Cupid and fair Venus so 'ententyfly', 'withoute guerdon ever yit' – in other words, because he has been unrewarded (whether by love or royal gift is deliberately ambiguous). Then follows the famous passage already quoted, describing how he studies far into the night because he must work during the day, and so knows nothing of how the world goes. As a reward he is to be taken to the House of Fame, where he will find news of love, and all the variety of love's experience. The poet, whom the Eagle clearly identifies by calling him Geoffrey (l, 729), refuses to believe that this is possible; whence follows the Eagle's brilliant exposition of the properties of sound. It finishes with the Eagle's amusing crow of self-satisfied triumph, after which he shows the poet the heavens, 'gladding' him with his explanations. It is characteristic of Chaucer that as he looks about and sees the 'airish beasts' and the way the clouds, rains and winds are made, he breaks out

> 'O God', quod y, 'that made Adam,   *I*
> Moche ys thy myght and thy noblesse!'
>
> (*HF*, 970–1)

It is equally characteristic that when the Eagle is anxious to inform him about the names of the stars, the poet says he is too old to learn. The Eagle points out how useful such knowledge will be 'when thou redest poetrie', but Chaucer says he will rely on the writer's words, and that anyway he is so near the stars that they will blind him if he looks at them. Then he is landed at Fame's 'place', so concluding Book II.

WHAT IS FAME?

The Third Book also begins with an invocation, an interestingly modest disclaimer of 'art poetical'. The poet dreams he comes to a mountain of ice, with many half-melted names written on it. On this uncertain foundation is perched a castle wonderfully adorned, bustling with all kinds of people, including heralds, jugglers, classical heroes and heroines, all dancing and springing about. Within is the magnificent Hall of Fame, and Fame herself, sitting on a ruby throne, varying in height from human size to one reaching the heavens, reminiscent in appearance of some of the creatures described in Revelation, the last book of the Bible. The hall is upheld by pillars carved in human form (like Gothic cathedrals, such as the porches at Chartres). These figures, upholding the Hall of Fame, are the great writers of the past.

Groups of people come up to the Goddess Fame. She grants or withholds worldly honour quite without regard to desert. The poet himself is asked why he is seeking fame. He replies in a dismissive way as already noted. But what *is* he doing? someone asks him. 'That will I tell thee,' he says. It is to learn some new tidings, *he does not know what*, either of love or similar glad things. What he has seen so far he already knew and is nothing to the point. His unnamed questioner replies with another question: 'What are the tidings that you have thus brought here, which you have heard? But no matter, I see what you desire to hear.' This is the sort of mysterious inconsequentiality which makes the poem so exasperating, and suggests either 'private jokes in panelled rooms', or that Chaucer never really worked out what he wanted to say. He is taken to the House of Twigs, a vast hall built of wickerwork, continually going round – another extraordinary image. In it is a tumultuous crowd of people exchanging whispers, rumours, stories, which themselves take on a kind of corporality. This is the House of Fame in the word's Latinate sense of Rumour, where he is to see such strange sights and hear such new things as will console him for the distress he has endured so cheerfully, having been so empty of all bliss since Fortune destroyed his heart's rest. It is the Eagle who tells him all this, thus harking back to the earlier passage where the poet was told of Jupiter's pity. His sadness may be due to the frustration of his poetry caused by the pressure of business which ties him to his office accounts all day when he would prefer to be reading. At least, strange sights and 'tidings', whether these be 'news' or 'stories', would seem to be a rather more satisfactory reward for one who was denied freedom and learning, than for one who was unlucky in love. The poet goes about inquiring eagerly for certain news – which he hints is now known pretty widely (another puzzle) – when there is suddenly a rush to one corner of the hall. A man of great authority steps forth . . . and the poem breaks off. What message the man of authority could have delivered is unknown. It seems quite possible that it eluded Chaucer. The poem must have been very near its end; it has suddenly risen to a climax, demanding a really striking announcement, yet there seems nothing that could have been a satisfactory literary climax. The notion that the poem is written as a deliberate prelude to some *real* announcement seems wildly impractical. We cannot tie the poem to any external event, as we can *The Book of the Duchess*.

The poem is an exploration of love and fame, and for all the frequent lightness of tone, and confidence of manner, the darker side of both is prominent. The poet is eager for stories about people, but the disorderliness of humanity is distressing, and the ambivalence of worldly values is painful.

The flight into the skies is an ancient religious and literary motif, an image of aspiration, of desire for higher experience, for a larger point-of-view, greater knowledge, for paradise, where men are free and spontaneous and good, out of time. Yet Chaucer also mocks this; treats it with scientific realism; rejects the sublimity which he is offered and perhaps yearns for, refuses to be 'stellified' (ll, 584–92). Knowledge of the stars he will have, but as an earthly astronomer, not as religious prophet or classical god. To use the anthropological terms of Mircea Eliade, Chaucer refuses the role of *shaman*, priest, magician, prophet, with access to other-worldly experience: he chooses this life, this earth, these people. Whatever the difficulties or the sorrows, he chooses with self-deprecatory humour the actually human. The reason, we may guess, why the man of authority has nothing to say is because Chaucer cannot bring himself to put authoritative words into his mouth. What could be important enough?

The poem is an interesting contrast and comparison with *The Book of the Duchess*. Each implies a courtly situation. The earlier poem has a death to mourn: the later one is entirely cheerful. Although death (of Dido) and sadness are touched on, if closure of plot is always a metaphor for death Chaucer refuses to acknowledge both. If the poet's self is constructed in *The Book of the Duchess* with a certain art, so it is in *The House of Fame*, but we might almost add that it is also deconstructed, removed from poetic dignity while Fame is rejected and scorned. Love is supposed to be the topic of both poems, but we do not reach it in *The House of Fame*. It is indeed a strange and fascinating poem, whose wealth of detail can be no more than mentioned here.

ANELIDA AND ARCITE

Love continues to present its puzzles and its pains. A good many poems about love are poems of discontent. Love itself is so often unreciprocated or betrayed, and the lover has time on his hands to write about it. Such discontent may also reflect other forms of discontent or sorrow in life. There was a tradition of sorrowful poems of love which was as powerful, and as natural, as the equally noticeable number of modern pop-songs of various kinds about unsatisfied love. In the fourteenth century the poems were more formal, and called 'complaints', like the words first spoken by the man in black in *The Book of the Duchess*. Chaucer had written such poems early: *A Complaint unto Pity*, and *A Complaint to his Lady*. They have something of the feeling, for us, of 'periphrastic studies in a worn-out poetical fashion', to quote T. S. Eliot. *The House of Fame* is one attempt to escape, by going back to the love-vision again, and looking at it in the light of Dante's and Boccaccio's poetry. Another attempt is the poem *Anelida and Arcite*. It starts off splendidly, modelled on Boccaccio's epic, *Teseida*:

Thou ferse god of armes, Mars the rede . . .

We immediately notice the more powerful, expansive five-stress line, forming the seven-line rhyming stanza which came to be called rhyme royal, and which Chaucer probably based on the model of Boccaccio. It is the first example in English of this splendid metre, which combines the spaciousness needed for storytelling with the capacity to rise to lyric intensity. The influence of Boccaccio's *Teseida* is plainly apparent, for there is to be a story attached to Theseus, who is the principal person in and gives his name to *Teseida*. But Chaucer's story here rapidly dwindles into one about the love of Queen Anelida betrayed by the false Arcite, and concludes with a 138-line 'Complaint' spoken to her, whose content is entirely in the old-fashioned French manner, though it is a miracle of verbal dexterity in the new stanza form. Here again Chaucer has tried and failed to assimilate Italian content and style.

THE LIFE OF SAINT CECILIA

Since Chaucer refers in the *Prologue F* to *The Legend of Good Women* to writing the life of Saint Cecilia 'with other holiness' such as the translation of Boethius's *Consolation* (424–6) it must have been written before 1386, and being written in the seven-line stanza may be grouped with other poems like *The Parliament of Fowls* and even *Troilus and Criseyde*. It used to be thought of as early and not very good, being a saint's life and partly based on a passionate virginity, neither of them easily comprehensible subjects to modern readers. It makes a piquant contrast to Chaucer's other perhaps contemporary poems and Chaucer apologises for what may be a certain perfunctoriness in its execution:

> Yet preye I yow that reden that I write,
> Foryeve me that I do no diligence
> This ilke storie subtilly to endite
>
> (78–80)

because, he says, he is translating it. It is true that he seems not to 'amplify' his source, and it may not have so intensely appealed to his imagination. Yet three stanzas before, he writes, apparently with feeling, in the Invocation to the Blessed Virgin Mary,

> Now help, thow meeke and blisful faire mayde
> Me flemed wrecche, in this desert of galle ...   *banished exile; bitterness*
> And though that I, unworthy sone of Eve
> Be synful, yet accepte my bileve.   *faith*
>
> (57 ... 63)

His soule is in prison troubled by the contagion

> Of my body, and also by the wighte   *weight*
> Of erthely lust and fals affeccioun.
>
> (72–3)

Well might the author of *Troilus and Criseyde* feel such qualms, until he came to the very end of that poem. The same sentiments are found in the prose *Retractation* at the end of *The Canterbury Tales*, and Theseus in *The Knight's Tale* speaks of 'this foule prisoun of this lyf' (I, 3061). This is a vein of thought deep in the culture of the times and deep in Chaucer, in perpetual tension with this-worldly pleasures. Some earlier lines of the Invocation are indebted to Dante, but those just quoted, though commonplaces, are nevertheless put together by specific choice. Chaucer also did choose to write the saint's life, and did so very successfully, if without expansion.

The reference to reading is noteworthy: taken literally it suggests more voluntary effort on his part. Any other interpretation, like the wrigglings around the obvious meaning of 'son of Eve' are mere cavillation, partly arising out of the odd later placing of the poem among *The Canterbury Tales*, and the persistent anachronistic desire of critics to see personal subjective expression driving the tales.

The Prologue with its Invocation is obviously written by a man and so, from the general tone, is the Life. To appreciate the poem and its assumptions we have to adjust our feelings to a different society. Many societies have regarded sex as 'dirty', not least because, as Yeats writes,

> But Love has pitched his mansion in
> The place of excrement.
>
> > (*Crazy Jane Talks with the Bishop*)

(But equally, 'Fair and foul are near of kin.' Dirt may be power.[1]) Purity may also be power. In the early days of Christianity it was through virginity that women attained power and influence.[2] Granted the magical, or supernatural, element in the saint's life, the story of St Cecilia is a stirring one, vigorously told, asserting the intelligence and power of a noble Roman virgin, who gladly endures martyrdom. It is a tragic story in which death is eventually swallowed up in victory. It can hardly be called feminist in a modern sense, because Cecilia's strength appears to be that appropriate to a man, but no other pattern was available to Chaucer or his immediate or remote sources. In all it is a poem that in its direct strength does not merit the neglect with which earlier critics (and earlier versions of this book) treated it.

NOTES

1. Mary Douglas, *Purity and Danger* (London, 1966).
2. Kate Cooper, *The Virgin and the Bride: Idealized Womanhood in Late Antiquity* (Cambridge, Mass., 1996). A similar situation continues in modern times in northern Albania where 'sworn virgins' have the status, privileges and work of men. See *The Daily Telegraph*, 6 February 1997, 15.

Chapter 11

The Parliament of Fowls:
Communality and Conflict

The uncertainty of direction and the failure to conclude *The House of Fame* were not so great as to lead Chaucer utterly to disclaim it, for he takes credit for it (rather oddly) as a love poem in *Prologue F*, 417, to *The Legend of Good Women*, and he revokes it with the rest of his secular work in *The Retractation*. Only three manuscripts and two early prints of *The House of Fame* survive, however, while for the next poem, *The Parliament of Fowls*, there are 14 manuscripts and Caxton's print. It is clearly more successful. It is complete and more controlled, though it too has its underlying puzzles, as well as pursuing the same quest. In it Chaucer shows a deepening Italian influence. Boccaccio now becomes more important. Boccaccio's most important gift, no doubt in conjunction with Dante, is to show the way to the more expansive five-stress line of ten or eleven syllables, with rhyme. From now on Chaucer counts syllables like an Italian or French poet, and good English accountant. In this poem he uses with fully developed skill the seven-line stanza, rhyming *a b a b b c c*, the so-called rhyme royal. The poet's choice of metre is highly important both technically and symbolically. It tells us so much about his power and feeling. Here Chaucer is confidently expansive, has much to say, and in control. His diction also becomes more elaborate.

The date is uncertain within a year or two. A favourite argument, urged with renewed vigour by Professor L. D. Benson, is that it reflects a courtly marriage proposal for the young Richard II, and other possibilities have been urged. It would be wise to recognise Chaucer's close mesh with courtly knowledge and business, while it is also impossible to deny the echoes of ordinary life heard in this apparently artificial Valentine poem. But we must also recognise in Chaucer's work a certain detachment from the more intimate concerns of court politics, and the poem could be accounted for as one of several Valentine poems, by Chaucer and the French poet,

Oton de Graunson. Political interests may tie the poem to a date in 1382. The enigmatic reference to the planet Venus (113–19) may favour this date. 1382 is at any rate about right as a date in the course of Chaucer's poetry and life so far as we can plot them. It is worth remembering that this was also a period of great social unrest, and that the Peasants' Revolt took place in 1381. That too may be in the background, along with Parliamentary debate. So this is an even richer poem in life and literary content, still centring on the quest for meaning and arising out of a residual discontent.

The passage of time has further enriched the treasure of the poet's mind. Part of the impulse to write arises from the genuine discovery of a book, old but new to him. It is the substantial Commentary by Macrobius on the text which it preserves, *The Dream of Scipio*, written by the famous Classical Latin orator, Cicero. Chaucer discovered that Scipio was not a king, but a noble Roman, and the whole book excited him: it seemed to offer some sort of answer to his perennial searching of the mystery of love and the common good. He can now express his feeling more precisely with the aid of another great book, apparently recently read:

> For bothe I hadde thyng which that I nolde,   *did not want*
> And ek I nadde that thyng that I wolde.   *also had not what I wanted*
> (*PF*, 90–1)

This neat expression of a very common human feeling and situation is itself lifted from *The Consolation of Philosophy* by Boethius, which Chaucer has now obviously absorbed, as he has absorbed Dante and the Cicero–Macrobius *Dream of Scipio*. The range of Chaucer's mind had been notable in *The Book of the Duchess* by way of lists, references and sources. It was even more remarkable in *The House of Fame* through use of earlier love-visions, knowledge of earlier writers, response to the crowds of medieval entertainers and much else. Now he introduces what may be called a roughly philosophical dimension. This is no dry-as-dust intellectualism. Like any true intellectual, scientist, scholar, Chaucer's thought is driven by feeling, concentrated in the question of love, radiating out from that into the many concerns of human relationship.

The poem has the mixture of seriousness and levity so characteristic of Chaucer's poetry. There is a genuine desire to understand the contradictions of life, a concern for ultimate meaning, quite explicitly expressed. Yet there is also delight in variety, interest in the multiple world, an appreciation of both the sensuous and the comic.

A modern critic may ask whether it is not merely naïve to take this series of poems, and this particular poem, as a genuine personal expression of a genuine search for wisdom. Is not Chaucer striking an artistic pose, presenting a puzzled narrator-puppet while he ironically pulls the strings? To think so would create an even greater problem. What would be the point of such trickery? If we suppose it to be mere trickery we stifle any possible recognition of the poetry. By super-subtlety we would deny what the poet says. No one surely now thinks that to respond to a poet's apparent intention within the poem is a mere fallacy? Granted, there may well be more to a poem than apparent intention, but that is where we must start.

In truth it is easy for a normal person to respond both to the underlying purpose of the poem and its entertaining series of events and descriptions. Chaucer is often enigmatic, subtle, sly, ironical, but his poetry is not difficult. There is always an immediate meaning, whatever echoes and afterthoughts may be aroused. In the present case, since all sensitive people are at times discontented with their lot, and most intelligent people at some time are puzzled by the inherently self-contradictory nature of experience, the poem starts from a recognisable human dilemma. How do we reconcile the conflicting claims of love? How do we achieve the common good? Or even more simply, we are invited to see how the most direct and well-intentioned human emotions lead to communal discord.

In *The Parliament of Fowls* Chaucer is not overtly posing philosophical problems, nor making a social analysis, nor advocating a political programme. He is telling a sort of story, but he does indeed have a general theme – that of personal discontent – and the consequent search for an answer. The problem of love, of personal relationships, is at the core, but this leads to the wider problem of conflicts about love, and ultimately of conflict in society. Chaucer's preoccupation is primarily courtly, and with courtly dilemmas, with the nature of romantic love, but we with knowledge of the contemporary social discontent in England may hear the cries of peasants in the background of the expressed discontent of most (not all) of the lower orders of birds. We see contradiction within what should be communality. The effect is achieved through a most adept collocation of sources, a kind of *collage* – personal introduction, summary of a severe philosophy, a beautiful park, a warm temple with bright images, a lively 'parliamentary' debate, a vulgar argument, a song of spring. In the end there is a kind of hope holding all these elements together. It is always wise to postpone a painful decision you do not have to make, and meanwhile the search can still go on.

Chaucer begins *The Parliament* with exclamations on the nature of art, but he deliberately and jestingly misleads us in the first line or two, and soon deflects well-established comments on the nature of art to say that it is the art of love *he* is talking about. An educated courtly audience or reader is presupposed. Then he switches back to the old book he had discovered, in which he read so eagerly 'a certeyn thing to lerne', for the whole day (his duties to the Customs referred to so ruefully in *The House of Fame* do not seem to have burdened him so greatly here). *The Dream of Scipio* itself is then summarised. Scipio is carried in a dream to a point in the heavens from where he can see the utter triviality of the whole earth and its concerns. But a man may win to the bliss of heaven. How to get there? 'Know thyself first immortal,' and work for the common good (ll, 73–5). It is a secularised version of religious truth.

Macrobius wrote in Latin about 400 AD, and like Boethius preserved in relatively elementary form something of the science and art of Classical Antiquity on which men could build after the collapse of Roman civilisation under barbarian attack. His commentary is concerned with the scientific concepts that might be educed from Cicero's *The Dream of Scipio*, such as the roundness of the world, of which he preserved the knowledge for the whole medieval period, and the importance of certain numbers. Chaucer read the Commentary by Macrobius with interest and makes incidental use of some parts, but for his poem he takes the core of it, Cicero's *The Dream of Scipio*, as the centre of his eager search. But he finishes the book with the couplet already quoted, that he had what he did not want, and lacked what he did want.

Why was he disappointed? Partly perhaps at the banality of the message, for we all know what we ought to do, most of the time, and that we ought to be good. It may be true, but it rarely illuminates, consoles, inspires or compensates us. More specifically, there is no word about love, and love is the subject of major interest.

The poet falls asleep and dreams, and as he writes 'now' of the dream he had 'then', he invokes 'Cytherea', the name he uses when he wants to indicate the planet Venus, who, he says, made him dream this dream, and whom he asks to give him strength to write. Astronomy and astrology were seriously studied together in the fourteenth century, as will be shown further in the next chapter, and Venus is both a mythological personification to adorn the poetry and a genuine almost personal planetary force. According to astrology, Venus the planet influenced love, friendship, affection, company, domesticity, sexual intercourse, pleasure and also, if unpropitious, the miseries of love. The planet Venus now becomes the poem's guiding star, and though the invocation is light-hearted, it is not ironical. Chaucer has achieved at last an appropriate lightness of tone that is not merely flippant or, as in *The House of Fame*, verging on the extravagantly facetious, but is strong and fresh.

In the poet's dream Scipio, who gave such worthy but perhaps unattractive advice in Cicero's book, comes to show the poet not heaven nor hell, but a wondrous park, with a twofold promise on its gates; first that

> This is the wey to al good aventure,   *events*
>   (*PF*, 131)

but also, just opposite,

> Th' eschewing is only the remedye!   *avoiding*
>   (*PF*, 140)

A witty allusion to the words on the gates of Hell in Dante's *Divine Comedy* is included. The vast majority of Chaucer's earlier readers would not have realised it. It is a joke that Chaucer is having with himself, to label the park of love and life with the same phrases as the domain of Hell. The park is delightfully and not ironically described. This section is largely translated from another recent discovery, Boccaccio's *Teseida*. Chaucer improves on his original, making Boccaccio's abstract words flower into colourful, lively images. The lovely garden is refreshed by light sweet breezes and the ravishing melodies of birds; it is adorned with blossomy boughs, green meadows, flowers white, blue, yellow and red – an Earthly Paradise. It symbolises the bright expectant springtime of young life and love; clearly, also, it stands for the whole created world, and the birds which later appear symbolise both human society and all created beings. Part of the implicit message is the unity of all creation, human beings, living creatures, the organic world of flowers and trees, as God originally created the harmonious whole.

After describing the temperate freshness of the whole park, where there is no 'grievance of hot nor cold', no night nor bitter weather, and no man is old or sick, the dreamer sees Cupid with his followers, Pleasance, Aray, Lust, disfigured Craft, and so forth. Behind these is the temple of Venus, the mother of hot desire. Her temple, in contrast to the freshness outside, is filled with sighs and rich with a thousand sweet odours. Priapus, the lustful god, stands 'in sovereyn place', shameful, ludicrous, obscene, with a *double-entendre* on 'sceptre':

In swich aray as whan the asse hym shente   *shamed*
With cri by nighte, and with hys sceptre in honde.

                                                              (*PF*, 255–6)

(This is another witty allusion, this time to a story by Ovid.)
Venus lies in a 'private corner', all but naked. She disports herself
with Richesse who, according to the English *Romaunt* (5993ff.), will
have nothing to do with poor young men, who are the stable and
steadfast lovers of whom the real god or lord is Cupid. On the walls
of the temple are painted stories of those who have suffered bitterly
for love. Infatuated and betrayed love, sometimes illicit, is portrayed
everywhere – though as a misfortune, not as a crime. Chaucer adds
to *Teseida*'s list of lovers some of those placed by Dante in Hell in
the Circle of the Lustful: Dido, Cleopatra, Helen, Achilles, Paris,
Tristram. Troilus is also added to these sufferers, without a hint from
Dante or Boccaccio. He must already have been in Chaucer's mind.

The temple of Venus therefore shows love only as infatuation,
lust, shame, misery, betrayal – indeed, as a justification of Scipio's
condemnation of the world. Her temple is an anomalous, discordant,
disordinate element in the paradisal garden of love. Should any doubt
of this exist in the mind of a modern reader, we may refer to
Boccaccio's own *Chiose* or notes, issued with *Teseida*. It does not
seem likely that Chaucer's copy of *Teseida* contained these notes, but
a later age may be grateful for the guidance they give to the general
effect Boccaccio aimed at. The *Chiose* devote pages to the signific-
ance of the Cupid and Venus passage, attributing allegorical mean-
ing to every detail. It may be doubted whether Chaucer would
have been much interested in this excessive allegory, but there is no
doubt about the general implications of the Temple of Venus.
Boccaccio says:

> Venus is twofold; by the first can be and should be understood every
> honest and legitimate desire, such as to desire a wife in order to have
> children, and desires similar to this; and this Venus is not meant here.
> The second Venus is she through whom all lasciviousness is desired, and
> who is commonly called the goddess of love; and *she it is* whose temple
> and other qualities belonging to it are described here by the author, as
> appears in the text.
>
>   (G. Boccaccio, *Teseida*, edited by A. Roncaglia
>   (Bari, 1941) 417ff. (*My translation*))

The dreamer makes no overt comment on this ill-omened temple,
but walks out to comfort himself. We imagine the pleasure of the

fresh air again, after the scented warmth inside. So far he has seen little to assuage his discontent. However, he now sees the goddess Nature,

> a queene
> That, as of lyght the somer sonne shene
> Passeth the sterre, right so over mesure
> She fayrer was than any creature.
>
> (*PF*, 298–301)

The garden is the garden of Nature, created by God, the world that was originally good. This is St Valentine's day, when every bird must choose his mate at the council held by the great queen, Nature. All the birds are present. So many are they that the dreamer has scarcely space to stand and they are all in their proper social rank, from the noble hawks to the plebeian cuckoo and goose. True community, for such a culture, requires hierarchy and order. Nature, the 'vicar', or deputy, of almighty God, commands them to begin to choose their mates, and he that is most worthy shall begin. In such a community it is assumed that the male will make the first advance. There is only one condition: that whoever is chosen is not to be constrained against her will. Then the famous debate begins, for the three noblest birds who speak first all love the same formel eagle.

At once the problem of contradiction even within love appears. The birds speak in the high-flown language of the court. They address the beloved not as a mate, but as a 'sovereign lady'. They humble themselves to the dust before her, claiming rather her pity than her love, though they are fierce enough towards each other. They all claim the reward of the lady's love: one in particular for his truth, one for the length of time of his service, one for the intensity of his devotion. Each invokes in his own way the law of social reciprocity as a return for his humble service. But their argument goes on for so long that the lower orders, who cannot choose before their natural lords have done so, become impatient. Eventually certain birds are chosen to give the opinion of each class as to who should have the formel: the spokesmen are the noble falcon, the 'unnatural' cuckoo, the turtle-dove loyal in love till death, the vulgar and stupid goose. Their speeches are masterpieces of dramatic truth and variety – noble, selfish, loving, foolish, according to the speaker, and tinglingly alive. But their speeches are no help, and Nature gives it to the formel eagle to decide for herself – though Nature's advice is that she should choose the royal tercel, as the noblest. The formel, however, asks for a year's grace, and so the solution is postponed. The other birds then choose their mates, and fly happily away after singing in honour of Nature the lovely roundel:

> Now welcome, somer, with thy sonne softe.

The poet awakes, and betakes himself to other books, always hoping that some day he will meet something by which he will 'fare the better'. He makes no other comment, and it seems unlikely that he himself has resolved the problem which haunted him at the beginning.

We can now, however, at least see something of its terms. The birds represent the human community. They have the quality of an animal fable, in which animals or birds speak and may even be understood by human beings. There is no problem of communication between creatures, human and other, in the unity of creation. The problem lies in mutually incompatible desires. Just as the Temple of Venus represents lascivious love, so Nature represents legitimate love. The figure of Nature, developed from the Latin poem *The Complaint of Nature* by the twelfth-century theologian Alanus de Insulis, is the key to the latter part of the poem. She is God's deputy

> That hot, cold, hevy, lyght, moyst and dreye   *dry*
> Hath knyt by evene noumbres of acord.
>
> (*PF*, 380–1)

She knits together the diverse elements of the world by the bond of Love, as Boethius explains in the *Consolation*. Nature here is the expression of God's creative activity. Whatever she ordains is good, and what is more, she is in command (617). And love, pleasant love, is what she commands when she tells the birds how,

> Ye knowe wel how, seynt Valentynes day,
> By my statut and thorgh my governaunce,
> Ye come for to cheese – and fle youre wey –   *choose*
> Youre makes, as I prike yow with plesaunce.   *mates*
>
> (*PF*, 386–9)

Yet Africanus (and a good many others including Boethius) had commanded medieval man 'That he ne shulde hym in the world delyte'. Here is an important contrast of authorities in the poem. Another important contrast lies within the garden of love itself, between good love and corrupted love; Nature and Venus.

The poem thus presents first the major problem of the dualism of the world, then the subsidiary comment on the two kinds of love. We see these not in terms of logical conflict, but rather as masses of light and shade are balanced against each other in a picture.

The love debate itself has its conflicts and contrasts, too, some of them set within each other. There is a social conflict – easily enough appreciated in the turbulent years before and after the Peasants' Revolt. We cannot doubt here where the poet's convictions lie, for it is Nature (i.e. by implication, God) who ordains the ranks of society. There is also, on the most obvious level, the fashionable *demande d'amour*, the question of love; who should win the formel? There is yet another question, inherent in the contest between the suitors – the paradox of love itself as set forth on the gates of the park. Love causes both happiness and unhappiness. In large part, the unhappiness of love is caused by the lascivious Venus – love unrestrained by modesty. But even under Nature there is unhappiness. She is good, and gives us instincts which it is both our pleasure and our duty to satisfy. Yet even in following Nature there is frustration and unhappiness, as there must be for the unsuccessful suitors. The irony is that this afflicts pre-eminently the noblest and worthiest. The lower orders, with their coarse lack of sensibility, their desire primarily for a mate, find no such frustration, and depart happily. Chaucer puts the problem even more plainly in another Valentine poem of the same period – that witty, astrological poem, *The Complaint of Mars*.

To what fyn made the God that sit so hye,	*end*
Benethen him love other companye,	
And streyneth folk to love, malgre her hed? . . .	*constrains against their will*
Hit semeth he hath to lovers enmyte,	
And lyk a fissher, as men alday may se,	
Baiteth hys angle-hok with som plesaunce,	
Til many a fissh ys wod til that he be	*mad*
Sesed therwith; and then at erst hath he	
Al his desir, and therwith all myschaunce.	

(CM, 218 . . . 41)

That last line is a crisp poetic summary of life's paradox.

What is the total effect in *The Parliament*? Chaucer, like other medieval writers of debates, deliberately leaves the problem open. The satirical humour of parts of the debate does not detract from the genuine seriousness beneath. The strain between the two ways of life, the way of Acceptance, the way of Denial, he does not finally resolve till the end of his life, when, old and tired, he takes the way of Denial and condemns his non-religious writings. But in this fruitful period of mature manhood, conscious of and delighting in his powers and the richness of the world, he very strongly leans towards the way of Acceptance. Nature is good, and genuine love is good, since ordained by her – that is the overwhelming impression left by *The Parliament*.

Chaucer himself called the poem *The Parliament of Fowls* and the debate has always and rightly been considered the heart of the poem. The whole poem is itself a debate about the nature of love, though the movement of thought is by association and contrast, rather than by direct logic. *The Dream of Scipio* gives a world picture in which the world is despised – a view of great authority in Chaucer's day. By contrast, the park of Nature represents the world as God's own lovable creation, and under his law, which has Biblical warrant and was increasingly felt in the fourteenth century. Within the park the pictorial or dramatic descriptions of Venus and the noble and common birds all show contrasting aspects of or attitudes to love. It is typical of Chaucer's method of writing poetry that he presents these contrasts in the form of descriptions with a high degree of surface decoration, and that he leaves an appreciation of them and of the underlying principles of connection and contrast to the reader's wit and imagination. He creates a set of 'states of feeling' which interact and come to fruition in the reader's own mind. He does not argue a case – it is no lecture on love's philosophy. The birds' arguments are more dramatic than logical; they are contrasts in attitudes. Although the ostensible subject of debate is who should marry the formel, the actual subject of what the common birds say is the nature and value of love. And the delightful comedy of their argument only enhances the genuine seriousness of the fundamental issues, which are deeper still. *The Parliament* is one of the richest and most remarkable poems of its length in the English language.

Just as *The Book of the Duchess* marks a new start for English poetry, *The Parliament* represents the point of take-off. It blends together without strain a great amount of learning, gathering up the whole European tradition. Its tighter form is attained by returning to the shape of the thirteenth-century French love-visions, much shorter than the thin volubility of Machaut, and by employing the device of the 'question of love'. Yet this is done under the powerful Italian influence, which gives a far stronger stride to the verse. Even so, Chaucer has achieved his own independence of form and content.

His self-mocking manner disguises a tremendous absorptive power and an extraordinary mastery. This mastery of compression of many materials without any congestion in a short poem of 699 lines was now ready to be deployed over a much greater length.

The poem is a St Valentine's Day poem. There may well have been annual celebrations of St Valentine's Day in the court, for there are a number of other Valentine Day poems, like *The Complaint of Mars*, and several in French by Oton de Graunson, a Frenchman often at Richard's court.

The poem attracts us particularly by the comic dramatic realism of the debate, and its wonderful sense of daylight and open parkland. We rejoice in the feeling of heightened yet ordinary life. This like a beautiful landscape rests on the massive structures below the surface. Before seeing how Chaucer further deploys his mastery in a great long narrative we need to survey the geology of this poetic country, the underlying intellectual structures which sustain so fertile and colourful a surface. We need to turn briefly to the philosophy, science and mythology, deeply interesting in themselves, which so greatly contribute to the interest and the human warmth of the poetry.

Chapter 12

The Fair Chain of Love: the Consolations of Philosophy and Venus

HOW CHARMING IS DIVINE PHILOSOPHY?

Chaucer's interest in the world extended from the appearances of people and love and ordinary life to the underlying difficult intellectual theorising. His interest was secular. He had not been to the university, and he was not interested in the high-powered theology that developed in Italy, Germany, France and Oxford in the thirteenth and fourteenth centuries. His mind was of a more worldly, less abstract turn, and his dominant interest in love was clearly no pose. It would no more have been satisfied by scholastic analytic philosophy than it was by *The Dream of Scipio*. On the other hand, science interested him greatly, especially astronomy, of which some kinds of astrology were part. He was interested in dreams and their classification, as well as in other scientific knowledge which he picked up from Macrobius. Medical, historical, grammatical knowledge he picked up from such encyclopedias as those by Vincent of Beauvais, the *Speculum Historiale, Speculum Morale* (*Mirror of History, of Morality*), or from Bartholomew the Englishman's *De Proprietatibus Rerum* (*On the Properties of Things*). He had a passion for knowledge and thought. But like a concerned scientist today he was driven further, to attempt to understand something of the nature of the world. His sceptical, questioning, yet constructive mind needed more than emotional religious devotion could offer him. He read with passion for there were problems that needed to be solved. In the same spirit today an educated man or woman of the world, interested in the developments of the arts and sciences, dissatisfied with the apparently baseless speculations of theology, not concerned with the professional philosophy of the universities, will read difficult though non-specialist books and articles on general questions about life.

There was a fair amount of choice of such books open to Chaucer, some of which he made use of in *The Canterbury Tales*. He tells us in

The Prologue to *The Legend of Good Women* ('F' version, written about 1386) that he had translated 'Boece' and also a devout work by the ancient Church Father Origen on Mary Magdalene, as well as *The Life of Saint Cecilia*. In the 'G' version of *The Prologue*, written about 1395, he adds that he had translated the gloomily entitled *Wreched Engendrynge of Mankynde*, otherwise entitled *De Contemptu Mundi* (*Of Contempt for the World*), by Pope Innocent III of the twelfth century. These are works, like the *Tale of Melibeus*, of morality, and indicate not only a continuing but a deepening concern. The 'Boece' is far the most massive influence on his poetry. This is not surprising, for it had been a work of major European importance ever since written in the sixth century. Manuscripts, printed versions, and translations are numerous. In England it held sway until the end of the seventeenth century and Milton was influenced by it. King Alfred in Anglo-Saxon times, and Queen Elizabeth I both translated it. It was philosophy, and consolation, for the intelligent non-specialist layman.

BOETHIUS

The Consolation of Philosophy builds into its own text something of the circumstances in which it was written, and the work is a classic example both of how much we gain from knowing something about the circumstances of an author and the conditions in which his book was written, and of how much of such essential real information could be written into the text itself in earlier literature, mingling fact and fiction.

Boethius was from an old Roman family, and after the conquest of Rome by the barbarians he served the Emperor Theodoric. He was exceptionally well read in Greek philosophy and his translations of some elementary treatises formed the basis of the later medieval developments in philosophy and logic. He was a Christian and wrote several influential theological tracts. He also had an exceptionally fortunate political career and the joy of seeing his two sons made joint consuls. Then, when he was at the height of Fortune's wheel — an image he himself invented — disaster came. He fell from the Emperor's favour, and after a period of imprisonment in Pavia he was cruelly put to death in 524, still only 44 years old. While in prison he wrote his greatest work. It draws much of its force from the tremendous reversal of fortune that had overtaken him in his own life. The point of writing it was precisely to 'console' himself, to come to terms with the nature of existence, to make sense of an apparently senseless world, to account for suffering and evil, and to see how to overcome them.

Boethius, though no doubt sustained by his Christian faith, which underpins his work with the belief in a benevolent Creator-God, attempted to meet the problems of evil and mutually incompatible goods through the exercise of natural reason, which for him meant relying mainly on the classical pagan philosophers, Plato and Seneca. Consolations had been written in classical times, but the elaboration and power of Boethius's work is unique, as at first was its dialogue form addressed to himself.

THE FORM OF *THE CONSOLATION OF PHILOSOPHY*

The *Consolation* is written in elaborate and quite difficult late-classical Latin. It is divided into five books, and each book is divided into alternating sections of prose and verse, called 'proses' and 'metres', though Chaucer translates all into prose. This form, in conjunction with analytical content, is sometimes called Menippean satire, or an anatomy: it was very influential, especially in the twelfth century, and the work of the twelfth-century theologian and satirist, Alanus de Insulis, already referred to, follows it carefully. *The Canterbury Tales* also may be thought of as a Menippean satire, or anatomy, both analytical and creative, in verse and prose.

A striking feature of the *Consolation* is that the author presents himself as a character within it. It begins with a metre; in Chaucer's translation, 'Allas, I wepynge, am constreyned to bygynnen vers of sorwful matere, that whilom in florysschyng studie made delitable ditees . . .' He reproaches Fortune. All this refers to his situation in prison. The following prose then describes how he then sees 'a womman of ful greet reverence', of great beauty, sometimes of human size, sometimes seeming to reach to Heaven. Her beautiful dress bears two Greek letters which signify both active and contemplative life. But part of her dress has been torn by men. The lady sees the poetical Muses approach the bed of Boethius to help him write his complaint, but she drives forth their flatteries with scorn. She is the Lady Philosophy. Her dialogue with Boethius is conveyed in the successive proses, punctuated by beautifully meditative metres.

This opening is peculiarly effective and was immensely influential. The author is shown as an inferior character within his own work, a Narrator of what happened and what was said to him; and yet he is also the real person who is outside the whole work and is writing the words attributed to the superior character as well as those attributed to his lesser self of the past within the book. We have here the ambiguity of author/*persona* which was developed into a characteristic Gothic device by so many European poets in the thirteenth and fourteenth centuries.

The device is very effective because it creates, in the *Consolation* as in so many later poems, a complex instrument of meaning and audience control. Because the 'mask' of the writer, the *persona*, is inside the poem, the audience is enabled more easily to identify with him, his sorrow and ignorance. In so far as they do so, their feelings can be worked on and they can be instructed. They also identify with the superior person in the work, adopting their superior knowledge and greater power. The result is that readers or audience both dominate the writer (in the work) and are dominated by him (from outside). There is also a progression. The *persona* begins as inferior to the writer *now* because he was *then*, in the past, ignorant and stupid. The work charts the progress of the *persona*, or rather the progressive narrowing of the gap between *persona* and writer and, consequently, the removal of the initial inferiority of the *persona*. At the end *persona* and writer are united in understanding. It is a model of the 'construction of the self'.

In identifying with and following the progress of the *persona*, the audience also repairs its inferiority, is agreeably instructed, and finally becomes at one with the writer. A satisfying unity of feeling and idea is achieved at the end. The work is never totally self-enclosed, like a printed book, of whose author we are as entirely ignorant, as you, dear reader, are of me, except in so far as you can guess about me from my manner of writing. (If you consult the blurb you are going outside the text, into the context, and you almost certainly have done this if you are sensible, because all books need to be read in personal and historical context if the author's full meaning is to be understood.) With as much knowledge of context as possible, the creative, sympathetic participation of the audience or reader in the text is then necessary for full understanding. The initial presence of the modest, suffering, ignorant *persona* is an encouragement to participate. The duality of the author/*persona* creates an attractive blend of realism, and fiction: a blurring, or fluidity, of limits.

A GREAT LADY INSTRUCTS THE AUTHOR

The situation in which, in the work, a great, superior lady instructs the inferior author became a favourite literary device in medieval literature. The Lady is a sort of Jungian Anima, or mother-figure, within the mind of the author, in the *Consolation*. She is a similar personage in the very Boethian *Complaint of Nature* by Alanus de Insulis. In Langland she is Mother-church. Mutations are possible and fruitful. In Dante's *Divine Comedy* the beloved lady Beatrice is the equivalent. In *Pearl* the lady who instructs the author is his own transformed dead daughter. The authoritative yet protective female figure appears in Chaucer's work as the Virgin-Mother of *An ABC*, as already noted, and by way of Alanus, as Nature. There is a trace of her even in Blanche the Duchess. Queen Alcestis in *The Prologue to the Legend of Good Women* is a related figure. She is the counterpart of women-as-victims, the betrayed ladies whom Chaucer lists so often and for whom he has so evident a sympathy.

The dominant authoritative figure within the work of art, and the *persona* of the author, also within the work, who receives instruction, are both (like all fictional characters) projections of the writer's own mind. They represent an argument within himself, in his own mind, between two points of view, two aspects of the divided but self-conscious self, in which he attempts to adjust himself to the reality which the later 'higher', more philosophical part of him perceives, to win over his recalcitrant, earlier, lesser physical self, and to achieve a wholeness within which he will overcome sorrow with reconciliation. Chaucer sees this very well, even if he makes little use of the figure of authority, and his *Troilus* in particular is influenced by the attempt to reconcile ourselves to painful reality portrayed by the *Consolation*.

THE CONTENT OF THE *CONSOLATION*

The *Consolation* is a complex work, proceeding by question, argument and answer, and only its main themes and questions can be summarised here. Book I centres on the essential question, if God exists and is good, where does evil come from? Book II is concerned with Fortune, a concept which Boethius did much to elaborate, and concludes with the remarkable poem, metre 8, which Chaucer also translated into verse and incorporated as the climax at the end of Book III of the *Troilus*, celebrating the bond of love which holds all things in the world in harmonious unity. Book III of the *Consolation* discusses what goods bring true, as opposed to uncertain, happiness. Books IV and V deal with the problems of free will and destiny.

The subject matter of the *Consolation* may be summed up in Milton's description of the Fallen Angels, who reasoned high

Of Providence, Foreknowledge, Will and Fate –
Fixed fate, free will, foreknowledge absolute –
And found no end, in wandering mazes lost.
Of good and evil much they argued then,
Of happiness and final misery,
Passion and apathy, and glory and shame –

(*Paradise Lost*, 559–64)

though Boethius did not lose himself in the labyrinth. Boethius's first and undisputed premise is belief in a good and all-powerful God, who can do no evil, and who has created the world. This granted, he is obviously faced with two great difficulties. First, how can a good God have allowed so much misery and evil to enter the world? Second, since such a God must know *everything*, he knows the future. If God knows now what is going to happen in the future, then the future must be fixed, and nothing we can do can alter it. (This connects with the first problem, since it ultimately implies that God makes us do evil as well as good, whether we will or not.) The horror of this predestination, this determinism, appals Boethius, and he spends much time confuting it. Indeed, a great deal of the philosophy of the Middle Ages was concerned with it, and the philosophical poets, Dante and Jean de Meun, write about it. It is one of the dominant themes of learned controversy in England in the fourteenth century, and Chaucer often refers to it.

Boethius solves the problem of pain and evil by saying that although we all rightly and naturally desire happiness, we seek it under the wrong forms (as in the love of wife and family, of wealth and power, of natural scenery, of the arts). True happiness is the Good, which is God, who only is permanence. We should therefore love God alone; and to do this we must master ourselves and our natural passions. If we master our passions, we shall be free from the trammels of the world, and so shall find true happiness and freedom in God. The ultimate lesson is one that many modern scientists would accept: namely that 'reality' is essentially 'mind-stuff', and that mind is superior to matter.

He solves the problem of predestination by first pointing out that eternity is quite different from time-going-on-for-ever. It is outside time. Everything on earth, past, present and future, is in God's eternal Now. Second, he says that it is a man's passions only which are part of the normal chain of inevitable cause and effect. Once his soul has freed itself from the domination of the passions by loving the divine, man's will is free.

This bleak summary of the central thought of the *Consolation* conveys nothing of its delight – the noble conception of an all-wise, loving Creator, of the loveliness of the world as created by God, and as continually maintained by him. There is an inevitable dualism in the *Consolation* which is of extreme importance in appreciating both Chaucer's thought, and that of the Middle Ages as a whole. God is good, and therefore His creation must be good: yet we know that so much is bad. Should we, therefore, in loving God, despise His world? It seems wrong to undervalue the world, since God made it 'and saw that it was good', but if we love the world, do we not inevitably forget God, loving his gifts instead of Him?

Most thinkers in the Middle Ages tended to emphasise the need to be on the safe side, and to despise mundane affairs. The dualism of medieval Christian teaching could provide an agonising problem for an intelligent, sensuous and pious man – especially in matters of love. However, at this full flowering period of his life, Chaucer was most attracted by the possibility of synthesis. The possibility of reconciliation is inherent in the *Consolation* itself, as may be seen from two important passages which Chaucer later put into poems. One of these, already referred to, is praise of 'the bond of love' (II, metre 8). The other is praise of God's creative activity. Boethius in *Consolation* III, metre 9, says that the world is perfectly made, and is governed and controlled by God's everlasting Reason, which binds the elements in harmony in 'the fayre cheyne of love'. This is the basis of Theseus's great speech in *The Knight's Tale* (*CT*, I, 2987ff.).

These and similar passages emphasise the goodness of creation and the divine source of love. Human love and marriage appear as part of the divinely maintained order of things. Love and reason here spring from the same source. The possibility of reconciling the inherent tension between them was further improved by the teaching of astrology.

DATE AND QUALITY OF THE TRANSLATION

The precise date of Chaucer's translation of Boethius's *Consolation of Philosophy* is uncertain. It was probably done some time about 1380, although it is likely he knew the book some years before that, and much of its substance had been conveyed in the *Roman*. The translation was written with scholarly care, and he consulted a French translation and commentary, and perhaps other commentaries, for many existed in Latin.

Chaucer's care is such that at times he is awkwardly literal, but the work is in general, though not easy, a masterpiece of English prose. His task was the more difficult in that there were virtually no precedents in English for this kind of prose. He was not content only with a literal translation, important though that was to him. He seems to have used rhythmical devices based on the patterns of the *cursus* (or rhythmic ending) of Latin prose, and other rhetorical adornments like alliteration and word-echo, to dignify the style.

OXFORD INTELLECTUAL SCEPTICISM AND EMPIRICISM

The *Consolation* was simple and unprofessional compared with the power of thirteenth- and fourteenth-century scholasticism, but that in itself made it available to Chaucer, a courtier and a literary man, not a professional philosopher and theologian. Yet Chaucer, with his remarkable intellectual sensibility, used the *Consolation* in a way that echoes some of the main concerns of fourteenth-century thought, which centred on problems of determinism and free will, and which were notable for the beginnings of English empiricism. His Oxford connections may have helped him here. In the early fourteenth century Oxford was the dominant centre of European thought. Ockham, who developed both a sceptical rationalism and a passionate fideism (two sides of the same coin) was an Oxford man. Ockham separated faith from rational enquiry – a process which seems to appeal to the English tradition, for Francis Bacon did the same in the early seventeenth century. Ockham also opposed 'Realism' (which confusingly was more like what is now called Idealism). Ockham was a Nominalist, asserting the importance only of individual particulars. A number of fellows of Merton College in Oxford did important scientific and theological work. Bradwardine, who was one of them, and died as Archbishop of Canterbury in the Black Death, wrote a vast tome on free will and predestination, though of this Chaucer in *The Nun's Priest's Tale* says he cannot 'bulte it to the bren': cannot sort it out. What does seem clear is that Chaucer caught something of the new spirit of rational enquiry without needing deep professional acquaintance with its detail. He had numerous Oxford connections (as not least *The Miller's Tale* shows). His taste for what modern thought calls 'realism', which resembles what medieval thought called Nominalism, may be in part a kind of echo of Oxford Nominalism. He eventually shared the fideism, the faith without reason, that inevitably accompanies rationalism even today, though the terms are different.

OTHER INTELLECTUAL INTERESTS AND
CHAUCER'S ATTITUDE

Chaucer's other general interests also reflected the advanced move-
ment of the age. He could have acquired his alchemical and medical,
even his ornithological, knowledge from Vincent of Beauvais's encyc-
lopedia. In so far as interest in religion is intellectual Chaucer had a
characteristic sympathy with Lollardy. Lollardy was a major growth-
point of the spirit of the fourteenth century. It was extremely literal-
istic, therefore radical, and anti-ecclesiastical, anti-traditional. It was also
passionately simple-minded, and Chaucer's association and sympathy
stop far short of commitment. He had other secular interests of a
different kind. He was astonishingly well read in secular literature,
and in secular history, in Latin (though mostly in Ovid apart from
anthology pieces), and in French and Italian. He might almost be
thought of as our first professional literary intellectual, except that he
was not paid for being so. His intellectual imagination is classicising
and historical rather than romantic and mythopoeic. He is an import-
ant example of the development of the lay spirit in the fourteenth
century.

As already noted, another deep interest was in astronomy, where
though he was amateur he was far from superficial. Astronomy was
scientific, but in so far as astronomy was inextricably entangled with
astrology, which had close connections with classical mythology,
Chaucer's scientific interest also very obviously fed his philosophical
and poetical interests.

One of the constant notes of the *Consolation* which must have
especially appealed to Chaucer is the praise of the beauty of the
starry heavens, which are the perfect example of the beauty of the
natural world when it obeys God's laws. They are the embodiment
of the serenity and radiance and perfect order – those brave translunary
things – which are so notably lacking in our sphere beneath the
moon.

By Chaucer's day there was a very considerable accumulation of
astronomical knowledge. The movement of the stars was very well
recognised and plotted out; prediction was possible; tables for cal-
culating stellar movements, and such instruments for observing the
height of the stars as the astrolabe – though not yet the telescope –
were all in relatively common use. Chaucer's ability in arithmetic
would have made calculations easy for him. It is worth repeating that
all this demands a high degree of literacy. Numerical tables *must* be
written down.

As it happens, the model of the universe then formed by astronomers was wrong. It was the model going by the name of Ptolemy, an astronomer of the second century AD. In the Ptolemaic universe the earth is the centre, tiny, relatively dull, unmoving but subject to change, decay and death. Around this centre were thought to be a series of rotating concentric transparent spheres, in which were successively fixed the planets and the sun. These are the 'heavens', which, for example, Dante moves through on his way to Paradise. The nearest sphere and planet is that of the moon, which provided the limit of corruptibility. Outside the moon and successively outside each other are the spheres of Mercury, Venus, the Sun, Mars, Jupiter, Saturn. Then comes the sphere of the fixed stars, which is the general scattering of stars about the sky in their slow-moving constellations. Outside these eight spheres is a ninth, the *Primum Mobile* or First Mover, whose function is to transform the love of God into the energy which moves the stars, whose movement produces the harmony of the spheres.

Among the fixed stars is a particularly noticeable band of constellations which go all round the sphere like the seam on a cricket ball. This band is called the Zodiac. When we look up from earth we can see various planets at different times against a different background of Zodiacal constellations, for they all travel roughly the same path round the Earth, at slightly different speeds. When planets could be seen against a particular constellation, or sign, of the Zodiac, they were thought to have a particular relation to it, and to have a special effect on events on earth.

Although we know that the Ptolemaic model is wrong, most of us know that only because books tell us so. If we cannot work great telescopes, etc. we are happy to take the modern picture of the universe on trust, on the authority of scientists, incomprehensible though space must be. Medieval men did the same, and accepted the authority of experts. With the instruments at their disposal the Ptolemaic model in fact better explained the observable movements of the stars than did the new Copernican model of the sixteenth century. Only further theoretical refinements, and the invention of the telescope in the early seventeenth century, justified the later model.

Chaucer would have loved the telescope. His technical and practical interest in the mechanics of astronomy is illustrated in his *Treatise on the Astrolabe*, which was the principal instrument, with some resemblance to a quadrant or sextant, used by medieval astronomers for measuring the height of the stars. It is an elementary treatise, mainly translated, but with some attractive personal notes, which Chaucer wrote for his 'little son Lewis'. It is unfinished. Perhaps the boy died. It was written about 1392, when Chaucer was at the height of his poetic powers, and shows how seriously he took both the astronomy and his fatherly obligations and interests. He modestly comments in his prefatory remarks to Lewis that 'I n'am but a lewd compilator of the labour of olde astrologiens, and have it translatyd in myn Englissh oonly for thy doctrine. And with this swerd shal I sleen envie.' All the same, the very idea of undertaking such a work was original, and the work is a milestone in the history of English scientific prose.

There is also in existence a similarly technical treatise, finished, called *The Equatorie of the Planetis*. Only one manuscript exists, and in a margin of one page is written the name 'Chaucer'. It has been suggested that the manuscript is in Chaucer's very own hand. The language would correspond to his period and dialect, and the spelling seems quite likely to be his. The work is quite impersonal but an important part of a notable movement of scientific English prose of which Chaucer was in the forefront. There has been much extremely learned study of the *Equatorie*, notably by Dr Karen Schmidt, and two schools of thought contest whether or not Chaucer wrote it. The issue is important for our general view of Chaucer, but alas absolute certainty evades even Dr Schmidt, though others are more positive for or against. I myself am undecided.

Astronomy is scientific, specialist, non-evaluative, based on calculation: in a word, 'modern'. It was, however, inextricably interwoven, in the fourteenth century (as Chaucer knew, and illustrates by his abrupt withdrawal in the *Astrolabe*) with astrology, which is a quite different matter. Astrology is concerned with evaluation, it has a moral quality, it affects the whole of life, it is in a word 'archaic', not only in being ancient but in representing those hopes and fears which are always part of the human condition. We must now turn to a brief consideration of astrology in the fourteenth century.

ASTROLOGY

The Moon unquestionably influences the tides, and the Sun controls our seasons on earth. It was inevitable that from earliest times other stars too should have been thought to control events on earth, and the fortunes of men. This is astrology. The power of astrology to meet some requirement of the mind and imagination is witnessed today, when so many popular newspapers and magazines in advanced industrial societies publish horoscopes and astrological predictions, which many people believe. Astrology is demonstrably rubbish, but its modern prevalence may help us sympathetically to imagine the situation in the fourteenth century when, in the conditions of the time, it could not be seen to be rubbish, but was regarded as a master-science. All men accepted it. The more learned the scientist or theologian (they were often combined in the same person) the more firmly he believed that the weather, the crops, the very stones of the earth, and all animal life including the animal part of human beings, were governed in their properties by the stars. The theory of astrological influences was the fourteenth-century scientific theory of the normal working of cause and effect now explained in terms of Newton's and Einstein's laws of dynamics and so forth. Medical men, scientists, politicians, merchants would have been incompetent if they did not either know some astrology or (in the two latter classes) consult the experts.

The troubled and harassed years of the fourteenth century gave a great impetus to men's desire to know the future, and so perhaps to be able to control their fates. But the possibility of knowing the future immediately raised the problems of predestination faced by Boethius, while orthodox Christian doctrine was irrevocably committed to belief in free will. Furthermore, the aim of controlling man's outer environment, rather than his inner spiritual state, is one which any religion must regard with misgiving. Hence, there was a good deal of religious writing against science, in particular against astrology, not so much because it was thought to be untrue, as because it was thought that it might lead men on the wrong track. Those parts of the science which tended to destroy belief in freedom of the will (judicial astrology) or which appeared to truckle with supernatural (and probably evil) agents were especially condemned as magic. It is generally agreed that science and magic spring from the same impulse of the mind to control the external rather than the internal world, and it often seems that what men call magic is really faulty science. Astrology, to fourteenth-century minds, merged imperceptibly into magic, but it was difficult to draw the dividing line. This explains the many contradictions and confusions in writers on the subject, and Chaucer's own *volte-face* in the *Astrolabe* (II, 4), where after he has gone on from astronomical information to the discussion of fortunate and unfortunate aspects of the stars, he suddenly says, 'Natheles these ben observaunces of judicial matere and rytes of payens, in whiche my spirit hath no feith.' The crux of the problem lay in questions of morals and ethics. Philosophical and religious problems were not so obvious in the case of, say, weather predictions. The orthodox view with regard to men's actions may be summed up in the words of St Thomas Aquinas:

> The majority of men, in fact, are governed by their passions, which are dependent on bodily appetites; in these the influence of the stars is clearly felt. Few indeed are the wise who are capable of resisting their animal instincts. Astrologers, consequently, are able to foretell the truth in the majority of cases, especially when they undertake general predictions. In particular predictions they do not attain certainty, for nothing prevents a man from resisting the dictates of his lower faculties. Wherefore the astrologers themselves are wont to say 'that the wise man rules the stars', forasmuch, namely, as he rules his own passions.
> (*Summa Theologica*, I, I, 115, 4 Ad Tertium (5.544). Quoted by T. O. Wedel, 'The medieval attitude toward astrology', *Yale Studies in English* (Yale, 1920), lx.)

Chaucer does not make his heroes 'wise men'.

The stars, therefore, are thought to form a person's character and often to motivate his desires and actions. In Chaucer's work at this period there is little emphasis on *resisting* the course guided by the stars. The reason is that God's Providence – or as he puts it in *The Knight's Tale*,

The destinee, ministre general,	
That executeth in the world over al	*carries out*
The purveiaunce that God hath seyn biforn	*providence*
	(*CT*, I, 1663–5)

which controls the whole world with the 'chain of love' – must intend all for the best. There is a strong streak of optimistic determinism in Chaucer's thought at this time. Since Love is what guides the world and maintains its order, as both Boethius and the Gospel of St John say, the planet of love – Venus – assumes particular importance. Venus the planet was regarded as the scientific or immediate 'cause' of love not only between human beings, but of the 'love' which guides the mating of animals, and even the attraction asserted by the force of gravity (for to the fourteenth century the whole material universe was in a sense 'alive', almost sentient). Moreover, Venus was the Goddess of Love in much of the classical literature which Chaucer knew so well.

MYTHOLOGY AND MYTHOGRAPHY

By mythology here is meant stories about the gods. Every age has them. By the time they come to be thought of as 'mythology', rather than as sacred stories, scepticism has crept in. A further stage is reached when men collect and compare stories about the gods, make dictionaries of attributes, analyse their meaning. This further stage is called mythography.

THE CLASSICAL HERITAGE

For the Middle Ages the Biblical stories which make the foundation of Christianity were literally true and sacred, although they could be allegorised, interpreted and retold. The classical heritage was different. There were many pagan gods, and in the first few centuries of the Christian era many people still took them seriously, and even invented new ones, like the goddess Fortune. The ancient gods and goddesses, Jupiter, Mars, Venus, Mercury, etc. were still strong enough to be violently attacked by St Augustine in his *The City of God* (413–27 AD). The attacks by him and others were successful, and by the sixth century the gods were finished as sacred powers. This released them for other valuable purposes in the Christian Middle Ages.

The gods were also characters in stories. Originally these were presumably sacred, but as early as the Greek Homer's time, the seventh century BC, in his *Iliad* and *Odyssey*, the gods are portrayed in a fascinatingly human style, even if regarded as divine. By the time of the Latin classical writers, Virgil and Ovid (with many others), stories of the gods could present them in many different ways, from serious to comic. The earliest comic story on record is about them, and is found in Homer. The goddess of love, Aphrodite (in Latin, Venus) was married to the ugly, lame god of smiths, Hephaistos (in Latin, Vulcan). She had an affair with Ares (Latin, Mars), god of war. The jealous husband by his art wove a metal net so fine it could not be seen and hung it over the bed. Then he trapped Aphrodite and Ares together and displayed them naked to the other gods. They laughed as much at the jealous husband making public his shame as at the lovers, while Hermes (Latin, Mercury) said that he would not mind being in Ares' position. This story as told by Ovid became the most famous story about Venus.

On the other hand, in Virgil's *Aeneid*, Venus is rather the beautiful, tender, anxious mother of both Cupid and Aeneas. Aeneas had a mortal father. Stories varied as to who Cupid's father was. The stories of the gods, like all myths and folktales, existed in numerous different forms. They are traditional stories, and the very act of retelling a traditional story both repeats the old and introduces something new. The Christian church was the great educational force in the Middle Ages, and it had no choice but to use pagan Latin texts, as already noted, as the most refined instruments of education. Hence the use of Virgil and Ovid. In the early centuries there was continuous unease about the intrinsically non-Christian nature of the texts, and the subject matter of many of the stories, such as the one just quoted about Venus. By Chaucer's time this unease had largely though not entirely disappeared. Reference to pagan gods was commonplace, and it was well understood that they were either fictional characters, or allegories, or planets, or in some cases poetical references to God himself. Thus, Jupiter (Jove) might be either a fictional character, an allegory, a planet, or an educated way of referring to God in a story. (In the nineteenth century Englishmen might still use the mild oath 'By Jove', instead of the less polite 'By God'.)

THE SCIENTIFIC BASIS

There were two general reasons why names of some of the pagan gods should have become Christian commonplaces. One will already have been realised by the reader. The names of a number of them had been given to certain stars to identify them, especially the planets. In origin perhaps the influences attributed to planets had been taken over from the gods with whom they had been associated, as Venus planet of love, and Mars of war. By the fourteenth century the actual planet was thought to be the source of the influence, which might be strong or weak according to the planet's apparent relationship in the sky to other planets and stars. Chaucer's *Complaint of Mars* is a witty conflation of planetary movements and influences with the love-story. The poem has a basis of astronomical truth, and is adorned with humanising mythological fantasy. Though non-religious, there is nothing anti-Christian or particularly pagan about it, except in its remote origins, and these would not have occurred to fourteenth-century readers.

THE MYTHOGRAPHERS

Besides astronomy and astrology, the other main reason for the Christianisation or, at any rate, for the sterilisation of pagan qualities in classical mythology, was the work of the mythographers. Mythographers, that is, scholars, had begun to analyse myths long before the birth of Christ. The stories are often so strange that they need interpreting. One favourite way of interpreting was attributed to a scholar called Euhemerus, whose work, now lost, argued that the so-called gods were really supremely successful mortals whom others had by mistake come to consider divine. Euhemerism is still used occasionally by some as an explanation for myths. Another line of interpretation was to consider the stories as allegories of various kinds. Commentators on classical texts developed many theories. Cicero in *De Natura Deorum* (*On the Nature of the Gods*) wrote an influential book incorporating different points of view. The school-book *De Nuptiis Philologiae et Mercurii* (*On the Marriage of Philosophy and Mercury*) by Martianus Capella in the fifth century uses mythology to attempt to enliven a dry description of the Seven Liberal Arts. There were many others.

FULGENTIUS TO BOCCACCIO

From the point of view of the Middle Ages the basic mythographer was Fulgentius, whose *Mitologiarum Libri Tres* (*Three Books of Mythologies*) appeared in the fifth century, and whose remarks were endlessly repeated by later writers. He takes the stories and allegorises them to show that they 'really' mean quite different physical or historical events, or moral concepts. A good example of the method of Fulgentius is given by his interpretation of the famous mythological episode of the Judgement of Paris. Paris was a Trojan prince. Some time after his judgement, to be described in a moment, he eloped to Troy with the beautiful Helen, wife of the Greek king Menelaus, whom Paris had been visiting. Menelaus in order to reclaim Helen started the Trojan war, in which the Greeks after ten years' fighting utterly destroyed Troy. The judgement of Paris which preceded all this was made when this princely shepherd was visited on his lonely hillside by three beautiful naked goddesses, Minerva, Juno and Venus (to give them their Latin names), and told to decide who was supreme. He chose Venus, goddess of love. Fulgentius interprets this as an allegory of the soul's need to choose between the contemplative life (Minerva), the active life (Juno), and the voluptuous life (Venus). He then Christianises the story by interpreting it as an allegory of the Fall of Adam (because of his love of Eve) as told in *Genesis* II, with Jupiter signifying God.

Fulgentius is remarkable for describing for the first time the appearance of the gods, and indicating the significance of their characteristics. They paint Venus naked, he writes, either because she

sends away naked those who are addicted to her, or because the
crime of lust cannot be concealed, or because it is only suitable to
the naked. She has roses because they are red, and sting, like lust, the
red coming from shame, the sting from sin. As roses please for a
while then fade, so lust pleases for a moment then always departs.
She has doves with her because they are notoriously lecherous. They
paint her floating in the sea because lust in the end suffers shipwreck.
She carries a conch-shell because this creature is totally immersed in
copulation. Fulgentius also tells and allegorises the story of Venus
and Mars.

Just as Augustine's powerful attack made it impossible to take
Venus seriously as divine, and thus paradoxically made it theologi-
cally safe to read about her, so Fulgentius's condemnatory allegory
made her morally respectable because she showed up how bad lust
is. Theologically and morally safe, scientifically acceptable, the later
career of Venus was highly successful, so that she could in the end
represent God's own love, and be presented by Boccaccio and Chaucer
as a classical representation of the Blessed Virgin Mary, Empress of
Heaven and Earth and Hell.

It is impossible to follow here all the mythographers and poets
who wrote about Venus in the Middle Ages. One Albricus Philo-
sophicus wrote an account based on Fulgentius and others, but limited
mainly to descriptions, leaving out allegorisation, which may be the
source of Chaucer's description in *The House of Fame*, ll. 130ff.
Chaucer is rarely interested in allegory: he prefers the historical or
scientific fact 'without glose' (commentary).

To conclude this account of mythography we may take as an
example Boccaccio, a little older than Chaucer, so rich a source for
him, yet such a contrast. Boccaccio, like Chaucer, but earlier in life,
turned away from the vernacular poems and stories at which he was
such a genius, and devoted the rest of his life to religion and scholar-
ship. In particular he collected up all the stories of the gods, and tried
to classify and interpret them, like a fourteenth-century version of
the immensely influential modern French scholar, Professor C. Lévi-
Strauss. So contemporary at all times is mythography. Boccaccio
wrote a vast compendium in Latin, *De Genealogia Deorum* (*Concerning
the Genealogy of the Gods*), which was copied, reprinted and translated
frequently during the next four centuries in Europe. Chaucer either
did not know it, or was not interested in it. But though Chaucer was
antipathetic to allegory, he could not avoid being susceptible to the
kind of meanings that might be implicit in traditional figures in
literature. And he would have relished the ambiguities.

Boccaccio's discussion of Venus in the *De Genealogia Deorum* is typical of his method and material. He is not quite clear how many Venuses there are, but it is vital to realise that there are more than one. The first is the greater Venus, sixth daughter of the Sky and the Day. Boccaccio comments on the many confused stories about her, but as they have been deduced from the properties of the planet, he says, he will first describe what the astrologers say. The core of the matter is this. Since as a planet she appears fixed in the sky and moving with it, she seems to be produced by it, hence her father is the Sky. She is called daughter of the Day because of her brightness. Since God made nothing in vain, he made the stars 'in order that by their movement and influence, the seasons of the passing year should be varied, mortal things generated, what generated should be born, what born fostered, and in time should come to an end'. The effects of Venus are those of 'love, friendship, affection, company, domesticity, union between animals, and especially the begetting of children. . . . Whence it may be admitted that by her are caused the pleasures of men.' When she attends marriages she wears the girdle called the Ceston, signifying love, friendship, eloquence and caresses. 'This bond is not carried if not in honest marriage, and therefore all other coupling is called incest.' At times the astrologers say she is associated with the Furies, and this is especially liable to happen in spring when 'not only brute animals, but also women, whose complexion is for the most part warm and moist when spring comes, incline more strongly towards heat and wantonness. Which inclination, if modesty does not restrain it, may be converted into fury.' The Furies may also be said to come when there is bitterness or deceit or desertion in love. Venus can also indicate mere sexuality, and the lustful are born under her domination.

The second Venus is the seventh daughter of the Sky, and mother of Cupid. By her Boccaccio understands the *lascivious* life, and she signifies sexual intercourse. He then quotes verbatim the condemnatory passage from Fulgentius about Venus, summarised above.

The third Venus, eleventh daughter of Jove, was wife of Vulcan, mistress of Mars, mother of Aeneas. Some think she was the same as that lady of Cyprus who was wife of Adonis. But Boccaccio thinks not. It was this latter lady, a yet different one, who invented prostitution in order to cover her own promiscuity, and was thus a fourth Venus.

All this is a great muddle. By including as many references as possible, without having any serious analytical method, Boccaccio has piled up a huge heap of miscellaneous material, a mere aggregation, with only the most superficial order. He did this for all classical mythology. The very fact of extensive accumulation, however, made his work attractive to many scholars in the late fourteenth and fifteenth century, and it went into numerous printed editions. It is the immediate or ultimate source of almost all classical mythography in Europe and there were still schoolbooks in plenty in the eighteenth century peddling simplified versions.

One advantage was that we could find almost any interpretation we wanted in Boccaccio's work. Inconsistencies and incompatibilities have their uses when there is an attempt to sum up an intensely complicated matter either in art or exposition. We have already seen an example from Boccaccio himself in the *Chiose* to *Teseida* (above, p. 138). These were admittedly written before he had started his great mythological compendium, but he must have already had some idea of the many aspects of Venus because they were familiar both from poetry and voluminous earlier mythographers. In the *Chiose* he chooses to simplify Venus into two figures, the good and the bad. The course of history had paradoxically made it possible to think of Venus, the goddess, or the allegory, or the power, of love as on occasion entirely good. Venus could be made to represent the love expressed by God towards his creation. Venus herself could represent, in her beauty, the fair chain of love. Cupid too could take on respectability as the God of Love, and from being represented as a child was seen as a handsome young hunter and king, as in *The Prologue to the Legend of Good Women*, but that is too long a story for the moment.

The essence of the matter is the secular, educated, courtly representation of love as noble and worthy, part of the divine unity and consistency of the universe. Clerical writing continued its normal misogynistic message for the most part, though not all of the hostility to sexual love was foolish or against nature. That again is a matter not to be dealt with here. The assertion of the goodness, and the divine origin, of sexual love became an important element in Chaucer's poetry and the courtly culture he was part of. Philosophy and the stories of love could be reconciled – up to a point. There was much that the fair chain of love could bind together. Some ideas and attitudes would never submit to be so bound. There was as always the risk of contradiction and conflict. That question must be postponed for the consideration of love and death which the fair chain of love binds together.

Chapter 13

The Tale of Palamon and Arcite: Love and Death

Chaucer had bought at least three books in Florence in 1374. One was Dante's *Divine Comedy*; the second was Boccaccio's *Teseida*; the third was Boccaccio's *Il Filostrato*. The *Divine Comedy* he read and referred to in detail but it was an end in itself, with one exception (in *The Monk's Tale*), not raw material he could work on. Boccaccio's more human less perfect narratives were more malleable. *Teseida* offered some brilliant passages, an interesting story, and a tantalising challenge in form. Chaucer had tried to use something of *Teseida's* splendid diction and expansive narrative in *Anelida and Arcite* and had fallen back defeated on his earlier French manner. He had been more successful in *The Parliament of Fowls* by simply taking a few excerpts with which to create the glowing sultry picture of Venus and her train as part of the brilliantly varied *collage* out of which he created that poem.

Although the connections of *Palamon and Arcite* seem stronger with Chaucer's earlier rather than with his later poems there is one marked change which points forward to later poems – its metre. Like *the Legend of Good Women*, *The General Prologue* to *The Canterbury Tales* and some other later poems, it is written in the five-stress, mainly ten-syllable rhyming couplets which Chaucer was the first to use in English, and which proved so hard for his fifteenth-century followers to imitate. As with the change from the four-stress line of *The House of Fame* to the five-stress line and seven-line stanza of *The Parliament of Fowls* the change of metre signals a development. The couplet has a broader, more flexible sweep. It is less lyrical, but better for description and varieties of discourse. It is more 'realistic' within obvious limits. It is more rapid in narrative. It could be that *Palamon and Arcite* was originally written in rhyme-royal stanzas, but there are no signs of revision. It may have been written after *Troilus and Criseyde*, thus modifying but not seriously disturbing the line of development I have suggested. At all events the choice of metre is significant of the wider horizons coming into view – though even so some mists will return with *The Legend of Good Women*. There is no simple line of development in a great poet's work.

Teseida continued to present Chaucer with a tempting subject, a strong inner structure, and an impossibly verbose form, in which Boccaccio had imitated the artifice, and length, of Virgil's *Aeneid*. Chaucer now met the problem by taking the centre of *Teseida*, modifying it, and ruthlessly cutting out the artificial early Renaissance flummery. He 'medievalised' the story, as in C. S. Lewis's phrase, he 'medievalised' Boccaccio's *Filostrato* to make *Troilus and Criseyde*. Chaucer reduced *Teseida* to *Palamon and Arcite* (the names of the heroes) though he expanded *Filostrato*. Of course he did not think of himself as specifically 'medievalising': the idea of 'the Middle Ages' had not been invented. But nor was he in his own terms bringing Boccaccio's poems in any sense up-to-date. Both poems were set in ancient pre-Christian times and that was no doubt part of their attraction, for it avoided awkward theological problems, and distanced the action to a period already established as romantically interesting in Classical Latin literature. At the same time the period allowed a chivalric colouring, for the Age of Chivalry was always in the past. The local modern detail of chivalry was available for any period. The topics of love and arms were perennial for Chaucer though he recognised that manners and language might change over a thousand years, as he remarks (*Troilus*, II, 22–49).

So he stripped out the essentials of *Teseida*, saw the story both in terms of medieval love-romance and as presenting 'philosophical' dilemmas of the kind that interested him in *The Parliament*, and called it *Palamon and Arcite*, which is how he refers to it in *Prologue F* of *The Legend of Good Women* (420–1) written in 1386, adding 'thogh the storye ys knowen lyte'.

It is possible that the story was less popular in his own day than others of his works, but that did not prevent him from allocating it to the Knight when, a little later, he came to devise *The Canterbury Tales*. I have little doubt that if the idea of the competition among the *Tales* had been carried through, *Palamon and Arcite* as *The Knight's Tale* would have won the prize. For several centuries *The Knight's Tale* has been regarded, as Dryden called it, 'a noble tale'. It is indeed a many-splendoured thing.

Yet for most modern readers it is the most repellent or, at least, hardest to swallow. Everything in it displeases: the leisurely pace, the chivalric fighting ethos, the glow of description, the pains of love, the conflict of lovers and death of one, the homely but lengthy philosophising about making a virtue of necessity, the stereotyped characters, the mythological decoration, the genial authority of Duke Theseus. Woe to the teacher who has to put it over. For example, many modern intellectuals dislike the pomp and circumstance of rituals, colourful processions, bands, the jingling horses and bright uniforms of, say, the Household Cavalry. Not only the apparent glorification of war but the glamour of special dress for special occasions is disliked, as non-utilitarian, economically unproductive. Modern intellectual values are utilitarian, egalitarian, altruistic, and individualistic to the point of hostility to communal expressions of identity.[1] Such modern intellectual values descend from our paradoxically vilified Puritan forebears and are to be cherished, but they are a narrow band of individualistic artistic expression. Assertions of community are as vital to personal identity as is individualism. Thus, the pomp and glory of Theseus's march after a successful war is glorified by the poet in a brief colourful passage ending, like the triumphant tap of a drum

Thus rit this duc, thus rit this conquerour	*rides*
And in his hoost of chivalrie the flour.	*flower*
	(I, 982–3)

But after all, we might argue, Theseus has just returned from what for all we know was an entirely unjustified attack on 'the reign of Femenye' – the realm of women – and has captured their queen. What recompense is it to her that he marries her? When he is appealed to by the widows of warriors slain by Creon, the poet represents him as overcome by pity and immediately, instead of returning home, going off to fight another war and make more widows. And we are expected to approve. For many moderns all this has only been made acceptable by claiming that all is ironical, the story is a dramatic speech by the Knight who is a mercenary thug, nobility is degradation, pathos is ridiculous, bravery mere violence, piety platitudinous and hypocritical. The liberal humanist atheist pacifist ethos of our day finds nothing to respond to in the poem. That is natural enough, but it disregards what we know of history and ancient stories and human nature, as a glance around much of the world even today, let alone over history, immediately suggests. Chaucer has by his own standards protected Theseus from the accusation of undue aggressiveness, by giving only a cursory account of fighting, and by emphasising Theseus's pity for the women in their justifiable complaint that they are forbidden to bury or burn the corpses of their husbands.

There is simply no evidence for an ironical reading, and every reason for taking the poem straight, like it or not. *Palamon and Arcite* is the product of that medieval Europe briefly described at the beginning of this book; the product of the tiny élite of a small community, hierarchical, patriarchal, aggressive, religious, passionate, loyal, irrational, like virtually every other pre-industrial agrarian community that humanity has created. The same attitude of mind is found in Shakespeare, though modern productions normally distort it in the interests of modernism. It is widespread in other medieval literature, though since medieval culture was intensely contentious other points of view were also expressed.

Many clerics, Lollards, and some laymen like Gower, condemned variously war, chivalry, tournaments, crusades, love, serfdom, the behaviour of the rich and courtly, as well as normal human sinfulness, and those later bawdy comic poems of Chaucer's that we now value so highly. On the other hand, though actual kings and nobles might be condemned, it was impossible to conceive of society as being other than hierarchically ordered. Democracy, egalitarianism, statism were beyond social imagination and possibility. In short we must accept differences and read the poem for its glamour, pageantry, pathos, studying it as we would any archaic society that was both 'other' and deeply different, yet connected with us by powerful links of human continuity. It is like travel in a foreign land. In making discoveries about the other we learn more about ourselves and enrich our experience.

Palamon and Arcite was written about the same time as *Troilus and Criseyde*. *Troilus* is more closely connected with *The Legend of Good Women* which as it were grows out of the *Troilus*, while *Palamon and Arcite* is more closely connected with the earlier *Anelida and Arcite* and *The Parliament of Fowls*, both of which testify to the fascination which *Teseida* at this stage held for Chaucer. Both *The Parliament* and *Palamon and Arcite* treat of rivalry in love, and the deeper questions of life and love which rivalry produces. It is convenient, at least, and seems to follow a natural development, if we assume that *Palamon and Arcite* was composed before *Troilus and Criseyde*, which puts it (if *The Parliament* was completed about 1382), within the next year or two. At about the same period, Chaucer seems not only to have translated Boethius's *Consolation* but to have used it to deepen his treatment of questions and stories.

Although *Palamon and Arcite* is more familiar as *The Knight's Tale*, it was written before the Knight was created in *The General Prologue* of about 1387, and beyond its chivalric ethos has little to do with him. Compared with *Troilus* it is a little more schematic, yet has a broader range through the person of Duke Theseus, and has altogether less inwardness than *Troilus*. Although not particularly warlike, it convincingly portrays the sustaining ethos of Chaucer's culture, what later Othello calls the 'pride, pomp and circumstance of glorious war' (III, iii, 355), as well as conveying with even more force what Othello elsewhere refers to as war's harshness and cruelty. War could not be glorious if it were not also horrible; bravery cannot exist, or at least, appear, without danger.

Another reason for taking *Palamon and Arcite* here is to avoid the trap of reading it as expressive of the Knight's subjective character, or attempting to read the Knight's character back from the poem. This is the dramatic fallacy which derives from reading *The Canterbury Tales* as if they were expressive of independently conceived personages speaking of their own volition independent of the poet, as if the tales were speeches in a play, though the critical habit derives more truly from the nineteenth-century novel of character. (It is a view I have contested without much success for 50 years but, as the modern novel and drama become less 'realistic', so may this type of reading become less prevalent – though it is justified by some parts of *The Canterbury Tales* as will be shown.)[2]

In *Palamon and Arcite* as we have it as *The Knight's Tale* the four lines *CT*, I, 899–92 near the very beginning must have been inserted by Chaucer when he fitted the poem into *The Canterbury Tales*. They follow the very unknightly metaphor of the author as a ploughman with weak oxen, which, however, is in tone with Chaucer's usual self-deprecating narrative style. The last two lines of the poem, *CT*, I, 3107–8 could fit any social situation. These latter are characteristic of Chaucer's normal imitation of orality referred to earlier. Elsewhere there is ample evidence that the poem is conceived of as a written poem issuing from the poet Chaucer, which he did not bother to revise except at the very beginning. For example, the poem contains no less than five references to writing or 'editing' (I, 1201, 1209, 1380, 1872, 2741) spread throughout the poem. There are plenty of references to speaking, but this is natural throughout many centuries of written or printed discourse. Here we have particularly clear examples of Chaucer's playing with the variations between orality and literacy, noticeable throughout his work.

To follow for a moment the personalised narration of *Palamon and Arcite* introduces its essential quality, and its connections in sentiment and attitude, with a variety of Chaucer's other poems. We may note that the teller of *Palamon and Arcite* even addresses

Ye loveres, axe I nowe this question

(1347)

in a way very like the style of *Troilus and Criseyde*, e.g. I, 22, or
of *The Prologue* to *The Legend of Good Women* (F 69) and totally
inappropriate to the ostensible pilgrimage-audience. The division of
Palamon and Arcite into four parts, unlike any other Canterbury Tale,
the style of the visual descriptions, that strange *occupatio* (that is, the
apparent refusal to describe), here used of Arcite's funeral pyre (2919–
64) all have a curious flavour suggesting relationship to a written
source, different from most of the other *Tales*.

Yet the narrative style and attitudes are not radically different
from Chaucer's other work. For example, the teller wishes to make clear
that he refers to the Ovidian character Daphne in one passage, calling
her *Dane*, and says explicitly he does *not* mean *Diana* (2062–4). This
explicitness, surely unrepresentative of the Knight, recalls the Pardoner's
insistence that definitely Lamuel, *not* Samuel, is the person *he* is
referring to in another passage (*CT*, I, 585), which is equally unrep-
resentative of the Pardoner's character. Such remarks are meant for
readers and scribes, rather than for hearers. They betray a certain con-
cern for precision and care for the text unconvincing as a character-
istic of Knight or Pardoner but entirely typical of Chaucer the poet.

In another *occupatio*, the teller of *Palamon and Arcite* refuses to give
details of the feast (2197–205) just like the teller of *The Man of Law's
Tale* (*CT*, II, 701), the teller of *The Squire's Tale* twice (*CT*, II, 63–
72, 278–90), the teller of the *Legend of Dido* (*LGW*, 616–22) and in
a different way, the teller of *The Wife of Bath's Tale* (*CT*, III, 1073–
8). These references tell us about the poet's attitude through various
'voices' to courtly festivity, and though characteristic of Chaucer
they are not special to the Knight.

The relatively frequent use by the teller of the tale of the first
personal pronoun is particularly noticeable in the explicit and self-
conscious management of the actual narrative of *Palamon and Arcite*.
It begins very early, when 13 lines after the tale has begun the teller
remarks

And thus with victorie and with melodye
Lete I this noble duc to Atthenes ryde
And al his hoost in armes hym bisyde.
And certes, if it nere to long to heere   *were not*
I wolde have toold yow fully the maneere
How wonnen was the regne of Femenye, etc.

(872–7)

In this poem of over 2000 lines there are more than 80 narratorial interventions of this kind, often expressing the need not to bore the reader or hearer, or leaving one part of the action and turning to another, careful not to forget to tell something. These are characteristics found, for example, in *The Man of Law's Tale* (*CT*, II, 246−8) or in *Troilus and Criseyde* (V, 195−6, 841). In *The Knight's Tale* the teller is learned in many examples from old books but says he will spare us the mention. There is no reason to think the Knight learned in this way, and every reason to know that Chaucer is. He is a confident manipulator of the narrative, entirely in control, explaining to us what he is doing, daringly entering into the very narrative when he describes the paintings on the walls of the temples as seeing them himself. The sense of a personal narration is so strong that we can legitimately project back from the poem a sense of the character of the teller, which is very different from projecting the assumed character of the Knight on to the poem. What sort of teller does *Palamon and Arcite* construct?

Chaucer's confidence in narration is common with traditional story-tellers. As is also common, such self-characterisation as he projects is rather social, general and consensual. He has traditional flippancies about women (2284−8, 2681−2), like those, for example, in *The Man of Law's Tale* (II, 708−14) which is balanced in *The Man of Law's Tale* by a similar flippancy about husbands (II, 271−2), all equally indecorous in a serious context.

In a rather similar way he is dismissive about death, in a way not uncommon to those societies where death is common, and balanced, as again can be observed in some more 'archaic' societies today, by the extravagant grief of mourners, and found elsewhere in Chaucer.

The agnosticism about souls, of which the teller is no *divinistre* (2811) reminds us of the similar agnosticism about Heaven and Hell at the very beginning of *The Prologue* to *The Legend of Good Women*. There is nothing very daring about this rather commonplace secular attitude. It is a recognisable vein in much of Chaucer's poetry.

Another aspect of traditional secular wisdom is expressed in Egeus's brief speech, stoical and appropriate (2843−9). The speech is often condemned as platitudinous, but it is true in its own limits and only the criteria of the New Criticism caused familiar but unpleasant truths to be thought ridiculous in poetry.

The teller of *Palamon and Arcite* well evokes the bright colours and the corresponding dark shadows of the chivalrous life. He is sympathetic to its glamour and vividly evokes it in too many passages to quote. The self-glorifying panoply of chivalry is an aspect of that need for ceremonial and ritual which is felt in all societies. Theatricality is intrinsic to all social life.

It is not always the case that public ritual is a sign of internal weakness. Some modern critics regard ritual as concerned with ostentatious inessentials, and not economically productive. For earlier societies there was an intrinsic connectedness and coherence between outer and inner, the spiritual and the material. The doctrine of the Eucharist is a prime example. Certainly it was questioned, but the whole concept of cosmic unity and order had not broken down. The speech of Theseus, so difficult for modern minds to accept, witnesses to this order. Order is always threatened beneath the moon, and suffering is everywhere present, but that is not the whole story.

Suffering but also the heroic endurance of suffering is at the heart of the perception of the world in *Palamon and Arcite*. Suffering is most vividly imaged in pain and death; endurance of them, and the certainty that just as woe follows joy, then joy may follow woe, is at the heart of *The Knight's Tale* as it is of Theseus's great speech which accepts the contradictions of life, because as he says, we have to. This life is indeed a 'foule prisoun' (3061) from one point of view, but as Theseus says

> after wo I rede us to be merye.   *advise; cheerful*
> (3068)

Joy and woe are traditionally represented in tales of war and combat, imaged here in the social and literary stylisation called chivalry. Everywhere in *Palamon and Arcite* the teller is sympathetic to the glamour, colour and high ideals of chivalry. The dying Arcite generously commends Palamon the 'gentil man' (2797) for his

> trouthe, honour, knyghthede,
> Wysdom, humblesse, estaat, and heigh kynrede,
> Fredom, and al that longeth to that art.   *Generosity*
> (2789–91)

It must be clear by now that the teller of *Palamon and Arcite* is the poet Chaucer, the same poet who tells in his own poetic person the earlier poems, and *Troilus and Criseyde*, and *The Legend of Good Women*. There is no dramatic colouring or psychological expression which constructs the Knight as story-teller.

On the other hand *Palamon and Arcite* was later not unsuitably attributed, by the light fictionality of story-telling, to the Knight, because it is clear that Chaucer shares the same chivalric values as those he attributes to the Knight. That we may passionately dislike these values should not lead us to impose modernistic anachronisms, modern political programmes, on Chaucer's works.

THE STORY OF *PALAMON AND ARCITE*

The story goes straight to the point, summarising many hundreds of Boccaccio's lines in a few dozen. 'As olde stories tellen us', it begins in the traditional way – once upon a time – there was a duke called Theseus, lord of Athens. He has conquered the Amazons, married their queen Hippolyta, and brought back her and her young sister Emily. Just as he arrives home a band of ladies, widowed in war at Thebes, ask him to avenge them on the tyrant Creon. Immediately, as true knight, he swears to do so, and turns for Thebes. We see the magnificence of a great king off to war, such as Edward III must have appeared.

The rede statue of Mars, with spere and targe	*shield*
So shyneth in his white baner large	
That alle the feeldes glyteren up and doun	*fields*
And by his baner born is his penoun	
Of gold ful riche, in which ther was ybete	*embroidered*
The Mynotaur which that he slough in Crete.	*slew*
Thus rit this duc, thus rit this conqerour,	*rides*
And in his hoost of chivalrie the flour	*army*
Til that he cam to Thebes and alighte	
Faire in a field, ther as he thoughte to fighte.	

(*CT*, I, 975–84)

In his victorious battle two young Theban knights are captured, all but dead, and Theseus imprisons them for ever in Athens in a tower. They are two cousins and dear friends, Palamon and Arcite (the latter pronounced and sometimes spelt Arcita).

One day in May they see from their prison the beautiful golden-haired Emily at dawn gathering white and red flowers and singing. Palamon is the first to see her and is as it were stung to the heart. Palamon hardly knows if he has seen a woman or a goddess. Arcite then sees her and is equally affected. Alas, they then quarrel, each claiming – how hopelessly – the primacy in love, because Arcite argues that Palamon is disqualified by not knowing whether Emily was woman or goddess. Arcite says that anyway lovers always break the law for love. He is much the tougher and more ruthless of the

two young men, as well as the second to see Emily. A friend pro-
cures his release, with ironical consequences, for it places both young
men at the extremes of grief: Palamon because still in prison, Arcite
because free, but banished from Athens. However, Arcite returns
secretly and works his way up the ladder of advancement at court,
though still no nearer Emily. Then Palamon escapes, and Arcite, out
Maying and sorrowing, accidentally meets him in the grove where
he is hiding. They all but fight. Palamon, however, has no armour,
so Arcite in his chivalry brings him next day all the armour and
weapons he needs. They meet and arm each other in stony silence.

Ther nas no 'good day', ne no saluyng	*was not; greeting*
But streight withouten word or rehersyng	*repeating*
Everich of hem heelp for to armen oother	*each*
As freendly as he were his owene brother.	

(*CT*, I, 1649–52)

They fight madly. Theseus, out hunting in the company of Hippolyta
and Emily, finds them. He is at first in a noble rage with them, and
condemns them to death. The Queen and Emily go down on their
bare knees to beg for pity for them, in a scene which recalls Froissart's
famous story of how Queen Philippa successfully begged Edward III
for mercy for the burghers of Calais. (The fiery, amorous but mag-
nanimous Theseus might be a portrait of Edward III.) He forgives
the two young men, who agree to meet in a year's time each with a
troop of supporters to fight for Emily. Theseus has some fun at their
expense. How great a lord is love, he says. Here are Arcite and
Palamon, who might be living royally in Thebes, and who know
that I am their mortal enemy, and here they are, in my presence,
fighting each other to the death:

Who may been a fool, but if he love?

(*CT*, I, 1799)

But this is yet the beste game of alle,	
That she for whom they han this jolitee	
Kan hem therfore as muche thank as me.	*owes*
She woot namoore of al this hoote fare	*knows; hot business*
By God, than woot a cokkow or an hare.	

(*CT*, I, 1806–10)

In a year's time the lists are set up, like a great theatre, precisely
measured, and temples of Mars, Venus and Diana are set up. These

are magnificently described, though mainly emphasising pain and sorrow – a reminder of the hardness of life underlying all the splendour. The poet participates so keenly, though not ironically, that he continually says in his description, 'I saw' this and that. He makes it all vivid and present to the mind. Arcite prays to Mars for victory; Palamon, who cares nothing for victory, only for Emily, prays to Venus; Emily, who would prefer the life of virginity, and loves hunting,

> And for to walken in the wodes wilde
> And noght to ben a wyf and be with childe
>
> *(CT*, I, 2309–10)

prays to Diana that Palamon and Arcite may be reconciled and neither want her; but if it must be so, let him have her who most desires her. There is real sympathy for the pathos of woman's lot here. Since the poem is a fiction about pagan times these prayers come to the respective god and goddesses to whom they are addressed, in particular Mars and Venus, each of whom by a sign in the temple grants what is asked. The requests of Palamon and Arcite are incompatible, so Mars and Venus are referred by Jupiter to the gloomy Saturn, who promises that each will get what he or she asks for.

SOME INNER STRUCTURES OF THE STORY

The pagan surface of the story is supported here by the inner structure of scientific truth (as it then appeared) according to which the gods are really the planets, who really do influence people's lives. There is also an ironic pattern within the story: you get what you ask for, but it may not turn out to be precisely what you want. Arcite wants Emily but he asks for the means, victory, not the end, marriage with Emily. These inner structures of the story do not mean that the story is allegorical: they are not *more* real than the literal meaning, but are the depths below the shining surface, and are part of the whole meaning.

THE STORY RESUMED

The preparations for the tournament are told with unparalleled realism and conviction, and the fighting vigorously described in a pastiche of the rough alliterative style (ll, 2600–13). And Arcite wins.

What of Venus's promise then? Saturn sends an infernal fury from the ground which startles Arcite's horse as he rides in triumph, and he receives his death-injury. The description of his sufferings is as detailed and realistic as the description of earlier splendour. The women shriek as he marries Emily on his death-bed, and he generously reconciles himself to Palamon, in a moving speech.

The extravagant sorrow shown by all is corrected by Theseus's aged father, Egeus

> That knew this worldes transmutacioun   *changes*
> As he hadde seyn it chaunge both up and doun,
> Joye after wo, and wo after gladnesse,
> And shewed hem ensaumples and liknesse.   *illustrations*
>
> (*CT*, I, 2839–42)

The ups and downs of earthly fortune are a favourite reflection with Chaucer.

> This world nys but a thurghfare ful of wo
> And we been pilgrymes, passynge to and fro.
> Deeth is an ende of every worldly soore.
>
> (*CT*, I, 2847–9)

This Boethian and medieval Christian commonplace is repeated at the end of *Troilus*, and is echoed in the Boethian lyrics 'Fortune' and 'Truth'. We should not expect life to be all roses. We should not mourn too much. Chaucer keeps the speech of Egeus short, but there is no reason to believe that its tone is ironic and self-mocking because it is a commonplace. It is the basic stoic acceptance of life-with-death that underlines both pathos and comedy, and is paradoxically comforting.

Arcite's pagan funeral pyre is described in great detail in that strange device known as *occupatio* in Latin rhetoric, or refusing at great length to describe. It is an example of Chaucer's virtuoso rhetoric, very effective for those with an interest in pure artistic skill. Eventually, after years of mourning, Theseus summons Emily and Palamon to marry. Palamon deserves to succeed. He saw Emily first. He was less ruthless. He prayed for the end, the love of Emily, not the means, the victory in the tournament. Chaucer changes Boccaccio's characters around to bring this about. But the point is that the two young men are nevertheless closely similar. The deeper pattern of the story embodies the unspoken proposition that we stand a 50–50 chance of success and happiness in life.

The conclusion is brought about by a noble Boethian speech by Theseus, encouraging Palamon and Emily to make the best of 'this wrecched world', 'this foule prisoun of this lyf', which is, however, bound by 'the faire cheyne of love'. Death is inevitable, but Arcite made a good death. Why begrudge him his welfare? So let us make a virtue of necessity,

> And after wo I rede us to be merye   *advise*
> And thanken Juppiter of al his grace.
>
> (*CT*, I, 3068–9)

Chaucer's resolute realism will no more deny joy than sorrow.

SPECTACLE AND IMPLICATION

The variety of vivid description in *Palamon and Arcite* can only be experienced and enjoyed by leisurely reading. There is also plenty of generalised comment by the poet, as in his comment on

> The destinee, ministre general,
>
> (1663)

or such a flippant remark as the apparent fuss women make when their husbands die (2817–26), or the sententious wisdom of Egeus and Theseus towards the end of the poem. Descriptions are characterised by typical hyperbole

> Infinite been the sorwes and the teeres.
>
> (2827)

The generally sententious style maintains the collective wisdom:

> For pitee renneth soone in gentil herte
>
> (1761)

one of Chaucer's favourite lines, along with another favourite, preceded by the poignant general question underlying the whole story

> What is this world? What asketh men to have?
> Now with his love, now in his colde grave,
> Allone withouten any compaignye
>
> (2777–9)

'Company' is a word that echoes through the poem. It is a society where the collective group, not individuals, holds the supreme values. This kind of general sentiment is independent of local detail. Arcite died like a gentleman but his body was burnt in a glorious pagan funeral pyre, not left in a cold and solitary grave.

Repetition (and a form of it, duplication, in the almost identical young heroes) and memorialisation are inherent in style and structure. *Palamon and Arcite* is a stylised monument to chivalry, a chivalry of the past, whatever light it may throw on the present as inspiration or strengthening recollection. And like monuments of brass and marble these in rhyme have little subjectivity of personality, though they give the pang of personal remembrance in the present.

Theseus's speech could be condemned as a pseudo-philosophical papering over the cracks of self-contradictions in an inadequate worldview, or as a witness to the 'crisis of chivalry' in the fourteenth century, or as self-regarding meaningless platitudes. To do so misunderstands its nature and purpose. It is in fact religious and practical, put into the mouth of a benevolent pagan king. Chaucer could not make it overtly Christian, as he did the ending of *Troilus and Criseyde*, because it is a dramatic speech within the historical fiction. Nor could it be philosophical in any modern sense. Its keynote is a stoical acceptance of the internal contradictions within earthly existence, where good is inextricably mingled with evil, joy with sadness. It asserts that acceptance of necessity can be converted to a personal virtue. For human beings it is only sensible to make the best of things, to see the advantages that there may be in any death or any life. These unfashionable and always unpleasant truths bear repetition, especially when they are expressed with sympathy and understanding. Muscatine has emphasised the poem's and Theseus's over-riding concern with order, and most of us, as we look at history past and present can sympathise with the desire for order. Order, like any other benefit, is not achieved without cost. Pagan natural reason, as mediated through Boethius, accords with the underlying Christian concept of a mysterious but ultimately beneficent providential order, to be accepted with faith and trust. In the poem Theseus is himself the instrument of providential order on earth, and does all he can to establish and maintain it, while he is also characterised as a bluff, chivalric, humanly impetuous medieval king – a veritable Edward III in his best days. The profound psychological power of the Biblical and medieval ideal of God as king, the king as God, underlies the feeling here.

What maketh this but Juppiter the kyng
That is prince and cause of alle thyng?

(I, 3035–6)

Jupiter is here referred to as the First Mover above all planets, not as god-planet, in which capacity he does not figure in the poem. It is easy to accept such usage when using a poetic mythology which suits the pagan setting and the underlying astrology but which neither Chaucer nor we take literally. It relies on the frequent medieval use of the name Jupiter for the Christian God. That we moderns have no faith nor trust in Providential order need not prevent us from recognising the human appeal of Theseus's speech. We can respond sympathetically to its strength, beauty and pathos. It is unsentimental and admirably clearsighted: an uncomplaining acceptance of the good and bad of life, with willingness to make the best of things. And death finally is both victorious and swallowed up in victory, part of the contrast of bright and dark portrayed in this hard, brilliant chivalric world of war, hunting, love, worship, extravagant feeling, stoical endurance, translated literally and metaphorically from past to present, part of a stream of historical consciousness.

One part of that consciousness which strikes a modern reader particularly strongly is male domination and especially that Emily has no choice either to marry or not to marry, nor whom to marry. She is powerless over herself though she exercises a huge force of attraction to the young men. She has even fewer individualising traits than they. This is part of one underlying theme of the story: the force of necessity. You have to make the best of it, 'a virtue of necessity'. It is not only society but nature at its simplest that denies individualism. The force of evolution (unknown of course to Chaucer) has little care for individual preferences, and earlier societies, however they struggle to modify nature, must recognise, to survive, that natural force. 'The world must be peopled' as Jean de Meun and others recognised. Women must breed, and in this society in order to do so women of the highest classes must marry. The young men are carried along by a biological force, modified and made more humane by such social constructs as the conventions of love but not fundamentally altered – how could it be, if the will to survive is to persist? It is this harsh necessity which *The Knight's Tale* presents, modulates, ponders over, recreates and memorialises. Society marks it with beauty and meditation, because such a society cannot, as modern people can, reconstruct nature. It has to co-operate with the universe.

NOTES

1. Charles Taylor, *Sources of the Self: the Making of the Modern Identity* (Cambridge, 1989).
2. Important and powerful critics who differ begin with Kittredge and of recent years include Professors Lee Patterson and Marshal Leicester. C. D. Benson supports it. See Select bibliography.

Chapter 14

Troilus and Criseyde I:
From a View to a Death

Troilus and Criseyde was written about the same time as *The Knight's Tale*, the mid–1380s, shares the same assumptions, but is even more personalised. The poet presents himself dramatically, yet he is not a named actor within the poem as in the earlier poems. The process of withdrawal has gone further. The sense of participation in the feelings the story evokes is, however, even stronger. The poet is the traditional story-teller, retelling a story which moves him at times deeply, which he himself claims not to know in every detail, though sometimes he can report the inmost secrets of a character's mind.

The basis is a translation of Boccaccio's *Il Filostrato*, written some half-century earlier. Chaucer treats it even more ruthlessly than *Teseida*: sometimes he translates line by line, sometimes runs roughly parallel, at other times totally diverges from, and in general greatly changes. For all the poet's claimed reliance on the 'authority' of ancient writers he takes only what he wants – the attitude of a conqueror rather than a dependent. The poem is most richly stored with all Chaucer's wide reading and his experience of daily life. He did not need and did not use the rather close translation into French prose attributed to one Beauvau, as some scholars have claimed. Coincidental readings are trivial and the French was almost certainly written in the middle of the fifteenth century.

Though close in time to *The Knight's Tale*, *Troilus and Criseyde* has a narrower, more personal focus – less pageantry for example – and a wider human reference. There is much closer and more inward presentation of character, a delicate analysis of love and sadness, yet also a touch of fabliau humour, and in many places an ambiguous tone. There is both on the part of the poet and also placed in the speeches (unrealistic though it may be) a Boethian seriousness of tone. Above all there is a powerful sense of the narrating poet, so much so that some critics have taken the poem to be, in the end, *about* the Narrator, the teller (not the poet). But we must not forget that in the end it is the poet, elusive, ironic at times, genuinely moved at times, who tells the story. One thing worth bearing in mind is the natural assumption (implicitly challenged by modern criticism) that the poet chose to write the poem because he himself was moved by the story. He felt for the 'inner story' which by his genius he perceived and created out of Boccaccio's more superficial though highly readable poem, which combines sexual titillation with misogyny. Chaucer 'saw' the course of events much as Boccaccio, who was himself helped by earlier versions, devised them. It had to be that story. But Chaucer saw the characters differently. He created for the first time in English a set of believable young people about whom we may have different and changing views. It is, astonishingly, a sort of historical novel, though not, in the end, truly novelistic. We are aware of Trojan society, but all is presented through the shifting perspectives, sympathies, jokes, withdrawals and advances of a poet who with all his seriousness is at times coquettish.

In *Troilus and Criseyde* the poet is telling a story, but a story is more than just an interesting narrative – it does other things too. It images and recovers life and death. In *Troilus and Criseyde* Chaucer is doing all sorts of things: working something out of himself, lovingly contemplating a beautiful woman, exploring a young man's love and integrity, watching true human feelings and human treachery, recreating domestic life, wondering how free we really are to do and be what we want, touching on the beauty and sadness of life, looking at life from different points of view.

It would trivialise this great poem to think of the poet here 'constructing himself', for all the strong sense of his presence. He is too confident. He *is* constructed, without self-consciousness, after many years of practice. He constructs, or rather, reconstructs, the characters differently from Boccaccio, but that is another matter, to be discussed later.

The poet's mastery, range of tone and confidence are carried by superb use of the rhyme royal. It follows Boccaccio's similar stanza and at times the translation is amazingly close, even occasionally so as to give an Italian flavour to words. Sometimes Chaucer is forced by the metre into a few empty phrases, and word-order naturally is changed as required to suit the demands of rhyme. Though rarely does a sentence move across a stanza division, the verse flows freely and musically, at times with lyrical expressiveness, and with the exception of letters, songs and some long speeches has a steady narrative flow. The diction is remarkable for its range from ordinary everyday colloquialism to the use of a number of words recorded for the first time in English, sometimes homely, more often grand, more polished – but always the diction of a highly educated courtier, never a pedant or a scholastic.

The poem has more relationships than might be suspected with *The Book of the Duchess*. It is a repetition, a recapturing, of the course of life. Starting with Troilus's first sight of Criseyde it goes from this view to his death, a metaphor of a whole life, though going beyond life. A re-telling is in the narrowest sense a repetition, but Chaucer's *Troilus* is also a variation on the universal theme of love and death. The structure is repetition, with variation, of sorrow, but with the interspersed joyousness of the superb central third book of the five into which the poem is divided. Because of sorrow and death so much of bright life is captured standing against the shadow. Light and shadow are in conflict, but the contrast within the whole gives the nature of life.

Chaucer both cuts and expands his source, re-forming the story so that it is the fullest treatment of the search for, indeed achievement of, happiness and its loss in all his work. This is the poem in which Chaucer meditates most fully on that deprivation of love, the loss of the loved one, and the consequent feeling of bewildered betrayal, which is so powerful an impulse for the searching intellect in the earlier poems. For the loss to be fully felt, the joy of its realisation must first be experienced. That joy itself is only to be gained by effort, and expectation, and desire, by painful yet bitter-sweet struggles. The full confrontation of the bitterness of loss forces acceptance, perhaps a transcendence, or at least detachment, and a sharp change of perspective, over the whole of life. The change of perspective at the end, inconsistent as it is with much that is said and felt in the course of the poem, is to be accepted as inconsistent. Only by accepting inconsistency can the paradoxes and ambiguities of life be portrayed. Yet there is a continuity, a recovery, implicit in the whole poem, which in the end is not about Criseyde's betrayal but about Troilus's *trouthe*; that profoundly complex notion of Chaucer's and his culture, of loyalty, faithfulness, stability, as well as the modern notion of truth as opposed to falsity. *Trouthe* is sometimes used as the word for God. Rarely is it a quality found in this life. Yet sometimes, somewhere, in some one, it may be found, and may redeem the world.

For all the variety of attitude and experience in the poem, for all Chaucer's engagement in it as writer, as poet, for all the feeling in the poem, the poet does not write as a participant, though many critics would have him to be so as Narrator. Boccaccio claims that the story expresses his own feelings for his beloved. Not so Chaucer, who is only the 'servant of the servants of love' (I, 15), a sympathetic onlooker, as he makes clear especially at the beginning of the poem. He takes his favoured marginal position in order to see and sometimes comment on what goes on at the centre.

The best way to think of Chaucer the poet in this poem is as the *Expositor*, the presenter of a play, who also comments on the action and is, though not an actor, as it were, present on the stage and deeply engaged sympathetically with the action. Such an Expositor, called *Contemplatio*, appears in the Hegge (or Coventry) Cycle of plays. *Expositor* introduces the Chester Cycle. In the Digby *Conversion of St Paul* the introductory character is even called *Poeta*. In other plays there is a similar character, *Prologue*. The essentially dramatic nature of Chaucer's genius, combined with his compulsive desire to comment, are exactly summed up by this crucial but neglected aspect of medieval drama.

There are other aspects of *Troilus and Criseyde* which are reminiscent of the drama. The characters often speak with vivid immediacy, especially Pandarus. Criseyde's last speech is a soliloquy astonishingly like the last speech of a character in a medieval play, even ending, as if leaving the stage,

> But al shal passe, and thus take I my leve.
>
> (V, 1085)

And yet the most dramatic section is formed by the first 56 lines of the whole poem, an Expositor's prologue, a masterpiece of introductory prevarication and provocation, with yet another version of that typical mixture, personal commitment and reserve, of seriousness and levity, knowledge and ignorance, deference and control, marginality and worldly knowingness, which helps to make up Chaucer's teasing ambiguity.

Troilus was known as a youthful hero from antiquity, and famous for having loved a woman (in the past called Briseida) who left him for the Greek hero and enemy, Diomede. His story had been told or referred to many times. In case we do not recall the story Chaucer expresses its essence in the poem's first line,

> The double sorwe of Troilus to tellen.
>
> (I, 1)

This is the full story and the double sorrow is also the backdrop of all the intrigue, the delights of love, of which we are told.

At last, after all the flirting with the audience which the prologue creates, placing the reader among them, the Expositor begins, with due deference, his story.

> Yt is wel wist how that the Grekes stronge   *known*
>
> (I, 56)

and we are led into remote pre-Christian yet known history (or we are flattered by the belief that we know it). Troilus is one of the princely sons of Priam, king of the doomed city of Troy. He is young – say 16 (the same age as Edward the Black Prince when he commanded the right wing at Crécy) and after Hector the bravest warrior in Troy. Troilus still practises an adolescent mockery of those who are in love, until one day at church during the festival of spring, he sees the beautiful Criseyde and is at once smitten with desperate love.

Criseyde is a young widow, whose age we are never told, but which is surely near to that of Troilus, or a little older. She stands modestly yet assuredly by the church door, with black dress and glorious golden hair.

> Hire goodly lokyng gladed al the prees.   *crowd*
> Nas nevere yet seyn thyng to ben preysed derre   *praised more highly*
> Nor under cloude blak so bright a sterre.
>
> (I, 173–5)

She is rich and independent but isolated, for her father Calkas is a great lord and priest of Apollo who by calculation, presumably in astrology, foreknows that Troy will be destroyed and has deserted to the Greeks.

Troilus sickens with love for the all but unknown lady and eventually in his misery retires to his bed – a bedroom being the only place of any privacy in Chaucer's world. A song of lament is attributed to him, one of the many lyrical moments of the poem, like an aria in an opera and (as Chaucer's audience could not know) based on a sonnet of Petrarch's.

The poet imputes to Troilus all a young man's sensibility in heightened terms. What a fool he is, he tells himself, and what a fool others will think him, and so he goes on, repeating the name Criseyde, as the poet says in a neat combination of hyperbole, amused deflation, and sympathy that recalls the attitude of Theseus in *The Knight's Tale*,

Til neigh that he in salte teres dreynte.   *drowned*
Al was for nought: she herde nat his pleynte.
And whan that he bythought on that folie
A thousand fold his wo gan multiplie.

(I, 543–6)

A friend called Pandarus comes into his room unexpectedly and hears him groan. Alas, says Pandarus, have the Greeks frightened you, or have you become devout and suffer from remorse for sin? He asks this as a wild improbability to make Troilus angry and throw off his sorrow, for he knows there is no braver man. So Pandarus makes his first appearance in English fiction, as a vivid dynamic speaker, undescribed, very much what he says and does, purely dramatic. He is an emotional, shrewd, friendly, energetic man. He well nigh melts for sorrow and pity for Troilus, who replies with a comic languidness to his briskness. But Pandarus is Criseyde's uncle, and will make Troilus's case with her. Friend and companion of the young warrior Troilus, but no fighter himself, uncle of a grown woman, he occupies an ambiguous position as to age, in the action, and in the moral scheme. These, with Criseyde, are the main characters. These men in concert but in very different ways, are those who are to act on Criseyde. Yet she, by being herself, is the cause of and reason for the action, even if only acted on. The male–female relationship is very complex.

This little scene is the first of dozens of examples of domestic realism in the poem, again for the first time in English. The realism of setting and dialogue carries in itself material of further significance as to character and action.

Here we may pause for a moment on precisely those deeper implications, for it is sometimes hard for the modern reader to sympathise with Troilus. Even if some modern young men may experience similar feelings they may receive little sympathy. Modern love is differently regarded. Troilus may seem to capitulate too easily, to wallow in factitious adolescent despair (though even today young people commit suicide because of disappointed love). Troilus's helpless passion may seem childish, psychologically a regression to the infant's desire for the mother. Or it may be represented as no more than self-indulgent young masculine lust. Or it may be represented as a dangerous obsession. It is possible to stand back, rely on modern concepts and take such views of the series of events. The sexual revolution from the 1960s onwards, the freedom of social and sexual intercourse between adolescents, in modern Western society, the decline in traditional morality and constraints, the modern collapse of concepts of faithful love in or out of marriage, all create a gulf between modern Westerners and traditional Western moral and social assumptions (let alone traditional Eastern and Islamic moral and social assumptions).

More complicated still, Chaucer is not telling a moralistic tale in the ordinary sense. He is telling a known story from antiquity of how a royal prince sought a mistress, and that was common enough in fourteenth-century England and later. But he chose to tell a story about love, not sexual adventure, and love, even when sexually driven, is a moral force. And despite the 'social construction' of character, and the changing human heart, there are some continuous human characteristics, among them sex, love and even the shyness of some adolescent boys.

No writer of the fourteenth century was more interested in love than Chaucer. Some of the complexities of the patterns of love in Chaucer's version of his own culture have been discussed above in relation to his earlier poems, especially *The Book of the Duchess*. The pattern is further developed and explored in the leisurely conduct of the action in *Troilus and Criseyde*. It will be further explored in several of *The Canterbury Tales* but nowhere with the depth, tenderness and sceptical reserve found in *Troilus and Criseyde*. There will also be in that poem a development, lacking in *The Book of the Duchess* for obvious reasons, of the purely physical aspects of sex. Traditionally men were accepted as having strong sexual desires and women not. On the whole, sex was considered to be 'dirty' (hence the modern concept of 'the dirty joke') and women of good reputation were expected, as being more refined creatures than men, to feel this more strongly. So feminine modesty was socially 'constructed', though no doubt for most women for good evolutionary reasons such self-protection has a biological base as well.

As is clear from *The Book of the Duchess* and *The Parliament of Fowls*, what was special in Chaucer's concept of love (and not his alone) was that if genuine it would last a lifetime. We might say it had been confused with marriage, even though detached from marriage. In practical life in the fourteenth-century royal court things were very different, but all the literature in French and especially English romances sustained the essentially adolescent and indeed noble ideal of absolute faithfulness in love for a lifetime. Tragedy came from the destruction of the ideal either by death or desertion.

Chaucer called his 'little book' about Troilus a 'tragedy', taking the word from Boethius and being the first to use it in English

(V, 1786). The story line is soon told. As already noted, Troilus falls in love with Criseyde: too shy and good to seduce her himself, they become true lovers helped by the machinations of Pandarus and enjoy three years of happiness. Their love is celebrated by a Boethian song of joy attributed to Troilus who wishes their love may be part of the harmony of the universe. Then Criseyde's father, Calkas, asks the Greeks to demand her in exchange for a hostage and to Troilus's utter grief she is sent to the hostile Greek camp, refusing to elope with Troilus before. There she is seduced by the slick womaniser, Diomede, and eventually denies her love for Troilus. She laments her own 'untruth', her reputation to come as 'false Cressid'. Troilus remains true to her and dies in battle. By an astonishing reversal of the poet's narration he is then shown as ascending somewhere into the heavens and, looking down on those mourning for him on earth, laughs at such grief and all our blind desire for pleasure. The poet as Expositor comes forward at the very end, as he has done on other occasions to different effect, to condemn in Christian terms the pagan joy and goodness of love that earlier, especially in the third of his five books, he has seemed to praise. It is an ending whose inconsistency has caused much debate and even indignation.

So long and great a poem contains many elements that cannot be discussed here. Something about the characters and critical attitudes to them will go some way to the heart of the matter.

Chapter 15

Troilus and Criseyde II:
Characters and Critics

We rightly think about the characters of *Troilus and Criseyde* as if they were real people, however careful we may be to think in terms of the poet's art. There is no other way to discuss them, yet we must also take into account the poet's manner of presenting them. Most fundamentally we have to remember that we are dealing with a received story, a series of events, whose outline and outcome the poet could not change if it were to remain *that* story. We need also to remember the conventions, implicit and explicit. Many causal connections are omitted. Much that was taken for granted we miss, and we take for granted certain elements that did not exist, like the desire for complete consistency and unity in a work of art.

We may forget that we are dealing with a really different pre-industrial society, or alternatively insist too strongly that there is no such thing as a natural instinct, that all is 'socially', and consciously, 'constructed' in a character. But someone, some essential self somewhere, however rudimentary, has to begin the process of the creation of the person. Manners and sentiments and language change, as Chaucer himself points out (II, 29−49). In 1936 C. S. Lewis in *The Allegory of Love* argued against the fallacy of 'the unchanging human heart'. Different ages and people do feel and act differently. But as Chaucer and Lewis and many people in between them tell us, we must accept and sympathise with difference. We should not be less tolerant or curious than those Middle Ages which are so often accused of narrow-minded intolerance.

Criseyde is the character on whom most critics focus, because though she is necessarily passive and worked upon, the physical and psychological actions all centre on her. All the European tellings of her story, from earliest times to Shakespeare[1] with the possible exception of Chaucer, condemn her. As a heroine she fulfills the conventional and convincing requirements, which date back to the Greeks, of a beautiful woman: young, fair-haired, of medium height, of admired figure. Her fascination in Chaucer derives from his presentation of the slow progress of her love, led on by Pandarus, the trusting relationship with Troilus, her sorrow at parting, and the slow failure of her love for Troilus.

But for Chaucer and the structure of the poem the central interest is Troilus. In the end as at the beginning Criseyde is marginal, and unless we understand Troilus we shall miss the point. We shall also miss the point if we fail to sympathise with the complex values of love and constancy, both secular and religious, that underlie the poem, as profound a contemplation of love and time as that of Proust's in *A la recherche du temps perdu*, though a good deal clearer on the surface.

In Book I the main interest lies in the psychological state of Troilus, presented in terms of fourteenth-century love-sickness, and in the cajoling of Pandarus. In Book II the interest shifts to Criseyde when Pandarus visits her sitting with her ladies and hearing read the *Romance of Thebes*. We see Pandarus's affectionate teasing, his hints about good news, Criseyde's anxiety about the siege, her disappointment that the good news is only that a young man is in love with her. Pandarus leaves and she retires to her private room to think about it, not without some natural pleasure, but with no conceit. Then follows a passage which in its delicacy and ambiguity is essential to the development of the poem, but which has received such different interpretations that both the passage and the history of its criticism, deeply intertwined, require detailed consideration.

Criseyde, in her private thought, and on her own, then sees Troilus pass on his return from battle, in rich armour, but with his shield and helm battered, his horse wounded so that to spare it he rides slowly, cheered by the people, and altogether

So lik a man of armes and a knyght

(II, 631)

so young, brave, handsome, chivalrous, that she is intensely impressed – 'Who gave me drink?' (II, 651) she exclaims, referring to that powerful medieval image of feelings as a drink, whether a love-potion like that immortalised by Tristan and Yseult, or a drink of bitterness and suffering. She blushes and thinks that it would be a pity to slay such a one 'if that he mente trouthe' (II, 665), which again seems a natural, even sensible thing to think. Up till now the impressions upon Criseyde, from Pandarus's wily prompting to the sight of Troilus, have come from outside, and have been received with natural interest and cautious pleasure by Criseyde. Her wavering meditations are left for us to judge, if we want to. The poet does not appear to be directing our responses and in consequence we are left to follow with interest, without moralisation, and judge according to our own prepossessions and prejudices. These are her own private thoughts, unknown to anyone else except the here omniscient poet, not subject to social evaluation, tentative, totally uncommitted by action.

Now the poet breaks in to say that some envious person might think that this was a sudden love: how could she so quickly love at first sight? The poet, or at least the text, insists that it was not in fact sudden, but was first of all an inclination to like Troilus, through which love eventually 'mined' its way in. There was no sudden love.

Now myghte som envious jangle thus:	*envious person chatter*
'This was a sodeyn love; how myght it be	
That she so lightly loved Troilus	
Right for the firste syghte, ye, parde?'	*yes, by heaven*
Now whoso seith so, mote he nevere ythe	*may he never thrive*
For every thing a gynnyng hath it nede	*needs a beginning*
Er al be wroughte, withowten any drede.	*done; doubt*
For I seye nought that she so sodeynly	
Yaf hym hire love, but that she gan enclyne	
To like hym first, and I have told you whi;	
And after that, his manhod and his pyne	*torment*
Made love withinne hire for to myne	*mine*
For which by process and by good servyse	
He gat hir love, and in no sodeyn wyse.	*way*
	(II, 666–79)

Chaucer is here playing with sequential time as he does in a more general way throughout the whole poem. We see each moment of the action in the light of a larger sequence of consequences.

More immediately in this passage we have behind it the convention, and the fact, that young men or boys (Troilus being about 16 years old) can and do fall in love at first sight, but that chaste young women have more sense; or at least, appear to shy boys to have more sense. As we have seen, young women in Chaucer do not even love; they may eventually pity the successful suitor, and so reward him with the jewel of themselves. Chaucer also has to work against the audience's foreknowledge of Criseyde's unfaithfulness.

So Criseyde's response is important. We might well think that it was no sin to love Troilus at first sight. It might not be a sin, but it might be foolish. That was the understanding of the situation for many centuries, and there were good religious, social and practical reasons to justify female caution. Yet we all know that the heart has moods and inclinations entirely private, and at their beginning much better kept so. They may fade, or be mistaken. So a sensible young woman, in those days, and let us think of Criseyde, already a widow, as about 18 years old, when a young man said 'I love you', did not immediately believe him, or respond outwardly at all. The poet, it would seem, wants to preserve Criseyde from the least imputation of wantonness. She may have been married, for we all know, like the Wife of Bath, at the age of 12, to some 'old kaynard', but now he is dead, and unlike the Wife of Bath she is no merry or wanton widow. Chaucer is not telling us about such a one. In this he is going against the grain, both of his source in Boccaccio, in the earlier account in Latin by Guido, and later in Shakespeare. The nineteenth and early twentieth century shared Chaucer's sympathy, as I do, but post-war critics have implacably denigrated her. The change of view among twentieth-century critics is a most interesting spectacle.[2]

In his notable popular book published in 1915, G. L. Kittredge[3] takes the passage quoted quite straight. He follows the novelistic tradition of late nineteenth-century criticism, responding to characters as real persons, the source of the action. This is not quite true of traditional literature, where knowledge of what takes place precedes the creation of characters, so that Chaucer has partly to counter an early possible impression of what kind of a person Criseyde is. But the response to character as such is one of Chaucer's great achievements, and to Kittredge it looked as if here Chaucer is genuinely defending Criseyde. Or at least it did so until the advent of the New Criticism. As has been earlier mentioned (pp. 95–6) the New Criticism saw the essence of poetry as irony, and had no recognition of the oral, as opposed to the printed, basis of traditional poetry. The New Criticism retained the idea of a 'character' generating speech and action, but now it was often or usually to be understood ironically. The effect is to have two levels of meaning, implying two 'speakers': the simple, or stupid one who speaks the literal sense, and the real one, the poet. Hence a poem is often treated as implicitly a dramatic monologue, spoken by a fictitious person. In the nineteenth century Browning often used such a device, though his dramatic monologues were recognisably such. In the twentieth century the device has been imputed to Chaucer, and latterly to other poets, so that we have all poetry uttered by a Narrator, not a poet.

This question has already risen in connection with Chaucer's earlier poems, where the poet is indeed a character within his own poem. But criticism has extended the notion to *The Knight's Tale* and *Troilus and Criseyde*. Chaucer's active speaking, or imitation of speaking, the poem, as it were the dramatic Expositor, is a considerable justification for the idea of the Narrator, except that there is no reason to accuse the Expositor of being either a fool or an ironist. The modern notion of the foolish Narrator has been most popular in connection with *Troilus and Criseyde*, and has been deployed very effectively in criticism of the passage just quoted. Why, it is asked, should Chaucer try to defend Criseyde from the accusation of sudden love? We would not have brought it. The historical answer is that Chaucer is a genuine Expositor, who has to contend against an earlier characterisation of Criseyde as false, and that in the convention followed by Chaucer no truly lovable woman falls for a man at his first approach. She has to be won. The more modern answer is that Chaucer is being ironical. The passage therefore is now said to have two meanings: first, the superficial and false one of defence; second, the true one which by raising the question at all casts doubts on Criseyde's integrity. The superficial meaning is thought of as spoken by the simple-minded, naïve Narrator. The Narrator was effectively introduced by E. T. Donaldson in a brilliantly witty essay.[4]

The Narrator in Donaldson and in a huge number of critics ever since has a quite clear character. He is a bumbling fool. Donaldson describes the passage in question and particularly the poet's comment in such a characteristically witty way that by the time he has called it 'sententiously fuzzy', 'wordy', yet of 'laborious precision', indicating that the prurient Narrator is 'himself looking forward to the love affair' and finally 'much confounding' the reader's mind (all in his essay reprinted in *Speaking of Chaucer*, pp. 66–7) we have an apparently plausible yet in fact misleading character sketch of the Narrator as a dramatic character (both 'fuzzy' and 'precise') fumbling and bumbling his way onwards: but to what?

If Donaldson's brilliant exposition is analysed in cold blood, what is he really saying? Is he saying that the Narrator denies that Criseyde fell in love with deplorable suddenness because the Narrator is a fool who says what is the opposite of the poet's true meaning, which is that Criseyde really did fall in love with deplorable suddenness? And if she genuinely fell in love, is that very shocking, especially to modern thought? But why should the poet's remark be attributed to a dramatic *persona* within the poem who has not so far been evoked? It assumes that no text is written in good faith. Why should the so-called Narrator's claim that Criseyde did not fall too rapidly in love make us suspicious unless we approach the text with hostility, as if we were interrogating a lying witness? This is what has been well called 'the hermeneutics of suspicion'.

Donaldson is a forerunner of Deconstruction in this respect. He is, in fact, not much interested in Criseyde. Donaldson's main interest is in the Narrator. He says that Criseyde 'is seen almost wholly from the point of view of a Narrator who is too terribly anxious to see only the best in her and not to see the worst even when it is staring both us and him in the face . . .' (p. 68). Donaldson devotes the next few pages to the Narrator's favourable treatment of Criseyde and argues that here Chaucer interferes with the work of his Narrator whom he says 'He has created not quite in his own image' (p. 68). How does Donaldson know what is the degree of likeness between Chaucer the poet and his Narrator? Above all, how do we tell when it is the poet speaking and not the Narrator (or *vice versa*)? Donaldson inadvertently, like every other critic, sometimes speaks of the poet himself as origin of the narrative, without telling us in any way how we know when either the poet or the foolish Narrator is speaking. The short answer for almost every critic is that when they wish to put an interpretation on the text contrary to what the text says, they attribute the text to the Narrator and distort its meaning. Donaldson argues that the Narrator strives laboriously to palliate Criseyde's behaviour and goes on 'Chaucer standing behind him jogs his elbow, causing him to fall into verbal imprecision or into anti-climax or making his rhetoric deficient, or making it redundant – generally doing these things in such a way that the reader will be encouraged almost insensibly to see Criseyde in a light quite different from the one that the Narrator is so earnestly trying to place her in' (p. 69).

In short, when Chaucer is writing what is in Donaldson's view bad poetry we recognise that the Narrator is speaking. Our passage about 'sudden love' is now strangely characterised, like many other passages in the poem, as instances of 'rhetorical failure'. To read those many critics following Donaldson's line you would think that practically all of *Troilus and Criseyde* is bad poetry, because it is the expression of the Narrator. We are never told how to distinguish between the good and the bad poetry except by Donaldson's criteria, and Donaldson's criteria are the criteria of an advanced print culture as expressed in the local and now *passé* form of the New Criticism. They totally disregard the nature of that oral poetry which Chaucer so assiduously imitates, and where he had his roots. To deplore 'sententiousness' or 'repetitiousness' (redundancy) is to apply the criteria of print to orality, and to beg the question of what is good poetry. Sometimes anything sensible, sympathetic and easily recognised as such qualifies as bad poetry.

The strange paradox of Donaldson's essay is that though he proclaims how fond he is of Criseyde he uses the concept of the Narrator remorselessly to call her into question and to condemn her. For him 'the woman's a whore, and that's an end on't'. Whenever the text excuses her, Donaldson attributes it to a sentimental foolish Narrator who has got the story wrong.

There are so many mysteries about the Narrator. We are told 'He does not let himself appear in the woefully pathetic scene between Criseyde and her uncle' (p. 73). How do we know he is 'there', if he does not let himself 'appear'? If such is really the case, however, this would argue some artistic subtlety on the part of the Narrator telling the story but concealing that very fact. Is this the same bumbling sentimentalist who so clumsily intrudes elsewhere? How do we know that it is the Narrator (not the poet) who is narrating but not appearing? What verbal or other signals are there? Is an indication of the self-concealing Narrator the absence of the first personal pronoun? Apparently straightforward descriptions without the first personal pronoun are attributed to the Narrator (e.g. Book V, 180–2). But in other places the text contains the word 'I' and is attributed to the Narrator, as in the passage we began by considering (II, 673). Donaldson implacably persecutes Criseyde through the figure of the Narrator. He does it by attributing a deliberate effort on the part of Chaucer the poet to write bad poetry in order to signal to the reader not to take seriously remarks favourable to Criseyde. This could be thought of as dramatic poetry of a sort, but it is very strange. In fact, it is nonsense. But it fits strangely well into the centuries' long denigration of Criseyde, to which Chaucer is such an interesting exception.

The other great Chaucer critic, almost contemporary with Donaldson, is Charles Muscatine whose *Chaucer and the French Tradition* (1957) has been immensely influential as an instrument of the New Criticism.[5]

When Muscatine writes 'Chaucer handles (Troilus) functionally . . . Troilus is described in conventional hyperbolical terms', Muscatine appears to be writing about Chaucer the poet, and is surely correct. But after that song for which Muscatine tells us 'Chaucer [*sic*] adapts a sonnet of Petrarch', we find that the poem is being told by a Narrator. It turns out not to be Chaucer after all who describes the characters. The narrative of the poem is in the hands of a character who is closely related to the fictional action like the first person Narrators of the dream poems. The Narrator turns out to be a character inside the poem, though oddly enough none of the other characters notice or, as they well might want to, object to his presence. (They never notice or speak to him, or engage with him on the same level of fiction, or any other.) So that the hyperbole by which Troilus is described is after all not Chaucer's but the Narrator's and the Narrator is said to exist within the fiction to such an extent that he could, though as it happens he never does, interact with the other characters. According to Muscatine, the Narrator is also a commentator and of course stupid. For example, we have 'the Narrator's apparent obtuseness' (p. 136). But why is it only apparent? Is the Narrator really being clever? It is true that Muscatine calls the Narrator a 'fugitive' character (p. 137), and indeed this is the trouble. He comes and goes and who is to know apart from the critic whence and when he does so? There are no verbal signals at all to tell us when we are to understand he is speaking; only the critic's say-so. In practice Muscatine often, as in his superb discussion of Pandarus, totally forgets the Narrator but then on other occasions Muscatine uses the Narrator to condemn the principal characters.

Muscatine's interpretation of the key passage with which this discussion has begun is closely similar to Donaldson's. The Narrator is deliberately querying Criseyde because he is a mouthpiece of somebody or other. As Muscatine points out, in the twelfth-century poem *Eneas* 'There is no question of the suddenness of Love's assault' on the heroine, but when we come to our key passage in *Troilus and Criseyde* he says 'Chaucer's Narrator complicates the effect'. He says 'The dramatic action and the editorial comment together produce a kind of controlled ambiguity that is increasingly apparent as the poem progresses' (p. 155). This remark is itself highly ambiguous. But since the Narrator must, in his stupidity, be different from the poet, we are presumably meant to understand that the poet condemns Criseyde. Or is the Narrator, stupid as he is, the same as the poet? The critic takes a strong moral line in condemning Criseyde – Muscatine and Donaldson have much less sympathy for her than has the Narrator, or of course, in my opinion, Chaucer, or myself.

Almost every later critic who discusses *Troilus and Criseyde* takes up the view presented by Donaldson and Muscatine, frequently quoting what has now become this key passage from which we have started, and repeating the same judgement.[6]

The Narrator in one essay is said to treat Criseyde in Book II with 'bantering hostility'. The concept of the Narrator always results in denigrating Criseyde. Winthrop Wetherbee's *Chaucer and the Poets* (1984) is the culmination of the general development.[7] The Narrator is described as the principal character in the poem. His development has proceeded by fits and starts and the poem is a character study of the Narrator who now happily emerges with a new-found sense of purpose. In this last stage he achieves a perspective on poetry itself (p. 20). Presumably, since at the beginning of the poem when the poet insists on the sadness of the story, it must here be Chaucer the poet himself who is speaking, how we know that the poet gives way to the Narrator in the fourth stanza is unclear. It turns out later that the Narrator knows Dante. But there are multiple other confusions of narrative level.

Wetherbee argues that the characters are controlled by somebody or other 'like a Broadway director'. What is the poet doing? Where is the Narrator standing on this Broadway stage? He is said to cast aspersions on Criseyde's sudden love and to continue speaking up to line II, 686. The next line begins 'Now lat us stynte of Troilus a throwe.' This stanza so begun uses the word 'I' and introduces comments on Criseyde's state of mind followed by her long internal soliloquy. It is a marvellously delicate passage. It is not in fact attributed by Wetherbee to the Narrator. Who tells it? Can it be the poet Chaucer? When did 'the Broadway director', who could have but did not control his leading lady, take over, and when did he withdraw? When does the stupid Narrator appear and when does he disappear, though he is regarded as the detractor of Criseyde in our significant lines? To take yet another example, Elizabeth Salter[8] attributes the same few lines to the Narrator without telling us how and when he comes in, and says his comment is quite gratuitous. Whatever does this mean? Does it mean that it is wrong, and that we should disregard it? What then is its function there? Is this a defence of Criseyde, against the Narrator's attack? Have we here a justification of Criseyde, made against the assumed grain of the text? What then is the status of the text?

Rather surprisingly, the recent tidal wave of feminist criticism which ought to have drowned the misogynistic Narrator allows the Narrator still to float. Dinshaw's *Chaucer's Sexual Poetics* (1989), for example, takes the usual line on the passage concerned.[9] She speaks of − I quote again − 'the Narrator's interjection in Book II, his defence of Criseyde against potential detractors [which] functions to close gaps that haven't even opened': it is said to be a massive explanatory effort designed to answer questions before they have arisen (that is, questions that begin to nag the Narrator himself). Feminist criticism would do well to rescue Criseyde from unjust misogynistic criticism by abandoning the device of the Narrator, and some more recent criticism has begun to do so.[10]

What then are we to make of the presentation of Criseyde? The great advance made by the New Criticism, leaving aside the critical brilliance of Donaldson and Muscatine, was to make us aware, through the paradoxically misleading device of the Narrator, seen as a character *in* the fiction, albeit invisible to, unheard by, the other characters, of the artistry and perhaps the artifice of the poet. Much of the wealth of meaning in Chaucer's poetry does come from what may be called irony, but is preferably called ambiguity. Irony can be quite definite, and the clash between overt and covert, or manifest and latent, meanings can be quite sharply defined. Ambiguity is not so clear. It is not vague. It is the sense of multiple possibilities within the poet's words, of several implications. It is an open figure, with some relation to metaphor and is perhaps the equivalent of metaphor. Chaucer's poetry relies much less on metaphor than does that of Romantic and later poets, but much on ambiguities whose elements can, paradoxically, often be quite clearly defined.

THE AMBIGUITY OF CRISEYDE

Ambiguity is of the essence of Criseyde. Chaucer presents a character quite different from the beautiful lusty young widow of Boccaccio. Since he takes over her story there is, as often in the retelling of a traditional story, as noted elsewhere, as it were a gap between the action (which is predetermined by the story) and the character as reconceived by the present storyteller. (The same thing happens quite frequently in Shakespeare though there is no space to develop that argument here.) As modern people we are passionately interested in linking cause to effect, in analysing causes, establishing motives and origins. Hence the interest in psychoanalysis, since motives and causes of action in people are deeply mysterious. Hence also modern introspectiveness. Earlier literature has not developed the same self-consciousness. Characterisation as such follows simple stereotypes and the subtleties we are aware of are more readily to be found built into the story structures, as I have argued elsewhere.[11] But Chaucer, like Shakespeare, is quite remarkable for his interest in individual characterisation. He is often surprisingly modern, though unsurprisingly not always, and not always in ways we expect. *Troilus and Criseyde* has often, since the nineteenth century, been thought of as a novel, and it is easy to see why. The three main characters, Troilus, Criseyde and Pandarus, are reconceived by Chaucer as quite different from the stereotypes presented by Boccaccio. Criseyde is the most interesting to us. Troilus, as will be shown in a moment, is based on a different stereotype of an ideal, well realised and seen with unusual inwardness. Pandarus arises from the necessities for the plot of the changed characters of Troilus and Criseyde and is best noticed as he functions in the course of the story.

In medieval culture the roles of the sexes, or as modern style prefers to call them, 'genders', are clearly defined at all levels of society. The ideal for a young aristocratic woman was to be a virgin until married, then faithful to, virtually the property of, her husband. The virginal ideal is even exaggerated by Chaucer in such poems as *The Book of the Duchess* and *Palamon and Arcite*. She is passive as to action, but powerful as an icon of ideal beauty and goodness. Inactive herself, placed 'on a pedestal' by young male adorers, she is the source of even frenzied action by the young men, as *Palamon and Arcite* illustrates to an extreme extent. Their love derives more from the subjective biological compulsion within young men and its idealising tendencies than the objective unique beauty and goodness of the young woman. Others can observe her without being transported – a phenomenon that Troilus himself notices and derides at the beginning of the poem before he is suddenly stricken by his own obsession with Criseyde. This is not to deny the real beauty, charm and goodness of many young women, or deride the natural attraction of these qualities for young men. They are the natural, we may even say transhistorical base, on which the culture constructs further qualities, or on which young men, more precisely, build further fantasies. The experience of being in love is not given to all, but to those to whom it comes it may well be the most significant, or at least, the most memorable, experience of their lives. In everyday life it comes to women as well, but in Chaucer's poetry, as perhaps in fourteenth-century courtly culture generally, it is limited to men. Chaucer's genius in *Troilus and Criseyde* is to show in Criseyde a realistic, inner-directed, domestic portrayal of the medieval heroine who becomes a realised young woman in a conceivable society. Being a beautiful young woman she is, as she says of herself,

I am myn owene womman, wel at ese –
I thank it God – as after myn estate   *with regard to my wealth and rank*

Right yong, and stonde unteyd in lusty leese,   *free in pleasant pastures*
Withouten jalousie or swich debate: *argument*
Shal noon housbonde seyn to me 'Chek mat',
For either they ben ful of jalousie,
Or maisterfull, or loven novelrie.   *new lovers*

(II, 750–6)

This meditative speech, put very convincingly in Criseyde's thoughts – she clearly has no regrets for her husband – illustrates the constraints put on married women, from which she is free. Yet she also reflects, why should she not love, she is not a nun, especially as she is beloved by the worthiest of knights, provided she herself always keeps 'myn honour and my name' (II, 762). Then she goes on to reflect what a miserable constraint love itself may be. Much of this is suggested by Boccaccio's text which undoubtedly helped Chaucer here, but he refines and elaborates her thoughts and sets the passage in an extended context partly formed by Pandarus's persuasions which are entirely Chaucer's invention. In particular, as Chaucer and Boccaccio both see, she is caught between on one side the urgent persuasions of Troilus and the cunning devices of Pandarus, and on the other her vulnerability as a woman and the demands by her society on her honour.

In the brief summing up of the characters of Troilus, Criseyde and Diomede – significantly not Pandarus – that Chaucer later provides, she is fully and beautifully praised, and said to be

Tendre herted, slydynge of corage.

(V, 825)

To be 'slydynge of corage', 'changeable' is a comment on how she has behaved, rather than a description of her character. The comment is not in Boccaccio and Chaucer probably drew the suggestion for it from earlier tellers of the story, but it is not, as some have taken it, *the* key to her character, not 'a fatal flaw'. It is part of the general vulnerability and passivity forced upon a tender-hearted woman. But she herself recognises that she has lost her honour, which is her loyalty to Troilus (V, 1058–85), and the poet continues independently of Boccaccio

Ne me ne list this sely womman chyde   *I do not wish; simple*
Forther than the storye wol devyse . . .   *narrate*
And if I myghte excuse hire any wise,   *in any way*

For she so sory was for hire untrouthe
Iwis I wolde excuse hire yet for routhe.   *certainly; pity*
                                                              (VI, 1093 . . . 9)

The teller of a received story is constrained by its general course, and
it is the general course of the story which has attracted the teller to
tell it again, however he modifies it. And the teller takes an attitude
towards his own recreated characters. There seems no reason to take
this statement by the poet as an ironic condemnation of Criseyde or
as a peculiarly fatuous remark by a foolish and uncomprehending
Narrator within the fiction. It sums up the ambiguity inherent in
Criseyde, that such a person should behave in such a way. There is
no reason why we ourselves should not pity Criseyde, and, like
Troilus, continue to love her, nor any reason why we should not
believe that the poet's pity is genuine.

TROILUS

There can be no ambiguity, or ambivalence, on the other hand, in
Troilus's attitude to Criseyde. It is the nature of his obsession, and
one still found at times in actual life, that whatever she does he
cannot stop loving her 'a quarter of a day' (V, 1698). But if there
have been differences in the judgements on Criseyde there have been
even wider differences in the judgement of Troilus, as Western soci-
ety in the late twentieth century has oscillated in value-judgements
and largely abandoned those of previous centuries.[12] Judgements
of Troilus in particular have varied. Windeatt gives an admirable
account of his character, and a summary of varied reactions.[13] For
centuries Troilus was seen, if commented on at all, as the noble
if tragic lover, 'true Troilus'. Then he was derided, for example, by
D. W. Robertson, along with all medieval lovers, as the stereotype
of foolish immorality, sexual love being so regarded by many medi-
eval theologians and apparently by Robertson himself. A number
of critics have found Troilus extravagantly self-indulgent in grief,
or unduly timid. Lambert finds him boringly and exasperatingly
faithful.[14] More recently political feminist critics have condemned him
and his whole male-dominated culture as predatory, lustful, insecure,
competitive, selfish, so emotional as to 'invite psychoanalytical atten-
tion', little better than a rapist. His love is continually called in ques-
tion by being placed within quotation marks, 'love'.[15] By contrast,
most of my young women students used to regard him as a feeble
creature, 'a poor sap', 'a wimp'. There is some justification for all

these views if we stand back outside Chaucer's culture and judge by purely modern standards. But that is not the best way to understand what Chaucer means.

Not all recent critics have despised Troilus. Donaldson, for example, emphasises Troilus's *trouthe*. Mann notably expounds the growth of a trusting relationship between Troilus and Criseyde, and I myself have always maintained that he is a sympathetic and noble figure.[16] We have to remember that he lived in a small agrarian-based society, which was, like almost all such societies, to repeat the simple truth yet again, hierarchical, aggressive, male-dominated, religious, with various other, to us, socially deplorable characteristics. Troilus fits the pattern of an idealised and idealistic young man in such a society. Although it cannot be true that individuals are entirely 'constructed' by society, for 'society' is not an entity with a single will but a complex of forces, many of them being mutually inconsistent individual wills and choices, it is nevertheless obviously true that we are all largely formed by the multiple influences of the societies we live in. We who live in liberal bourgeois democracies, where tolerance is a main virtue, must tolerate less tolerant, archaic societies, such as the archaic societies of the Middle Ages.[17] A study of Troilus in this spirit shows what Chaucer calls 'manhood' and that Troilus accords with it. Troilus's manhood is a more delicate and complex condition than the word 'masculinity' implies, though 'masculinity' as a concept, rather than as a quality, has been frequently referred to in the criticism of the late 1990s, and is often condemned by critics.

YOUTH, ROYALTY AND MANHOOD IN THE FOURTEENTH CENTURY

'Masculinity' as a word has become prominent as a product, appropriately enough, of feminism and gender-studies. Though first recorded in English in 1748 it has not been much used, and when used it has often had slightly derogatory, and French, connotations. Now it seems to be used as an apparently value-free scientific term, though it tends to retain its disagreeable – and French – associations, for example with violence.[18] It has also tended to be used, along with the adjective 'masculine', with specifically sexual implications. Thus Aers writes of what he describes as Troilus's fantasies of rape, and of his swoon at Criseyde's bedside, that they are 'the product of "drede" (III, 706–7), fear lest his masculine identity so heavily dependent on performance in the sexual domain, might not, as it were, stand up' (129). There is simply no evidence nor any reason to suppose that Troilus may fear sexual impotence. His love is naturally sexual, and Chaucer makes of it also a social and personal construct, and superstructure, of great complexity. Troilus's 'masculinity' is better described by Chaucer's word (and that of many later English writers) as 'manhood'. That, and the equivalent word 'manliness', were both used until very recently to express the ideal behaviour men should aim at. It was not primarily sexual in implication.

To be in love is not essential to Troilus's identity, nor to the general concept of manhood. He is fully himself when he is seen at the beginning of the poem 'guiding' his young knights, looking at ladies, and mocking lovers. It is typical of adolescent boys' behaviour. Equally typical is his precipitate falling in love. The poem is remarkable for the way it constructs Troilus's love and manhood to give an individual cast to the ancient ideal of the brave man who is a 'lion in the field and a lamb in the hall'.[19]

It is important to recognise Chaucer's assumption of Troilus's youth, already noted, but to be emphasised. His behaviour might be thought more extravagant in a man of 25 than in one of 16, though men of all ages may make fools of themselves in love, as Theseus remarks (*CT*, I, 1799). And royalty always has a certain recognised licence. It will be remembered that when John of Gaunt, Chaucer's contemporary, married the Duchess Blanche at the age of 19, he had already had a mistress and an illegitimate child (above, p. 79).

English courtly society in the fourteenth century is the setting of *Troilus and Criseyde* and it was dominated by adolescent values in all their vigour, generosity, petulance, passionate egoism. These values are not limited to the period of adolescence, but that is their period of greatest prominence, and even today most modern popular fiction is dominated by them. Adolescence is probably the most interesting and intense period of our lives. The actual concept of adolescence did not exist in medieval thought, though 'youth' was recognised. Our modern notions of adolescence were then subsumed into young manhood.[20] Clerics might disapprove of most of these values but had little notice taken of them then as now. Even older men and women subscribed to them. Ideals of romantic love and extravagant bravery were shared by all, if not practised, as is the way with ideals now as then. Princes had their mistresses and took part personally in battles from an early age.

Edward III asserted his position as king by a coup against his mother's lover, Mortimer, in which he personally took part when he was 17, in 1330. He had married Philippa of Hainault when he was 16 and she probably 14, in 1328, a political marriage but something of a love-match too. Their son Edward the Black Prince (so called from the sixteenth century onwards) was born in 1330. In 1346 he at least nominally commanded the right wing and vanguard of the army in the great victory of the English at Crécy. He distinguished himself in the hand-to-hand fighting, and though he was at one time beaten to his knees and almost captured, he recovered and showed the great physical strength, bravery and skill of the Plantagenet line. The poem *Wynnere and Wastoure*, composed only a few years after, describes him in splendid armour and says 'he was ȝongest of ȝeris and ȝapest [liveliest] of wit' (119). All this at the age of 16.[21] He did not marry until he was 31, but by then had an illegitimate son. His brother, John of Gaunt, born in 1340, took part in Edward III's campaign in 1359–60, as did Chaucer, born about the same date or a little later. Gaunt took a leading part in the fighting in December, aged 19, and it will be recalled that even Chaucer, whom we may suspect was no fighting man, strayed sufficiently close to the enemy to be taken prisoner. Richard II, born January 1367, became king in 1377. In June 1381, aged 14, he gallantly confronted the rebellious peasants at Smithfield when men in his entourage, much older in years, seem to have been stricken with fear.[22] In 1385 Richard headed an army which invaded Scotland and devastated Edinburgh. In 1382 aged 15 he married Anne of Bohemia who was 16. At her death in 1394 he raged tempestuously and had their favourite palace at Sheen destroyed. Richard's behaviour was more extravagantly emotional than Troilus's, and he was then 27.

Troilus fits well into this pattern of behaviour of royal princes. Chaucer goes out of his way to emphasise his fighting prowess. True, he is second to Hector as 'holder up of Troye' (II, 644), but no one could displace Hector from his supreme position in any version of the Troy story. To be second only to Hector is the highest praise. There is nothing realistically unlikely about Troilus's return from battle, looking as knightly a sight as Mars the god of battle, and well able to attract Criseyde's admiration,

> So lik a man of armes and a knyght
> He was to seen, fulfilled of heigh prowess,
> For both he had a body and a myght
> To don that thing, as wel as hardynesse;
> And ek to seen hym in his gere hym dresse
> So fressh, so yong, so weldy semed he   *vigorous*
> It was an heven upon hym for to see.

(II, 631–7)

The admiration expressed in the text here has no signs of irony, and there is no need of an uncomprehending Narrator. The admiration accords with the ideals of the time. Troilus's helm and shield are cut to pieces (and surely it is perverse to read this as symbolic of his psychic vulnerability, any more than of a young fighter-pilot in 1940 returning to base with his plane full of bullet holes). The people cry out in his praise

> For which he wex a litel reed for shame   *modesty*
> When he the peple upon hym herde cryen
> That to byholde it was a noble game
> How sobrelich he caste down his yën.   *eyes*
>   (II, 645–8)

No one has so far suggested that all this is meant ironically as spoken by the stupid Narrator in order to denigrate Troilus, though that critical method has been frequently employed in the adjacent lines in order to denigrate Criseyde. The description sums up Troilus's manly prowess in terms of unequivocal, and natural praise – that being the only mode of thought open to Chaucer. There is a genuine touch of non-ironical genial humour in observing Troilus's entirely proper embarrassment, youthful for all his manliness.

History provides an interesting real-life analogue to this princely embarrassment. After the victory at Crécy the king asked prince Edward what he thought of going into battle and fighting, and whether he thought it good sport. The prince according to the chronicler 'said nothing and was ashamed [*honteux*]'.[23] This shame was modest embarrassment, not the humiliation of conscious wrong-doing. He had done extremely well, like Troilus. All the passage describing Troilus's return from battle is Chaucer's invention, fully in accordance with contemporary courtly and chivalric culture. Boccaccio does not provide this glamorous spectacle of Troilus as a basis for Criseyde's musings on Pandarus's information about his love for her. After hearing his praise, then seeing him, she naturally rehearses to herself his good qualities, including his handsomeness and *gentilesse*, and most of all that 'his distress was all for her' (II, 659–65). In other words, the sight of him is connected with all the praise given to him by Pandarus, and her own social knowledge of him, including the fact that he loves her. The poet is then looking forward to Criseyde's eventual love for him says that eventually it was 'his manhod and his pyne (i.e. torment)' (II, 676) that made her love him. The two qualities, manliness and the pain of love, are significantly joined here: neither one without the other would be enough. That he suffers for her is a guarantee of his love for her, but here we may first note the emphasis on 'manhood'. It is 'manliness', not simple 'sex-appeal'.

TROILUS'S MANHOOD

The reference to 'manhood' just quoted is the first ever made in Chaucer's work and has no counterpart in Boccaccio. A second follows at a most interesting stage in Book III, after Troilus, lying sick in bed, has had a satisfactory interview with Criseyde in the house of Deiphebus. It is not true that Troilus has feigned illness, 'For I am sick in ernest, douteles' (II, 1529) as he says.

Muscatine long ago pointed out an interesting partial analogue for Troilus's taking to his bed and his interview with Criseyde.[24] It is the story of Amnon's love for his half-sister Tamar (II *Samuel*, 13), which according to D. W. Robertson was well known in the fourteenth century. The first point to note is that Amnon is reported to be genuinely 'sick for his sister Tamar' and becomes noticeably lean (v. 4). In this Troilus resembles him. There is nothing feigned or unmanly in being sick for love of a woman. The second point to note is the great contrast between Troilus and Amnon. Amnon commits a rape. Troilus is so overcome with love and shyness that he forgets all the fine words he has prepared. The poet, and the reader, both a little distanced from the character though seeing as it were over his shoulder may be a little amused at this, but the poet tells us that Criseyde liked him none the less well for it, as seems natural enough.

Since she therefore to some extent accepts him, Troilus is cured of love-sickness and burns with sharp desire of hope and plesaunce, but 'He nought forgat his goode governaunce' (III, 427).

This self-controlled Troilus is a different side of his character, consequent on the certainty of being loved. He continues to do his full duty as a soldier though he suffers the pains of love. All this is Chaucer's own, from III, 428 to III, 1295. These lines take the place of stanzas 21 to 29 Parte Seconda in Boccaccio's *Filostrato*, in which Criseida makes arrangements to let Troilo secretly into the house and swiftly goes to bed with him. Chaucer has nothing of this. The actual arrangements are made by Pandarus. Criseyde is entirely innocent of them. Boccaccio's stanzas 30 to 32 relate his Criseida's flirtatious coyness in abandoning her last garment, which Chaucer follows only at a great and discreet distance in III, 1296–1316.

The long, beautiful, complex account by Chaucer of 'sweet, reluctant, amorous delay', including Troilus's swoon, has been much discussed, notably by Jill Mann[25] who illustrates most clearly the dilemma and conflicting feelings in Troilus, torn between desire and honourable refusal to coerce. This is manhood, the manliness which includes gentleness, generosity and if necessary self-sacrifice. It is referred to by Mann as exemplifying 'the feminised hero', whose role is passive, who forbears coercion, and whose surrender to love is the sign of a noble generosity. 'Feminised' does not mean 'effeminate'.[26] Convincing as is Mann's exposition here, the word 'feminised' has its dangers as well as its virtues. It is valuable in pointing out the possession by Troilus of those sterling virtues of constancy, patience, gentleness, goodness and fortitude which Chaucer more frequently incarnates in women, but it may lead us to forget how seriously the traditional male stereotype for many centuries also incarnated these same virtues in the chivalric ideal of manliness, which included being a 'lamb in the hall' and in which domineering sexual prowess has no part. The example of the Knight in the *General Prologue* to the *Canterbury Tales*, so powerful a fighter, so 'gentil' in ordinary life, is highly relevant. The ideal is reiterated in the poet's praise of Troilus as a 'manly' knight. When Criseyde has her second glimpse of Troilus passing by, 'God woot wher he was lik a manly knyght' (II, 1263), he appeals to her the more in that he humbly salutes her and blushes. She is aware of his *gentilesse*. There is a combination of traditional chivalric virtues here, of the lion and the lamb. Later, with similar oxymoron, Troilus displays 'manly sorwe' before Criseyde. The last use of the word 'manly' in the poem tells how Troilus, when he prepares to ride out with Criseyde when she is handed over to the Greeks 'gan his wo ful manly for to hide' (V, 30). He continues to conceal his sorrow as far as the public is concerned, though the poet gives us full access to his private sorrow in his letters to Criseyde and his talk with Pandarus, so that we have perhaps too strong a sense of self-indulgent grief.

Troilus refuses to carry off Criseyde when he learns that she will be sent to the Greeks. True, he weeps, and Pandarus, whose ideas of manhood are simpler, says why don't you simply elope with her? But Criseyde refuses and Troilus too rejects the notion for good practical reasons, and because of his respect for Criseyde's honour and her own refusal.

Honour is a very complex notion, different for men and women. If Troilus ran off with Criseyde it would ruin her honour but not affect his, because women's honour depends on sexual faithfulness and men's honour depends primarily on their bravery. This is very unequal, but is the way of the world in all pre-industrial societies. The theme of honour is very important in the poem,[27] but Criseyde's honour is the crucial matter. She is in a terrible bind. Even her affair

with Troilus if known would destroy her honour. Hence their re-
fusal to act in a way that would acknowledge the affair. Chaucer
consistently emphasises Troilus's bravery, and by implication his
honour, but that is not in question nor, as Chaucer says, what the
poem is about (V, 1765–9). What distinguishes Troilus is that under
the guidance of love he himself will not seduce Criseyde. On the
contrary he yields to her all power. The superiority, the 'governance',
of the beloved lady, and the humility of the lover are part of the
convention of romantic love, part of Chaucer's 'medievalising' the
Filostrato, as C. S. Lewis remarked,[28] but conventional as they may
be, it is important to recognise that the lady's status is genuinely
superior and humility in love is genuine in Troilus. His surrender of
all power to Criseyde is not feeble but is the product of choice and
self-control. It prevents him from carrying her off to save her from
being sent to the Greeks. So she goes to the Greeks.

To call it 'surrender' may inadvertently suggest unwilling capitu-
lation. It is true that Troilus is said to be hit by the arrow of the
god of love (I, 209), 'For may no man fordon the lawe of kynde'
(i.e. of nature) (I, 238). His passion is entirely natural and to that
extent involuntary. Love spared him in no way 'But held him as his
thral lowe in destresse' (I, 439). Yet equally Troilus's own thought
and intention develop his passion. Following his first sight of Criseyde
there are a couple of hundred lines, partly suggested by Boccaccio
and partly original with Chaucer, tracing most delicately the balance
of involuntary and voluntary love, and the way that Troilus reorgan-
ises his actions in the service of love, as for example his increase of
ferocity against the Greeks, not because he hates them, but in order
to please Criseyde better with his renown (I, 477–83). All this is
interlarded by the poet with half-humorous warnings about love,
both its irresistibility and its danger. In the course of this almost
Proustian passage about love it is said of Troilus, 'Thus took he
purpos loves craft to suwe' (i.e. to follow) (I, 379).

In these matters nature and nurture (or culture) interact. Troilus is
represented as a more than willing victim of natural impulses but he
equally naturally *chooses* to follow the combined natural and social
construction. Too much has been written misleadingly about 'the
code of courtly love', but there is indeed a literary social construct,
of behaviour in love, without being an external compulsion, that
Troilus follows. It is best illustrated by Chaucer's interesting short
poem now called *The Complaint of Venus*, translated with considerable
alteration from a poem by Oton de Graunson. The 'complaint' is to
Love about jealousy. It is spoken by a lady expressing her own love

and praising the knight she loves. It could be Criseyde speaking at the height of their love about Troilus whom she praises, in its applicability. The conventionality is here of value as establishing the norm. Every wight, says the lady, praises the knight's *gentilesse* (three times repeated). The lady takes pleasure in thinking of his honour, nobility, humility, *gentilesse*, and dear purchase of noble suffering, down to loss of appetite and 'change of hewe and contenaunce' (31), just as Troilus 'changes his hue' 'sixty times a day' (I, 441). Conventional this may be but also authentic. Love-sickness was a recognised ailment,[29] and does not indicate Troilus's lack of manliness. Its symptoms could be hypocritically imitated, as Diomede shows, but though that may be 'manly' in one sense, it is a world away from Troilus's manly and knightly *trouthe*, i.e. his loyalty in love.

Troilus's total devotion has been called the 'infantilisation of Troilus, a desire to be bound', 'a desire for a metaphysical seigneur', while of Troilus's Boethian meditation in the temple it has been remarked that 'Reading the Boethianizing attempt in Book IV it is hard not to conclude that no form of thumb-sucking, however sophisticatedly abstract, could defend the knight against the anxieties that flood over him.'[30] The imputation of anxiety to men has become a fashionable critical ploy by which the attribution of anxiety is made yet another cause for condemnation. Anxiety is a natural feeling. It is quite reasonable, indeed, quite sensible, to feel some kind of anxiety about all sorts of real or potential difficulties and threats. The biological value of such anxiety is that it may prompt us to take some evasive or remedial action. Aers is correct in saying that Troilus, foreseeing the loss of Criseyde, is anxious. Troilus does then propose various remedies, all of which she rejects. There is no justification in the text for attributing to him nameless and by implication childish, and by further implication reprehensible, fears. Quite the reverse: once Troilus is in love 'Alle other dredes weren from him fledde/Both of th'assege and his savacioun' (I, 663–4). The poem is quite explicit that love drives out other even legitimate and appropriate anxieties.

Troilus's only desire is for Criseyde's

> compassioun
> And he to be hire man whil he may dure –
> Lo, here his lif, and from the deth his cure.

(I, 467–9)

Troilus may suffer from being in love but his love focuses his desire and relieves him, says the poet, of all other anxiety. When he wins

Criseyde's love he has no anxiety at all. In Criseyde's own terms (IV, 1674–8) Troilus's 'gentil herte and manhod', and that his 'resoun bridlede [his] delit [i.e. sexual appetite]' and his 'moral vertu grounded upon trouthe' are so fully built into his character, such a combination of a noble nature and a consciously idealistic nurture, 'following the art of love', that he has no choice but to be himself, and this is the essence of both his misery and his manliness. The tragedy of Troilus is caused by his virtue, that is his 'trouthe' and his 'gentil manhode', not by any moral flaw. So the reader may think in reading the story, and as I believe Chaucer intended. Yet other readings are possible. Troilus himself in the long philosophical soliloquy in Book IV (based directly on Boethius) comes to the conclusion that he has no free will and that

> Thus to ben lorn, it is my destinee.   *lost*
>
>   (IV, 959)

This long soliloquy is far from characteristic 'thumbsucking'. It is not realistic characterisation in order to represent Troilus as a philosophical young man. He certainly is not. Nor of course is it a joke by any Narrator. It represents in wide terms one of the underlying problems both of life and of telling a known story: what degree of personal freedom do human beings possess? The soliloquy is put in Troilus's mouth as representing his feelings, not as realistic expression. It discusses one of several questions underlying the poem. The answer that the poet might give is not so simple as Troilus's, but maybe Troilus is right. A modern view of his situation could be that he is the victim of an extreme example of the kind of involuntary sexual obsession that many (not all) men suffer from, and call it love. Most men either recover from or at least contain the obsession, but not quite all. In Troilus's case, if he is really subject to an irresistible obsession, then there is no virtue in his 'trouthe'. He cannot help but love Criseyde, as he says himself. We might argue in a modernistic way that he could only have maintained the virtue of 'trouthe', of loyalty and stability, if he had fallen *out* of love with Criseyde, and yet remained true to her even if, perhaps, he had fallen in love with another lady. It may be with some perception of this that Aers derides his philosophising as 'philosophical thumbsucking', as infantilism, excessive reliance on 'the mother'. Aers too sees Troilus as a 'wimp'.

In the concept of 'fine amour', of total devotion to the 'service' and the 'worship' of a woman there may arise a dangerously filial element. This can be faintly seen even in *The Book of the Duchess* and much more clearly in *An ABC*. In the latter poem, since it is directed to a supernatural but actual mother, and not suppressed or unrealised, the psychological danger is minimal. In other stories it is not. The reader must decide if Troilus is 'infantilised'. Chaucer presents him in terms of his own courtly culture. My own view is that since Troilus recognises his own plight, though he is tormented by jealousy, he is not rendered childish unless jealousy is considered always childish. Is Othello 'infantilised'? Chaucer himself recognised a potential infantile element in certain kinds of obsessive love in a typically comical way in *The Miller's Tale* as already noted (above p. 105). The portrayal of Absalom is in total contrast with that of Troilus, and to that extent illuminates the character of Troilus. Troilus is neither 'infantilised' nor 'feminised'. But then – and again the reader will have to judge – it is possible that Chaucer himself, in the *volte-face* at the end of the poem shares, at the last, Aers's robust lack of sympathy for Troilus, though not his contempt. Chaucer places Troilus after his miserable death in some vague heaven from where Troilus derides those who weep for his death (some of us readers?) and all who follow the 'blinde werk' of the passion of love, such as those of us who sympathised with both the sorrow and joy of Troilus. But why should Troilus go to heaven? In what did his 'moral vertu' and his 'trouthe' really consist? For Chaucer they are the fundamental virtues. Let the story conduct the reader's feelings through the whole gamut, from the first view, to the death and beyond.

NOTES

1. *The European Tragedy of Troilus*, edited by P. Boitani (Oxford, 1989).
2. A more extensive discussion which my present treatment summarises is Derek Brewer, 'Some Aspects of the Post-War Reception of Chaucer: a Key Passage, *Troilus*, II, 666–79', in *Expedition nach der Wahrheit; Poems, Essays and Papers in Honour of Theo Stemmler*, Hrsg S. Horlacher und M. Islinger (Heidelberg, 1996), 513–24.
3. George Lyman Kittredge, *Chaucer and his Poetry* (Cambridge, Mass, 1915), 16, 109ff.
4. E. Talbot Donaldson, *Speaking of Chaucer* (London, 1970), 68–83.
5. C. Muscatine, *Chaucer and the French Tradition* (Berkeley and Los Angeles, 1957), 133.
6. Many examples can be found in *Chaucer's* Troilus, *Essays in Criticism*, edited by Stephen A. Barney (London, 1980). The repetitiousness of criticism is extraordinary.

7.   Winthrop Wetherbee, *Chaucer and the Poets: An Essay on* Troilus and Criseyde (Ithaca and London, 1984).

8.   Elizabeth Salter, '*Troilus and Criseyde*: a reconsideration', in *Patterns of Love and Courtesy*, edited by John Lawlor (London, 1966); reprinted in *Critical Essays on Chaucer's* Troilus and Criseyde *and his Major Early Poems*, edited by C. David Benson (Milton Keynes, 1991) (hereafter C. D. Benson), 92–119, reference on p. 99.

9.   Carolyn Dinshaw, *Chaucer's Sexual Poetics* (Madison, 1989). Elaine Tuttle Hanson, *Chaucer and the Fictions of Gender*, Berkeley, Los Angeles and Oxford, 1992, 115, makes less use of the Narrator.

10.   Barry Windeatt, *Oxford Guides to Chaucer*: Troilus and Criseyde (Oxford, 1992); for example, 182. It is not to his purpose to discuss in detail our particular passage. See also Jill Mann, in Benson, as note 8, 149–63; and Murray J. Evans, ' "Making strange"; the Narrator (?), the ending (?), and Chaucer's *Troilus*' in Benson, as note 8, 164–75.

11.   Derek Brewer, *Symbolic Stories* (Cambridge, 1980).

12.   The following few pages summarise Derek Brewer, 'Troilus's "gentil" Manhood', in *Masculinities in Chaucer*, edited by P. Beidler (Cambridge, 1998).

13.   Barry Windeatt, *Oxford Guides to Chaucer*: Troilus and Criseyde, (Oxford, 1992), 275–9.

14.   D. W. Robertson Jr, *A Preface to Chaucer* (Princeton, NJ, 1962). Mark Lambert, '*Troilus*, Books I–III. A Criseydan reading', in *Essays on Troilus and Criseyde*, edited by Mary Salu (Cambridge, 1979), 105–25.

15.   David Aers, *Community, Gender and Individual Identity* (London, 1988), Ch. 3: 'Masculine Identity in the Courtly Community: The Self Loving in *Troilus and Criseyde*'.

16.   Jill Mann, *Feminist Readings*: Geoffrey Chaucer (London, 1991).

17.   An illuminating introduction to this approach is by Aaron Gurevich, *Historical Anthropology of the Middle Ages*, edited by Jana Howlett (Cambridge, 1992). Nevertheless, we should not exaggerate the differences of fourteenth-century society from our own, particularly from Western society up to the mid-twentieth century, still vivid in the memory of such as the present writer.

18.   Clare A. Lees, Introduction, xi–xii, in *Medieval Masculinities: Regarding Men in the Middle Ages*, edited by Clare A. Lees, *Medieval Cultures*, Vol. 7 (Minneapolis and London, 1994).

19.   The lion/lamb stereotype is widely invoked. In English an early example is the praise of the hero at the end of *Beowulf*. The portrait of Chaucer's Knight in the *General Prologue* to the *Canterbury Tales* spells it out (I, 43–78). At the other end of the time-scale we find the same sentiment in the threnody for Lancelot in Malory's *Le Morte Darthur*, *The Works of Sir Thomas Malory*, edited by E. Vinaver, revised by P. J. C. Field, 3rd edn (Oxford, 1990), III, 1259.

20. James A. Shultz, 'Medieval Adolescence: the Claims of History and the Silence of German Narrative', *Speculum* 66 (1991), 519–39.

21. *Wynnere and Wastoure* in *Middle English Debate Poetry*, edited by J. W. Conlee (East Lansing, 1991). R. W. Barber, *Edward Prince of Wales and Aquitaine* (Woodbridge, 1978), 17, 64–6.

22. Derek Brewer, *Chaucer and His World* (London, 1978, reissued Cambridge, 1992), 133–51.

23. R. W. Barber, *Edward Prince of Wales and Aquitaine* (note 21), 68.

24. Charles Muscatine, 'The Feigned Illness in Chaucer's *Troilus and Criseyde*', *Modern Language Notes* 63 (1948), 372–7.

25. Jill Mann, 'Troilus' Swoon', *Chaucer Review* 14 (1980), 319–35.

26. Jill Mann, *Feminist Readings: Geoffrey Chaucer* (London, 1991), 166.

27. Derek Brewer, 'Honour in Chaucer', in *Tradition and Innovation in Chaucer* (London, 1982), 89–109; Barry Windeatt, *Oxford Guides to Chaucer*: Troilus and Criseyde (Oxford, 1992), 244–6.

28. C. S. Lewis, 'What Chaucer Really Did to *Il Filostrato*', *Essays and Studies* 17 (1932), 65–75; repr. in R. J. Schoek and J. Taylor (eds) *Chaucer Criticism*, ii, Troilus and Criseyde *and the Minor Poems* (Notre Dame, Indiana, 1961), 16–33.

29. Mary F. Wack, *Love-sickness in the Middle Ages* (Philadelphia, 1990).

30. David Aers, *Community, Gender and Individual Identity* (London, 1988), 147.

Chapter 16

Troilus and Criseyde III:
The Lore of Love

Troilus and Criseyde merits further detailed consideration. The outline of the events in Book I has already been given. The essence of it is the beginning of Troilus's love, the beginning of Criseyde's favourable response, the consequent improvement in Troilus's already noble character caused by the hope of successful love.

BOOK I: COMMENTARY

Though the modern reader may well be as interested in love as the fourteenth-century reader, our responses will be very different, especially after the sexual revolution. Chaucer himself recognised this at the beginning of Book II, and comments in a remarkably modern way about the fact of historical change. Language changes over a thousand years, and words then

That hadden pris, now wonder nyce and straunge	*value; foolish*
Us thinketh hem; and yet thei spake hem so	*they seem to us*
And spedde as wel in love as men now do;	*succeeded*
Ek for to wynnen love in sondry ages	*also; various*
In sondry londes, sondry ben usages.	*customs*
	(II, 24–8)

This suggests that Chaucer himself recognised some degree of extremism in his portrayal of Troilus, and wished also to protect his story from being judged on too simply contemporary grounds even then. Chaucer's art is always heightened, and he makes as it were an experiment in *Troilus*, testing an extreme hypothesis of love.

The Church had early set its face against sex save for the purposes of procreation. There was much to be said in favour of that, considering the times. But it cut off from religious support, except through sublimation, some of mankind's most passionate and imaginative experience in personal relations. It is true that mystics used the imagery of marital sexual love to describe the highest form of spiritual union with God, but they did so only by paradoxically relegating actual sexual love to a low level of esteem. Again, the great theologian, St Thomas Aquinas, praised sexual love: but the normal run of moralising and devotional writing, more in touch with what people are actually like, normally condemned it. Sexual love, therefore, became a purely secular sentiment, only tangentially related to religious love, and treated with hostility by religion. Since religion set most of the dominant 'official' values of the culture, love became 'unofficial', though as it was practised by the highest in the land it achieved in purely secular terms the dominance which literature reflects, especially in Chaucer. Official secular culture in this respect could rival and oppose official ecclesiastical culture for a time.

Like religion, love inevitably involves suffering. This is partly because any ambitious enterprise involves self-discipline, forgoing short-term pleasures in favour of long-term advantages, persistence, and consequently some incidental pain. More deeply, passionate desire itself, when unsatisfied, is deeply painful as well as deeply attractive. Hence the ancient but true cliché of the bitter-sweet nature of love. Suffering is intrinsic to it.

The greater the suffering, the greater the joy of accepted love. It becomes the acme of human happiness, the goal to which all turn.

All this is most characteristic of human experience in youth, when society is less interesting, administration a bore, and social bonds are felt to be restrictive rather than supportive. Yet still for most people the heart of their satisfaction in life is to find satisfying personal relationships in the secular world.

So it is that in Chaucer's poetry the concept of the 'craft of fine loving', as he calls it in *The Legend of Good Women* (544) or 'Love's craft' (*Troilus*, I, 379), combines the desire to please, the desire to win a lover, and a highly moral set of feelings. It is both natural and socially 'constructed'. In *The Legend* it is Alcestis who teaches the craft of fine loving and specially of 'wifehood the living'. She is a faithful wife, and the poem, being about faithful women, is unusual in giving the initiative to women. In the case of Troilus himself, the instructor of faithfulness will be his own heart, and the instructor of the ways and means of wooing Criseyde will be Pandarus. Marriage is irrelevant, and it is taken for granted that love is so private as to be secret. No one likes his innermost feelings to be the subject of gossip and jest.

THE CONDUCT OF THE STORY

The conduct of the story in Book I is leisurely. The poet as Expositor works his way slowly into the story, first presenting himself, then allowing the characters to take over as dramatic figures. He is much more interested in the significance of small but crucial events than in a series of stirring events. The poem is concerned with feeling, not action. Thus, the first glimpse of Criseyde by Troilus (I, 273) is explored in a passage extending from I, 204 to I, 308. Chaucer is the Samuel Richardson, the Henry James, the Proust of the fourteenth century. And, as Dr Johnson said of Richardson's work, if a man were to read *Troilus* for the story alone he would hang himself. The immediate moment is to be savoured. It is no use being in a hurry. The tiny event of Troilus's first sight of Criseyde is preceded by a mythological reference to the God of Love, an adornment, with a touch of comedy, suitable for the local colour of a pagan past, but part of fourteenth-century contemporary fancy, too. Then the poet reflects on the nature of life:

> O blynde world, O blynde entencioun,
> How often falleth al the effect contraire
> Of surquidrie and foul presumpcioun.   *pride*
>   (I, 211–13)

This dignified language is followed in the next stanza by a reference to horses:

> As proude Bayard gynneth for to skippe
> Out of the weye, so pryketh him his corn,
> Til he a lasshe have of the longe whippe
> Than thynketh he, 'Though I praunce al byforn
> First in the trays, ful fat and newe shorn   *harness*
> Yet am I but an hors and horses lawe
> I moot endure, and with my feres drawe',   *must; companions*
> So ferde it by this fierse and proude knight . . .
>   (I, 218–25)

The comment is in one sense serious enough, yet it has a flicker of amused sympathy, not derogatory of Troilus, but a little detached. Further reflections follow; a general description of Criseyde, and of Troilus's feelings. Then Troilus leaves the temple and goes back to his palace, where he soliloquises on love. There is a psychological comment on how he makes 'a mirror of his mind' in which Criseyde appears and he thinks of her; then follows the *Canticus Troili* (song of

Troilus), the translation of the only one of Petrarch's famous sonnets to Laura which Chaucer seems to have come across, which lyrically expresses the self-contradictory nature of love.

The style of all this varies from the elaborate, the exaggerated, to the plain. It is never dull. The plain, which comes near to ordinariness but is always slightly different, carries the sense on without difficulty, though the needs of the metre often require alteration of the natural word-order. The elaborate is found in the use of less usual words, often recorded in this poem for the first time, or very early, in English, like *entencioun*, first found here, and *presumpcioun*. The passage containing these words is a good example of Chaucer's *sententious* style, uttering traditional wisdom, usually seriously, of which the proverbs that Pandarus uses so much are another example.

Those parts of the style that are exaggerated, or hyperbolical, are often so in traditional ways, expressing exaggerated ideas, as that Pandarus nearly 'melts' for pity and woe, or Troilus is nearly 'drowned' in tears. Ordinary excited colloquial speech often expresses such exaggeration, which no one in their senses takes literalistically. Chaucer occasionally also expresses himself more extravagantly in complex imagery, or even in strained metaphor. An outstanding example is the line

N'yn him desir noon other fownes bredde.

(I, 465)

(Desire bred no other fawns in him): i.e. sexual desire aroused no other wishes in him. The idea of subsidiary wishes as fawns, the young of deer, is attractive but strange. Not surprisingly it gave the scribes a lot of trouble and they produced many variations.

BOOK II: THE STORY

We begin with another invocation, this time not to a Fury but to Clio, muse of history, and the promise that we will sail out of these black waves. The poet disclaims responsibility for his story – it is a received story, a piece of history, autonomous, though there is also irony in this assertion, for though a man may not have responsibility for inventing a story, he certainly has for passing it on. Chaucer dramatises his narrative by presenting so many different attitudes of his own towards it. He proclaims his own ignorance anew, and here at the beginning (ll. 22–8) occurs as part of his apology the stanza already noted discussing historical change in language and manners.

We are then told that the date is May 3rd, traditionally unlucky, but a date Chaucer uses several times. Pandarus himself is suffering as much for love as Troilus, tossing and turning in bed all night for sorrow. But he gets up early, finds out by astrology that the time is propitious and visits Criseyde. She is in her paved parlour with two other ladies, hearing her niece read to them about the siege of Thebes. Their meeting is joyous, but she will not dance because she is a widow. They draw aside for private conversation and there follows a marvellous scene of several hundred lines (up to line 595) in which Pandarus slowly breaks to her, at first to her genuine dismay, the news that Troilus loves her. They fence in conversation with wit and slyness; the poet sees into their minds, they each try to gauge what the other is up to.

Equally fascinating, though more beholden to Boccaccio's original, are the succeeding passages in which Criseyde first sits in her own room on her own to think about it all, then sees by chance Troilus returning from battle, richly armed

> So lik a man of armes and a knyght
>
> (II, 631)

in the passage earlier discussed whose interpretation is now so disputed. Criseyde is shown arguing with herself in an entirely convincing way. Why should she get involved, she asks herself. She is perfectly happy, free and independent, and love is 'the most stormy life'. But she is fatally divided between hope and fear. She walks out into her beautiful formal garden with her three nieces, walking along the sanded alleys between the blossoming green boughs, and one of her nieces, the bright Antigone, sings a song of love, that makes Criseyde feel what bliss there is between lovers, while when she goes to bed

> A nyghtyngale, upon a cedir grene
> Under the chambre wal ther as she ley,
> Ful loude song ayein the moone shene   *against; bright*
> Peraunter, in his briddes wise, a lay   *perhaps; bird's way*
> Of love, that made hire herte fressh and gay.
>
> (II, 918–22)

She dreams a dream in which an eagle tears out her heart and leaves his own in hers – traditional but almost Freudian symbolism.

The remainder of the book continues with Pandarus rushing between Criseyde and Troilus with extraordinary joy. On one occasion to Criseyde

He seide, 'O verray God, so have I ronne!   *run*
Lo nece myn, se ye nought how I swete?   *sweat*
(II, 1464–5)

He gets them to write letters to each other (in Criseyde's case the first that ever she wrote) and advises Troilus on his epistolary style, including how to blot the letter with a few tears (l. 1027). Pandarus asks the honourable and generous Deiphebus, an elder brother of Troilus, to give a large dinner party (ostensibly to arrange help for Criseyde, for a problem purely invented by Pandarus), to which, besides others like Paris and Helen, Troilus will be asked. Pandarus will arrange a private interview between Criseyde and Troilus at which, he exhorts the shy Troilus, he must

Now spek, now prey, now pitously compleyne . . .
Somtyme a man mot telle his owen peyne.   *must*
(II, 1499 . . . 1501)

Pandarus then arranges for Troilus to show sickness, so that Criseyde may see him alone in a bedroom in Deiphebus's house. All this is arranged with zestful bustle by Pandarus and ingenious detail. The domestic intrigue of this second book is really very like a novel in its realism, its chain of cause and effect, and vivid dialogue. The book finishes delightfully with Troilus about to be visited alone by Criseyde, longing to declare his love, and asking himself,

O myghty God, what shal he seye?
(II, 1757)

BOOK II: COMMENTARY

Our sense of individual characters and relationships is built up in this book on the basis of realistic domestic and personal detail, much of it, like Pandarus's visit to Criseyde, invented by Chaucer and inserted into the story. The poem approaches the nature of a novel because the characters seem to create the events, and it is no accident that most of the actions of Pandarus, from his first talk with Criseyde to the organisation of the meeting at the dinner party, are Chaucer's invention. None of this invention is of a traditional literary kind. Pandarus manipulates both Troilus and Criseyde, though he is continuously respectful to both. He refers to Troilus as 'my lord', and usually begins a conversation with him, however flippant, using the respectful second person plural 'ye' (e.g. 1. 943), though he soon switches to the familiar second singular. He and Criseyde always speak to each other using the respectful plural form. Troilus always uses the singular, as to an inferior, to Pandarus, while throughout the poem Troilus and Criseyde use the plural form to each other. These subtle usages illustrate something of the subtlety of relationship. The action in this book, apart from Pandarus's bustle, is mostly in Criseyde's mind.

CHARACTERISATION

The characters take on clearer Chaucerian shape, except that it is of the essence of Criseyde's character that it is malleable, responding to the pressures on it, ambivalent, therefore charming and interesting. Troilus has already been discussed at length as constituting the corner-stone of the story, the stable element. Both these characters, but especially Troilus, are traditional types (none the less true or interesting for that) whom Chaucer has realised with sharp realism. He has changed them from *Il Filostrato*, making Troilus both more warrior-like and more shy than his Italian counterpart, who unlike Troilus is sexually bold and experienced. From this change arises much of the greatness of the poem, for it enhances Troilus's goodness as a young man, allows Criseyde to dally longer in 'sweet reluctant amorous delay', introduces more philosophical reflection, and causes the need for Pandarus's activity.

The story requires that Troilus should seduce Criseyde. This is taken for granted in Boccaccio, and willingly assented to by his heroine. But Chaucer's Troilus is too good and too shy, his Criseyde too cautious, for such promptness, and Pandarus has to do Troilus's dirty work for him, as they both acknowledge a little later (III, 239ff., especially 253–5). Pandarus says that if what he has done were known, everybody would say he had committed the worst treachery possible (III, 278). Thus, in a deeper sense, Criseyde and Troilus are independent characters with an archetypal relationship, while Pandarus is, in the end, created by the need for action between Troilus and Criseyde, so that he *is* what he *does* and *says*, no more and no less. Since we know most people only in such a way, by what we hear them say and see them do, this makes him very immediate to our imaginations, and very 'solid'.

If ever there were a character like one in a novel, we are tempted to think, Pandarus is he. Yet it is not so, because what we know of him is only his functions, not his essential being. Thus, we know he is Criseyde's uncle. This is Chaucer's invention; in Boccaccio's poem he is her cousin. He needs to be Criseyde's uncle, not cousin, because Chaucer conceives of Criseyde so much more subtly than Boccaccio does his heroine. She is not the type of amorous widow, as eager for an affair as her Italian boyfriend. Therefore, Criseyde has to be persuaded, and therefore Pandarus has to be cunning, socially adept, and with some authority over her. He is her financial adviser and, as she says, her best friend, whose duty it is to *prevent* her having a lover (ll. 411–12). He is *in loco parentis*, as no cousin of equal age could be. He is only her uncle because Chaucer needs him to be so in order to persuade her to love Troilus. We see this more clearly when we recall how Criseyde's isolation, consequent on her father's desertion, is emphasised at the beginning of the poem. On that occasion Pandarus is not mentioned, because his function as go-between, literally as pander, has not yet arisen. (It is not accident that the function of bawd has taken his name in England.) He must presumably be her mother's brother, rather than the brother of her father Calkas, whom he never mentions, and whose defection is not said to bring shame to him. Genuine family relationships are not important in the action and Chaucer leaves them out, for his poem is not after all, a novel, and its realistic surface covers an inner structure of romance, of relationships between two people only. Criseyde in Book II appears to be far from isolated, with, apart from Pandarus, her three nieces who live with her, and her friendly relationships with Deiphebus, Paris and Helen, apart from Hector.

The impressionistic nature of the poem thus causes some paradoxes of character. Not least important for the vividness of Pandarus as a character is that there is so much we do *not* know about him, as is the case with so many of our acquaintances in real life. The action of the story between Troilus and Criseyde does not require him to appear as a soldier, so in this society of soldiers, though he is the closest friend of one of the greatest soldiers, we know nothing about his fighting ability or lack of it. We hear that he is in love, and is unsuccessful and unhappy in love, but the lady is not needed for the relationship between Troilus and Criseyde, so she does not appear.

Although Pandarus shares many of Troilus's activities, and thus would seem to be of about the same age, as he is in *Il Filostrato*, he is *in loco parentis* to Criseyde, and is very much more knowledgeable in all sorts of ways than Troilus, so he also seems older than either. We have ambiguous clues to his age. He seems both middle-aged and young. The ambiguity does not worry us because it arises out of the action itself, and is not irreconcilable to natural possibilities, but to recognise it is to be reminded again that the story is about the relationship between two archetypal characters, and that the character of Pandarus is not in itself of any intrinsic significance.

REALISM AND SOCIETY

The same paradox of practical social surface realism without naturalistic depth (not as a fault in the poem, but as part of its quality) is to be seen in the social circumstances sketched in Book II. We are given a delightfully vivid glimpse of social life in Chaucer's Troy, and as it must surely have been among courtiers in their grand houses along the Strand in Chaucer's London. Enough detail is given for us to begin to describe this society, with its visits, and acceptance of ladies on equal footing in an easy and gracious politeness. It is sociable, rather emotional. People touch each other often in friendly manner, like modern Italians. Helen, for example, in charmingly womanly fashion, puts her arm round the apparently ailing Troilus (l. 1671), not amorously, but as a friend, in a society where people feel strong personal warmth. The paradox is that this society, though so vividly presented, only appears when it impinges upon the relationship between Troilus and Criseyde, either as help or hindrance, and the essence of their affair is its evasion of all social structures. It is a relationship of love alone, a bond purely of personal feeling. That is what the poem is about.

WORDS AND THE POET'S ATTITUDES

Feeling in the poem is conveyed by words, in expression *by* the characters; in letters and speech *between* them; and in narrative and comment *about* them, by the poet to us. Pandarus is most eloquent, a well-trained rhetorician, as Troilus and Criseyde are not. He gives Troilus excellent advice on how to write a letter, keeping to the point, but still arousing feeling. Pandarus's rhetorical art to some extent associates him with the poet himself, of whom, it might be said with only a little extravagance, that he himself has to act as a bawd between Troilus and Criseyde, since he has to bring his freshly conceived characters together, and he has had to invent, in the new character given to Pandarus, the means by which they are brought together.

A number of critics have seen some similarity between Pandarus and the poet. Each acquires a character by his relationship to the action. The poet's character, like Pandarus's, varies in relation to different aspects of the story; it is ambiguous, and contains inherent inconsistencies. He expresses approval, at one stage, as we shall see, of what he seems to disapprove of at another. Yet since these differences arise from the facets of the action, like flashes from the many different facets of a well-cut diamond, they are all part of the same brilliance. The poet, like Pandarus, is a literary intellectual, a dramatic presenter, an Expositor, drawing speech from the other characters, urging on the action and commenting on it. Both poet and Pandarus love the sententious style, larded with proverbs. Both have zest and fun and a wicked sense of humour. (The poet mocks his own love of rhetoric with a rhetorical joke, ll. 904–5.) Yet Pandarus is a character *within* the action, whom the other characters recognise, and the poet is not. Pandarus is less than, and in the end, quite different from the poet. When the relationship between Troilus and Criseyde finally breaks down he will have nothing to express but angry frustration. His *raison d'être* as a character will disappear, while the poet will go far beyond, conducting Troilus up to the heavenly harmony of the spheres, then able to turn away even from him to address his learned friends and pray to God. As Pandarus rightly says, echoing the rhetoricians, 'th'ende is every tales strengthe' (l. 260).

BOOK III: THE STORY

We end Book II with Troilus palpitating with nervousness about what he shall say to Criseyde. Was he not, says the poet amusedly, in a 'kankedort' – a strange word, still not properly understood, though its general meaning of being in a 'fix' is clear; those scholars who discuss it are still themselves in a kankedort.

Book III begins on a new note, a triumphant hymn to Venus, based on a later passage from *Il Filostrato*. Then we resume with Troilus in bed, going over in his mind what he wants to say, Pandarus pulling Criseyde in by a fold in her dress, peeping in between the curtains that enclose Troilus's bed, and seeming almost to weep. Troilus tries to spring up, while Criseyde gently lays hands on him to press him back. All that he wants to say flies out of his head. Criseyde perceives and understands his tongue-tied embarrassment very well, and loves him never the less for it. He manages eventually to express what the poet calls his manly sorrow, and Pandarus weeps as if he would turn to water. The talk between the three is serious yet with a touch of pure social comedy, quite without satire or irony. In a moment's sober comment when Criseyde has gone Pandarus remarks to his 'alderlevest lord' (best loved lord) and 'brother dear' that he has done for him what he will never do again for anyone, be he a thousand times his brother.

> That is to seye, for the am I bicomen   *thee*
> Bitwixen game and ernest, swich a meene   *go-between*
> As maken wommen unto men to comen
>
>   (III, 253–5)

that is, a bawd, what is henceforth called a pandar. Troilus reassures him, and says he would do the same for him, even if it were to concern his own sister. The whole conversation is of the greatest interest for the way in which the whole affair may be thought of. Troilus asserts his total devotion, and they settle down to sleep, for Pandarus has had a pallet made up for him in Troilus's room (ll. 299–31).

A plan is then devised for Pandarus to hide Troilus in his house and invite Criseyde to supper. He does so on a night when a most unusual conjunction of stars (which occurs once only in 600 years and occurred in May 1385) promised exceptionally heavy rain. So Criseyde, half against her will, certainly without her foreknowledge, is persuaded to stay. Troilus is introduced into her bedroom, in one of the richest, most interesting scenes in all English literature. He is fearful, solemn, devout, she surprised, Pandarus comically urgent. Troilus pleads his love, and faints. Pandarus throws him into bed with Criseyde, says 'Do not faint now, whatever you do,' and retires to read 'an old romance' by the firelight. Troilus has been told by Pandarus to tell some lies about his jealousy of one Horaste, which Criseyde repudiates, and Troilus in lyric speech – again, we are re-minded of the long expressiveness of operatic arias at the point of action – praises Citherea (Venus) and celebrates 'Benigne Love, thow holy bond of thynges' (l. 1261). Now at last he seizes Criseyde as a hawk seizes a dove. She is fully won, and though their subsequent meetings are few and secret, each is full of joy. Troilus improves still more in manly conduct, in honour, generosity, kindness, even in being well-dressed, achieving fully all the beauty and joy of the ideal courtly life (ll. 1716–36). The book concludes with Troilus's great song in praise of cosmic love (ll. 1744–71) based on Boethius. Troilus expresses the wish that his love may be part of the great bond that unifies and harmonises the universe – that Love, as Dante says in the last line of *The Divine Comedy*, which moves the sun and other stars. It is an aspiration, not an assertion, on the part of Troilus – the operative word in the song, *Bynd*, is in the subjunctive mood, expressing a hope, not in the indicative, expressing a *fact*.

BOOK III: COMMENTARY

There is far more in the book than can be summed up in brief commentary. It moves from the lyrical intensity of sincere passion, to sensual appreciation, gently comic comment, and slightly bawdy innuendo. There is evidence here for almost any attitude towards love one likes to mention, from moral condemnation to reverence to secular and cynical revelling in sensuality.

The vehicle of most of these attitudes is the self-dramatising poet's narrative, which includes comment of all kinds. Though the sustained realism is unrivalled in English literature until we come to Defoe, the poet remarks that there simply is not space and time enough to record everything fully, and anyway it would be boring (ll. 491–504). And though the poet knows at times the inmost thoughts of his characters, he deliberately distances himself, with a touch of humour, at the very climax of sensual joy. He claims only to be translating from his author, whom he has earlier called 'Lollius' (I, 394), not altogether seriously, but he effectively throws all responsibility on to the reader:

> For myne wordes, heere and every part,
> I speke hem alle under correccioun
> Of yow that felyng han in loves art,
> And putte it al in youre discrecioun
> To encresse or maken dymynucioun
> Of my langage, and that I yow biseche.
>
> (III, 1331–6)

He gives licence to the critical fashion of the 1980s for 'deconstruction', for reformulating the work of art in the reader's own image. He disclaims, or pretends to disclaim, responsibility, especially moral responsibility, for the story at least at this point. The reader is called on fully to participate, to imagine and create for him- or herself, and is flattered by the imputation of greater knowledge and experience. The requirement is genuine in that all poetry, all art, can only live if the reader, or viewer or hearer, brings personal knowledge, experience and sympathy to come part of the way to meet the artist. It is also more specific to Chaucer, in that he is generally not didactic, but rather questioning, exploratory, ambivalent. Nevertheless, if he *really* rejected responsibility he would not write at all: if the readers were *totally* independent they would not read at all.

Both poet and reader necessarily practise an ironic complicity. Chaucer's awareness of playing with this complicity is part of his many-layered poetic meaning, and of his humour.

HONOUR

The domestic and social realism of the poem continues strikingly and delightfully in Book III. One aspect of it which develops more strongly, and relates to character, is Criseyde's insistence on the maintenance of her honour. Almost the first thing she says to Pandarus, in Troilus's presence, in reference to his long first speech is

> Myn honour sauf, I wol wel trewely,   *provided my honour be preserved*
> And in swich forme as he gan now devyse,
> Receyven hymn fully to my servyse,
> Besechyng hym, for Goddes love, that he
> Wolde, in honour of trouthe and gentilesse,
> As I wel mene, eke menen wel to me,
> And myn honour with wit and bisynesse   *common sense and energy*
> Ay kepe.
>
> (III, 159–66)

Honour is mentioned three times in eight lines. The concept of honour in traditional societies is complex and almost totally lost in modern society. It is an aspect both of primitive individual integrity and of primitive collective social cohesion. Honour so to speak looks both inwards into the personality and outwards towards society. Honour is what the individual needs to exist as an effective person, and is simultaneously the recognition by the social group that that quality is actually present. The qualities in question are the primitive masculine and feminine qualities: for men bravery, for women virginity, and these qualities have already been noted in Chaucer's heroes and heroines. They are vital to life at a high level in traditional society, though some sections of society have no honour to gain or lose, for example, priests and peasants.

Criseyde, like all of Chaucer's heroines, is much concerned with her honour. She talks about it more than any of them, and the pathos of her story is that she, who is concerned above all with her honour, will lose it. The problem of this essentially two-sided honour is that if only one side is felt to exist, the whole is called in question. If a man is brave or a woman chaste but their social groups cannot, or refuse to, believe that they are, how far does *honour* exist? *Goodness* may and does exist without social recognition, we may perhaps say, because it is seen by God; but honour is purely worldly, which is why the Church, especially in England, always regarded it with suspicion and some hostility. On the other hand, if society believes you to be brave or chaste, that is as good as truly being so, as far as honour is concerned, until you are found out. If you are found out you are treated with derision, and cast out from your group.

Criseyde ultimately gets herself into something like this last situation, partly because she cares so much about the external social aspect that she neglects the internal quality. She is very vulnerable. As a widow she is honourable in solitude. By sleeping with Troilus she loses the internal quality of honour, since she is not married to him. That is why the affair must be kept secret, *because if nobody knows* (and nobody except Pandarus and the reader does) *she may be said to retain her honour* from the social point of view. Honour is partly what people think about you and the respect they accordingly grant you.

There is another aspect of honour not so far mentioned. That is, keeping your word. It might be argued that this is not really honour but loyalty or truth or faithfulness; it is at least so closely associated with the integrity that is part of honour that it must be considered with it. The significance of loyalty can be seen most clearly in the case of a married woman's honour. Her honour obviously does not reside in her virginity; her honour resides in her faithfulness to her husband. This is part of the social nature of honour, for her husband's honour also depends on her faithfulness to him. If she is unfaithful to him, she loses honour, and so does he. A cuckold is universally an object of derision. Since sexuality is not itself part of a man's honour, the seducer is not dishonoured. This example again shows that honour is by no means always the same thing as goodness or justice. Nor is it dishonourable to deprive another man of honour, either by defeating him in battle or by dishonouring his wife, though either act is risky since it may well provoke battle and death.

The complexity of Criseyde's position consists in this: she has given her honour as it were into Troilus's keeping. If the affair is known, she is dishonoured but he is not.

Troilus, however, is nothing if not loyal. The poem is as much about his loyalty, called *trouthe*, as about Criseyde's ultimate disloyalty. For Criseyde will eventually lose honour by abandoning Troilus for another man. That will be her dishonour, not primarily her loss of chastity in sleeping with Troilus when not married to him. But there will be more paradoxes before the story is finished.

LOVE AS A PURELY PERSONAL RELATIONSHIP

Why does Troilus not marry Criseyde? The simplest, true, answer is that the story does not say that he did, and the story has a traditional 'given', historical character, which does not allow events to be changed. If the events were changed it would be a different story, not this one. The question does not arise in Boccaccio's story about a lusty and lustful young pair. Chaucer creates the problem because he makes both Troilus and Criseyde more thoughtful, more complex and more moral. He seems conscious of the problem when he emphasises at the beginning of Book II how different were manners and morals in time past. In his own day, in literature at least, marriage would be the normal object of such a wooing as that of Troilus. But Chaucer never mentions marriage in the poem, and in life in his own day, as opposed to literature, liaisons of the kind which Troilus, who is a prince, is seeking, were, as has been said, usual for princes. The goodness, not the amorousness, of Troilus is the stumbling-block.

Chaucer's presentation has nevertheless the advantage already remarked: that the interest is concentrated on the personal relationship independent of any social support or compulsion. Chaucer presents the romantic ideal of a purely personal relationship, independent of social obligation or constraint, and as such it is highly relevant in the late twentieth century. Social bonds differ from personal; when divorce was difficult they maintained marriage and the marital relationship independent of the respective parties' personal wishes. A purely personal relationship depends on both partners maintaining a continuous wish, or abiding by a personal, not a legal promise. If personal volition is all, and it fades for one of the partners, as it is likely to, then the promise, and the other partner's personal wish, may be treated as of no account, as Troilus found. The rational answer then is for the deserted person to change their wish, as now often happens; but we are not all rational, nor can we all control our wishes. So it seemed to Boethius, and to Chaucer, and to Troilus, that the flesh, or the stars, and not the rational mind, controlled desire; and sexual love is seen as the greatest of all desires.

LOVE AND DESTINY

Book III is a curious mixture. It begins and ends with noble hymns to love which are not ironic, while Troilus's sincere love is brought about by a deceitful intrigue. We cannot doubt the nobility of love. The hymn to Venus at the beginning is a wonderful combination of mythology, astrology, historical local colour, and an almost religious warmth of feeling. Of Venus, goddess, and planet, the poet says

In hevene and helle, in erthe and salte see
Is felt thi myght,

(III, 8–9)

as if she were the Virgin Mary, Empress of Heaven, Earth and Hell.
Troilus, a pagan, solemnly invokes all the gods, including Hymen,
god of marriage, and shows a serious piety which deserves respect
and from which he never swerves. It is an intrinsic irony that the
love-stories of the gods he invokes are all of rape, atrocity and
disaster, with nothing of the faithful tenderness that Troilus himself
never fails in. He regards himself as totally committed to Criseyde
though they are not married. When they are together she fully
avows her love with complete sincerity, but never with such fervour
of religious conviction.

Is their love a product of fate or manipulation or chance or their
own choice? The poet deliberately creates an ambivalent sense that it
is both inevitable and yet chosen. At the crucial moment when
Criseyde proposes to leave Pandarus's house after supper in the
downpour of rain, the poet apostrophises Fortune, another mytho-
logical figure:

But O Fortune, executrice of wyrdes	*agent of destiny*
O influences of thise hevenes hye,	
Soth is that under God ye ben oure hierdes	*shepherds*
Though to us bestes ben the causes wrie.	*beasts; hidden*
This mene I now, for she gan homward hye	*hurry*
But execut was al bisyde hire leve	*carried out without her consent*
The goddes wil; for which she moste bleve.	*remain*
	(III, 617–23)

In other words, Destiny controlled her through the stars. But Pandarus
had calculated that effect from the stars, in the form of the rain,
when he invited her. *Wyrdes* is not a pagan concept but an aspect of
Destiny, which is controlled ultimately by God, as Boethius argues.
So here is a strong sense that Criseyde is helpless. But when Troilus
later that night amorously in bed seizes her and says there is no
escape for her, she prettily answers

Ne hadde I er now, my swete herte deere	
Ben yold, ywis, I were now nought heere.	*been yielded*
	(III, 1210–11)

Here, at least, she willingly co-operates with the universe. Destiny as
always remains a mystery.

BOOK IV: THE STORY

> But al to litel, weylaway the whyle,   *too little, alas that it should be*
> Lasteth swich joie, ythonked be Fortune.   *thanks to Fortune*
> (IV, 1–2)

So begins Book IV, in sharp contrast to the calm joy in which Book III ended. Criseyde, we have always known, will desert Troilus, and this sad foreknowledge has always been a dark background to the brightness of the moment. Now the sun goes out and clouds come up. The poet prays to the Furies to help him finish this fourth book in which he will show Troilus's loss of both life and love. He was obviously translating and remoulding with a copy of *Il Filostrato* open on the desk before him, knowing the general outline of what he was planning but changing the details of the plan as he went along, guided by his response to the story at the moment. At this stage he is still with the fourth of *Il Filostrato*'s eight books. He presumably intended to cut *Il Filostrato* as radically as he had cut *Teseida* for *The Knight's Tale*, and tie it all up in one last book. As it proved, the subject matter of loss and betrayal made too deep an appeal. It invited long expressions of sorrow on the part of the characters, and much philosophical questioning of choice and destiny. The long irony of Troilus's self-deception, the precise calculation of time, the chance of a really striking ending: all appealed very strongly to Chaucer both as man and as artist. The fourth book became immensely long (as had happened proportionately with the last book of *The House of Fame*), so he cut it at l. 1700 and made the rest of it a fifth book, without noticing, or without bothering to change, the promise to finish made at the beginning of the fourth.

Criseyde's father, Calkas, asks the Greeks if they will arrange to have his daughter sent to him. They grant him the Trojan prisoner, Antenor, to use for exchange, and the proposition for this unfair deal is put to the Trojan Parliament. Troilus is present and in agony. He feels he cannot say anything because Criseyde would not wish him to betray any special interest. The noble Hector resists: she is not a prisoner, he says; tell the Greeks we do not sell women here. But the crowd wants Antenor. Little do people know what is best for them, says the poet, for it was Antenor who later betrayed Troy (l. 204). But Hector is outvoted, and Criseyde must go. Troilus goes home distraught. Pandarus too is distressed, but after all, he says to Troilus, why are you so mad? You have had what you wanted. There are plenty of other ladies in the town.

If she be lost, we shal recover an other.

(IV, 406)

The poet remarks that Pandarus merely uttered such sentiments in order to prevent Troilus dying from sorrow (a good example, acknowledged by the poet, of how what Pandarus says arises directly from the needs of the action between Troilus and Criseyde. He himself has no stable views, no 'stable ego of character' as they have, which is another reason why he seems so modern a character.)

This went in at one ear and out at the other, says the poet, as far as Troilus was concerned. He is wholly Criseyde's whom he will continue to serve till he dies.

Criseyde hears the rumour that she must go with dread, since she cares nothing for her father and everything for Troilus, but she dare ask no one for confirmation. A crowd of silly women come to congratulate her, but she weeps distractedly and they think it is because she will miss them. When they go she curses her fate and the prospect of separation from Troilus, in a complaint, reproaching the 'cursed constellation' of her stars. How shall she live without him? Pandarus visits her and she tells him of her sorrow. Pandarus once thought to himself how dim she was (II, 271–2). Now he tells her that since women are 'wise in short avysement' (IV, 936: i.e. 'good at quick consideration' and the earliest recorded use of *avysement*) she should be able by her wits to find a way out of the difficulty.

Then he looks for Troilus and finds him in a temple, in despair, arguing with himself whether there is such a thing as free will and coming to the conclusion that there is not:

> For al that comth, comth by necessitee
> Thus to ben lorn, it is my destinee.   *lost*

(IV, 958–9)

This is expanded by a long argument with himself which is a versified translation from Boethius, *Consolation*, V, prose 3. The passage was probably an expansion inserted by Chaucer at a slightly later stage of composition, between what are now lines 960 to 1086, but were once 960 and 961. The passage is an extreme example of the variability of form of the *Troilus*, which can range from detailed realism to this philosophical argument which makes only the slightest concession to dramatic propriety, and sometimes even violates it. The passage represents by logical argument the actual turmoil in Troilus's mind, and is part of the Boethian deepening of the poem.

Pandarus is genuinely impatient with such depair. Has Nature made you only to please Criseyde, he asks in exasperation (1. 1096)? And it is true that such devotion as that of Troilus has something of supernature in it, as well as something supine. Pandarus wants to see some action. So Troilus visits Criseyde. They are speechless for woe; she faints and after lamenting he draws his sword to kill himself. Though this may all seem very extravagant it is translated from *Il Filostrato*, but medieval romance is full of strong feeling and in all centuries and cultures there have been young people prepared, sometimes successfully, to commit suicide for love.

Troilus is saved by Criseyde recovering and calling to him. They go to bed to talk things over like an old married pair. This is in Boccaccio, but the very long speech by Criseyde (ll. 1215–414) is much expanded from Boccaccio's quite brief report of her speech. The style, which combines the colloquial, the sententious and the learned, like a gloriously varied aria, is entirely Chaucer's: the subject matter of lines 1317 to 1414, plus the next stanza, is Chaucer's own without any corresponding lines in *Il Filostrato*. Criseyde says, echoing Pandarus in both word and idea (from IV, 935–6), that being a woman she is 'avysed sodeynly', and that they ought not to make half this woe, for she has a plan. She will return of her own accord from the Greeks. She reveals a foolish over-confidence which complements her usual and more sensible nervousness. Chaucer, having taken the framework of event from Boccaccio, fills it in with his own substance of Criseyde's motive and attitude, his own further colouring of style. Criseyde is shown to be touchingly inventive and enthusiastic about how she shall manage and what she shall say. Chaucer adds the comment, as Expositor, ll. 1415–21, that she really meant what she said, and that she intended to be true. Is this remark ironical? I do not think so, though others do. The later event, which we already know, turns sincerity into an ultimate irony, but need not impugn her present actual intention.

Troilus is dubious, and in language more humble, expressive and religious than that of Boccaccio's hero Troilo, prays her to elope with him, since, as Boccaccio's hero does not mention, Troilus has, 'vulgarly to speken of substaunce' (1. 1513), enough money. So the discussion goes to and fro, enriched with much comment. Criseyde rightly says her life would be impossible if she lived with Troilus openly: her reputation for chastity would be besmirched for ever. She emphasises that she will return on the tenth day of her exile. She also warns Troilus against making love to any other woman in her absence, because she would be so distressed if he were untrue – an extra emphasis by Chaucer which is part of the irony of the total narrative, since we know that it is Criseyde who will prove unfaithful. She also emphasises that she has loved Troilus not for his position or power, but for his 'moral vertu, grounded upon trouthe', his 'gentil' (i.e. noble) heart, and his manhood (ll. 1672–4). The sentiment does credit to both lovers, and has the effect of emphasising the centrality to the story of Troilus's own natural goodness and 'trouthe'. Then Chaucer inserts an extra stanza, not suggested by Boccaccio (ll. 1660–6) in which Criseyde says that she will always behave, since he has been so true, 'That ay honour to me-ward shal rebounde.' Chaucer's Criseyde is always concerned for her own status and there is more narrative irony here. They lament and make love. Dawn comes; Troilus must dress and go, in deepest sorrow.

BOOK IV: COMMENTARY

The characters are enriched still further and more facets of Criseyde's character are shown dramatically. As with people in real life there is no single key to her personality. She is loving, gentle, nervous, spirited, rash, well-intentioned; but her governing concern, as Chaucer envisages her, is with her honour, which ought to be, but is not, associated with her 'truth', i.e. faithfulness. Her concern determines her actions, and it is a general irony that she who is more obviously concerned than any heroine in Chaucer with her honour is the one who notoriously loses it because she is untrue. Troilus rages against Fortune and is unshakably true, but honour does not come into the question for him.

THE EXPLORATION OF A DILEMMA

Although the characterisation is rich, the essence of Book IV is a realistic version of a *demande d'amour*, a question of love; in other words the main point of the book is to express dramatically a frantic exploration of possible ways out of a distressing dilemma. The three characters discuss many possible courses of action, even marriage, or the violent abduction of Criseyde; too many to summarise here. Character or circumstance foils each possible solution, and we attend with sympathy to the expression of passionate frustrated feeling, while contemplating the apparently ineluctable course of events.

VARIATION OF STYLE

In this exploration of possible solutions the style is wonderfully varied. There are realistic touches of description, as in the mention of the knight who guards the door of Troilus's darkened room (ll. 351–4); there are vivid colloquial touches, as Troilus calling himself a 'combre-world' (l. 279) (an expression invented here by Chaucer and only used again by Hoccleve), and Troilus referring to 'nettle in, dock out' and 'playing rackets' (ll. 460–1) with love; or Troilus described as paying deep attention with 'heart and ears spread out' (l. 1422). But in general the style in Book IV is less naturalistic, less dramatic, and more abstract or general, more intellectual. The extreme example is Troilus's soliloquy in the temple, where for a while all naturalistic imitation is abandoned (ll. 960–1078), but Criseyde's long speech, and the poet's comment, ll. 1254–421, express high sentiment in a high style, which makes no attempt at novelistic imitation, though mingled with more homely notes. The learned words *conclusioun* (l. 1284) and *redresse* (l. 1266) (each of which Chaucer used several times later but are first recorded in English here); *mocioun* (l. 1291); and the strange *amphibologies* (l. 1406), (meaning 'ambiguities'), are examples, which could be much extended, of an intellectual vocabulary.

This fourth book contains much less comment by the poet. Nor does there seem any need to attribute irony or mockery to such comments as there are. On the other hand, the promises of faithfulness by Criseyde are examples of what may be called dramatic or narrative irony, because we know, though she does not, that the future will show them to have a different, opposite meaning to what she at present intends.

BOOK V: THE STORY

Book V begins without an invocation but with two stanzas of solemn comment in high style added by Chaucer and not in *Il Filostrato*, which also begins here at Book V:

Aprochen gan the fatal destyne	*fated*
That Joves hath in disposicioun,	*at his disposal*
And to you, angry Parcas, sustren thre . . .	*three sisters*
The gold-ytressed Phebus heigh on-lofte	*golden-haired; aloft*
Thries hadde alle with his bemes clene	*bright*
The snowes molte, and Zepherus as ofte . . .	*melted*
	(V, 1 . . . 10)

There is no question here of a stupid, pretentious, ironical or cynical Narrator. The poet speaks grandly, a dignified *Expositor*, *Contemplatio*, or *Poeta*, independent of the action but sympathetically engaged with it. We know the story: these premonitory introductory chords lead into the last act.

Fatal destiny does not mean '*deadly* destiny'. 'Fatal' simply means 'Fated'; what happened. There is no notion here of a Hardyesque malicious Fate, or of a modernistic fatalism. Destiny is the expression of Providential order, which by a poetic fiction we think of as the action of Fortune (*Boece* IV, pr. 6; *LGW*, 2580; *Troilus*, III, 617). It may be painful because to us beasts here below the causes are hidden. The world is both tragic and good. The poetry here expresses a natural human mood, for which the underlying logic, such as it is, must be sought at much greater length in the *Consolation*, or in theology.

The Greek Diomede is ready to fetch Criseyde, who feels her heart bleeding, in this extravagantly if traditional expressive image which Chaucer adds to his source. Troilus accompanies her to the gate, hiding his sorrow, and his anger when he sees Diomede, in a manly way. Chaucer both adds to and cuts from his source as usual, tending to add a Gothic extravagance to the expression of feeling, and adding equally Gothic concrete detail, as when Troilus takes Criseyde's hand 'full soberly', 'And Lord! so she gan wepen tendrely' (ll. 81–2), details which are not in Boccaccio.

Diomede, as he takes the bridle of her horse, thinks to himself – for the poet here knows his inmost thought – that he may as well have a try at seducing her, if only to make the way seem shorter. So he courts her immediately in an odious unconscious parody of the high love-language of Troilus, swearing to her, 'as a knight', that he will be 'her own man', never having loved a lady before, but now unable to strive against the God of Love – though he only asks to be her friend and brother. The speech is not exactly a joke, either by Diomede or the poet, yet there is an almost painfully comic wit in the dramatic aptness of expression of this cynical, treacherous womaniser. Criseyde is so distracted that she pays little attention, but all the same, with her usual readiness to collaborate with whoever is urging her, she thanks him, accepts his friendship and says she would gladly please him and will trust him. We see that she is effectively already lost. All this passage, which is both social comedy and personal tragedy (ll. 92–189), almost a hundred lines long, is inserted between stanzas 13 and 14 of the fifth book of *Il Filostrato*. And then she is warmly welcomed by her father.

Troilus returns to Troy and rages, soliloquising in torment, in a long speech plus poetic comment added by Chaucer between two lines of *Il Filostrato*'s Book V, stanza 21.

The poet continues,

Who koude telle aright or ful discryve	*describe*
His wo, his pleynt, his langour, and his pyne?	*torment*
Naught alle the men that han or ben on lyve.	
Thow redere maist thiself ful wel devyne	*guess*
That swich a wo my wit kan nat diffyne.	*intelligence; express*
On ydel for to write it sholde I swynke	*labour*
Whan that my wit is wery it to thynke.	

(V, 267–73)

The refusal to describe is a rhetorical device, which characteristically of Chaucer calls on the reader to participate. There seems no reason to doubt that the poet does genuinely sorrow for Troilus. If we, as readers, not only of this poem but of other stories, feel sorrow, as we surely do, for characters in distress, then equally surely the writer too must feel genuine pain, or else why should he write? Art objectifies and distances our feelings, but also extends and enhances them precisely in this way, by imaginative participation in fictional sorrows and joys, which yet may be more 'real' to us than real life.

Yet we also notice here that the poet, by his very comment, withdraws himself, and us, a little, from full participation, even as he invites it. The address to 'thou reader', a habit perhaps caught from Dante, is also interesting as inconsistent with other addresses apparently to an attentive *audience*. This is another example of the Gothic multiplicity of perspective.

A very beautiful stanza of a quite different kind immediately follows with sharp Gothic contrast:

On hevene yet the sterres weren seene	
Although ful pale ywoxen was the moone . . .	*become*

(V, 274–5)

It is translated from Boccaccio's *Teseida*, with suggestions from the *Consolation*. In this fifth book are a number of such beautiful evocations of the starry heavens.

Pandarus comes to assuage Troilus's sorrows and speaks with his customary colloquial and sententious vehemence, fullness of information, and worldly *savoir-faire*. Ten miserable days must pass before Criseyde will return. Pandarus makes Troilus spend a sociable week at the house of Sarpedoun, 'to lead a lusty life in Troy'. Social life is torment to Troilus and Chaucer makes us intensely aware how slowly the time passes for Troilus. He visits Criseyde's house, that desolate palace (Chaucer constantly heightens the social level and physical circumstance, as well as the feelings expressed: in Boccaccio the 'palace' is only a 'house').

Pandarus, like Boccaccio's Pandaro, is completely sceptical about Criseyde's return, but unlike Boccaccio's young man does attempt to console Troilus in a mixture of kindness and hypocrisy that is humanly entirely convincing.

Troilus sickens, soliloquises, makes another song, and walks on the walls to look at the Greek army (a concrete detail not in *Il Filostrato*). And

> Upon that other syde ek was Criseyde,
> With wommen fewe, among the Grekis stronge;
>
> (V, 687–8)

moving lines, translated straight from Boccaccio except that 'strong' is substituted for Boccaccio's colourless 'armed'. But for the next hundred lines Chaucer considerably expands the direct speech given to Criseyde, making her more sympathetic, and pathetic, in her distress. She weeps and sickens, and reflects in Boethian style on the nature of happiness. Meanwhile Diomede gets to work on her. Chaucer makes his cynicism and progressive success quite clear.

At this stage Chaucer, following a hint from *Il Filostrato* which actually occurs some 30 stanzas later in the Italian, slots into the narrative formal descriptions, physical and mental, of Diomede, Criseyde and Troilus (ll. 799–840), with an effect of summing-up. Then on the very tenth day, as Chaucer, not Boccaccio, tells us, Diomede makes another attempt on Criseyde, with a subtle mixture of bullying, threatening, flattery and cajolery, reminding her of the fate that her father himself foresees for Troy. He even reminds her of his own high lineage (l. 931). What a contrast to Troilus. Criseyde cannot but be polite. She temporises, but Chaucer shows her saying she will speak with Diomede 'tomorrow', which was when she had promised to be back in Troy. The hundred lines from l. 995 correspond to only three stanzas, that is, 24 lines, of Boccaccio, and are a masterly expression of the complex development of Criseyde's thoughts and feelings, when she goes to bed beneath the beautiful starry skies and turns over in her mind what this 'sudden Diomede' has said. Her soliloquy is a wonderful passage of psychological drama and finishes most remarkably

But al shal passe; and thus take I my leve.

(V, 1085)

Such speeches are a familiar rhetorical device, but it is hard to avoid the impression that Chaucer has been thinking of her as a character on a stage, giving a soliloquy. She is vividly before us on the stage of our minds, all ordinary realism left far behind. But truly, says the poet, in what is almost a farewell comment, no authority tells us how long it was before she actually forsook Troilus for Diomede. The comment is neutral, as it were historical, distancing her. The poet continues in his role as sympathetic storyteller in the stanza already quoted above (pp. 198–9) concluding,

Iwis, I wolde excuse hire yet for routhe.

(V, 1093–9)

The tone seems genuinely sympathetic. Her fault is plain. 'Trouthe' is the highest value. Yet of course only the reader and author *outside* the frame of the work, beside Troilus inside it, know that she is untrue, for her affair with Troilus is quite unknown to every other character *within* the fiction.

Chaucer has taken us far beyond the tenth day, and the narrative returns to Troilus on that very day. We now see him against the background of the desertion which is yet to come, to sympathise with the sickness of hope deferred. Criseyde has in every sense left the scene, and the story continues centred only on Troilus, on a foreboding dream he has, and an exchange of letters with an increasingly deceitful Criseyde. Chaucer draws swiftly to the end, making no use of long passages by Boccaccio in *Il Filostrato* describing Troilo's misery and a visit from Trojan ladies to Troilo. Chaucer adds Cassandra's foreboding interpretation of Troilus's dream, more historical and mythological allusions, and more addresses to Fortune. In particular the poet comes forward more and more as Expositor, referring to his sources, summarising events, steadily withdrawing us from close participation in the action. Criseyde is given one last indirect appearance by means of her most deceitful letter (ll. 1590–632). This is entirely Chaucer's invention, though he draws on earlier material from *Il Filostrato*, and illustrates her degeneration. A brooch that Troilus had given Criseyde is captured from Diomede. Troilus is at last convinced of her unfaithfulness and yet, he says, with profound human truth, he cannot find it in his heart

To unloven yow a quarter of a day.
In corsed tyme I born was, weilaway.

(V, 1698–9)

This is not in *Il Filostrato*. Troilus must suffer.

Swich is this world, whoso it kan byholde:
In ech estat is litel hertes reste.
God leve us for to take it for the beste.

(V, 1748–50)

The poet speaks movingly. Such true and appropriate comments arise naturally from the story. That they are not original, but are part of traditional wisdom, part of common human experience, seems their strength, though some critics consider them to be commonplaces intended to arouse our derision.

As the poet moves increasingly into the foreground, the persons of the narrative become more distant. The long slow withdrawal is amazingly rich. The story is finished, but not the poem. There is a lightening of tone, with an injunction to the poem itself, first as 'a little book', then implicitly as a person itself (as stories seemed 'persons' to Chaucer), to kiss the footprints of the great poets of the past: Virgil, Ovid, Homer, Lucan and Statius.

There is an astonishing last flourish. Troilus is killed by Achilles, reported in one line (l. 1806), and his soul is taken up into the heavenly spheres, to laugh at those who mourn his death, and to go wherever Mercury shall place him. And then again a surprise, as the poet says emphatically, in a moving stanza with repetitions like a tolling bell, yet ambiguously, so that we are uncertain if it is praise or blame, such was the end of Troilus. What was his suffering worth, what relevance had it? The poet counsels young fresh folk to love the true God. The heathen gods are mere 'rascaille'. The poet then dedicates this courtly poem to his middle-aged learned friends, the poet 'moral Gower' and the 'philosophical Strode', and concludes with a noble prayer to the Trinity, translated from Dante.

BOOK V: COMMENTARY

Book V is an artistic *tour-de-force* and a most moving account not only of the sadness of betrayal, the sickness of hope deferred and extinguished, but also of a robust modification of tragedy. The *story* is a tragedy, but the *poem* is something larger, longer, more varied.

THE ENDING

The ending has attracted a great variety of response. It is not, as it is sometimes described, an epilogue, a mere tailpiece, nor a palinode, a rejection of what has gone before. It is the expression of yet another point of view, another response; and though it may be the last, it does not deny the truth, within their own terms, of the joys and sorrows and interim values expressed before. The long-drawn-out ending is a deliberate disengagement from the story, held together by the poet as Expositor, who continues to comment on the action. The flight to heaven, adapted from *Teseida* and not in *Il Filostrato*, is an immense strengthening of the poet's exposition, rather than a part of Troilus's story. Its placing is very deliberate. It both condemns and validates Troilus's love, which is inseparable from his 'trouthe'. The ancient motif of the flight to heaven suggests both questions and answers, which are obliquely followed by the injunction to love Christ. None of this should be taken as ironical. It would be too silly, as well as historically impossible. But it does leave a fascinating set of underlying ambiguities, opening out multiple perspectives within this extraordinary poem. As in so many of the greatest stories we are left with the sense of a profound enigma at the heart of it, which prompts a series of different yet related answers, none final.

THE USE OF THE *CONSOLATION* IN *TROILUS*

The essence of the *Consolation* is that mind is superior to matter. Its two main topics are, first, 'what is true happiness', which Chaucer calls 'felicity'; and, second, how to obtain it in the light of our material conditioning, both inner and outer, which amounts to what Boethius calls Fortune, Destiny. In *Troilus and Criseyde*, Criseyde is more interested in 'felicity', Troilus in fate and free will. Troilus is in the position of the 'lesser' Boethius, inside the *Consolation*, though Troilus, unlike Boethius, never becomes reconciled to his destiny.

Criseyde is clearly aware that worldly happiness is only false felicity (e.g. III, 813–17). According to Boethius true felicity consists in *gentilesse* and *trouthe*, which is exactly what Criseyde says she loves Troilus for (IV, 16, 72–4). *Trouthe* is for Chaucer the highest, most complex quality, which can refer to God himself, as in Chaucer's short poem with that title. But Criseyde, though she can recognise *trouthe*, does not possess it. She is always worrying about what other people think, but you can only find *trouthe* inside your own mind (though it is not subjective, or limited to yourself alone); and you must have peace with yourself, as Boethius says (II, p. 4, as also does Pandarus, I, 893). *Trouthe* is that inner integrity which assures loyalty to what is outside ourselves.

We can only love *trouthe* 'outside' us if we have it 'inside' us. Now it is clear that Troilus has *trouthe*, yet comes to disaster in his life, as did Boethius himself. It must be because of Troilus's *trouthe* that after death he goes, if not to heaven, which the poet is not explicit about, yet presumably to bliss, although the poem ends in condemnation of pagan life and of 'feyned loves'.

Boethius has as it were a circular model of the spiritual universe, the opposite of the Ptolemaic model of the physical universe (above, p. 153). In the Ptolemaic model earth is the almost dead lump at the centre, with Hell inside it at the very mid-point. Above the moon all is stable and beautiful in the successive starry spheres which mediate God's plans for earth. In the spiritual globe by contrast, God, not the earth, is the centre; next comes the sphere of Providence, which is God's planning, and outside that, Destiny and Fortune, which are the physical universe of appearances, the ups and downs, the chains of cause and effect, of ordinary life. In practice for Chaucer, Destiny and Fortune are the same. Fortune is the poetic personification of that level of reality represented more philosophically by Destiny.

Boethius claims that man can either stay at the level of superficial ordinary experience, the level of Fortune, or he can move 'inwards' towards God's providence. Fortune is chaotic yet unfree, bound by chains of material and astrological causation. Moving towards God is towards love and freedom (they must go together for, as *The Franklin's Tale* will tell us, 'Love wol nat been constreyned by maistrie', 'Love is a thyng as any spirit free').

There are plenty of paradoxes and problems here, but one of them is particularly significant. Boethius represents himself inside the *Consolation* as at first arguing in Book V, prose 3, that men cannot have free will to choose the good if God foreknows all, since if he can know it now, it must be bound to happen. Therefore there is no real choice for men. This is the longest speech by Boethius within the whole *Consolation* and is clearly of great intellectual and emotional significance to Boethius; so it is to Chaucer, for Troilus's repetition of part of Boethius's argument here is the largest single section that Chaucer directly borrowed from the *Consolation*. Boethius's argument contains a logical fallacy which his mentor, the Lady Philosophy, analyses in order to break out of the circle of necessity. She thus convinces Boethius of his mistake. But Chaucer does not employ the refutation, since he is concerned with the dramatic relevance to Troilus, who uses and believes the demonstrably false argument of Boethius without correction. Troilus, though good, is not represented as learned, and this long philosophical excursus as already noted is not part of a naturalistic characterisation. His speech represents the nature of his feelings as the good rationalist pagan 'who found no end, in wandering mazes lost'.

This raises important points for understanding the intellectual nature of the poem. We, the audience, are clearly meant to dissociate ourselves from Troilus's point of view, while sympathising with his sorrowful dilemma. He accepts a total determinism which we know to be mistaken. Yet the course of the poem, of which we know the outcome from the very first line, if not before, may seem to exemplify Troilus's deterministic view. We are therefore, *vis-à-vis* the poem, in a position like that of God *vis-à-vis* the world, while in a sense the poet, in the poem, is like the philosopher who has to reconcile God's (the audience's) foreknowledge of the outcome with local immediate participation in the hopes, fears, lives and potential freedom, of the characters. Both choice and necessity must be seen to coexist. This involves the shifting of perspectives upon the narrative events, which has already been remarked. To put it another way, to do justice to the complexity of the action different attitudes are required to different parts of the poem. For example, the attitude to love expressed or implied in the whole of Book III is different from that at the end of the whole poem. This is the nature of a 'Gothic' poem which, unlike a novel, straddles fiction and reality. The unity of the poem lies in the continuity of the story as presented by the Expositor; different persons may validly judge the events differently, and so may the poet himself at different stages of the story, in various contexts. The events are presented with, and for, sympathetic rationalistic participation, though the degree of participation, or distance, between us and the events, varies. The realistic non-mythic, or non-folkloric story, told mainly in terms of naturalistic cause and effect, here serves Chaucer much better than a mythic story would have done. The chain of cause and effect so efficiently linked in *Troilus and Criseyde* provides a connected, coherent, continuous and almost self-enclosed simple structure, round which the poet as Expositor can wind a much less continuous or consistent commentary, which is certainly not self-enclosed since it can address itself to actual living people (Gower, Strode) and evoke real, non-fictional standards. The commentary at any point tends to take its tone from the nature of the specific action being described, but then relates that action to the audience or reader.

The chain of cause and effect is an effective Boethian image of worldly events. The various attitudes taken towards them by the poet contribute to our sense of wonder, our speculations, and our own sense of the possible alternatives and choices. The poem is always presented for our godlike contemplation; we always know more than the characters, and the poem cannot fully exist unless sustained by our godlike loving participation, just as the world itself, in Boethius's and Chaucer's thought, could not exist without God's sustaining participating love.

THE QUESTION OF LOVE

In the question of love Chaucer goes further than Boethius. Although Boethius does indeed write nobly of the bond of love throughout the world, the general effect of his work is to recommend an ascetic denial of the world for the sake of loving God. Troilus loves Criseyde who represents worldly joy, the gifts of Fortune, and is badly let down as we expect. The paradox is that because of his virtue, his *trouthe*, he cannot cease loving Criseyde. Stable people cannot just switch love off – not even Pandarus can. Stability is the crucial value for Boethius, as it was for Chaucer. It is an aspect of *trouthe* (cf. *Consolation* III, m. 11.), an aspect of God, dwelling within oneself. What makes worldly felicity false is precisely its own transience, its instability. Troilus's stability involves him totally with an unstable person: a painful and hopeless paradox. The simple answer to the paradox at the end of the poem is that it is less painful and more satisfying for stable true love to direct itself to the only really stable true person, to wit, God. But the totality of the poem's commentaries, in whatever way we resolve or fail to resolve their logical inconsistencies, adds up to a more complex assertion of the reality of the joy of human love, even if it is transient. This thought is at best only implicit in Boethius. Chaucer brings it out much more fully.

The usefulness of the *Consolation* to Chaucer lay in its rational appeal within the general Christian tradition. Scholasticism was rational, and no doubt Aquinas was a greater thinker than Boethius. But for Chaucer Boethius with his literary flavour was a better teacher than Aquinas, and was secular; he was neither ecclesiastical nor technically philosophical, nor theological. Had he been so Chaucer would have lacked training and perhaps sympathy to understand his work. Being secular the *Consolation* was historically apt for a poem set in pre-Christian times; even more, it could bypass what by

Chaucer's time was the rather sour asceticism of the ecclesiastical tradition.

This great long poem was Chaucer's supreme artistic achievement in which tradition is handled with startling originality. Having achieved it Chaucer went on to different kinds of work, of even greater originality, but first he followed the vein which he had in fact almost exhausted.

Chapter 17

The Legend of Good Women: Cupid's Saints

It is reasonable to believe that Chaucer finished *Troilus and Criseyde* about 1385, himself aged about 45 and at the height of his powers, not tired but eager to proceed. There were so many possibilities open to the poet for whom every new poem was an experiment, and whose mind was full of stories, thoughts and questions. *Troilus and Criseyde* must have caused some little stir in court-circles because the next substantial poem, *The Legend of Good Women*, in its *Prologue* presents a vision of the mighty God of Love – the medieval Cupid, a bold, handsome young man – who reproaches the poet for bringing love into disrepute. (There are two *Prologues*, referred to as F and G, to be explained later. Here we refer to the earlier, F.) The poet, says the God of Love, has made wise folk withdraw from him because the poet has translated the *Romance of the Rose* 'that is a heresy against my law' (F 330) and has told the story of Criseyde which makes men distrust women who are 'as true as steel' (F 332–4). The likely date for *The Legend* is therefore about 1386. The god has with him a glorious Queen, incarnation of the daisy, or marguerite, who rallies to the poet's defence, says he didn't know what he was doing, etc. After some sharp words about the deceitfulness of courtiers she lists Chaucer's own works which have made ignorant folk delight to serve love. She refers to the *Death of Blaunche the Duchess*, *The Parliament of Fowls*, 'the love of Palamon and Arcite' though the story is little known (F 415–21), many love-lyrics, Boethius, the *Life of Saint Cecilia*, and a great while ago, *Origen on the Magdalen*.

All this lodges the poet himself, not a stupid Narrator, but a self-mocking half-real half-fantasised *persona*, in a courtly environment, where 'the woman question' was a real issue, if also the subject of some teasing. The court was far from the powerful misogyny of some clerical writers, but probably all traditional societies, being male-dominated, have some ambivalence towards women.

The *Prologue* is delightfully relaxed and lighthearted, with the poet's references to spring and how he leaves his books to enjoy worshipping the daisy. It is highly personal in Chaucer's most mature vein of self-deprecatory humour. The god and his queen do not appear until a couple of hundred lines after the beginning, during which the poet has rather extravagantly proclaimed his love of the daisy in May and his allegiance to the Flower in the courtly game of Flower against Leaf – another social anchor for the lightly floating fantasy.

The god's accusation is not taken very seriously – witness the Queen's defence – and provokes no sign of anxiety. There is behind no hint of the savage political campaigns that would soon be fought around Richard II, to be noted later. There is no sense of urgency. The translation of the *Romaunt*, and *The Book of the Duchess*, had been written some 17 years before. We have a recapitulation of Chaucer's whole writing career, triggered by the reception of *Troilus and Criseyde* and presumably by the arguments it caused about women, their nature, their 'stability' – arguments that as we have seen continue, centred on Criseyde, to modern times, nowadays reinforced by the new feminism, which had its precedents in Chaucer's day. Throughout the fourteenth and fifteenth centuries there were arguments especially in France about whether *Le Roman de la Rose* was or was not anti-feminist – la Querelle de la Rose. Similar arguments continue today about *The Legend of Good Women*, which is another of Chaucer's odd poems. The *Prologue* is superb, though some questions arise. The separate stories are rather different but also fascinating in their internal variations of tone, and the consequent uncertainty of how to take some parts of them.

The Legend of Good Women tells the stories of classical heroines deceived and ill-treated by men but showing constancy and goodness according to Chaucer's own version. The stories constitute a poem of profound repetition, recapitulation, of the experience of loss and betrayal. Indeed the repetition has been felt by many readers to be too great at the superficial level, since each of the nine stories extant repeats the same pattern. Commemoration is unlocked by 'the key of remembrance' (F 26) held by old books which we ought to believe, says the poet, 'there we han noon other preve' (F 28). That line is typical of the enigmatic qualifications inherent in the poem. How sceptical is it? Translation too in the deepest sense is involved. The poet translates and thus transforms. His versions are very different from some traditional accounts.

Several lines of thought and feeling come together. In earlier poems Chaucer has listed women betrayed, and there seems no reason to doubt that their plight aroused his sympathy, and that the reiteration of the theme, and its gender-reversal in *Troilus and Criseyde* corresponded to some deeply felt pain in himself – a pain that few people will have completely missed in their lives, but noticeable in Chaucer. The main source of these narratives of pathos was Ovid's *Heroides*, letters supposed to have been written by the betrayed heroines and a source of literary interest and controversy in the medieval schools. Alongside these secular narratives ran the huge river of saints' lives, probably the most popular of all medieval literary genres, sacred or secular, of which many told of the heroic endurance and ultimate miracle-working power of holy women. Though these stories emphasised passive rather than physically active heroism for obvious reasons, their heroines often argued fiercely and effectively. They give a powerful image of a certain kind to women. Again we must recall how widely religious feeling percolates through a traditional culture, colouring so many acts and thoughts in as it were a casual taken-for-granted way. 'Normal' piety was not so intense, so highly strung, or intellectualised, as the serious devotion of the theologian, or of the female recluse, or mystic, which arose out of it, and which everyday religious practice accepted without necessarily closely following it. Saints' lives in particular may be regarded as religious folklore, not in any dismissive sense by those of us who are trying to understand this different culture, but in the sense of something appreciated, often fantastic, yet in some sense believed, and accepted, if not acted upon, in ordinary everyday life.

Chaucer responded to this popular veneration of saints quite wholeheartedly. He wrote, as he tells in the *Prologue* to the *Legend of Good Women* the *Life of Saint Cecilia* and later incorporated it into *The Canterbury Tales* as the *Second Nun's Tale*. It was not difficult therefore to blend sacred and secular elements of feeling, especially of pathos, in his rehearsal of the stories of betrayed classical heroines. At the same time, just as we have noticed the association of laughter with death (above, p. 101) so we may note Chaucer's irrepressible levity at times in the *Legend* like that found, for example, in *Palamon and Arcite* in the account of Arcite's death. Our post-Reformation, post-Counter Reformation, post-industrial, seriousness, fragmentation and almost complete loss of religious feeling finds it difficult to blend so many apparently incompatible attitudes together without one destroying the other. Traditional societies are less logical but can be more 'holistic'. Chaucer is also exceptional in the vividness, not to say the hyperbole, with which he represents his culture. The extreme pathos, the irreverent mockery, at times what seems the

satiric and ironic posturing of his style, are hard to keep in balance
with his genuine enjoyment, delicacy of perception, true sympathy,
and sombre reflections on the hardness of life.

To sum up, the *Prologue* is deservedly, at least in parts, among the
most famous passages of Chaucer's poetry. In it he again displays
and exploits his own enigmatic subjectivity, his courtly environment,
and particularly his consciousness and pride of being a varied and
important author, though without Humanistic didacticism and arro-
gance. Composition of the individual legends is the task which the
God of Love imposes on Chaucer and they are intriguingly different.

THE PROLOGUE TO THE LEGEND OF GOOD WOMEN: ITS VERSIONS AND DATES

The Prologue is one of Chaucer's most delightful poems, with its own
independence and a quite extraordinary mixture of old and new. In
substance it is something of a throwback to the old-fashioned French
love-vision, and several French poems about the marguerite are
followed at times quite closely. But the metre is the new five-stress
rhyming couplet and the manner is that of Chaucer's maturity, often
apparently only half-serious. The jests go along with a real tender-
ness and beauty of description. The preciosity of daisy-worship is
indulged without becoming mawkish, or being sneered at.

The poem was sufficiently interesting to Chaucer for him to have
two goes at it, and *The Prologue* exists in two versions.

The first survives in 11 manuscripts or parts of manuscripts and in
Thynne's edition. The best of these manuscripts is Bodley Fairfax 16,
a notable anthology of Chaucer's minor poems. This version of *The
Prologue* has therefore been labelled F. The second version appears in
only one manuscript, University Library Cambridge Gg. 4.27, the
biggest manuscript collection of Chaucer's poems in existence. Its
spelling is odd but its texts are usually very good, and close to the
originals. Hence this version has been labelled G. Each manuscript is
of the early fifteenth century (and like many others, is now available
in facsimile). The first version, F, must have been written, because of
the content, sometime after *Troilus*. There is a kind of dedication to
Queen Anne, for Queen Alcestis says,

> And whan this book ys maad yive it the quene
> On my byhalf, at Eltham or at Sheene
>
> (*Pro LGW*, F 496–7)

(Eltham and Sheene were favourite royal palaces not too far from Westminster.) Since Anne died in 1394 *The Prologue* must have been written before then, and it seems reasonable to date it soon after the completion of *Troilus*, around 1386, before the beginning of *The Canterbury Tales*, which has been plausibly suggested as around 1387. The later, G-version of *The Prologue* omits the reference to the Queen and was probably produced some time after 1394. Not every scholar agrees that F is earlier but the cumulative literary evidence is overwhelming and has now been authoritatively reinforced on textual grounds by Kane and Cowen. Naturally, all manuscripts contain scribal errors and the solitary G-text of *The Prologue* is not free from them. Typical scribal errors have now been classified and identified by Kane and Cowen, and the remaining differences of G from the scribally edited versions of F can be confidently attributed to Chaucer himself.

THE FURTHER CREATION OF THE POETIC SELF

In *The Prologue to the Legend of Good Women* the poet tells us very clearly about his own personal tastes and habits. He makes explicit his love of books, in an extension of his earlier manner in *The Book of the Duchess*, *House of Fame* and *Parliament*, making deliberate play with his own personal character.

> On bokes for to rede I me delyte.
>
> (F 30)

Only in May, when the birds sing and flowers bloom, farewell his book and his devotion, and he walks the meadows at dawn to observe the daisy, the flower of all flowers. Granted that this derives from French poems devoted to the cult of the marguerite, it seems fairly specific to Chaucer's own situation. There is a reference to Saint Valentine (F 145) which may associate *The Prologue* with St Valentine's Day celebrations. A reference is made to the divisions of the Flower and the Leaf (F 72), which were court parties or associations, probably with some political overtones. In F, Chaucer seems to declare for the flower (F 82), but in the revision he adds a passage which denies adherence to either side (G 71–80). Whatever its significance, the brief reference stands the poet against a courtly social backdrop.

Chaucer tells us how he retreats to his house at dusk and sleeps in a little arbour he has had made in his garden. We are bound to feel that all this refers to his new house at Greenwich, then so near the meadows. He has a couch made up for him on a bench of turves. This is a touch of personal domestic circumstance which gives a base for the dream-fantasy to come, just as it did in *The Book of the Duchess*. Servants are props to individualism, implying a person's authority and confidence. As so often, we do not know quite how seriously to take what he says. He fell asleep, he says, 'within an hour or two' (F 209) – surely a wry joke about an uncomfortable bed, a touch of irresistible comic realism? Then he dreams of the god of love coming to him over the meadows, hand in hand with a queen, both clad in green, she with a golden fret upon her hair, and a crown with white 'fleurons' – the small protrusions of medieval royal crowns – which were made of pearl, and resembled the petals of a daisy. The queen is the human transformation of a daisy, charmingly described in the height of courtly fashion. She is yet another of Chaucer's *grandes dames* who are also beautiful, young, authoritative, yet kindly, an important element in the complex image of women he creates throughout his work. Both the god of love and his queen speak with royal condescension to the poet. The god reproaches him. The queen defends him in a beautifully patronising way, and they eventually commission from him the stories of ladies loyal in love. The commissioning is unique in Chaucer and suggests an actual command or request from a patron and patroness of a kind completely lacking elsewhere in his poetry. One aspect of Chaucer's modernity is his normal freedom from patronage. Perhaps he was not free here. But the commissioning is not a reward: rather as it were a fine in kind, to make up for transgression.

WHO DOES ALCESTE REPRESENT?

But who was the queen? We later learn she was Queen Alceste, famous in Greek Antiquity for her loyalty to her husband, whose death she took on herself. Who does she represent in the *Prologue*? A natural guess is that the god of love is King Richard II and Alceste Queen Anne. It may be so, but it seems odd that she should suggest that the poems be presented to the Queen, that is Anne, at Eltham or Sheen. The God of Love was not married, and the Classical Alcestis famously had a husband. Possibly Chaucer intended a compliment to the Queen Mother, Joan, once the Fair Maid of Kent, now the widow of the Black Prince, with whom it is possible that Chaucer served in Aquitaine. Whether or not this very pretty scene represents an actual reproach and commissioning of compensatory stories by some great lady, no outcome is suggested. Despite the courtly scene the result will be stories written to be read, not orally presented. They will be privately consumed, even if presented formally as a book. All is internalised. The scene is allusion rather than allegory, and teases us with its possible meanings. Whomever the god and the queen may allude to, the poet permits himself a fairly light-hearted dramatic portrayal of them, not disrespectful, but far from obsequious.

THE NAKED TEXT

The Prologue has many interesting literary points. Chaucer's listing of his works as a way of claiming and so to speak signing them has already been noted. The G version has the additional item of *The Wretched Engendring of Mankynde*, a lost work, but witness to Chaucer's continuing pursuit of serious, not to say gloomy, devotional subjects, in his maturity, which accompanied his equally vigorous development of the far from moralistic bawdy comic stories in *The Canterbury Tales* at the same time.

Chaucer emphasises his interest in old stories, and his desire to revere and believe in them. But in the revised version, G, he is more clearly ironical about this – 'leveth hem if you leste' (believe them if it pleases you) G 88. It is here that he declares his intention for the narratives that will follow: to declare them in 'the naked text'. He aims at narrative literalism, without allegory. The plain or naked text, without the 'glose' – without, that is, the interpretation that came to signify falsification or flattery or deceit – appealed to Chaucer, and he always uses the word 'glosing' unfavourably. The point is important for the general understanding of Chaucer. Some critics have given extended allegorical readings of Chaucer's poems and in this they are surely mistaken. It goes against the grain of all his work. To admit as much is far from denying some conscious or unconscious symbolism and far-reaching implications which are by definition characteristic of great works of art, as they interact with those who hear, read or see them.

THE REVISION OF *THE PROLOGUE*

The revision itself gives us a unique opportunity to see Chaucer at work on the craftsmanship of writing, and at the same time gives us some insight into his changing attitudes. The structure of F is somewhat rambling, and there is an awkward confusion between Alceste and 'my lady' (cf. 249ff., 432 and 540). G does a certain amount of tidying up and the confusion about Alceste is removed. In F the subject of the fashionable controversy between the Flower and the Leaf is approached in 72, but is not actually developed until 188–96. In G these two references are consolidated in 65–78. Chaucer now takes neither side. We may notice here as elsewhere that Chaucer, at least in his later years, somewhat distances himself from the court. In one short poem (to be mentioned later, *To Scogan*), he seems to regret his isolation, but elsewhere there is evidence of withdrawal and even condemnation. No doubt he was inconsistent in his attitudes, especially if he was, while writing the G revision, in what amounted to retirement in the mid-1390s in Greenwich. Chaucer is notable for divided or multiple attitudes. Many elderly people both hanker after and criticise the activities in which they can no longer take part.

In G the dream starts earlier. The effect of this alteration is to put the famous description of the beautiful morning and the charming anthropomorphic behaviour of the birds *inside* the dream. This is an improvement. The morning, for all its freshness, is nothing like the chilly hours just following dawn of an ordinary English May morning. It has the warmth and sweetness of a kinder clime, as in the French literary tradition, and is much easier to accept as part of the dream. The general effect of this and other structural changes is to consolidate, to make the development less wandering and casual.

G also develops certain matters more lightly touched on in F. In the earlier version Chaucer says that a king's subjects 'are his treasure and his gold in coffer' – a very appropriate sentiment for a customs officer. In the later version he substitutes six lines about the duty of a king to hear his subjects' complaints and petitions. This is an echo of increasing resentment about and criticism of Richard's irresponsible and autocratic behaviour. Nevertheless, in G the central occasion of *The Prologue* seems to be taken less seriously. As he grew older Chaucer was even less able to refrain from a little mocking with a solemn face. In the long and important insertion, G 258–312, he gives the God of Love a much livelier and fuller speech. The god accuses Chaucer of heresy against him, although he remarks that Chaucer owns a lot of books telling the lives of women, 'and ever a hundred good against one bad':

> What seith Valerye, Titus, or Claudyan?
> What seith Jerome agayns Jovynyan?
>
> (G 280–1)

This is a joke at the expense of the God of Love. What Jerome said against Jovinian is touched on in the *Wife of Bath's Prologue*. He and 'Valerian' (i.e. Walter Map), far from praising women, were perhaps the most satirical and effective of all the many libellers of women in the anti-feminist Middle Ages. Chaucer loved them as much as he loved the tales of noble women. Here he is deliberately making a fool of the God of Love. He makes other ironical additions. The queen defends him by suggesting that he translated poems, and 'knew not what he was saying'. On the other hand Chaucer cut out F 152, which is rather a feeble joke about sex.

Most of the alterations are obviously aimed to improve the sense and the poetry. Thus, he cut out the last 25 lines of F. They are somewhat verbose and are little loss. At the beginning he much modified the expression of his love for the daisy. It is difficult not to sense some personal feeling in the early, F, version of this – perhaps it was a genuinely felt courtier's address to the Queen or some great lady. Chaucer may have modified it later because the Queen's death made it inappropriate, or even simply because the daisy cult was no longer a courtly fashion in sentiment which was current or still appealed to him. Some of the alterations at the beginning forced him to abandon the charming four-line song which in F introduces Alceste's attendants. Chaucer's willingness to abandon these excellent few lines in the interests of the whole is a mark of his maturity and self-confidence as craftsman and artist.

Other changes are often minute, but hardly less interesting. Thus, he tones down the rather mechanical emphasis on the brightness of the God of Love. For 'holiness' (F 424) he substitutes 'busy-ness' (G 412). Where F 348–9 describes love as a god who knows all, G 323–7 substitutes the remark that all is not true which the God of Love hears; but the condemnation of court gossips and flatterers appears in both versions and is a traditional criticism of courtly life, of a kind going back for centuries, no doubt well justified but never destroying the glamorous appeal of the court. Occasionally the alteration enriches the density of the text, as, for example, instead of the repeated word 'serve', F 326–7, he substitutes 'trust', G 253. The later version also writes at somewhat greater length of Geoffrey Chaucer himself, in the familiar image of an amiable simpleton, but nevertheless extending the work of 'self-construction' and a kind of 'subjectivity' or self-awareness of himself as a person who is a subject for poetry. There seems little profit in referring to the poet as the Narrator, implying that the real poet is someone quite different. On the contrary, we get a strong sense, in the revisions, of the actual poet at work.

In general, the revision gives a stronger sense of the poet's personality, a better construction, and a strengthened style. The G version is livelier in humour and also warmer in its praises of noble women. It varies much more in tone; some parts of G are more serious, other parts more flippant, than in the earlier version. Chaucer intensifies his source, even when it is his own earlier composition, as he intensified the style of *Il Filostrato*. Nevertheless, for all the tinkering, it is still the same poem. The wonderfully fresh sense of spring remains, with the poet's heart-warming confession of inability to read in that stirring time of the year. There is still the delight in books, together with a little more information on the books Chaucer has read or written.

Perhaps between the two versions of *The Prologue* Chaucer's interests turned away from the courtly subject of love and of the fundamental problems raised by love. He may have felt he had worked that vein. It is also a matter of common experience that as a man grows older he becomes less interested in fundamental questions, for willy-nilly he has made up his mind about them. Interest tends to turn from philosophy to ethics; from theories to facts. We may perceive this happening even in the difference between *The Parliament* and *Troilus*. We shall see it continue.

LET US NOW PRAISE FAMOUS PAGAN WOMEN

When we come to the stories themselves we find that there are only nine actual poems about these love's saints and martyrs, beginning, somewhat surprisingly, with Cleopatra, and continuing with Thisbe, Dido, Hypsipyle and Medea together, Lucrece, Ariadne, Philomela, Phyllis, Hypermnestra. In the *Introduction to the Man of Law's Tale* in *The Canterbury Tales*, undoubtedly written later, Chaucer gives another list of his works, along with a jest against himself, and lists 15 of these 'saints of Cupid', while in yet another list, his *Retractations*, written in a quite different spirit, he refers to his Book of the Twenty-five Ladies. He clearly wrote many if not all of the stories we now have after writing *The Prologue*. It may be that he intended to continue, but got diverted to *The Canterbury Tales*. It is also possible that some have been lost. It is clear from the state of the manuscripts that some of the stories (like some of those in *The Canterbury Tales*) circulated separately. Minnis[1] points out that the *Retractations* of *The*

Canterbury Tales show that some of Chaucer's other works have been lost. So may some of the individual poems of the *Legend*. But the last poem ends in mid-sentence, and that cannot be due to physical loss of a sheet or more. The fact that a further statement is promised but is non-existent is very like the abrupt stopping of *The House of Fame*. Chaucer was reluctant to give us his 'conclusioun'.

That most of the heroines may surprise the modern reader as illustrations of virtuous and loyal women has led some critics to assume, inevitably, that the poems are ironical, and the poet reluctant or bored, and even intent on introducing grotesquely obscene *double entendres*. Most of this is surely wrong, but as usual with Chaucer there is room for some critical disagreement. Readers may come to varied conclusions, though it must be possible to be proved wrong by recourse to vital evidence, even if we cannot be proved right.

A certain ambivalence, humour, and touches of irony in the *Prologue* have already been noted, and in the second version, G, some ten years later, the equivocal note is stronger. The poet is more detached from the court though still deeply interested in this particular poem, the *Prologue*, wishing to improve it. The poems themselves so vary in tone as they proceed as to encourage some critics to take them less seriously as a whole. But if there is one lesson to be learned in following the evolution of Chaucer's work it is that Chaucer constantly mixes elements, the serious with the comic, and that to do justice to all we must respond equally to all. The mixture will always be of different proportions and may give rise to different responses, but the reader's desire for unification, uniformity, consistency, will always over-simplify and impoverish. Chaucer is the supreme example of an internally self-contradictory – the modern North American word is 'conflicted' – culture, which nevertheless holds together and has certain attitudes in common more firmly than our own scientifically specialised age. Chaucer himself rejected fragmentation and chose consistency, uniformity and thus exclusiveness in his own *Retractations* at the end of his life, but luckily few have agreed with him, and the works he himself condemned escaped destruction. As already noted, what he calls 'the Book of the XXV Ladies' (or in some manuscripts 'XIX Ladies'), which must mean *The Legend of Good Women*, is included among those secular love-poems which are condemned in the *Retractations*. This must paradoxically encourage us to take them seriously, like *Troilus and Criseyde* and the others, as being poems about genuine love, however the tone may vary.

TROUTHE IS THE HYESTE THYNG THAT MAN MAY KEPE

The subheading comes from *The Franklin's Tale* (*CT*, V, 1479) un-doubtedly written later than *The Legend of Good Women*, thus illus-trating the steadfastness of Chaucer's own moral vision, underlying so many variations of attitude. 'Trouthe' is a highly complex concept but among other things it illustrates the supremacy of faithful com-mitment and integrity in personal relationships in Chaucer's and his culture's moral universe. That being so, the breaking of personal bonds is necessarily the greatest harm.

True lovers deserted by their beloved either involuntarily through death or wilfully by breaking their word are a constant theme in Chaucer's poetry. It is the subject of *The Book of the Duchess*; it occurs in *The House of Fame* prominently in the case of Dido and those listed in *The House of Fame* 388–426; it is the story of Anelida, and of those listed in *The Parliament of Fowls* 284–94; and it is extensively treated in *Troilus and Criseyde*. The theme was fashion-able in contemporary French poetry. Loss was a constant event in normal life. Life expectancy was low, disease endemic, war frequent: death was all around and people, especially courtiers, were as amor-ous, inconstant and unfaithful as ever. The insecurity of life and love bore heavily on those of any sensibility and with warm affections. Personal loyalty and stability were the virtues most highly praised, not only in love and friendship but socially in vows, promises and in the feudal obligations between lord and servant. Loyalty and stab-ility were the essential bonds of social reciprocity that should promote community and override self-interest, selfishness, tyranny. Those bonds were broken continually then as now. Plenty of poets and moralists condemned the viciousness of the times then as in all periods. So did Chaucer in some of his lyrics, in *The Parson's Tale*, presumably in his lost translation, *The Wretched Engendryng of Mankind* and, in terms of troth-breaking, *The Legend of Good Women*. But as with *Troilus and Criseyde* he was more moved by virtue than by vice, 'virtue in all her works most lovely'. He commends *trouthe* and only incidentally condemns treachery and betrayal.

It is reasonable therefore to accept that the general purpose of the *Legend* is what it claims to be. It asserts that women are capable of steadfast loyalty of love, as supremely shown by the heroism of Alcestis. Though she was not one of those who had been betrayed, she is fitly regarded as a Queen. At the end of *Troilus and Criseyde* Chaucer had promised

And gladlier I wol write, yif yow leste   *if it please you*
Penelopeës trouthe and good Alceste.

(V, 1777–8)

Each of the tales has, in effect, the same theme as *Troilus* (for *Troilus* is a story of true love, though reversed in sex), and is essentially a counterpart to *Troilus*. The tales certainly are not a repudiation of the so-called repudiation of love at the end of *Troilus*. They are written to assert the steadfast loyalty of women against what is said to be Chaucer's imputation of their falseness in the character of Criseyde. *The Legends* is thin when compared with Chaucer's other treatments of closely similar themes. There seems little doubt that in writing *Troilus* Chaucer had excised that sense of loss and betrayal which had haunted his early work from *The Book of the Duchess* onwards. But he did not at first realise that. Another reason for their relative thinness may have been that there seemed so many stories to be told that each was rather cramped. Like the later project of 120 *Canterbury Tales*, it was too ambitious a scheme. Moreover, all Chaucer's work shows how ready he was to change subject-matter and treatment. By contrast, the *Legend* has for him and us the major disadvantage of a single theme and type of subject matter. Chaucer seems to have liked variety above all.

LOVE AND MARRIAGE

The recurrent theme makes clear the centrality of marriage to Chaucer's general conception of love. Every one of the betrayed heroines has been married or been promised marriage. Love is genuine, thought to be mutual, and free from concepts of service and humility. The plight of those who are betrayed is rendered with genuine pathos. Chaucer does his best to stick to the bare essentials of plot and character, and concentrates on the personal relationships which as always are at the centre of his interest. Nor are these as monotonous as sometimes claimed; if the theme is the same the circumstances are all different.

Gower told several of the same stories in his *Confessio Amantis* and Chaucer's principal aim seems to have been to achieve a rapid, plain, brief narration of the kind in which Gower excelled. Perhaps Chaucer set out to imitate Gower. Like him he always maintains the interest in the succession of events. Chaucer's difficulty was in restraining himself from adorning and enriching the narratives, and in preserving the benevolent even tone in which Gower is so tireless.

Praise of pagan women, though a lesser theme than mysogynistic writing, had been known from antiquity even apart from Ovid, and had been repeated even in some of the most apparently anti-feminist Church Fathers, as Minnis shows. In the fourteenth century, besides Boccaccio's De mulieribus claribus (Of Famous Women), the classicising English friars of the earlier fourteenth century had written the lives of admirable pagan women. It was possible for them, as for Chaucer (as he had already shown in Troilus and Criseyde) to bring some historical understanding and sympathy to the different circumstances of those who had lived virtuous lives before Christianity. The problem of the saving of the virtuous heathen was widely discussed in the fourteenth century, as Dante and Langland witness in their references to the fate of the righteous heathen.[2]

Nevertheless, in such a 'dialogic' culture as Chaucer's, in which qualities are paired and opposed, it was inevitable that the virtue of 'trouthe' should be highlighted by emphasis on 'falsnes', as had happened in Troilus and Criseyde. The tales of good women emphasise 'trouthe' as the distinguishing virtue of women, and all the men are betrayers. Chaucer is quite prepared to adjust his 'sources' to make these points, and it is immaterial that the women whom he chooses to memorialise may be known in other accounts for different virtues and vices. In this respect his versions are indeed 'legend'. Saints' lives had a similar singleness of purpose, but Chaucer here is deliberately choosing pagan, pre-Christian and therefore secular examples. The morality is implicit in the narrative structure. As ever experimental Chaucer now tries out single-issue brief narratives. This is different from his more customary multifaceted and amplified style, and the strain shows. As an example we may consider the first poem, whose heroine is Cleopatra.

Boccaccio had presented her in his De mulieribus claris as completely evil but Chaucer's probable source is Vincent of Beauvais's Speculum Historiale, one of the books that the God of Love says Chaucer owns (Prologue G 307). Even here she is not presented very favourably. Chaucer, as in other cases, both relies on a source and changes it radically. Cleopatra still seems a curious choice but it is significant that Chaucer had added her, together with Troilus, to the list of those who had suffered for love in the Temple of Venus in The Parliament of Fowls (291). In the Legend she is presented as the image of faithful 'wyfhod', and commits suicide for love of the not always faithful Anthony who has already committed suicide. The poet insists that all this is 'storiall soth, it is no fable' (702). This assertion by its very emphasis perhaps paradoxically suggests some unease.

There are also signs of unease about the strict discipline involved.

The weddynge and the feste to devyse	*describe*
To me, that have ytake swich empryse	*undertaking*
Of so many a story for to make	
It were to longe, lest that I shulde slake	*omit*
Of thyng that bereth more effect and charge:	*carries more power and significance*

For men may overlade a ship or barge.
And forthy to th'effect thanne wol I skyppe,
And al the remenaunt, I wol lete it slippe.

(616–23)

Chaucer makes similar remarks elsewhere in his verse, but never at such length, and never with such a sense of burden 'Of so many a story for to make.' Nevertheless he cannot resist amplification in the superb virtuoso passage on the naval battle where he imitates the movement of alliterative verse (635–53).

PATHOS, GOODNESS AND MOCKERY

Pathos has not much modern appeal: witness many modern readers' response, or rather lack of response, to the sorrow of Troilus. Compassion is frequently invoked in the late twentieth century, but its objects are rarely the sufferings of virtuous aristocratic lovers or similar victims. Yet Chaucer's feeling for the sufferings of women seems absolutely genuine as fully expounded in *The Man of Law's Tale* of Constance and *The Clerk's Tale* of Griselda, though modern responses even here may turn into impatience with the heroines for allowing themselves to suffer. Pathos is evoked by the spectacle of the innocent and vulnerable subjected to mental or physical pain and to read of it unrelieved can be a painful experience in itself. What paradoxically makes it tolerable is the strength revealed in the sufferers which evokes our admiration.

The account of Thisbe is longer than most and genuinely affecting. Like others it has some touches of striking if slightly grotesque realism, as when Thisbe finds her beloved in the throes of death

Betynge with his heles on the grounde,	
Al blody, and therwithal a-bak she stert	*started*
And lik the wawes quappe gan hire herte.	*waves heave*

(*LGW*, 863–5)

The story of Dido is also told with some fullness, and worth comparing with the account from the *Aeneid* in *The House of Fame*. As in all these poems there is a refreshing response to goodness. Thus, Dido is attracted by the noble Aeneas:

> And saw the man, that he was lyk a knyght,
> And suffisaunt of persone and of myght,
> And lyk to been a verray gentil man;   *truly noble*
> And wel his wordes he besette can,   *apply*
> And had a noble visage for the nones   *at that time*
> And formed wel of braunes and of bones.   *muscles*
>
>   (*LGW*, 1066–74)

This is an admirable summary of the good qualities of a knight. The cumulative descriptive style with frequent use of *and* is one of the characteristics of Chaucer's later manner. The apparently simple style has more subtlety than at first appears. The conjunction of qualities given here expresses Chaucer's genuine ideal of the knight and gentleman, sympathetic to Dido. Yet the doubled use of the word 'like', the empty and possibly mocking phrase 'for the nones', and the comment on Aeneas's handsome physical appearance, such as Chaucer does not make for his real heroes, like Troilus, signals a satirical or sarcastic implication about Aeneas, as do other stylistic touches. Compare, for its subtle differences, the description of Aeneas with that of Troilus (*TC*, II, 631–7). Aeneas promises, or seems, better than he really is, as the story shows. This little passage is a masterpiece of veiled criticism of Aeneas.

And thus we come to the other aspect of the poems, a vein of mockery. In these stories Chaucer cannot altogether refrain from his usual habit of taking the story so seriously as to address the characters, or make exclamations about them. Critics rarely if ever speak of the Narrator in these poems, and quite rightly, because the concept gives us no new insight, but the narrating poet or Expositor is evident enough. An example, together with Chaucer's irrepressible tendency to hyperbole, is found at the beginning of the Legend of Hypsipyle and Medea where the poet addresses Jason:

> Thow rote of false lovers, Duc Jasoun   *root*
> Thow sly devourere and confusioun
> Of gentil wemen, tendre creatures . . .
> O, often swore thow that thow woldest dye
> For love, whan thow ne feltest maladye
> Save foul delyt, which that thow callest love.

Yif that I live, thy name shal be shove
In English that thy sekte shall be knowe,   *kind*
Have at thee Jason! Now thyn horn is blowe.   *Now the game is*
                                                                  up for you
                                                          (*LGW*, 1368–83)

None of this is in Chaucer's sources. The concepts are serious and
familiar enough, but the style, especially in the last three lines, is
irrepressibly lively. The horn is presumably that which in hunting
signifies the finding and death of the quarry.

LET US NOT PRAISE PAGAN GODS AND MEN TOO MUCH

The attitude expressed towards Jason appears elsewhere and may
remind us of the 'rascaille' of heathen gods referred to at the end of
Troilus. Although the stories are fascinating, Chaucer has a genuine
medieval contempt for the vices of pagan heroes and disgust at the
horrors which are the frequent subject matter of classical mythology.
He expresses this most forcibly in the *Introduction to the Man of Law's
Tale* when, after listing the stories in the *Legend* that he has written,
or is going to write, he draws attention to his refusal to write about
the incest of Canace and Antiochus. Although there again he
diverges into humorous asides, there seems no reason to doubt, in a
poet who so often expresses tenderness and pity, a real squeamishness
on certain topics, a real moral conviction that some things are be-
yond the pale. Of course there are exceptions to the disapproval of
pagan heroes and deities: Theseus, Palamon, Troilus, Hector among
men, and among the deities Venus, perhaps, though she is 'really' a
planet. And as he later shows in *The Canterbury Tales*, Chaucer has a
robust enjoyment of the physical and sexual mishaps of the tra-
ditional comic tale. But in the strange poem that is the *Legend*
Chaucer's idealism is in a sense the source both of his realism and of
his mockery of some of his characters. Idealism, pathos and mockery
come together.

RECULER POUR MIEUX SAUTER

Some critics have seen pervasive irony or even covert obscenities
everywhere in *The Legend*. Such a view is yet another example of the
attempt to foist a modernistic consistency or subversiveness or in-
decency on Chaucer's essentially variable work. But the uneasiness to
which I have several times referred and many critics have perceived

does seem to be shown in the more than usually frequent interpolations, the relative thinness, and the strain of so many stories all on the same sad theme. Taking into account Chaucer's natural taste for variety, the absence of any post-seventeenth-century sense of decorum, and the proximity of death and laughter noted earlier on (pp. 101–3) it is not surprising that, in the stories in the *Legend*, as was the case of the failed philosopher Oliver Edwards, otherwise unknown to fame, 'cheerfulness was always breaking in'.[3] The proximity of laughter to tears is a commonplace, but is notable in both Chaucer and Shakespeare.

The stories are very much a product of the Gothic sensibility in pathos and a certain risibility. They make an interesting contrast with Gower, who maintains a much more even tone, though he never put himself into such a ticklish straitjacket as Chaucer did in *The Legend*.

Chaucer in his stories was working the vein of love and desertion which he had so successfully mined in his previous poems. But he had both reverted to that theme and at the same time advanced beyond it, especially towards the notion, not original with him, of a collection of varied stories. The *Legend* is a sustained evocation of genuine pathos, drawing extensively on a great range of classical and other stories, with some corresponding variety, yet also with a new concision and drive. It is energetic, forward-looking, not tired. The style is often subtle. Were it not for Chaucer's other works we should admit without question that the *Legend* is a remarkably good, complex poem. The idea of a set of stories all on one theme was too constricting, but it led to the idea of a collection of highly variable stories. The metre, the so-called 'heroic couplet', was admirably set for broader narrative sweep. Narrow as it seems, and because it is so narrow, the *Legend* is a bridge to a much broader country of narrative.

NOTES

1. Alastair Minnis, *Chaucer and Pagan Antiquity* (Cambridge, 1982).
2. R. W. Chambers, 'Long Will, Dante and the Righteous Heathen', in *Essays and Studies* 9 (1924), 50–69.
3. James Boswell, *Life of Samuel Johnson* (1791), 17 April 1778.

Chapter 18

Prologue to *The Canterbury Tales*

IN FELAWESHIPE, AND PILGRIMES WERE THEY ALLE

It is the most famous group in all English literature. It seems so simple a device, a series of coloured cut-outs, distinctive, easy to understand. And yet all England is here, in the spring-time of leaf and crop, from the young sun and bird-song to the restless men and women thankful to be recovered from illness, eager to travel and pay their debt of gratitude. They are gathered in the welcoming big rooms of the famous Tabard Inn in Southwark, known to all, to start their cheerful pilgrimage.

The poet himself is soon one of their fellowship and thanks to his busy polite curiosity can give us a succession of separate sketches unrivalled for their crisp laconic vividness. The Knight he puts first, characterising him by love of chivalry, of

Trouthe and honour, fredom and curteisie.

(*CT*, I, 46)

Travelling with his son, the fashionable young Squire, and the yeoman, his servant and archer clad in green, the Knight must have been for all his modest appearance a great lord. Then the over-refined Prioress, imitating courtly manners, speaking the French of Stratford-le-Bow; and a couple of sturdy, prosperous worldly clerics, Monk, Friar; a well-dressed Merchant less prosperous than he looks; an Oxford scholar who has spent his scanty means on books rather than clothes; a jovial hospitable Franklin; a group of wealthy tradesmen; a ruthless master mariner; a learned and expensive doctor; the bold-faced Wife of Bath, expert in cloth-making; followed by the admirably conscientious Parson and the Ploughman his equally idealised brother, both low down in the social scale; and sharply changing again, the Reeve, Miller, Summoner, Pardoner and Manciple, all superior workmen, all rascals and churls, and grouped with them, as another self-deprecatory joke, the poet himself.

Almost all are clearly differentiated in various ways. Most clearly, they are all conceived as functions of what they do, not by their names, though in the course of the tales a few names appear, usually rather typical, like Alison, common in both senses of the word, as the name for the Wife of Bath. For no clear reason the only name mentioned in *The General Prologue* is the Friar's, Huberd. Chaucer specifically says that he does not know the Merchant's name, which makes us suspect that a specific person is aimed at. The descriptions have a lineage in the rhetoric of poetry, and especially in the literature of the 'estates', traditional descriptions of people in various ranks and positions of society.[1] To that extent they are impersonal types. But every reader gets a sense of a person in the portrait, though rarely of individual subjectivity, or self-consciousness. It is not as if we feel that they chose their functions: they just are.

Nevertheless they have individualising traits, and it is impossible not to feel that some models in actual life are being aimed at. Many years ago the Host of the Tabard was identified as Harry Bailly, a well-known citizen and innkeeper in Southwark. The Lawyer against whose writings no one could 'pinch' (*CT*, I, 326) may well have been a distinguished lawyer, Thomas Pinchbeck, whom Chaucer might have had a grudge against; the Shipman with his named ship may have been well known; the Cook may be a crack at Roger of Ware, a known cook; and so forth. Apart from Harry Bailly there is, with one other exception, no absolute certainty, but the sense of the reality of people, beneath the descriptive hyperbole (each pilgrim is the best of his kind, an expert in his function), is strong. The other exception of an absolutely real person, like Harry Bailly, is the poet himself, though at this stage he is not described; he is the unclassified observer. In the late nineteenth century the passion for 'realism' led to much speculation about the literal truth of the pilgrims and the actual locations of the pilgrimage route, culminating in Professor Manly's shrewd speculations about their 'real' identity.[2] More recently the fashion has been to discount the possibility of objective reality in art and life. Each view is unjustifiably extreme. There are two pilgrims, the Host and Chaucer, who certainly existed; of some others it is likely there was at least a model, occasionally of people whom Chaucer had reason to satirise on political (e.g. the Lawyer), moral (e.g. the Shipman), financial (e.g. the Merchant, who may have been a hit at Gilbert Maghfold, to whom Chaucer owed money) or purely personal grounds. Chaucer was composing a fiction and in his usual manner shifting among various points of view. The hints of real persons are only part of the wealth of meaning he has constructed, but they anchor it in an historical time and place, as well as in his own mind. One of the pilgrims is so dramatically envisaged that she approaches a degree of self-awareness, which will be further developed as the work progresses. The Wife of Bath even in the description of her in *The General Prologue* almost escapes into a dramatic life of her own.

The interest does not rely only on details of naturalistic description, of which there is too rich a profusion even to give examples here, where realism does not exclude fiction, and may even enhance it. There are other structures, inherent in Chaucer's mind, witnessed to by his writing, and related to his own nature and culture. Lists in traditional literature usually have an inner structure or several structures and messages. They are not a random sequence. *The General Prologue* is an extended list, framed by the wonderful spring opening which swoops down from the stars to the Tabard at the beginning, and at the end by the agreement at the festive suggestion of the Host of the inn to join in fellowship, to tell stories, and the early morning start to the pilgrimage. Within the frame comes the list of portraits as they may be called, apparently separate, yet in significant order or disorder. First, though, we should realise, they are notably a group. Separate as they seem, they have fallen into a company in fellowship (*CT*, I, 24–6) and the poet soon makes himself one of their fellowship (*CT*, I, 32). 'Fellowship' is a powerful word in Chaucer's poetry, linked with friendship and company. 'Company' is also an important word and Chaucer uses it more frequently. Both words signify the feeling for the strong social bond that holds people together (not always with good intent) in society and overcomes quarrels and rivalries. Most human beings depend on a social context: the ultimate sadness, even the horror of death, is summed up in one of Chaucer's favourite lines 'Allone withouten any compaignye' (*CT*, I, 2779) repeated several times almost verbatim, but extended by many other references to the sadness of being alone. On this occasion the Host says he has not seen 'so merry a company' this year (*CT*, I, 764), and they are united in a common purpose, serious yet cheerful, of pilgrimage to the sacred shrine. Chaucer does not sentimentalise the group-spirit. There are quarrels enough, the most serious reconciled by the Knight, the person of most authority, despite the Host's own bustling assumption of authority and sometimes fatuous commentary.

COMPETITION

Against this Anne Laskaya has argued forcibly that masculine competitiveness dominates both the general account of the pilgrimage, not only with quarrels but also in the way stories contrast with each other, and themselves portray competition.[3] In so far as any narration may be described as a struggle between teller and matter, competition may then fall into the category of propositions that are so generally true as not to be of much analytical use. It is the nature of life to be competitive and we see consciousness of this everywhere in Chaucer's work. The problem that interests him more in *The Canterbury Tales* is how to achieve reconciliation. In his culture competitiveness was particularly a male characteristic between men, often competing for a woman. Women may occasionally compete against men, with little chance of success, though such competition, and the success of wives in achieving domination, is a favourite subject of matrimonial jokes for many centuries, as several of the comic bawdy Canterbury Tales illustrate. More seriously, it is usually the female figure in Chaucer's poetry who attempts to achieve peace and concord between warring men, as Nature in *The Parliament of Fowls*, Queen Alceste in *The Legend of Good Women*, and Prudence in the pilgrim-Chaucer's own *Tale of Melibee*. Men are indeed quarrelsome and we shall see, for example, the sequence after the noble *Knight's Tale* broken by the interruption of the drunken Miller, who insists on telling his own derisive comic bawdy tale of rivalry between two young men for a pretty wench.

Fourteenth-century England was full of masculine disharmony, as was all Europe. What century has not been? Yet the 'fellowship' that Chaucer presents is genuinely a part of his poetic mind and his social and artistic creation. It perhaps accounts for the lack of sourness in what was often so evidently a satirical and detached attitude. Maybe the fellowship was more in his imagination than in actuality, but after all he was there (in some sense, however fictional the pilgrimage) and we were not. There is no longer quite the same questioning mind that works through his earlier poems, though the interest in and relish for diversity are undiminished, perhaps even stronger. He is now settled on the last stage of his journey through life, still in full strength, setting out not on a quest for the unknown but a pilgrimage, in gratitude, to the known destination of England's favourite saint, in that city of Canterbury that might be transmuted, if we will, to the way, as the Parson says

Of thilke parfit glorious pilgrymage
That highte Jerusalem celestial.

(*CT*, X, 50–1)

SOCIAL STRUCTURES

The three orders

Within this fellowship the deepest structure, most firmly set in Chaucer's mind, archaic, religious, social, not personal, is the vision of society as built of three interdependent orders: the fighting men, the priests, the labouring food-gatherers.[4] This concept was not limited to Chaucer or England and has its roots in antiquity, perhaps in the very beginnings of human agrarian society, when land, food and their physical and spiritual protection were the fundamentals of survival. In the later Middle Ages they translate into the knight who fights for all, the priest who prays for all, the ploughman who provides food for all. This wildly idealised social structure was an intellectual commonplace. Langland in *Piers Plowman* shares it. The peasantry, the most numerous and the poorest not surprisingly were inclined to reject it. Chaucer's Ploughman, however, knows his place, properly fulfils his function, and is contented. Similarly, the Knight is idealised as six centuries of readers have recognised as a true and perfect noble knight, where the very word 'knight' is in Chaucer's diction a word of praise. The priestly cast is presented in two equally idealised aspects: the scholarly learned Clerk and the Parson, the ideal pastor of his flock.

The idealised, essential characters are well established in convincing naturalistic detail. The Knight's career is just possible and has close similarities to contemporary figures, including John of Gaunt's son who eventually became Henry IV. The capture of Alexandria was hailed as the most resounding of crusading victories in the second half of the fourteenth century, though to modern sensibilities, and a few rare fourteenth-century ones, such crusading against Islam was wrong. Not so to Chaucer, though the Knight had also served Islamic lords, as was not unusual in fourteenth-century life and literature. Lines of loyalty were different then.[5] (Chaucer is *not* our contemporary.) The Clerk is convincingly characterised as a rather dry but devoted Oxford don. Chaucer had closer connections with Oxford than with Cambridge and may have known some of the famous Merton men, scientists and philosophers. The Parson and Ploughman are furthest from Chaucer's immediate experience but there is nothing false in their characterisation, even if such characters were rare. Indeed that is part of the point of their description.

Below the ideal

The paradox is that this ideal structure of a functionally integrated communal ideal is the basis of the varying degrees of satirical sharpness with which the pilgrims are viewed. Among the other clergy the sentimental pretty Prioress with her genteel social aspirations is only lightly mocked. The Monk, 'a manly man, to been an abbot able' (*CT*, I, 167), a hunter, an estate manager and so forth, who gave not 'an oyster' (*CT*, I, 182) for the vows that denied a monk freedom to wander, and forbad hunting, is treated more enigmatically, for the poet remarks

> And I seyde his opinioun was good.
>
> (*CT*, I, 183)

'Said', not 'say': in which of the poet's voices, omniscient Expositor or narrator, limited pilgrim-reporter, or any between them, is this remark made? The past tense suggests the pilgrim-reporter as speaker, as it were in polite conversation with the Monk, leaving the poet uncommitted. Bearing in mind the poet's own leaning towards secularity and serving the world, there seems a touch of sympathy in putting into words the Monk's attitude:

> How shal the world be served?
>
> (*CT*, I, 187)

At the same time there is equally a touch of derision in the extravagance of his fat shiny rich appearance. The lack of 'tone' in the line of approval and its ambiguity, take it how you will, is part of the poetry, of which enigma, not irony, under a cloak of simplicity, is the essence. The Monk certainly violates the ideal.

The Friar gets off less lightly as set against the original model for Friars, as established by St Francis, of devout chaste hungry poverty. The Merchant escapes from the fundamental frame of reference which obviously had no place, in its agrarian simplicity, for the newly evolving money economy which was part of the evolving capitalist system. Nor was there a part for the Lawyer, who is almost downright accused of fiddling the accounts – but lawyers have never been popular characters in literature, except in the novels of Sir Walter Scott, himself a lawyer. The understrappers of the ecclesiastical system, that unsavoury pair, the ugly unwholesome Summoner, and the swindling, effeminate Pardoner, are for slightly different reasons described with as near a savage zest as Chaucer ever came to.

They are part of the corruption of the ideal priesthood. The Summoner is an ignorant pig who oppresses the poor and will trade his whore for a quart of wine. The Pardoner offends particularly, not least in that he is physically effeminate, with a high-pitched voice and attempted fancy appearance, which in a highly masculinised society is enough to call down insult and revulsion on him. Chaucer says scornfully

> I trowe he were a geldyng or a mare.
>
> (CT, I, 691)

Neither can be meant literally. Castration of human beings was not a practice in fourteenth-century England, though the idea of eunuchs was known, if only through the Bible, and also from the East. And the Pardoner was obviously not a woman in disguise. But whereas for a woman to 'become' a man in this culture might be laudable, for a man even to be called a 'woman' was an insult (the present writer remembers hearing it being so used in a sporting crowd of men and in the British Army). Many modern feminists legitimately deplore the modern continuation of the same attitude. Chaucer here, as so often, and not surprisingly, articulates the dominant attitude of his culture, whether we like it or not.

Degree

The Franklin is another somewhat ambiguous figure. He may touch on the characteristics of a well-known country gentleman and politician such as Sir John Bussy from Lincolnshire. He is hearty, generous, does himself and others well. In so far as he descends from a line of figures in 'estates literature' Professor Mann rightly regards his portrait as not satirical, though it has a touch of Chaucer's amused detachment. Argument has raged over whether he is a 'gentleman'; there is no doubt that he is, but he may also be seen as part of another social structure in *The General Prologue*, the most practical of all the social divisions, that of 'degree'. It means rank, and was very well understood. The best example is the order of precedence in meals in hall given in such courtesy books as John Russell's *Boke of Nurture*, but there are other less conscious rankings, such as the rates of pay on campaign. Naturally, royalty, barons, knights come highest, the Franklin comes somewhere a bit lower, footsoldiers and peasants lowest. Clergy are distinctively ordered and slotted into the secular order. Chaucer apologises for not listing the portraits of the pilgrims 'in their degree'; as he says, 'My wit is short, ye may wel understonde' – the jesting poet obviously speaking here, as both poet and pilgrim (*CT*, I, 744–6). In fact in *The General Prologue* the order of degree is only slightly disturbed; the Knight comes first, the churls last.

Chaucer does not describe himself in *The General Prologue*, though later he gives some very interesting indirect comments through the patronising jesting of the Host:

> 'What man artow?' quod he;
> 'Thou lookest as thou woldest fynde an hare,
> For evere upon the ground I se thee stare.
> Approche near and look up murily' . . .   *cheerfully*
>   (*CT*, VII, 695–8)

Then follows the usual joke about his fatness. The Host is imperti-nently familiar to Chaucer with his 'thous', in contrast, for example, with his polite 'ye' to the Monk (*CT*, I, 3118) or Man of Law (*CT*, II, 33), or the Clerk (*CT*, IV, 2) – though not to the Physician or Franklin. We can grade the person's 'degree' in the Host's eyes by whether he uses the polite plural 'ye' or the familiar 'thou' to whom-ever he speaks to. Chaucer the poet and courtier amuses himself by exposing Chaucer the pilgrim to the Host's impertinence. It con-tinues the self-contained self-awareness and paradoxical reserve (since he also puts himself forward) of earlier poems. It is part of his poetic mentality. But we might also notice that Chaucer the man, one of the new class of literate laymen, is as hard to fit into any traditional category as Merchant or Lawyer, though he like them is a gentleman and on the upper end of the middle section of the ladder of degree.

Gentil and churl

The other social classification in *The Canterbury Tales* is that between 'gentils' and 'churls'. The 'gentils' are those who dislike coarseness – for example, they cry out when the Pardoner offers a tale

> Nay, lat hym telle us of no ribaudye,   *dirty story*
>   (*CT*, VI, 324)

whereas Chaucer the pilgrim or poet, in his pseudo-apology before *The Miller's Tale*, says plainly it is a churl's tale, which he regrets having to repeat, and asks 'gentil wights' either to excuse it or

Turne over the leef and chese another tale.   *page; choose*
                                                    (*CT*, I, 3169–77)

There is a clear distinction between gentry with refined tastes, and
the rest, which runs through English society, as one of the several
social classifications available until the first half of the twentieth
century – with uncertain but strongly felt boundaries.

Even here Chaucer is ambiguous. He calls *The Miller's Tale* a
churl's tale, but these *fabliau*-type tales are as courtly as romances,
and like romances appealed to a variety of classes. Chaucer's own
versions of these international comic tales are polished and more
rhetorical in the best sense than other versions. Chaucer and most of
his audience, including no doubt many ladies, appreciated them, and
they are not so foul-mouthed as some of the French courtly *fabliaux*.
Chaucer for amusement blurs the line between 'gentil' and 'churl'.
There is no doubt that he himself is 'gentil', and *The Canterbury Tales*
as a whole are designed for a courtly and 'gentil' readership.

Finally, we come to the Host. He is described as a seemly man,
not lacking in 'manhod' and fit

For to han be a marchal in an halle.

                                                    (*CT*, I, 753)

As a marshal is indeed his true function when at his suggestion the
pilgrims agree to the story-telling competition, with a supper for the
winner, and elect him, since it was not worth fussing about, to be
their 'governour' (*CT*, I, 813). This does not usurp the Knight's
natural authority. It would have been below the Knight's dignity as
the senior officer, so to speak, to do the sergeant-major's organising
job – especially as the troops turn out to be somewhat recalcitrant at
times. The Host is outside (like Chaucer) the ancient threefold divi-
sion, as also are the other townsmen like the Gildsmen. Like them
he is well up the scale in rank, being well-to-do, well established,
with authority, owning property. He is not a churl. Like Chaucer he
seems to move easily between the classes. Both of them are 'new
men'. But in character the Host has a vulgar *bonhomie* conspicuously
absent from Chaucer.

RHETORICAL DISLOCATION FOR LOCATION

The clash between fellowship and disharmony, order and disorder,
is illustrated in a literary way by the form of the actual portraits.

Longstanding instructions found in well-known rhetorical handbooks such as that by Geoffrey of Vinsauf quoted by Chaucer (e.g. *Troilus and Criseyde*, I, 1065–9, and, jestingly, in *The Nun's Priest's Tale, CT*, VII, 3347) laid down a formal structure of descriptive detail for a person from head to toe. Chaucer's own description of the Duchess Blanche in *The Book of the Duchess*, 855–960, is an example though even here it is already adapted and made more flexible, as well as more verbose.

None of the literary portraits in *The General Prologue* follows the strict rhetorical pattern though they are clearly based on it. Chaucer mingles details of dress, personality, occupation, biography in compressed descriptions which are all the more vivid for being apparently so casual. Usually, vivid unsystematic glimpses of appearance are given, which are often emblematic of the person's character – the Knight's stained tunic is the famous example. Others are the Wife of Bath's red stockings and bold red face, but there are examples everywhere. No visual description is given of the Parson or the Manciple alone, which illustrates no general principle, except the desire for variety, for they are given very different characters.

There are some fairly constant notes. Attitude to money is one. Type of speech is another. The acquisition of or interest in money are regarded unfavourably. The way a person speaks, or what they say, are indicative of character – and this, like so much else in *The General Prologue*, is a new departure in characterisation which deserves note.

MANUSCRIPT CULTURE

'This is a long preamble of a tale' as the Friar complains about *The Wife of Bath's Prologue*, but it is a foretaste of great riches to come. In order fully to appreciate the quality of the tales as they come to us from Chaucer's pen, it is well to remind ourselves of the conditions of manuscript culture. It is half way between the variability of speech and the relative fixity of print and this governs the nature of the Tales. Fifteenth-century scribes and early printers made a pretty good hash of the text, especially of the metre, and only during the eighteenth century did some notion of the regularity of Chaucer's metre begin to dawn. It was not even moderately firmly fixed until Skeat's great edition of 1894, which over-emphasised its regularity. Even now there is some debate. We now read the poems in the fixed form of print, which is a great blessing, but can mislead us, as has been earlier suggested (see p. 22) because Chaucer often imitated oral delivery, and the criteria of poems that are heard are different from those that have always been meant for the silent reader of print. (That so many modern critics think of the poetry as essentially printed can be seen by the way they point out that in their quotations the emphasising italics are theirs. Of course they are, because Chaucer had no way of italicising his writing. Nor did he underline for any reason. None of the three best and earliest manuscripts of *The Canterbury Tales*, the Ellesmere now at the Huntington Library in California, the Hengwrt at the Library of the University of Wales in Aberystwyth, and Gg. IV. 27 of the University of Cambridge Library, has any underlining.) These are big manuscripts. Ellesmere is particularly splendid, with the pages beginning each story being decorated with floriate borders, and the famous miniatures of the tellers, though attempts at literary criticism based on these sometimes clumsy and ill-proportioned figures are a useless exercise. Furthermore, the splendour of a manuscript is no index of its verbal accuracy. What must be emphasised, though not exaggerated, is the relative fluidity of manuscript culture itself, and the fact that Chaucer did not give final form either to the sequence of tales, nor, in some cases, to whom should tell them.

THE MANUSCRIPTS

Chaucer must have left a bundle of written papers, with stories partly in groups, partly on their own. Also, some stories were already in separate circulation, and he had continued to have bright ideas (*The Canon's Yeoman's Prologue and Tale* was clearly an afterthought, subsequent to *The General Prologue*). We have none of his preliminary notes, which may have been made on lightly waxed tablets, but his working copies of poems would have been loose sheets or pamphlets of paper or parchment which he bound up in booklets of at most a few stories at a time. When satisfied with what he wrote, he sent a section off to a professional scrivener to have one or more copies written out fair. Scribes were liable to make many mistakes, so Chaucer corrected the copy when it came back (scratching mistakes out with stone or a knife), cursing the scribe meanwhile. Much of this we know from the short poem which is the unenviable monument of his usual scribe, entitled *Chaucer's Wordes unto Adam, His owne Scriveyn*.

> Adam Scriveyn, if ever it thee bifalle   *scrivener*
> Boece or Troylus for to wryten newe,
> Under thy long lokkes thou most have the scalle, *may you have the scab*
> But after my makyng thou wryte more trewe   *unless according to*

So ofte a-daye I mot thy werk renewe,   *must*
It to correcte and eke to rubbe and scrape;
And al is thorugh thy negligence and rape.   *haste*

No critic has yet claimed that this poem is ironical and spoken by a Narrator, foolish or otherwise.

Even after correction many mistakes remained. We have none even of Chaucer's fair copies unless the prose *Equatorie of the Planetis* is his, and as that is technical prose it does not in any case help much. Scholars have established that Chaucer's spelling is reasonably closely represented in Ellesmere and Hengwrt, but not in Cambridge Gg. IV, 27. Even these manuscripts are copies of copies by a scribe not more than averagely careful. Scribes sometimes copied different sections from different exemplars, or compared or mingled exemplars: a process known as contamination. A late manuscript is usually more corrupt, but sometimes even a generally corrupt manuscript preserves a correct reading which generally better manuscripts have lost.

It must always be remembered that manuscripts varied greatly, and in Chaucer's time and for two centuries after his works came to the reader in a manner very different from the way we receive them now. Some manuscripts like Ellesmere are splendidly and regularly written in a dialect close to Chaucer's own, but others were less formal and could vary in dialect. The short minor poems in especial might be written in different informal hands over a period of years, like Cambridge University Library Ff.1.6, which has some late and scrappily written but quite good texts, for example of *The Parliament of Fowls*. Early printed texts resembled manuscripts. Not till Speght's edition of 1598 was there any attempt at glossary or notes, and then they were very inadequate. Chaucer came even as late as Shakespeare's time in a plain text, very corrupt, with variable spelling and negligible annotation. The little punctuation was very irregular and uncertain. The failure to recognise the function of final -*e* quite early in the fifteenth century, as well as the carelessness of scribes, caused everyone to think that Chaucer's metre was a rough 'riding rhyme', like the excruciating stumble produced by many students when they read Chaucer today. Modern editions purged of scribal error, with modernised capitalisation and punctuation, simplified spelling, careful annotation, are vitally necessary to our appreciation of Chaucer, but as noted above they may inadvertently and subtly misrepresent Chaucer by unconsciously invoking and instilling in us the characteristic expectations of a print culture, as well as more anachronistic qualities gathered from the printed books of later centuries.

The order of the *Tales* varies in different groups of manuscripts, and a very small amount of spurious text has crept in. The process of establishing a text is therefore difficult and highly technical. Some would argue that the very concept of a fixed text is misleading, and that might be true of the continuously rewritten *Piers Plowman*. Chaucer was as so often in advance of his time in insisting on the need for precision in writing his works, as the poem to Adam shows, and as appears in the stanza near the end of *Troilus and Criseyde*, which indicates some of the problems he himself was conscious of:

> And for ther is so gret diversite
> In Englissh and in writyng of our tonge
> So prey I God that non myswrite the,
> Ne the mysmetre for defaute of tonge,
> And red wherso thow be, or elles songe,
> That thow be understonde, God I biseche.

(V, 1793–8)

Needless to say, fifteenth-century scribes made plenty of mistakes even when copying this stanza. Modern editors, by laborious comparison and an ideal of accuracy shared only with Chaucer, not his scribes, do far better than they. But we are still uncertain of the internal chronology of the various stories in *The Canterbury Tales* and it is clear that Chaucer himself left the situation fluid, changing his mind, and switching the sequence about except for the first group of *General Prologue, Knight's, Miller's, Reeve's* and unfinished *Cook's Tale*. This fluidity, extending beyond sequence to who should tell the tale, defeats many modern theories and systems about characterisation or general message. Of the three main manuscripts Hengwrt, perhaps the earliest, has the least coherent sequence of tales, though good texts in detail. Hengwrt lacks *The Canon's Yeoman's Prologue and Tale*, but most scholars are agreed it is genuine. Hengwrt is the least 'edited' manuscript. Ellesmere, written by the same scribe, is better organised, not necessarily by Chaucer himself (but why not?), and a better shot at the whole work despite some blemishes. Gg. IV. 27 reproduces excellent texts (and is the only manuscript to preserve the revised form of *The Prologue* to *The Legend of Good Women*) but has eccentric spelling, and its own sequence.

THE SEQUENCE OF TALES

Chaucer did not group the *Tales* according to any intellectual system, but rather for the sake of variety. The whole work is a Gothic manuscript miscellany, like Robert Thornton's or the Auchinleck manuscript. Thornton was a Yorkshire gentleman and his manuscript, one of two written by himself about the middle of the fifteenth century, and now at Lincoln Cathedral, is a collection of poems and prose pieces, some of them secular stories, some religious meditations, of great variety. The Auchinleck manuscript is a great collection of romances which Chaucer may have known, now in the Scottish National Library in Edinburgh. *The Canterbury Tales* is a similar, though much superior, collection, and is, almost incredibly, the product of one extraordinarily diverse creative mind.

The intended sequence of tales can be made out to some extent by internal reference to stages of the journey between Southwark and Canterbury along the Pilgrim's Way. This was worked out by the scholar Henry Bradshaw in the mid-nineteenth century and followed by Professor Skeat in his now outdated edition, and earlier versions of this book. It still leaves inconsistencies, though it can be defended.[6] However, the earliest 'editor' of Chaucer was the scribe of the Ellesmere manuscript or his superior, and the order he follows is slightly different. The Ellesmere order has been followed in the now standard Riverside Edition, edited by L. D. Benson, and the sequence of tales and numbering used there is followed here. Ten blocks, or so-called 'fragments', which have some internal coherence, can be deduced from comparing manuscripts. The brilliant pieces of realistic comedy between tales, parts of various blocks, are sometimes called *Links*, and they with their specific references to place-names, and additional drama of interplay between the pilgrims, tell us something of the story of the pilgrimage itself.

It is generally assumed that the original plan was for each of the 29 pilgrims to tell two stories each way to Canterbury and back, but this proved impossibly ambitious and the pilgrimage ends as the Host calls on the Parson at 4 o'clock in the afternoon for their last tale. They would have been in sight of Canterbury (still to be seen from a hill on approaching from London). The approach to Canterbury makes an abrupt, moving but illogical end to the original scheme. Professor Pearsall suggests an opposite view: that the four-tale plan was a late addition to *The General Prologue* – in fact, another bright idea like *The Canon's Yeoman's Prologue and Tale* – 'postponing the bringing to an end of a project that had become coterminous for Chaucer with life itself'. The present ending is 'the conclusion of a plan that had been superseded. Chaucer's characteristic aversion to closure could hardly be more neatly expressed.'[7] This is surely over-ingenious. The sympathetic speculation that the project 'had become coterminous for Chaucer with life itself' agrees much better with the ending as we have it when the Parson sees the pilgrimage as a model of the way to the celestial Jerusalem. To think otherwise requires a rewriting of *The General Prologue* later than *The Parson's Prologue and Tale* for which there is no evidence. To devise a new plan of some 120 tales when only 24 had been completed by perhaps 1395 is to exaggerate even Chaucer's optimism, when by the normal standards of the time he was getting old. It also exaggerates his reluctance to close.

Of *The Canterbury Tales*, 20 come triumphantly to a close. If all stories may be metaphorically thought of as memorials that close in death (above, p. 101) then Chaucer as an ageing man was steering clearly towards death and as he might hope 'the celestial Jerusalem'. The contraction of the scheme of *The Canterbury Tales* to conclusion at Canterbury, whatever internal inconsistency it involved with the ambitious plan on setting out, has an imaginative satisfaction much deeper than the banal supper 'at hir aller coste' on return to the Tabard Inn. What an anticlimax that would have been, especially considering Chaucer's dismissive attitude to even royal feasts that we have several times noticed. Furthermore, the earthly closure of death could not be for Chaucer a final annihilation, any more than it was for Troilus. For Chaucer there would have been a literal truth in his own soul's destination after death, though what that destination might be he could not be sure. He took out the best insurance policy available in writing the *Retractation* at the end of *The Canterbury Tales*.

NOTES

1. Jill Mann, *Chaucer and Medieval Estates Satire* (Cambridge, 1973).
2. J. M. Manly, *Some New Light on Chaucer* (Gloucester, Mass., 1959).
3. Anne Laskaya, *Chaucer's Approach to Gender in* The Canterbury Tales (Cambridge, 1995).
4. For this and the other social structures of 'degree' and 'gentry' see Derek Brewer, 'Class distinction in Chaucer', in *Tradition and Innovation in Chaucer* (London, 1982), 54–72.
5. Derek Brewer, 'Chaucer's Knight as Hero, and Machaut's *Prise d'Alexandrie*', in *Heroes and Heroines in Medieval English Literature*, edited by L. Carruthers (Cambridge, 1994), 81–96.
6. The so-called 'Bradshaw shift' in the sequence has been defended by G. A. Keyser, 'In Defence of the Bradshaw Shift', *The Chaucer Review*, 12 (1978), 191–201.
7. Derek Pearsall, *The Life of Geoffrey Chaucer* (Oxford, 1992), 233. See also Charles A. Owen *The Manuscripts of* The Canterbury Tales (Cambridge, 1991).

Chapter 19

The Canterbury Tales I: Love and Rivalry; Tragedy and Comedy

THE RAW MATERIAL OF STORIES

Chaucer probably began to work seriously on the idea of *The Canterbury Tales* around 1386–7, when he went to live down in Kent. The idea of gathering stories into groups was fairly common. From Classical Antiquity comes the great example of Ovid's *Metamorphoses*. More collections of stories held together in a single framework came to be written in the fourteenth century. Gower was in the process of writing such a collection, the *Confessio Amantis*, and Chaucer's own *Legend of Good Women* is another example. A collection of short stories was perhaps the most characteristic form of fourteenth-century literature. It conveyed all kinds of literary effects. An audience, as opposed to a reader, can better understand and remember a short story than any other form of literary narrative. For the more sophisticated reader, a story could be analysed, and there might be as many as three or four levels on which a story might be understood. There were many folktales current of all kinds: pious, amusing, improper. A number of these, as habits of reading and writing spread, were caught up by literary men, all over Europe, and written up. Apart from what he might hear Chaucer also read many stories and he testifies in *The Prologue* to the *Legend of Good Women* (F 17–35) to his passion for stories. They appealed to him, both as typical man of his times, and as a literary artist seeking satisfactory forms. A collection of stories of different kinds obviously created an attractive variety.

Many stories were heard as oral narratives, or were developed orally from being read in some manuscript. Many other stories had been written down and recopied for centuries. In general it was the more serious stories which had been written down, and lighter ones told. Often a story was believed to be historical and therefore true simply because it was written down. The *Clerk's Tale* of patient Griselda is the subject of two illuminating comments in this respect, quoted by Professor Manly in his edition. One of Petrarch's friends doubted whether the story could be true. Petrarch replied that such stories as those of Alcestis (who went to the Underworld in place of her husband, and was rescued by Hercules) *seem* to be fables (*fabulas*) – 'Atque historiae verae sunt', 'but they are true histories'. The sensible fifteenth-century French citizen who wrote the *Ménagier de Paris* also tells the story of Griselda, and says, 'I do not believe it ever happened, but the story is such that I dare not correct or change it, for one wiser than I compiled it, and gave it its name.' There was a clear difference between the Latin 'fabula', meaning a fiction, and a 'historia', meaning true history. Yet whereas the plot itself could not be fundamentally altered, a great part of the aim of such rhetoricians as Geoffrey of Vinsauf was to teach how to dress up an old story in a new signification.

There was a venerable distinction made clear in medieval French literature (as at the beginning of *Le Conte de la Charrette* (or *Lancelot*) by Chrétien de Troyes) between *matiere* – the 'matter' or substance of the story – and *sen* – the manner of its telling, its attitudes, points of view, etc.; in general, the interpretation or spirit or theme of the work.[1] The distinction was made explicit by learned men but it is implicit in all traditional retelling of tales. Chaucer constantly alters the *sen* of his *matiere*. He has the term 'matter', which before *The Miller's Tale* he claims he cannot 'falsen' (*CT*, I, 3175), and that word often stands for the substance of his story. Chaucer uses the word extraordinarily often in *Troilus and Criseyde*, usually of literary material. The nearest verbal equivalent for Chaucer to *sen* is 'sentence' meaning 'inner meaning', as it occurs in the very relevant discussion in the *Prologue* to *The Tale of Melibeus* of the variants between the four Gospels which

Ne seith nat alle thyng as his felawe dooth,	
But natheless hir sentence is al sooth	*true*
And alle acorden as in hire sentence	*inner meaning*
Al be ther in hir tellyng difference.	

(*CT*, VII, 945–8)

'Sentence' is rather more restricted than *sen* to serious inner meaning, and is often opposed to 'solaas', which is entertainment pure (and impure) and simple, but the difference between basic 'matter' and verbal formulation and its interpretation is still inherent here. It goes against the more modern dictum that meaning is indistinguishable from actual words and that therefore paraphrase is impossible;

though that has its own related truth – different words, different implications at least. Chaucer's own works, almost all of them retellings, illustrate both concepts.

The division between words and matter held for style. Style was rightly regarded as consciously variable, a matter of choice, and not the unconscious and unchangeable expression of a person's mind. It was consciously chosen to be apt. Usually for 'high subject-matter' it was appropriate to write, as the Host says to the Clerk, in

Heigh style, as whan that men to kynges write

(CT, IV, 18)

The Host himself wants no elaborate figures of speech, only 'plain speech', suitable for the 'merry tale' he asks for: in other words, a low style. On the whole Chaucer observes this rule: high style comes, for example, in flowery passages in *The Knight's Tale*; low, or plain style in, for example, *The Miller's Tale* and other *fabliaux*. The style is accordant, or deliberately discordant, with the subject, it is less related to the speaker. *The Clerk's Tale*, though not 'low', is in a plain spare style. *The Man of Law's Tale* is more heightened, while for the purposes of burlesque Chaucer uses a high style for part of *The Nun's Priest's Tale*, for example, in the jesting apostrophe to the rhetorician Geoffrey of Vinsauf,

O Gaufred, deere maister soverayn, etc.

(CT, VII, 3347ff.)

The styles that the various storytellers use therefore tell us virtually nothing of their inner characters, though overall they tell much about Chaucer the poet. The various stories allocated to the pilgrims vary in their suitability, as will be seen, and the style suits the subject-matter. (See also below, p. 384, on *The Manciple's Tale*.) But some stories do to some extent suit their tellers.

Meanwhile, we may note that the tales that shall 'shorten their way' must be either instructive or amusing; either of 'sentence' or 'solas'. Stories of downright moral instruction in particular seem to have been relished by Chaucer and his audience almost as much as amusing anecdotes. What is missing is the idea of later Neoclassical literature, which continues through Romanticism even to the present day, that literature instructs *through* delight. Chaucer does not confuse comedy or art with moral uplift, and it is a mistake to try to find some edifying moral, allegorical or otherwise, intended in comic tales. Chaucer's dramatic audience is the group of pilgrims addressed as 'lordings' when the dramatic illusion is strong. This rather low-class appellation is never used by Chaucer in his own voice, as in *Troilus and Criseyde* and *Palamon and Arcite*, though oddly enough it recurs within the dialogues in *The Tale of Melibee*. Chaucer's real audience was composed of the members of the court, of important city merchants, of such clerics as the 'courtier bishops', and of such fellow writers as Hoccleve, a clerk in the Chancery offices, the poet and lawyer, Ralph Strode, the poet and small landowner, Gower, and courtly, perhaps other, ladies.

STORIES COME FIRST, CHARACTERS SECOND

The quality of Chaucer's genius and originality is especially clear in the use he made of the raw material and the ideas he shared with Gower and Boccaccio. It was natural to the Gothic spirit to attempt to gather in every kind of story, to put the serious subject by the amusing, the parody of the high style not far from the high style itself, the 'pious fable' by the 'dirty story' – in a word, to sum up as much of human experience as possible, to let 'contraries meet in one'. Even in Boccaccio's *Decameron* there are a number of serious and pious tales. Chaucer goes further than his contemporaries, however, in his variety; and especially in accounting for it by the characters of those who tell the tales. We may guess that his characters were first the product, so to speak, of the tales they were to tell. It is certain that Chaucer had some stories by him which were already written before the *Tales* as a whole were conceived. Clear examples are *Palamon and Arcite*, which became *The Knight's Tale*, and *The Tale of Saint Cecilia*, both mentioned in *The Prologue* to the *Legend of Good Women*.

It is important to remind ourselves again that all the tales existed in some form sometimes for centuries before Chaucer came to tell them. He is, like Shakespeare, the teller of traditional tales. As was the case with *Troilus and Criseyde* this did not prevent Chaucer from radically altering, and varying even the main drift, and the points of view from which different parts of the story are told, and the internal characterisation. But the received general structure remains, or it would not be that story, but another (whose general structure would be retained). Characters then more or less fit the actions allotted to them. They do not initiate action. Pattern underlies causation. There may be gaps in naturalistic cause and effect which do not bother us because we respond to the underlying pattern. There is always a play, perhaps a tension, between one telling of the same story and another. As in *Troilus and Criseyde* Chaucer may pull against his immediate source. And this process continues with our reading. Even a non-narrative critical account is a form of retelling, which may illuminate, or skew, the narrative it purports to criticise. (All criticism is itself a form of fiction.)

Boccaccio, most notably, had had the idea of assigning different tales in his vast collection, the *Decameron*, to different tellers, and to some extent he gave tellers the tales appropriate to their characters. Boccaccio has some tales in common with Chaucer, either from the general European stock, like *The Reeve's Tale* and its many analogues, or indirectly originating with Boccaccio himself, as with the tale of Patient Griselda, fashioned from folktale elements by Boccaccio, translated by Petrarch into Latin and by someone else into French. It is not clear that Chaucer knew Boccaccio's collection, but in any case Chaucer has a much greater variety of character and interest in character, than has Boccaccio.

Nevertheless the interest in the story in most, perhaps all, cases came first. Chaucer wanted to use the stories he had written, and knew a number of others he wished to tell. Perhaps he wrote *The General Prologue* to provide a series of pegs on which to hang the stories, and as it developed the whole scheme took off as a drama of its own, when characters, generated by some stories, developed their own interaction; then the whole scheme continued to develop under his careful fostering and pruning. We can see a good idea succeeded by a better, for example, when he substituted the present *Wife of Bath's Tale* for the tale we assume was originally given to her which is now called *The Shipman's Tale*. The change is apparent because the present *Shipman's Tale*, although unquestionably attributed to him according to the manuscripts, is written for a woman to tell. It belongs to the period of the *Tales*, and could only fit the Wife of Bath. Here is a case where the speed of Chaucer's own development as it were outpaced him; he had no time to complete the other half of his plan, and change the wording of *The Shipman's Tale* to make it accord with the new speaker. From similar inconsistencies in the text it is usually assumed that the prose *Tale of Melibeus* was first assigned to the Man of Law, and then later switched to its position as Chaucer's own second tale, perhaps to add its weight of contrast to the brilliant sequence of Fragment VII. When this was done, the Man of Law was given his present verse tale of *Constance*, though he promises to speak in prose.

The developments of the plan involving a change of attribution of the stories went hand-in-hand with Chaucer's writing of the links between the tales, which are a remarkable dramatic development. In them characterisation does in fact begin to develop as it rarely does within the tales. By contrast with the tales the links are genuinely original inventions, much as Shakespeare's own rare original inventions are knock-about popular comedy. The coarser characters quarrel, Miller against Reeve, Friar against Summoner. One tells a story against the other, churls tell churls' tales. Who shall say here which came first – such stories as make a pair and give rise to characters, or characters who quarrel, giving rise to stories in which they attack each other? In at least one case, the character came first; this is the Wife of Bath, for since she was presumably first meant to tell *The Shipman's Tale*, her present tale may be thought of as particularly hers, arising out of her character. Even so, it is not nearly so much the product of her character as, say, one of Hamlet's soliloquies is a product of his. Her tale of the conversion of a rapist knight is a fairy-tale, a wonder, told in a mood of delicate fantasy (though the plot was not invented by Chaucer). Delicacy is not one of the Wife of Bath's characteristics. To understand and enjoy the story and its placing to the full, the tale's reflections on sovereignty in marriage should be compared with the similar reflections – how differently expressed – in the Wife's own lengthy *Prologue* to her tale, which is very much more a product of her character. There is a most delightful contrast between her own comic and lusty coarseness which has its own rough charm, as well as satirising her own argument, and the varying jest, ethical seriousness and cheerful ending of her *Tale*. In the succession of *Tales* which follow hers (Fragments III, IV, V) the theme of marriage relationships is raised fairly frequently, though the sequence is not a conscious debate on marriage. But we shall miss some of the significance of *The Wife of Bath's Tale* if we do not recognise its contribution to the theme of marriage. Thus, only a part of its significance lies in its expression of character.

From this brief survey, it is clear that the essential quality of *The Canterbury Tales* as a whole lies in the interplay of stories, rather than in the interaction of the characters who tell the stories. The sequence of stories is similar to the events of a plot, and the characters are motivated so as to make their actions (i.e. their stories) seem suitable. By so regarding the *Tales* we better understand their design and distort it less. In the case of *Palamon and Arcite*, now *The Knight's Tale*, as we have seen above, by taking it as an expression of the Knight's character critics misread the literal text and import a whole series of anachronistic judgements about 'subjectivity', 'self-fashioning', 'the crisis of chivalry' and end up considering this magnificently colourful parade of noble and extravagant feeling about love and death as a poetic failure.[2] In some cases an inconsistency has developed between the character as presented in *The General Prologue* and the story he tells, as when the rich, fat, fashionable and self-confident manager, the Monk, tells his string of bookish and sententious Tragedies. Chaucer wanted to put them in. They express both a characteristic element of his literary culture and contain three of Chaucer's rare comments on current, political events, the murder of Peter of Spain, the murder of Peter of Cyprus, victor of Alexandria – which was the most resounding crusading success of the century (and the Knight's chief battle) – and the murder of the equally aggressive Bernabò Visconti, 'God of delit and scourge of Lumbardye' (*CT*, VII, 2375–406). The fall from prosperity to death of these three seems to be deplored. Both Peters are in addition called 'worthy', though modern historians rightly see all three as bad characters. Chaucer had probably met, or at least seen, all three. Other great persons whose fall from high estate is recorded were regarded as unequivocally wicked, as Lucifer, Nebuchadnezzar, Belshazzar. The central fact is the Fall, whether or not it was deserved. It interested Chaucer, as illustrating what might now be called sceptically a 'transhistorical' phenomenon: that is, an essential and continuing aspect of all life. The point here is that neither in range nor in what is said is the narrative expressive of the Monk's character. But its message of distrust in worldly prosperity was appropriate to a serious-minded cleric. It is phrased in too worldly a manner for the Parson, and anyway Chaucer was reserving something more powerfully didactic and parsonical for him. The Monk, as a monk, was the next best candidate as a teller, so the stories, very directly leading to death, are allotted to him. (That the doleful series is cut short by the Knight illustrates another aspect of how Chaucer, always afraid of his own tendency to go on too long, introduces variety, and a link shows character in action in a different way.)

The general conclusion of this survey, which might be much extended, is that there is above all a variety of purposes, perspectives, attitudes, materials in *The Canterbury Tales*. No one principle, no one point of view, and (as earlier versions of this book have maintained) no single 'dramatic principle' governs them all. It is a Gothic miscellany. The miracle is that it is recognisably the product of one single extraordinarily inclusive mind, even if that mind is sometimes divided within itself by inconsistency. The wealth of meaning in the stories is such that only a few can be discussed in detail. All illustrate many of the themes touched on earlier in this book, but apart from

The Knight's Tale we have finished with adolescent love stories. What follows is for grown-ups, whether the matter be serious or comic.

THE MILLER'S TALE

The contrast between *The Miller's Tale* and *The Knight's Tale* is very refreshing, and very typical of Chaucer. Though not a parody of *The Knight's Tale*, it also tells of two young men in love with the same girl. Since this is undoubtedly the greatest comic poem in English it will be worth discussing it in detail.

The plot of *The Miller's Tale* is as fantastic as that of any romance. It is based on a common folktale: variants of the story are found in several languages. A young Oxford student lodging with an old man tricks his simple-minded landlord, who has a young and beautiful wife, into believing that Noah's flood is coming again. So all three must spend the night in wooden tubs slung in the roof, in order safely to float out on the waters when need arises. The elderly husband falls asleep and the two young persons skip downstairs and into bed together. But along comes another lover of the wife, a fastidious, squeamish, village dandy. He serenades the wife and asks her for a kiss. The bedroom is on the ground floor, and she puts out her bottom which the unfortunate man kisses. It is a moment of awful comedy. He goes away in fury and returns with a red-hot piece of iron, a ploughshare. Again he serenades the wife. Her student-lover proposes to repeat the same exquisite joke, and puts out *his* bottom, and receives a jab from the burning-hot ploughshare; he withdraws with a scream of agony. To cool himself he shrieks for 'water!' The cry awakes the husband, who thinks the Flood has come and cuts the rope that holds his tub, and crashes to the floor, where he knocks himself out and breaks his arm. The wife and lover by their cries rouse their neighbours, and since many of these are students all take sides with the lover and tell the husband that he is mad, and laugh at him. Thus, he suffers, and the poem wastes no sympathy on him, concluding 'and thus his wife was seduced (though a blunter word is used), her lover scalded in the rear, and the dandy has kissed the lady's lower eye'.

I have told the story without names to emphasise how much the persons are roles or types: jealous old husband, lecherous student, lecherous village dandy, lecherous young wife. The wife is the centre of their attention, but the story is not about her: it is not even primarily about the men who circle round her as a sexual object: the story is, at its deepest or, as we may well say, at its lowest level, the articulation of a deliberately fantastic insult, common to all the languages of Europe, I should guess, in the Middle Ages; common even today, perhaps; the insult is the regrettable expression, 'Kiss my arse'. The insult is only funny in so far as coarse invective is funny, but there seems no doubt, to judge from the received history of comedy (as in the *Oxford Classical Dictionary*), that coarse invective is indeed the oldest form of humour. In the case of *The Miller's Tale*, however, the articulation of the insult into a fantastic story turns it into a classically comic structure; there is a reversal from top to bottom, if one may put it that way, yet in a context which prevents any tragic implications: the face-to-face human personal relationship of the kiss is grotesquely transformed, parodied and insulted; the spiritual or at any rate the emotional, imaginative, delicate, higher relationship of love is conquered by the grossly and disgustingly lower physical connection. Furthermore, the repetition of the first kiss by the burning second one produces further parody – we have all heard of burning kisses. And, of course, the further connection of the cry of 'water' brings down, lowers, the husband, in every sense. The very structure of the narrative is poetic. The story is a general lowering of the pretensions of the men; the wife never had any. In a way, it is a comic assertion of natural physical reality, though not of justice – an assertion of the reality of a young wife's natural lustfulness which is juxtaposed against the jealousy of a silly old man who would unrealistically restrain his wife, and against two deceitful and conceited young men, who want to exploit the wife's nature. We may well remember Aristotle's remark that comedy portrays people as worse than they usually are. Let us hope it is true. In origin the story is anti-feminist. All the men suffer: the woman unjustly escapes scot-free. The implication is that women trick men and make them suffer. But comedy is always ambivalent. And it always takes two to play the wife's game. So the story is not without sympathy for the wife. Chaucer is very sympathetic to women and he makes the wife very charming and attractive, though he mocks her too.

Chaucer's narrative is more complex than that of any other version. It is filled in, as ordinary popular literature is not, with descriptive detail of the highest artistry, so that we see the very dimensions of the physical setting. The characters are brought to life to enable us to enjoy the richness of the joke without going so far as to feel sorry for any of them. None of the analogues of this common folktale in any way rivals Chaucer's telling of the tale. There is, for example, a kind of poetry of absurdity in the way the carpenter is taken in by the tale of the tub. Some of the analogues miss this out completely; others attempt the impossible task of making the trick itself seem reasonable; Chaucer creates his carpenter as the very kind of man to believe such nonsense. The physical realism, the 'visibility' of characters and setting was never more brilliantly conveyed.

Comic poets particularly need to ground their fictions on territory familiar to the audience. This is an elementary principle, and thus the Flemish analogue of *The Miller's Tale* is set in Antwerp, the Italian in Naples, the *The Miller's Tale* itself in Osney near Oxford, a place well known to many of Chaucer's audience. The very house can almost be measured – the height of the window from the ground (an important point), the hole in the door of the student Nicholas's room big enough for a cat to pass though. We are conscious of the whole life of the village, as when we see the dandyish Absolon, who is also village barber and parish clerk, about his business and pleasure, or as when the old carpenter mentions with just the right touch of consternation that a man has just been carried dead to church whom 'last Monday' he saw at his work.

The characters are not pale shades, or types, as they are in the analogues. They are named. Alison is not simply the type of lustful and unfaithful young wife. Chaucer avoids the mistakes of the analogues. One analogue makes her a prostitute. This loses all the comic capital of the deceived husband and the need for secrecy. In another, the wife intends to receive three lovers in succession, which degrades the story. Chaucer's Alison has some individuality.

She is described with the same care as that with which Chaucer described the Duchess Blanche, though with greater art and to vastly different effect. Thus, she has the conventional and fashionable beauty of a white forehead, but this is how Chaucer praises it:

> Hir forheed shoon as bright as any day,
> So was it wasshen whan she leet hir werk.   *finished*
> (*CT*, I, 3310–11)

She wears an apron white as morning milk, plucks her eyebrows, and has a lecherous eye; she sings like a swallow.

> She was a prymerole, a piggesnye,   *primrose; a sweet little thing*
> For any lord to leggen in his bedde,   *lay*
> Or yet for any good yeman to wedde.
> (*CT*, I, 3268–70)

This must qualify as one of the most snobbish remarks in English poetry. There never was 'so gay a popelote or swich a wenche' (both of these nouns are 'low' words). She has a well-washed, luscious, vulgar (and genuine) allure. Chaucer does full justice to the allure as he does to the vulgarity. She is a comic figure to the courtly audience, and to us because our eyes by Chaucer's art are adjusted to his vision of her. The formal description of Alison is a kind of parody of the rhetorical portrait of the beautiful courtly heroine (above, p. 85) but here not the courtly element but the vulgar element is chiefly mocked, even if the very use of the courtly ideal for mockery shows some ambiguity of feeling about the ideal itself. Alison is amusing in action by descriptions such as that of her hoity-toity air (no more) when Nicholas begins his rough and direct wooing and by her speedy capitulation; by the way she gently struggles when firmly in his grasp, and promises only to cry out in the future.

The portrait of Absolon is painted with similar amused care and light satire. The village clerk and barber, he is a dandy, according to his lights, with a high-pitched voice and affected accent, and is, 'somewhat squeamish'. He is an amateur actor, and fancies himself with the women. His hair is long and curly. He wears the current fancy gear; in the fourteenth century it was the pattern of St Paul's windows cut on his shoes.

The character of the old husband is as remarkable for what is left out as for what is put in. Great care is taken to make him a clear, but decidedly background character. We are briefly told of his age and jealousy. We see his blend of respect and contempt for Nicholas's learning, his simple conceit of the practical man. We are made aware of his unthinking piety and clumsy good intentions. This is sufficient to make him real enough for the stratagem to have point, but not enough to make us think in terms of real life about the actual pathos, injustice and bitterness of his situation. All art depends on limitation of view and in this case the limitation is that of ordinary derisive popular humour without too much sympathy, reinforced by courtly snobbery about the antics of the provincial lower classes.

There is even more to *The Miller's Tale*. In it Chaucer makes fun of the miracle-plays, not only through Absolon, who used to play Herod 'upon a scaffold high', but also by larger allusions, for it was the Carpenters' Guild which usually put on, for obvious reasons, the play of the Flood. The language of the poem mocks the old-fashioned provincial English love-lyrics, with their use of what had become low-class hackneyed words like *gent* and *hende*. Polished rhetoric, neatly inverted, is used, as already noted, to mock a vulgar village-wench. It is altogether a most courtly poem, and Chaucer has the nerve to call it 'a churl's tale'. It does indeed share general popular feelings, but these are common to high and low. In the fourteenth century 'courtiers' were just as much part of 'the folk' as were peasants.

After all this it should not be necessary to say that *The Miller's Tale* tells us nothing about the Miller's character or status. Nor is it worth trying to turn it into an edifyingly Biblical allegory or ironical discourse. The style is direct and relatively plain, occasionally steering deliberately and perilously near the downright coarse. It is a contrast to, not a contradiction of, *The Knight's Tale*, though to that extent they are related and set each other off. It could be said that they have a kind of 'intertextuality'. It could be said that *The Miller's Tale* witnesses to 'transgression'; it breaks boundaries; but it is not 'subversive'.

The tale takes its place in the larger comedy of the pilgrimage in that it grieves the Reeve who, being a carpenter himself, takes to heart the misfortune of the carpenter of Osney. He falls into a self-pitying monologue about old age, spoken in a Northern accent fitting his Norfolk background (the Reeve being also probably an identifiable and unpopular character among Chaucer's friends). This poem and *The Miller's Tale* form as it were a diptych and *The Reeve's Tale* also deserves a somewhat full account to reveal the new reaches of Chaucer's art and its extreme enjoyability.

THE REEVE'S TALE

This time the setting is near Cambridge with its university, also well-known to Chaucer and his friends, though intellectually less influential than Oxford. And again the core of the narrative is a folktale, with many analogues, enriched by high art. The tale is set in the mill of the village of Trumpington. The village remains; the probable site of the mill is known; the fen is drained now but the mists still rise at evening from the damp meadows by the slowly flowing river.

The poem begins by describing Simkin the Miller in a realistic vivid portrait. He is proud, peacock-like, extraordinarily skilful, a bully and totally bald. The baldness is important. He is also a thief, as all millers were traditionally thought to be.

After this comes a portrait of his handsome wife, described as come 'of noble kin' because her father was the local parson. This is itself a joke, because the parson, being a cleric, ought to be celibate and therefore his daughter is illegitimate. She, like Simkin, is a snob in her degree and as proud and pert as a magpie. It is a fine sight to see them walking about on a holiday, brightly dressed. Simkin, the miller, is such a bully that nobody dares call his wife anything but 'dame' lest Simkin should beat him up. Forty-odd lines of description give us a wonderful character study of this well-to-do, efficient, proud pair whose pride is not entirely well-founded. The courtly audience might well laugh at the social pretensions of village worthies. They have a daughter 20 years old, of a lusty attractiveness, and somewhat improbably they also have a baby six months old. The miller reckons to marry his daughter well, since he is prosperous and she is of such distinguished lineage.

One of the miller's best customers is a Cambridge college, two miles away, the King's Hall. The King's Hall is referred to with remarkably convincing detail. (It happens no longer to exist because it was merged with a couple of other halls into Trinity College in the sixteenth century.) As the story tells us, the chief officer of King's Hall responsible for looking after the grinding of the College's wheat is ill, so two of the members of the College, both young men, called Alan and John, decide to take the grain to the miller and to make sure that the thefts which he has been committing shall not continue. They ride to Trumpington on a single horse with their grain and meet the miller and express the intention of supervising the grinding so as not to be cheated. The conversation between the two clerks and the miller is entertaining in itself. They have been there before, and know the miller slightly, though (a fine touch) they get his name slightly wrong. The students are characterised not only by the cheerful bumptiousness of young men, but also by the fact that they speak in a northern dialect, which always seems comic in the south. The miller puts up with their supervision and their condescension but he slips away and lets their horse loose, so out the two young men have to go to chase it, and only return in the evening, weary and wet. They know very well that their corn has been stolen. Moreover, it is so late that they are caught by the curfew and cannot return to College because they are locked out. They have to ask the miller to put them up and he, not without some jeering, agrees to do so when they pay for the food and drink, although he has only one room. His daughter is sent into the village for ale and bread, a goose is roasted, they have a splendid supper and the miller drinks so much that, as Chaucer says, he has varnished his bald head. It shines bright with sweat, and he is stupified, while his wife, on the other hand, has so wet her jolly whistle that she is

extremely merry. All three of the family, miller, wife and daughter
go to their various beds, fall fast asleep and snore resoundingly, having
allocated another bed in the same room to the two students.

The cradle of the baby is at the foot of the bed of the miller and
his wife. The noise of their snoring keeps Alan and John awake.
They talk and Alan (who probably studies law) says that law allows
them some compensation for the theft and humiliation which they
have endured that day. He creeps in by the daughter and shortly to
say it, they were soon at one.

John, as in all the other versions, lies gloomily awake on his own,
reflecting on what a fool he will seem when the story is told later.
Then he has a marvellous idea. He gets up and moves the cradle to
the foot of his own bed. Soon after this the wife arises to answer the
call of nature, payment for having drunk so much, and coming in
again, misses her cradle at the foot of her bed – 'Alas,' says she to
herself, 'I'd almost got into terrible difficulty, I nearly went into the
clerk's bed and then I'd have had a terrible time.' So she gets into
the other bed where she does indeed get an unexpectedly warm
welcome.

When Alan returns from the daughter's bed, he goes first to his
own bed, sees the cradle, thinks he is mistaken, gets into bed with
the miller, wakes him up, thinking he is John, and tells him how he
has fared. The miller, with a tremendous roar bellows out, 'Yea you
false scoundrel, have you so? Ah you false traitor, you false clerk.
You shall be dead by the dignity of God. Who dare be so bold as to
disparage my daughter who is come of such lineage?' He catches
Alan by the throat and they fight and roll on the floor like two pigs
in a bag until they fall on and wake up John and the miller's wife.
She cries to her supposed husband for help. John immediately under-
stands what has happened and gropes around the walls to find a
staff to help his friend. The wife does the same and knows the
interior much better than John. This is the passage which describes
the next events.

> This John stirte up as faste as ever he myghte
> And graspeth by the walles to and fro
> To fynde a staf; and she stirte up also,
> And knew the estres bet than dide this John,   *interior*
> And by the wal a staf she foond anon,
> And saugh a litel shymeryng of a light
> For at an hole in shoon the moone bright
> And by that light she saugh hem bothe two

But sikerly she nyste who was who	*did not know*
But as she saugh a whit thyng in hir ye.	
And whan she gan this white thyng espye	
She wende the clerk hadde wered a volupeer	*thought; night-cap*
And with the staf she drow ay neer and neer,	*nearer and nearer*
And wende han hit this Aleyn at the fulle	*thought to have*
And smoot the millere on the pyled skulle	*bald*
That doun he gooth and cride 'Harrow! I dye.'	*alas!*

(*CT*, I, 4292–307)

The rapid pace of the narration here keeps just ahead of our delighted anticipations. The miller has been punished once by Alan sleeping with his daughter, twice by John sleeping with his wife, and now, three times, with gloriously farcical appropriateness, since he is such a bully, by being hit on the head by his own wife. To have been hurt once is a shame, twice could be tragic, but three times is proneness to accident. It is absurd and, one might say, poetic. The students beat him up a bit more, then dress and go away. To crown all, the daughter gives them a cake of baked flour which is the proceeds of the theft of wheat which the miller has committed.

The passage quoted is an extraordinarily concrete and syntactically simple piece of story-telling. Of 15 lines no less than nine begin with *And* and two more with the similar word *But*. Only one and a half lines have grammatically subordinate clauses of purpose and explanation. There is a continuous series of concrete nouns which gives a vivid impression of simple solid appearances – a staff crashing down on a bald white skull. There is a huge predominance of one-syllable words and a very large vocabulary. Of the 75 separate words used 22 are nouns including the names John and Alan, 21 are verbs, and the remainder are other parts of speech, so that there is a high proportion of other words of action to nouns. There are only five adjectives and these are simple and structural. There are, however, 11 or 12 adverbs or adverbial phrases which outline and animate the action. For example, *up*, *fast*, *to and fro*, *near and near*. Although the vocabulary is concrete, full, simple, some key-words are repeated. The vigorous word *stirte* is repeated twice in the first three lines and the word *staff* is also repeated. *Light* is twice mentioned. It is great poetry but not at all our usual idea of poetic language. It is full and sinewy, with many links and associations with the rest of the action. It gives us the poetic culmination of the cross–patterned dualism on which the adventures of the night are based. Great artistry creates powerful effects in this poem, which is an extraordinarily full verbal realisation of a very complex pattern of place, people and events, much more logically connected than in the other versions of this story.

The poem creates a much more vivid sense of the world than we can get from the other versions. For example, only Boccaccio in his version of the tale, and Chaucer, provide names for most of their characters; but only Chaucer actually gives us a character sketch of the significant character, the miller. Moreover, he makes him a character who causes us to feel that even if he does not quite deserve all the punishment he gets, at least he is an unsympathetic person, a bully, who only gets what he has meted out to others elsewhere. Measure for measure is suitable for a miller. We also notice that Chaucer establishes a motif of pride coming before a fall, which is absent from the other versions. There is derision for social pretensions. In Chaucer's story the action is not premeditated by the two students and it has a freshness and spontaneity, and therefore an innocence, which is lacking in Boccaccio. Chaucer's version alone has the wife stun her husband by hitting him on the bald head with the staff, caused by thinking that his white bald head is the nightcap of one of the students. There is a comic irony of event in Chaucer's version whereby the wife, who is intending to help her husband, in fact strikes the culminating blow. Chaucer has a tremendous sense of the irony of circumstance. What is brought out by Chaucer's treatment of a traditional fantastic plot like this is the way in which he links the events and characters together. He is deeply interested in material cause and effect and in motivation and this gives him a remarkable modernity of outlook. In some ways Chaucer is in advance of Boccaccio. He is much more realistic and more interested in character. He is more atmospheric and more poetic in his treatment of a narrative.

THE COOK'S TALE

The pilgrim Miller's reaction to this tale is not told. It is the Cook who chimes in next, almost beside himself with joy at *The Reeve's Tale* and enthusiastically determined to cap it with one of his own. This begins with a description of the wild habits of a London apprentice called Perkyn Revelour which aptly illustrates how the interests of Court and City mingled in Chaucer's audience. We seem to be starting that comedy of City life which Chaucer could have written so well. But alas, he never wrote it, for *The Cook's Tale*, hardly begun, finishes abruptly, though strikingly. Perhaps three such tales in a row would be too much of a good thing. Chaucer never made up his mind about what should follow *The Reeve's Tale* and the whole Fragment ends here.

NOTES

1. For a full exposition see *The Works of Sir Thomas Malory*, edited by E. Vinaver, revised by P. J. C. Field, third edn, 3 vols (Oxford, 1990), vol. I, lxxiii–xciii.
2. See, for example, Lee Patterson, *Chaucer and the Subject of History* (Madison, 1991).

Chapter 20

The Canterbury Tales II: Constancy and Inconstancy; Love and Anger; Trouthe and Gentilesse

THE MAN OF LAW'S TALE

The contents of the next Fragment are in some doubt. It certainly begins with *The Man of Law's Introduction and Tale*. Chaucer seems not to have finally decided which tale should follow, as appears from the variants in the Epilogue to *The Man of Law's Tale*, and the omission of the Epilogue itself from many good manuscripts. The section begins with the curious Introduction to *The Man of Law's Tale*. There are several puzzles here. Why does Chaucer give a list of the contents of *The Legend of Good Women* through the mouth of the Man of Law – especially as it is a list different from the tales he had actually written? Then the Man of Law condemns two stories about incest. Chaucer's dislike of tales about such 'unnatural abominations' was probably genuine, and a similar fastidiousness appears elsewhere in the *Tales*, but is this passage merely a hit against his friend Gower, who had recently written these very stories? The Man of Law promises to speak in prose, though his tale is actually in verse, and *The Tale of Melibeus* was perhaps first assigned to him, but was later transferred to Chaucer. The Invocation which is the Lawyer's Prologue has nothing to do with his story of Constance, to which it makes hardly more than a grammatical bridge. The whole Introduction cries aloud the lack of revision.

Not so *The Tale*. It is written with care and elaboration. The 'matter' is a pious tale of folklore origin and again there are numerous analogues of 'accused queens'. Chaucer translates the story straightforwardly into verse from the Anglo-Norman Chronicle by Trivet, enriching the source here with borrowings from Pope Innocent III's *De Contemptu Mundi*, with touches perhaps from Gower's version of Trivet's work, and above all with his own understanding of how such things could come to be, with vivid evocations of speech and

scene, with his own pity for suffering. These rhetorical embellish-
ments arise naturally enough from contemplation of the 'moving
accidents' of the story. In this tale, in contrast with *Troilus*, there are
only two places where Chaucer is inclined seriously to suspect that
his source may be mistaken, both marked by the doubting phrase
'Som men wolde seyn' (II 1009 and 1086), where Trivet is in fact
quite unequivocal. Both these examples refer to minor details which
seem to Chaucer not to be in accord with what would have been
expected from the characters concerned.

This caution is the more striking in that the tale as a whole is of
the kind of impossibility that pious legend delighted in. It tells of
Constance, daughter of the Christian Emperor of Rome, who is
twice married to a pagan king, twice converts her husband, is twice
betrayed by an irreconcilably pagan mother-in-law, and twice com-
mitted to the sea in a boat without oars or sails. In each case she is
afloat for several years. Her first husband is killed by his mother but
she is eventually restored to the second. Such a plot does not aim to
reproduce a complexity of relationships. Its purpose is quite differ-
ent. Repetition is a favourite device of traditional literature and is
powerful in emphasising with variation the major point. Chaucer
handled it with all his mature skill. He accepts the miracles – he is
not misled by his capacity for realising detail into giving, as for
instance Trivet does, a list of stores for a three-year voyage. He sees
it as a Miracle of the Blessed Virgin, who supported Constance in
her trials. He comments now and again on the vicious men and
women who so afflict the pure and gentle Constance, taking the
material for these comments from the *De Contemptu Mundi* which he
had perhaps recently translated. With his remarkable historical sense
he takes the story seriously. He sets the action very vividly in its time
and place. The diplomatic overtures for a state marriage (which he
must have known so well); the geography of the seas around Eng-
land; the state of languages in England in about the fourth century;
the usage of courts; the felicities of home – all this and much more
is suggested or described.

Even more notable, as we would expect, are the very great beauty
and sympathy of the accounts of Constance. They have no artificial-
ity and there is perhaps nothing more exquisite in all Chaucer's
work than the passage, entirely his own, where Constance for the
second time is to be abandoned to the sea, on this occasion with her
baby (ll. 834–40). We see the very movement of her hand as she
draws the kerchief off her own head to put it on the child; another
phrase tells of the large crowd following her, sympathetic, but silent

and helpless. Her prayer is the most moving of all, where she asks pity for her child from that mother who saw her own child torn on the Cross, with whose woe the woe of no man can stand comparison. Yet in the end the world of Constance, for all its miracles, is recognisably part of the same world as that of *Troilus and Criseyde*. The same astronomical and astrological forces govern it under Providence. Constance is steadfast, as her name suggests, in her love of God, and neither pagan intellectual error nor pagan mythology intervenes between her and God; nor are virtuoso embellishments or distractions employed in the narration of what is practically a saint's life, though the poet comments plentifully as Expositor.

The story is exemplary, not allegorical, and the example of constancy is explicit. The repetitiousness of event in the story, though it does not contribute to such matters as characterisation, is necessary for making the point about endurance under repeated sorrows. We may also legitimately draw conclusions from the more general narrative structure which lies beneath, so to speak, the verbal surface or realisation. The propositions inherent in the structure of *The Man of Law's Tale* imply that mothers-in-law are difficult for daughters-in-law; and that strong opinions, especially strong religious beliefs, are divisive in families. The story implies the essential solitariness of religious belief, that ultimate internal value, which must justify itself when deserted by society, by friends, even apparently (as in the Crucifixion), by God himself. Constance is frequently cut off from society because she is a Christian, and we are invited to applaud this painful individualising lonely integrity, as in several other works of Chaucer.

Constance is the precise opposite of Criseyde. Criseyde is always thinking of her own honour. She is mainly governed by what other people (not Troilus, particularly) will think about her. In consequence the essence of Criseyde's character is that she cannot say 'no'; she is *slydynge of corage*, 'unstable'. To be able to say 'no' is often the measure of integrity. The irony for Criseyde is that although she always does what society or its present representative wants – Pandarus, Troilus, the Trojan Parliament, Diomede – she is even more completely sacrificed by society than Constance, who never yields. Criseyde wants to be loved by everyone and ends up loved by no one; Constance is difficult, but the best people love her. *The Man of Law's Tale* thus offers yet another variant of the favourite Gothic propositions that love means suffering and paradoxically often causes solitude, as it attracts jealousy. Truly life in the world is hard and full of tensions. Yet the *Tale* also argues that to the constant mind the physical structures of the universe are more sympathetic, more open to God's guidance, than people are. Constance is safer on the sea than often she is among men.

It is fitting that such an austere yet in the end encouraging tale should focus on a single character, and the single perfect flower of her loving fortitude. There are dozens of realistic and historical touches, such as the comment on Constance's Late Latin language ('A maner Latyn corrupt was hir speche', II, 519) which the Romano-British Celts of what is now Northumbria were able to understand. Another vivid passage is the comparison with the pallor of one who is being led to his death (II, 645–51). So the story is fully 'realised': but it quite properly does not seek to evoke the sense of interplay of character and society of such a work as *Troilus*.

It is written in the rhyme royal stanza of *Troilus*, which so beautifully balances meditative narration with lyric expressiveness. The poet addresses the reader or audience, and apostrophises the characters in the story, in his accustomed way:

> O Sowdanesse, roote of iniquitee!
>
> (II, 358)

> This Sowdanesse, whom I thus blame and warye   *curse*
>
> (II, 373)

recalling somewhat the manner of parts of *The Legend of Good Women*. It is part of the Expositor's technique of engagement from a detached position. At times it may seem artificial, but there is no reason to think it ironical. The Expositor is not represented as foolish or ignorant. There is a genuinely Chaucerian comment when Constance is married that

> thogh that wyves be ful hooly thynges
> They moste take in pacience at nyght
> Swiche manere necessaries as been plesynges
> To folk that han ywedded hem with rynges
> And leye a lite hir hoolynesse aside . . .   *little*
>
> (II, 709–13)

The assumption that good wives do not enjoy sex, and that holiness excludes sex, is very deep in Chaucer, though not always exclusive of other assumptions.

There is no reason anywhere in the poem to see it as in any way expressive of the character of the Man of Law. It was a poem

Chaucer had by him, which he rightly thought was worth preserving, and he attached it to a sober serious pilgrim on the grounds of general suitability.

Again Chaucer expresses his own and his culture's reverence for holy women and the mother-image. He writes from a male point of view and the heroic virtues that are praised are passive. A courtly Christianity that evades no hardship is propounded. There seems none of the internal questioning or self-contradiction that marks, for example, *The Clerk's Tale* and *The Franklin's Tale*. Though not a tragedy it ends very suitably and almost cheerfully in death, like so many good stories (above, p. 101).

Harry Bailly calls it a 'thrifty' (fine) tale and then asks the Parson for a tale. Receiving a rebuke for his swearing, the Host cheerfully calls out he 'smells a Lollard in the wind', and sees a sermon coming, but the Shipman bursts in to prevent so dire an outcome. The Shipman's introductory words have a witty pun on 'cockle in our green corn' based on the Latin *lolium*, 'tare', 'weed', which the orthodox associated with the word Lollard. But the Shipman goes on to deny his knowledge of Latin and proves it by mangling various Latin words. So the earlier wit we must attribute to the poet, not the character. Misuse of Latin words by the uneducated has always been a source of amusement to the English upper-classes. Both errors and amusement derive from the divisive wounds in communal national feeling inflicted by the Norman Conquest and which festered for centuries.

THE WIFE OF BATH'S PROLOGUE AND TALE

We now turn to a new section, a large one, since it may reasonably be held to be composed of Ellesmere manuscript Fragments III, IV, V. There is no link and we plunge straight in.

> Experience, though noon auctoritee
> Were in this world, is right ynogh for me
> To speke of wo that is in mariage.
>
> (III, 1–3)

And indeed the Wife of Bath's theme (for it is her cheerful, arrogant voice we hear) is tribulation in marriage – particularly the misery she has caused her five successive husbands. We have here a dramatic expression comparable in some ways to *The Pardoner's Prologue* but extending even further the feeling of a personal character. Here we do indeed experience some strongly individual feeling, all the more remarkable since the basic material is the long tradition of antifeminist mockery turned on its head.

To call *The Wife of Bath's Prologue* a 'confession', though it is partly that, is, as with the Pardoner, somewhat misleading because at least equally strong an element in the speeches is the much more ancient and human vice of boasting. Yet to represent vicious persons 'confessing' their sins in public, or revealing their trickery, as would never be done in real life, is a non-naturalistic but valid device of comic satire; and when the villains are made ridiculously to *boast* of their sins it is even more incongruous, comic and subtle. With the boasting, an aggressive element from character, author, and audience, enters into the sympathetic situation, and in the clash humour is born. The person confessing becomes more self-condemned partly because apparently also self-aware, and thus paradoxically deficient in moral self-awareness in so far as we can take morality, goodness, as self-evident. At the same time, such is fallen human nature, as illustrated daily in our newspapers, we tend to respond sympathetically to anyone in literature who is dashingly unrepentant, because they seem so vigorously alive, enviably capable of doing what they want to do. Falstaff, or on a different scale, Milton's Satan (in the early books of *Paradise Lost*) are two later and famous examples of such justified sinners and supermen.

Chaucer does not take us quite so far along the road which exalts personal will as the supreme value. Both the Wife of Bath and the Pardoner are ridiculous because they are making a foolish mistake by boasting, which is always amusing in those who normally exploit, to their own advantage, the mistakes, errors and follies of others. The balance in these characters is different, though. The Wife of Bath is predominantly sympathetic because her victims are not only old and rich (which is enough to damn them in the *fabliau* tradition), but also selfish and would-be tyrannous. Moreover, the Wife is loving after her lustful, domineering fashion, and we can easily see ourselves in her. The Pardoner by contrast is predominantly satirised.

These 'confessions' create that double image, that intersection of two incongruous planes of reference which is the essence of humour, and which creates that dual response in the reader, by which we recognise comedy, irony and poetry. 'Confessions' are not straightforwardly naturalistic, and to seek a straightforwardly consistent 'illusionist' interpretation, especially of those switches of attitude and perspective at the end of *The Pardoner's Tale*, as some critics do, is to be asking questions as mistaken as they would be in a Chaplin classic.

Comedy self-evidently has the self-sufficiency which our theories of imitation sometimes fail to credit other writings with.

Self-sufficiency does not mean the absence of realism. Comedy often points very sharply at well-recognised ordinary appearances, again as in a Chaplin film. Intensification and selection of detail constitute both realism and unrealism – another comic duality. The Wife of Bath's secular, boastful 'confession' is in parts marked by such an extremely naturalistic realism of presentation that she is even shown forgetting where she had got to in her ramblings. Yet this is also a taught rhetorical device. The basic structure of what she says is built on the framework, and sometimes the very words, of traditional clerical antifeminist tracts from St Jerome in the fifth century onwards. Some critics have puzzled themselves as to how she could have known the words of St Jerome and the rest. It has been seriously argued that since she knew no Latin she must have remembered the readings of her fifth husband. The problem and the answers are based on irrelevant novelistic, naturalistic premises, as if she were a real person. As well ask who gave the heroine of an opera singing lessons. The way she speaks is the medium, not the message; the Wife's knowledge of Latin texts is the equivalent of the music in opera; it is the product of the 'composer', not the character, just as much as the fact that she speaks in Chaucer's mature verse-line. Nevertheless, the Wife's *Prologue* is the *nearest* thing to sustained organic independently dramatic speech in Chaucer. Some strong degree of subjectivity, and to some extent an independent woman's point of view, may well be attributed to her. The wife was a favourite with Chaucer's readers years before his death, as well as ever after. In this respect she represents the climax of Chaucer's achievement in that dramatic narrative constituted by the links between the *Tales*, where in general we get nearest to the self-enclosed dramatic structures of later Neoclassical literature, with the wonderfully rich realism of ordinary life.

The Wife of Bath's Prologue is in itself a story about her life with her five husbands, how she married them, what a life she led them. This autobiographical thread links many comments on marriage, sex, money, dreams, etc., with realistic touches that evoke the social life of small towns surrounded by fields, the cycle of religious festivities, the easy adult sociability between the sexes in small English medieval towns. There is nothing in the *Prologue* about the Wife's taste for international pilgrimage and her experiences there, nor of her business of cloth-making. Nor is there any mention of family or children. She seems either to be childless or not to be bothered with children. The focus is limited to personal, specifically marital (with more than a hint of extra-marital) relationships, and in effect the proclamation of a fourteenth-century feminist manifesto. It is not only because of her modern feelings for the rights of women that we sympathise with her; it is because of her human enjoyment and gusto, her frank acceptance of life and love and of herself. She accepts the superiority of virginity, but makes a hearty plea for sexual pleasure in marriage. She reflects that sensible middle range of middle-aged conviction and behaviour represented by the medieval international comic tale, secular, resolutely cheerful, able to give and take hard knocks without resentment. She had tormented her fifth husband, the young clerk Jankin, who had responded by reading antifeminist stories to her out of his book. She had thrown the book into the fire. He gave her a clout on the ear which left her permanently deaf in that ear. And then they were affectionately reconciled (on consideration that she had the mastery), and loved each other and were true to each other. It is the stuff of the popular comic tale, yet, or therefore, granted some exaggeration, with a delightful sense of life. Here, if anywhere, it will be appropriate to speak in modern terms of gender, if we wish to, because her sexuality is so specific a key to Chaucer's representation of her in her *Prologue*. As already noted much of the general circumstance of her life is left aside. As with the Pardoner, the seed of her discourse is in *Le Roman de la Rose*, where the old woman, the bawd and former prostitute *La Vieille*, sketches a sort of autobiography. There are numerous other works in this vein, as pointed out by Professor Lee Patterson in his learned pages.[1] To the many misogynistic sources and analogues which paradoxically go to make up the Wife's *Prologue* we should add the savagely antifeminist little-known French *fabliau Le Leu* of the thirteenth century which shows how widespread was the recognition of such attitudes.

Several ingenious authors put the antifeminist arguments that go back to pre-Christian Classical antiquity, and the Old Testament, and were reinforced by such early Church Fathers as St Jerome, into the woman-speaker's own mouth. It is a device like making the Pardoner confess his own frauds, and is satirical. That is how the Wife's *Prologue* may have started in Chaucer's mind. But Chaucer's imaginative sympathy with women, and his increasing power of realising dramatically appropriate speech, turn it around. The garrulousness attributed to women becomes an entertainment. The *Prologue* falls into three general sections, the first a vigorously argumentative discussion of virginity and marriage, the second giving an account of

how the Wife comically bullied her first three husbands, the third
telling of the fourth and, particularly, how she caught her fifth,
Jankin the Clerk, half her age, whom she took for love, not riches.
It is the autobiographical turn which confirms the amused sympathy,
and creates the sense of a real person talking. Add to this the touches
of generosity, the capacity to see, if not to agree with, her old
husbands' point of view, the note of regret

> Allas, allas that evere love was synne,
>
> > (III, 614)

and the rueful reference to age 'that al wole envenyme' and has
taken her beauty and pith. These touches all lead us to sympathise
with her, and then we can admire the lack of self-pity when she says

> Lat go. Farewel! The devel go therwith.
>
> > (III, 474—8)

Now that the flour is gone, she must sell the bran, and so she will.
What admirable resolute energy. Some critics point out that her
Prologue uses masculine words and concepts, and that she is thus
'masculinised' in order to be acceptable. In the view of such critics
to be 'masculinised' is axiomatically bad, to be 'feminised' axiomati-
cally good. Such absoluteness of judgement is merely the mirror-
image of much stereotyped medieval misogyny. But the Wife rises
above that and even in her inconsistencies, or in the inconsistencies
of Chaucer's presentation, as with the portrayal of the Pardoner, she
is more complex and interesting.

The *Wife of Bath's Tale* springs out of her *Prologue* like a bullet
from a gun. It takes its direction thus, though the metaphor fails
because both *Prologue* and *Tale* have a reversal to the irrepressible
sexual vigour of the Wife at the end. The *Prologue* ends with her
mastery over Jankin, and since she says she will welcome a sixth
husband, refers to Jankin as in the past, and prays to God to bless his
soul (III, 823—7) it would seem that even the lusty Jankin could not
survive her. 'Wife' seems to be used in the general sense of woman,
though it is indeed as a Wife of a particularly vigorous and loqua-
cious ambiguity that the Wife of Bath has found literary immortality.

Her tale is undoubtedly meant for her and besides being most
interesting in itself has a somewhat ambivalent ending in relation to
her main theme of 'sovereignty in marriage'. The tale is the nearest

Chaucer comes to Arthurian romance and the world of fairyland, though he uses the reference to fairyland to make ironic references to the kind of fairies – in this case lecherous friars – found in the world nowadays. The action begins harshly with a knight of Arthur's court who rapes a girl. He is condemned to death for this outrage against women unless he can report to the Queen within a year and a day what women love most. The sense of the Wife dramatically telling the story is strong so far, even as she digresses into Ovid's antifeminist story of Mida, who could not keep the secret of her husband's two ass's ears. She tells how the knight wanders unsuccessfully and sorrowfully until almost the day of reckoning, when he catches a glimpse of four-and-twenty ladies dancing on a lawn by a forest-side, who disappear or metamorphose into a poor, filthy and hideous old woman. She will tell him the answer, on condition he will do whatever she asks. The answer is that what women most want is 'sovereignty', domination. The Queen and her court agree that this is right. The old hag asks for her reward, which to the knight's horror is to marry him. He cannot evade it, and in bed she gives him a long lecture on what is true nobility, which does not come from wealth or family, but arises from virtue, witnessed to by noble deeds. Nobility comes from God's grace. Low class, poverty, age and ugliness have nothing to do with the desirability of a wife. Glad poverty is honourable, age deserves reverence, and the ugliness of a wife ensures her faithfulness and humble obedience, for age and dirt are great guardians of chastity. But then the old woman asks, would he prefer to have his wife foul, old, true and humble, or have her young and fair and take the risk? He leaves the decision to her, thus yielding her the sovereignty. She promises to be both fair and good all the time. Cast up the curtain of the bed, she says, and see. They live in joy, and she obeys him in every way that can please him.

The narrative tone, which has become 'general Chaucerian', now reverts to the dramatic *persona* of the Wife of Bath, who concludes with a cheerful parody of the prayer that so often ends English romances, that

> Jhesu Crist us sende
> Housbondes meeke, yonge and fressh abedde
> And grace t'overbyde hem that we wedde.   *outlive*
> And eek I praye Jhesu shorte hir lyves
> That nought wol be governed by hir wyves.

(III, 1258–62)

This is not quite the moral of her tale, but trenchantly amusing, in Chaucer's vigorous plain style.

The Wife of Bath's Tale is again a version of a widespread traditional tale, and is individually modified. Chaucer's is the only version in which the hero commits rape in the beginning. (The touch of extremism, of forcing things to a limit, as with Griselda and here, is often to be noted in Chaucer.) The answer that the knight eventually finds is the exemplary part of the *Tale*. The answer is well suited to *The Wife of Bath*. It is also a good traditional joke, and from a man's point of view an antifeminist point. As with the Wife's *Prologue* the answer is poetically paradoxical in that it makes the Wife boast of that very quality, the wish to domineer, for which women have been traditionally condemned; her very defence is her guilt, or her guilt is her defence. The old hag's harangue in bed on the subject of traditional morality is true, but also comic in that situation; and then comes the dilemma between a wife who is old, ugly and true, or the reverse.

Gower also tells the story in *Confessio Amantis* but his version is more decorous. 'Gothic' would seem a mild style if we took Gower as its most characteristic exemplar. He has no nasty rape at the beginning, so he avoids the risk that Chaucer runs of totally losing our sympathy for the knight. At first Gower seems more natural and realistic than Chaucer. If Chaucer's poem were to be regarded as mimetic and naturalistic we might think that a woman of such parts and versatility as the heroine would hardly consider that to have a reformed rapist for a husband would be a satisfactory foundation for a happy marriage based on mutual esteem; even if it was, or especially as it was, some other woman whom he had raped. So Gower did not take that risk. He retains the traditional folktale dilemma between having one's wife beautiful by day alone, or by night alone; so he too is inevitably committed, by this fantasy, to an essentially non-mimetic plot. The situation creates a joke about sexual pride; more generally, a joke, or a series of questions, or propositions, about social reputation and real possession; about the relations between self and society, and social envy; about a particular variation of the broad theme of appearance and reality. Would you prefer to be thought, by your friends, or even more, by your enemies, to be in full possession of something every man desires, although really and secretly you have not got it; or be scorned, or ignored, for not having, what in secret truth you have? How self-sufficient and independent of others' opinions are you? How different is social appearance from personal reality and how much do you value one without the other?

Gower's is the traditional folktale dilemma, simpler than Chaucer's, more clear cut. All versions solve it in the same way, by the knight giving the choice to the lady, who having the choice chooses to be beautiful both by day and night. This ending suggests that appearance may be the same as reality if you do not assert yourself too egotistically, and that if you give a woman what she wants, she will give you what you want. It is a good, humane, optimistic, perhaps sentimental, folk solution; non-intellectual, non-clerical, pleasantly feminist. The solution may be a little too easy, partly because the dilemma is too schematic, clear cut, and with little moral implication.

Chaucer sacrifices the clarity of the folktale dilemma presumably because of his strong sense of reality and of the moral dimensions of human relationships. Granted that the story remains fantastic in that the old hag can magically transform herself into a beautiful lady, the dilemma that Chaucer proposes is much more profoundly natural in that it involves no magic alternations by night and day and it is quite possible in ordinary life to choose between marrying an old and therefore constant woman or a young flighty one. More issues, also, are in the balance. Sexual and social pride are involved, as before. But now also personal relationships are more at stake. Physical pleasure is balanced against the love and trust of a stable marriage. External values represented by youth are set against internal values represented by age. The question of risk arises. Do you want a safe marriage, guaranteed by your wife's age, or will you take the risk of marrying a young woman who may treat you badly, make you a laughing-stock to your enemies and an object of pity to your friends, and who may bear other men's children to inherit your property?

The Knight's readiness to accept his wife's judgement is the ultimate reversal of his brutal assertion of masculine domination by committing a rape. The knight has been educated to move from vile aggression against women to accepting female sovereignty. The significance of the rape is not as an index of character but as part of a pattern of events that show an action and make a proposition. Not its content but its message is significant. The knight is forced, by his situation, to an act of submission to, and faith and trust in a woman, the more striking for his earlier transgression. Though there is no naturalistic characterisation, the nature of actual behaviour is commented upon. The knight now has to treat his wife as a person in her own right, with her own responsibility to decide and act in a moral question of personal relationships; she is not merely a submissive adjunct to himself. He therefore takes a risk, though of a different, less egotistical kind, from the risk he might have taken had he made his wife's choice of what her identity should be for her, instead of properly allowing herself to decide for herself. You need equality (of age, as in other matters, for the knight is young), and you need faith, in order to sustain personal relationships, especially in marriage; if you have equality you cannot have certainty, which is why you need faith. The story says, optimistically, rather like *The Franklin's Tale*, that love that is non-egotistical, that does not seek to dominate, that suffers long, and is kind, must take a risk and trust the beloved, and will be rewarded by a corresponding faith and love. The old wife becomes young and beautiful and promises to be true. Perhaps there is a sense here that the right kind of love *makes* the beloved beautiful and desirable, beauty living in the eye of the beholder. The last word of the story proper is of the lady's obedience, surely very uncharacteristic of the Wife of Bath's sentiments. Then immediately there is a violent switch in perspective, in narrative tone, to the Wife as storyteller – one of the abrupt discontinuities of perspective so characteristic of Chaucer's Gothic art. The Wife gives her own cheerfully coarse interpretation of the story, understandably and comically off-centre, about lusty young men in bed.

The poem has Chaucer's usual range of point of view, subject matter and style. The satirical reference to friars as the only succubi nowadays modulates to the magical glimpse of the four-and-twenty ladies dancing on the grass, associated with the old hag but never explained – an unusual touch of fairy-magic in Chaucer. The comedy of the repulsiveness of the dirty old woman in bed with the shrinking knight is compounded by the noble sentiment and diction of her speech.

THE FRIAR'S PROLOGUE AND TALE

The Friar picks up the Wife's Tale only indirectly, in order to pursue a long-standing quarrel with the Summoner, so he tells a tale about and against a Summoner, which is lightly attached to his character as a Friar, traditionally hostile to Summoners, rather than to his specific personality. The story is a traditional tale with many European versions but Chaucer sets it in a specific social context, in the Friar's 'country', though we do not know where that was, and we may suspect some private joke. A vigorously active archdeacon, who punishes all forms of vice, has a Summoner 'ready to his hand', who is a most efficient and deeply corrupt rascal, using his power to tyrannise over the weak, letting lechers off for bribes in order to line his own pocket. One day, the Summoner, on his way to extort a fine from a poor innocent old woman, falls in with a very smart yeoman in a green cloak, who says he is also, like the Summoner, a sort of bailiff, living 'far in the North'. They immediately become sworn brothers, and confess their malpractices to each other, during which it emerges that the yeoman is really a fiend, whose home is hell. The Summoner is intrigued, not terrified, by such a companion, and asks him various questions about his life, which yield some fascinating information. They agree to work together, each taking whatever he is given. Soon they pass a carter, irritated with his horses, who consigns them to the Devil. 'Why don't you take them?' asks the Summoner. The reason is that the carter does not really mean what he says. They go to the poor woman, whom the Summoner threatens with the archdeacon's prison on a trumped-up charge unless she pays him 12 pence. She pathetically pleads her poverty, so the ruthless Summoner says that he will take her new pan. She curses both him and the pan to the Devil. The accompanying fiend asks him if he repents, but not he. Since the old woman really means what she says, away he is taken by the devil.

The story is a joke, a satire, an expression of anger against corruption and petty tyrants, a comment on over-confidence, and more fundamentally a story about real intention in speech. When do we really mean what we say? The inner structure of the plot is a popular wild comic fantasy. It embodies an underlying general, human and humorous sense that in the end the biter is bit, wicked men over-reach themselves, that corruption corrupts itself; that there is a hope for ordinary inoffensive goodness.

The style is predominantly plain and forceful. A fine example of how effective this style can be, without benefit of elaborate diction, glowing adjectives or complex syntax, is given by the couplet

> He was, if I shal yeven hym his laude,   *give him his praise*
> A theef, and eek a somnour, and a baude.
>
>   (III, 1353–4)

To give such praise is ironical; the use of the first person adds feeling and venom; the placing of 'somnour' between 'theef' and 'baude' turns the name itself into an insult, while to have one's function regarded as by definition despicable turns the knife in the wound. This delicately yet deeply cutting invective is powerful poetry.

The couplet is also a brilliant example of metonymy (as opposed to metaphor). A network of associations, of praise juxtaposed with blame, with theft and sexual corruption, is woven around the Summoner and his profession, creating a tapestry of derisive meaning. The regularity of metre, the predominance of monosyllables, with 'somnour' high-lighted as the only exception, the concrete yet general nouns, the clinching rhyme, the concision, all reinforce the strength of the couplet. The pleasure of much of Chaucer's poetry throughout his work is to be found in such relatively unobtrusive effects, which generations of colourful Romantic expression of cloudier emotions make it difficult for us consciously to recognise, and may even prevent us sometimes from enjoying.

THE SUMMONER'S PROLOGUE AND TALE

The Summoner on the pilgrimage is angry and insists on speaking against friars, beginning with a coarsely comic popular reference to where friars are kept in hell. This accords with the somewhat scatological nature of his tale, which is also modernistic in its comically arithmetical conclusion (above p. 18).

Although the Summoner, like so many other pilgrims, begins with 'Lordings', and thus demonstrates that his tale was certainly meant for *The Canterbury Tales*, and for its present place and speaker, the poem soon becomes told in the general Chaucerian narrative tone. The central incident suits the Summoner's coarse personality, but the varied interest of the subject matter, the subtlety of attitude, in no way correspond to, or express his personality.

A friar, brilliant in preaching and begging, is sarcastically described. He is accompanied by his man who carries a sack for the alms which they collect, and by a companion who writes down the names of those who give, so that they may be prayed for, on an ivory tablet, which is wiped clean as soon as they are out of sight. These companions we hear no more of.

The Friar comes to a house where he is always well-received, and where the husband is lying ill in bed in the main living-room. The Friar enters, drives away the cat from the most comfortable place by the fire, makes himself at home, and speaks in a most oily, canting way. The wife comes in and is embraced warmly by the Friar who

> kiste hire sweete and chirketh as a sparwe   *chirrups; sparrow*
> With his lyppes.
>
>   (III, 1804–5)

She offers a meal which he accepts with amusing hypocrisy:

Have I nat of a capon but the lyvere   *chicken*
And of youre softe breed nat but a shyvere   *slice*
And after that a rosted pigges heed –
But that I nolde no beest for me were deed   *dead*
Thanne hadde I with yow hoomly suffisaunce.   *sufficiency*
I am a man of litel sustenaunce;
My spirit hath his fostryng in the Bible.

(III, 1839–45)

The traditional satire on clerical hypocrisy and greediness, common
for centuries before and after, is laid on thick. The hypocritical tone
of voice is wonderfully hit off. The Friar assures the wife that he saw
the soul of her child, who she says died two weeks ago, borne up to
heaven – the kind of revelation given only to Friars, who are superior
in this respect even to kings, because they despise worldly pleasure.
He goes on in this vein in quite a long speech, expounding a 'glose'
on the very words of Jesus which indicates his particular approval of
Friars (III, 1920), and causes us to remember Chaucer's own contemp-
tuous attitude to 'glosing'. The Friar's host, Thomas, angrily com-
ments on how much he has spent on Friars and how little he has got
in return. He is answered by an entertaining sermon on not getting
angry, full of learned examples, which culminates in an order to
Thomas to be confessed. 'No', says Thomas, for he has already been
confessed by his local parson (there being always rivalry between the
local incumbent, and the wandering Friars who were accused of
giving easy penances for money). The Friar argues about the need
for money to build his church, and Thomas is beside himself with
anger at the Friar's 'false dissimulation'. He promises to give the Friar
what he has, and the Friar is eager. But there is one important con-
dition: that the Friar must promise to divide the gift exactly with all
the other Friars in his convent, convents being usually made up of 12
members. The Friar cannot wait, and swears on his faith to divide the
gift. He is invited to put his hand down into the bed behind Thomas's
back to find the gift, and when Thomas feels him groping around

Amydde his hand he leet the frere a fart   *gave*
Ther nys no capul, drawynge in a cart   *horse pulling*
That myghte have let a fart of swich a soun.

(III, 2149–51)

(Some acquaintance with draught horses is necessary to realise the
thunderous effect of the comparison.) The Friar starts up like a mad
lion, rushes off to the lord of the manor, and in the most outraged
manner complains to him before all the court of the trick which has

been played on him. The lord's lady would dismiss the grossness as a churl's deed done by a churl, but the lord is fascinated by the problem presented – how could a churl have the imagination to set such a problem? He meditates on questions of reverberation of air in a way which echoes, if we may put it that way, the Eagle's much longer disquisition in *The House of Fame*. A squire comes forward with a ludicrously ingenious solution, about using a cartwheel, which normally has 12 spokes, to the end of each one of which each of the friars shall lay his nose – the rest may be imagined. The lord, lady and everybody say that the squire has spoken as well as Euclid or Ptolemy – and the story comes abruptly to an end.

Although there are literary stories of what we may call the Satirical Inheritance, and a number of folktales about the catching or knotting of broken wind, there are no analogues to this tale. Although it bears all the marks of the international comic popular tale it is much more original and learned. The portrait of the Friar is broadly satirical, elaborately built up to a masterpiece of hypocrisy, so that his fall to a crude trick may be the greater. His character as such is only a broad sketch, but the amount of self-revelatory speech given to him etches in the few lines very deeply. The long sermon against anger, besides its intrinsic interest, further emphasises the self-contradiction when he is so totally unable to control his own. The wonderfully ingenious comic solution of the cartwheel appears to be totally original with Chaucer, and a remarkable illustration of what can only be called his scientific, and specifically his arithmetical, interests. No other poet in English could have invented such a story.

The story in common with most international comic tales both rejects and asserts. Like *The Friar's Tale* it satirises the abuse of the powers and values of the official culture by those whose duty it is to exemplify and maintain them. These tales attack the faulty bearers of the official culture, rather than official values themselves, by showing pride going before a fall, the biter bit, the enginer hoist with his own petard, the satisfyingly comic degradation of those whose moral quality does not live up to their superior position. The comedy indulges refreshingly in indecorous invective and fantasy. Such stories assert the common, commonsense secular values of ordinary honesty, allowing for a bit of honest deceit of those who deserve to be deceived. Neither Friar's nor Summoner's story is about sex. Both are placed in the ordinary everyday world of the community.

The style varies from the colloquial realism of the Friar's speech and some other plain speaking to the equally effective but surprisingly learned diction attributed to the 'churl', Thomas, when he says

This shaltou swere on thy professioun   *vows*
Withouten fraude or cavillacioun.   *quibbling*
                                                                    (III, 2135–6)

This is probably the earliest recorded use of the word *cavillacioun*
in English, though it occurs also in *Sir Gawain and the Green Knight*
(l. 2275), and must have been 'in the air' at the time. Similarly, the
word 'odious' (III, 2190) was just coming into use, and this is one of
the very earliest recorded uses. The range of vocabulary extends
from traditional earthy Old English words to the most up-to-date
new ones.

One of the most interesting uses of words is the Friar's mention
of 'suffisaunce', already touched on above (p. 26). It is one of
Chaucer's favourite words, meaning 'satisfaction' or 'sufficiency', first
recorded in English in *The Book of the Duchess* (ll. 702 and 1037) and
recurring throughout Chaucer's works in *The Parliament* (l. 637),
often in the *Consolation*, *Troilus* III, 1909, as already mentioned and
elsewhere in *Troilus* and *The Canterbury Tales*. It expresses both a
physical and a spiritual comfort and completeness: 'being satisfied'.
The phrase in *The Summoner's Tale* 'hoomly suffisaunce' is itself a
paradox which satirises the Friar, for 'homely' is a deprecatory word,
implying something not very grand. Its juxtaposition with 'suffisaunce'
and the phrase's reference to the delicacies which the Friar has just so
hypocritically ordered make an amusing set of inverted meanings and
implicit criticism.

THE CLERK'S PROLOGUE AND TALE

Although there is no explicit connection in the texts, all the manu-
scripts agree in having *The Clerk's Prologue and Tale* follow *The
Summoner's Tale*. There could hardly be a greater contrast (obviously
deliberate), yet each is characteristically Chaucerian and it would be
hard to say which is the better poem. In the fourteenth and fifteenth
centuries the intensity of feeling in the story which the Clerk tells of
Patient Griselda was very widely appreciated.

The Host regards the Clerk of Oxford just as many bustling
businessmen regard scholars: the Clerk is quiet, so he must be think-
ing, and in consequence must be miserable.

For Goddes sake, as beth of bettre cheere!
It is no tyme for to studien heere.   *think*
                                                                     (IV, 7–8)

He asks for a merry tale, of adventures, without rhetoric. The Clerk 'benignly' answers, and says he has learned a tale from Petrarch

> whos rethorike sweete
> Enlumyned al Ytaille of poetrie.   *enlightened*
> (IV, 32–3)

Such was Petrarch's fame in Europe at the end of the fourteenth century. He was the first really widely known man of letters, whose influence was strong until the seventeenth century. The Clerk represents that side of Chaucer which knows and values rhetorical skill, while the Host represents that other down-to-earth literalistic side of Chaucer which mocks rhetoric. The Clerk refers with admiration which we need not take as ironical to Petrarch's rhetorical introduction to the story. Chaucer here seems to go out of his way to pay tribute to Petrarch. Nevertheless he proceeds to tell his own version in a beautifully austere style.

The original tale, though Chaucer probably did not know this, was the last story in the *Decameron*, finished 1353. Boccaccio had fashioned it out of traditional folktale elements. Both Boccaccio and Chaucer, with their rather similar backgrounds of Court and City, work readily in the creative tradition of folktale (as Shakespeare, Scott and Dickens could later), while adding more individualistic and learned characteristics. The structure of this story moves away from the everyday domestic world of the popular comic tale into something nearer myth, and for setting it requires a wider range, from peasant's cottage to ducal palace.

The story caught the medieval European literary imagination and there are many versions in several languages for the next few centuries, including stage-plays, one in sixteenth-century England. Its dispersion in the first place was mainly due to Petrarch's late discovery of the tale and his translation of it into Latin prose, 1373–4. This is the version which Chaucer knew and worked from, though he also relied heavily on one of the two French translations.

So far all versions had been in prose, but Chaucer returns to his favourite rhyme royal, which suits the stateliness and intensity of the story well, without impeding narrative progress. We hear how an unmarried Italian marquis, Walter, of Saluzzo (30 miles south of Turin) is urged by his subjects to marry in order to secure the succession. They offer to choose him a wife from among the noblest and greatest in the land, but he insists on choosing his own bride. He selects the good and beautiful daughter, Griselda, of the poorest man in the

village by his palace. The people are astonished, and no one more
so than Griselda and her father. The ladies who must dress her for
her wedding hate to handle her old clothes. They have to comb her
tangled hair. She becomes a perfect wife, famous near and far for her
beauty, goodness and judgement. Soon she bears a daughter.

Now comes a strange desire upon the marquis to text the 'sad-
ness' of his wife. 'Sadness' is not sorrowfulness but stability, firmness,
a kind of spiritual solidity, a refusal to complain. It is the key quality
which the poem emphasises, and the word 'sad' is a key word,
occurring proportionately far more often in this poem than in any
other of Chaucer's works. The marquis reminds Griselda of her
humble origins, says his nobles resent them, and recalls that she herself
when married promised always to assent with patience to whatever
he desired. She accepts all this without expressing any grief. The
marquis is delighted at her response, but pretends to regard her
with disfavour, and commissions a 'serjeant' to take away Griselda's
baby. She kisses the child and is heartbroken, but gives her up with
Christian resignation, committing her soul to Christ. The marquis
ensures that his daughter is well looked after by his sister, Countess
of Panico near Bologna, while Griselda in ignorance of this maintains
her stoical goodness. Then she bears a son, whom Walter treats in
the same way, Griselda also bearing this with 'sadness'. After 12 years
more of marriage Walter tests Griselda again by saying that he has
now decided to reject her entirely and that she must return to her
father's house as humbly as she came. She replies with a noble dignity,
far from unfeeling, but without personal resentment, and goes home,
clad only in her smock, the people following her weeping. She is
faithfully received by her old father, who had always been suspicious
of the marriage, and who now covers her with her original old coat.

Then Walter decides to marry again, and tells Griselda to prepare
the palace for the new bride, since no one else can manage things as
well as she. Griselda prepares for the wedding. The bride and her
brother arrive, and all the people now say that Walter is no fool, for
the bride is so much younger and more beautiful, and will have finer
children. 'O stormy people, unsad and evere untrewe' (IV, 995)
comments the poet.

Griselda bears everything, including being asked to praise the new
wife's beauty, which she does – 'only' she adds 'do not prick her
with tormenting as you have done me. She could not endure advers-
ity as can someone poorly brought up.' Then Walter says 'This is
enough'; he embraces and praises Griselda, tells her that the new
'bride' is really her daughter, the brother her son. Griselda only then

breaks down into expressive feeling of motherly love, swooning and holding her children so tight that her grip on them can hardly be loosened.

> Thus hath this pitous day a blisful ende.
>
> (IV, 1121)

The story is told, says the poet, still translating closely, not that wives should follow Griselda in humility, for that would be insupportable, but that everyone should be constant in adversity.

That is not quite the end of the affair for Chaucer, but we may pause at this stage to consider this exquisite poem. At the most general level it is a story of suffering redeemed by constancy, like that of Job. God tests Job as Walter tests Griselda. 'Whom God loveth he chastiseth.' These are ancient perceptions, however disagreeable, about both the arbitrariness of suffering and some divine element in its infliction, which causes it to bear fruit if resolutely endured. These always hard sayings are even more so today. This redemptive passive suffering was also seen very much as a feminine virtue (except in the Crucifixion). Gothic 'feminism' is strong in *The Clerk's Tale*. The story is one of the heroism and triumph of Griselda. It is she who overcomes Walter. Nothing, however painful, however irrationally inflicted, can destroy her constant integrity or make her cry out or complain.

It is not too much to recall in connection with this poem the stories of those who have triumphed by endurance in the irrational martyrdoms inflicted in concentration camps in the twentieth century. Suffering and, in a few, the heroic endurance of suffering, are always with us.

The key to the poem is found in the use of the word 'sad'. It is primarily, and paradoxically, an *anti-expressive* word, or rather, perhaps, an expressive word used to signify the absence of the expression of feeling. This is a little unusual in Chaucer, because much of his poetry is concerned with persons, notably Troilus, but also others, who give way to their feelings and express them violently. (Neither *sad, sadly* nor *sadness* occur even once in *Troilus and Criseyde*.) The story of Griselda is designed to recommend an heroic Christian stoicism which sacrifices self and personal feeling to steadfast commitment to principle. It is conceived in terms of personal relationships. In order to exalt the nobility of Griselda's commitment to her promise, in order to present a worthy opposite that shall show her virtue to be truly heroic, and in order to show the value of the virtue by its cost in suffering, the story of Griselda sets the virtue of commitment, not against vice, for that is too obvious, in her case too vulgar, but against another virtue, or virtuous feeling, among the best we can know, the love of a mother for her children.

This confrontation of two virtues is what makes the exquisite pain of the story. This is why, fantastic as the story is in naturalistic terms, unconcerned with ordinary 'characterisation', it offers a complex model for a genuine life-situation of choice between two goods of different kinds. The story is not, in the end, an account of how an actual husband did, might, should or should not, treat his wife. It is not mimetic. It energises and explores a proposition about life, which is of great importance in the development of religion and civilisation, namely, self-control; 'You should not give way to your feelings.' The story of *Sir Gawain and the Green Knight* makes the same point. So does *The Physician's Tale* from the point of view of the father (below, pp. 341–50). That many modern people believe the opposite, or that the story of Griselda is an extreme and one-sided example, of which by his realistic and emotive telling Chaucer increases the tension, need not blind us to its nature or truth. The story is conceived not so much naturalistically as anti-naturalistically. This paradox must surely be what attracted Chaucer to the story. That the subject concerns the *suppression* of natural feelings in the name of a higher obligation makes the story of Griselda, which looks so much like that of Constance, really quite different, for in the story of Constance her natural feelings, especially those of motherhood, are always given free rein. Constance has plenty of sorrow in her life, but to use our present narrow loophole of the word *sad* for surveying this aspect of Chaucer's poetic world, we find that *sad* and *sadness* never occur in Chaucer's *Man of Law's Tale* of Constance, and *sadly* only once, referring to the foolish messenger's heavy drinking (II, 743). Constance is never *sad*, while Griselda is always so. 'Sad' occurs ten times in *The Clerk's Tale*, and only nine in all the rest of *The Canterbury Tales*.

The general meaning of the word in *The Clerk's Tale* may be further illustrated by comparing its use in the poem with the sources Chaucer is known to have used. When the fell serjeant comes to take away Griselda's baby daughter, apparently with the intention of murdering the child, the Latin version by Petrarch, the French translation of the Latin, and Chaucer's own version, which relies on both French and Latin, all emphasise that Griselda 'neither weep ne syked' (l. 545). She took and kissed the child, as Petrarch writes, *tranquilla fronte*, which is translated by the French as *de plain front*, and rendered by Chaucer as

With ful sad face

(IV, 552)

It is very difficult for a reader of modern English to avoid giving *sad* here the modern sense of 'sorrowful'. But the evidence of the sources, and of the general use of the word *sad* in English in Chaucer's time, all make a clear case for a meaning like 'calm'.

Chaucer's uses of the word *sad* do not depend on any specific word in his source. They are insertions or glosses. Thus, when Walter first speaks to Griselda, Chaucer adds the significant Biblical allusion to the 'oxes stalle' (1. 291) and the detail that Griselda fell to her knees

And with sad contenance kneleth stille.

(IV, 293)

Her endurance *so sad stidefast* (IV, 564) is part of a generally pathetic addition of Chaucer's own to the scene with the serjeant, and that she continued

evere in oon ylike sad and kynde   *uniformly*

(IV, 602)

is a further gloss on the statement in Latin, French and English, that she never changed. Again, when in all three versions Walter is astonished at Griselda's patience and, but that he knew her love, might have suspected her of hardness of heart or downright cruelty, Chaucer alone adds

That she hadde suffred this with sad visage.

(IV, 693)

Each of these last two examples comes at the end of a stanza, where Chaucer is forced as it were to pad out his text so as to give himself room in dealing with the briefer prose of his sources, and takes the opportunity to meet a possible criticism that Griselda may be unfeeling, and to give extra emphasis to the tone and the lesson of stoicism. Here the meaning must be 'calm'. There would be little point in asserting that she endured her afflictions with a face 'sad' in the modern sense. It would sound like a feeble apology, not the bold approving assertion it must be. A failure to realise Chaucer's meaning is the cause of criticism that condemns Griselda or the poem.

Chaucer emphasises that she does feel strongly, when Griselda is apparently to be banished in favour of a new wife. She was *tristis* (sorrowful) says Petrarch, and the French says nothing, while Chaucer says *hire herte was ful wo* (IV, 753).

But she is unshaken, unchanged, which is further emphasised when Walter sees her *constanciam, la constance et grant pacience*, translated by Chaucer in an unusual image as being

> ay sad and constant as a wal.
>
> (IV, 1047)

She could not be described as always 'sorrowful' as a wall. Chaucer's approval of the quality of being *sad*, his concept of it as stability, constance, calmness, sound judgement, is further emphasised by his independent use of the phrase *sadde folk* (IV, 1002), in a passage not based on the sources, to describe those who were not like the *stormy people*, who are, very significantly,

> unsad and evere untrewe.
>
> (IV, 995)

These words occur in an authorial and authoritative interjection which is not to be shrugged off as merely the words of a faceless 'Narrator'. *Sadde* here means 'sound, sensible, stable, unmoved by fickle feeling'.

The word 'sad' is associated for Chaucer with a number of other words, especially 'true' and 'wise', but also 'glad', 'good', 'kind', 'simple', 'stable' which establish its general aura of wisdom, stability, truth, goodness and even resolute cheerfulness. In Chaucer's work the association with the modern meaning 'sorrowful' is very slight.

Although he translates the story closely, Chaucer thus intensifies in certain respects its spirit. He adds clear religious overtones. He makes additions which cause the story to dig deeper into our feelings by its greater realism and humanity. Griselda is more vividly realised both as a peasant girl looking after sheep and as a sorrowful mother. Walter's relationships with his people are more convincing, the negotiations for his marriage (which was the kind of diplomatic business which Chaucer knew well) are fuller and correspond with actuality. Chaucer thus screws the tension up even higher. He allows for some naturalistic response, and perhaps attempts to forestall it by expressing an apparently personal sincere feeling. Whether we should attribute this to the dramatic character, the Clerk, or to the poet as

Expositor, is not clear. It is obvious and humane but not necessarily therefore facetious. It seems to me to express the poet's serious engagement – like ours – with his own fiction. He says there was little need to test Griselda.

> But as for me, I seye that yvele it sit   *it evil suits*
> To assaye a wyf, whan that it is no nede   *test*
> And putten hire in angwyssh and in drede.
>
> (IV, 460–3)

The comment on the 'stormy people' already mentioned (IV, 995) is another example. Fortunately even Chaucer manages to restrain his flippancy in what are for him these rare comments.

It is perhaps useful to remind ourselves of the extraordinary popularity throughout Europe for three centuries of this almost intolerably painful story. Some of it was no doubt due to a misogynistic sense that women should put up with anything from their husbands; some of it was due to the recognition of the *exemplum* that Petrarch makes of it, recommending patience, translated by Chaucer (IV, 1142–62), as living in 'vertuous suffraunce'. Some things disagreeable now, such as the grovelling tone of the people's request to Walter to marry, would be taken for granted (like flowery dedications in books a couple of centuries later) as the necessary style of address to a superior, that 'Heigh style, as whan that men to kynges write' (IV, 18) which the Host dislikes. In such a style sincerity is not an issue. Rhetoric and reality are the same public truth to which most people – officially – subscribed. The Host's dislike of high style reminds us, though, of the constant possibility of alternatives to any style, the potentially 'dialogic' nature, in Bakhtin's word, of all language. The interjections noted above, whether we attribute them to the poet or to the dramatic *persona* of the Clerk, hint at such alternative style and attitude. They are only hints; even with the interjections the tone of the poem is fully controlled as one of sober seriousness to which even the interjections contribute, as they do to the sense of engagement with the story. To this extent the story and style are appropriate to the Clerk as described in *The General Prologue*. Chaucer perhaps wrote the story particularly for the Clerk because the story interested him and the Clerk was the most likely speaker. But he did not write it to explore or express the Clerk's own personal character and subjectivity. *The Clerk's Tale* has much of Chaucer's own personal poetic manner. Beside the interjections already remarked on, we may note that the very beginning of the tale, where the sources remark on the youthful marquis's selfish pursuit of pleasure and refusal to marry, thereby upsetting his people, Chaucer goes further and adds 'I blame hym' (IV, 78), though this might indeed express the Clerk's moral seriousness.

Yet the deeper qualities of the tale are not characteristic of the Clerk. Such subjective feelings and attitudes as are expressed are essentially traditional, though Chaucer develops them with a sharper sense of Griselda as a person, a greater tenderness, that are his own. The actual subject-matter of marriage, motherhood, and a woman's heroic endurance are by no means typical of university clerks – rather the reverse. Nor is the literary interest in Petrarch which is attributed specifically to the Clerk in his Prologue at all characteristic of medieval university teachers and scholars, with their primary concerns with theology, law, medicine, and their low valuation of literature.[2] Griselda invokes the blessing of God's own death, as Christ, and as Father, on her child, in resigning herself to the child's imminent death (as almost every mother in the fourteenth century must have had to do for one or more children, when probably four out of five children died before the age of five). But Griselda does not pray to God for herself, as Constance does. Despite the religious and folkloric echoes it evokes, the tale is secular; it is not devotional, nor especially suitable to the Clerk. The previous tellers, Boccaccio the originator, and Petrarch, were not university men; the elderly Parisian bourgeois, who wrote Le Ménagier de Paris in the late fourteenth century as a book of instruction for his young wife and tells the story of Griselda, was a layman.

The story draws to an end, following the sources, by emphasising that the story is not designed to make wives follow Griselda's example in humility but to encourage everyone in his degree to be 'constant in adversity' and live in 'vertuous suffraunce' under God (IV, 1142–62). These stanzas are accompanied in the margin of the Ellesmere manuscript by their Latin original from Petrarch's version, the longest of several Latin glosses. Such marginalia may well be Chaucer's and witness to the seriousness with which he has taken the story, and his recognition of the prestige of its Latin source. Then the tone switches to a greater consciousness of the Clerk as teller, though in a more flippant style than we would expect of the Clerk.

> But o word, lordynges, herkneth er I go.   *one*
>   (IV, 1163)

'Lordings' is typical of the mode of address between the pilgrims, as noted above. The Clerk goes on to say ironically it would be hard to find more than two or three Griseldas in a town, so he refers his listeners to the Wife of Bath, and promises a song to cheer them

> And lat us stynte of ernestful matere.   *cease*
>
>   (IV, 1175)

The Clerk's 'character' of sombre seriousness has been flung to the winds by the poet, who has also allowed him to say 'er I go', which is entirely inappropriate in any realistic way to the group of pilgrims, whom he is not about to leave. It is more characteristic of an independent tale-teller – like Chaucer himself. So light is the fiction, and Chaucer has so to say usurped the Clerk's character. And this is but a bridge to the next six stanzas which conclude the tale, a wonderful technical *tour-de-force* of 36 lines using only three rhymes. It is headed *Lenvoy de Chaucer* and by a *volte-face* comparable with that at the end of *Troilus and Criseyde* it mocks one aspect of the story, though it moves to the comic against the serious, rather than as in *Troilus* from mixed comic to entirely serious. Considering the emotional tensions and the strain on belief that Chaucer himself has heightened in his telling of the story it cannot but be a relief that Chaucer himself, despite controlling his scepticism so firmly during the course of the story, should, like the modern reader, apparently react against it. But his reaction is different from what might be expected. Instead of being outraged by Walter's barbarism or Griselda's abandonment of her children, as are many modern readers, he jests at the very notion of submissive wives.

> O noble wyves, ful of heigh prudence,
> Lat noon humylitee *youre* tonge naille,
> Ne lat no clerk have cause or diligence
> To write of *yow* a storie of swich mervaille
> As of Grisildis pacient and kynde,
> Lest Chichevache yow swelwe in hire entraille!   *swallow*
>
>   (IV, 1183–8)
>
> (Chichevache means 'lean cow', lean because she fed only on patient wives.)

It is typical of Chaucer's ambivalence that alongside his real compassion, tenderness and feeling for women, alongside the implicit but genuine criticism that the story in all its versions offers of male dominance and competence (Griselda is a better, more efficient 'marquis' than Walter), nevertheless he finishes up with this ironic jesting, though even this is not simple antifeminism. There would be many a mature wife in his audience/readership who would enjoy its back-handed compliment. This is not the quiet, thoughtful Clerk speaking, nor a stupid Narrator; it is the poet himself, as the text tells us. Yet the envoy is picked up by the succeeding remarks made by the Merchant and is clearly meant to be part of the tale. The tale has been well concluded, but provides almost endless opportunity for comment and some variety of interpretation. Not every or any interpretation can be right – if that were so, interpretation or even reading the tale itself would be pointless. Which interpretation(s) is/are right remains for the reader to argue about. The ending that is also a prolongation by comic comment is without anxiety – certainly no 'male status anxiety' or anxiety about influence. It shows how confidently Chaucer could move between the levels of narration. He was not trying to create a consistently naturalistic illusion. He was a brilliantly versatile story-teller ready to exploit any device to stimulate the reader, to change pace, to alter the perspective, amuse, intrigue, delight his audience, and always ready, like all good story-tellers, to leave a core of enigma at the heart of narrative which continues to draw attention.

THE MERCHANT'S PROLOGUE AND TALE

The Envoy jestingly advises wives to make their husbands miserable. The Merchant, quite unexpectedly, takes this up, complaining of the cruelty of his own wife, to whom he has been married only two months. Perhaps this is some contemporary joke about Gilbert Maghfeld, or maybe it is a device to motivate a somewhat antifeminist tale, though as usual the implications of the story cut both ways.

For some reason this tale, like the Clerk's, is set in Lombardy in Italy (while the Summoner's and perhaps the Friar's are set in the North of England, and the Pardoner's and *Sir Thopas* are set in Flanders). *The Merchant's Tale* could hardly be more different from *The Clerk's Tale*, and is a deliberate contrast to show an erring wife. The central episode is again one of adult marital domestic comedy with a fantastic core of the kind familiar in the international popular comic tale, enriched by learning of many kinds, and a strongly ironic humour not likely to appeal to the young. After the brief plaintive Prologue in which the Host asks for a story about 'wyves cursednesse', since the Merchant knows so much about it, the story itself begins and continues without any sense of the Merchant himself telling it. It is not displaced autobiography, and some manuscript variations suggest that it may not have been originally meant for the Merchant.

An old and lecherous knight called January decides at last to marry. The poet with heavy irony puts into January's mouth praise of young wives for old men, and either continues January's speech, or speaks in his own poetic person (and the uncertainty shows how unimportant is the distinction) with general ironic praise for the superiority of marriage over bachelordom;

> For who kan be so buxom as a wyf?   *obedient*
>   (IV, 1287)

A string of not quite relevant examples follows. This is good traditional ironic humour on an ancient theme. January boasts of his youthful feelings — he is only white about the head, and that is but blossom on a green tree. His brother Placebo (Latin for 'I will please'), a flatterer who has been a 'court-man all his life' and who never disagreed with the great lords he has accompanied, confirms all January's opinions. Another brother, Justinus, whose name suggests 'justice', and who is presented as a teller of disagreeable truths, gives the traditional advice to a man who asks if he should marry — 'Don't'. January insists, and only worries that since one is unlikely to be happy both in the present world and the future life, wedded bliss may deprive him of Heaven. Justinus tartly replies that he should not despair; perhaps his wife will be his Purgatory. Remember, says Justinus, the Wife of Bath (who had boasted of being the purgatory of her fourth husband). Here is another amusing confusion of narrative levels, with a character *inside* the story referring to one who is outside that story.

January marries a maiden of tender age and 'small degree', that is, of low rank — not quite a lady. The wedding is splendid, and described with Chaucerian humour and verve, mingling Classical and Biblical allusion,

> And Venus laugheth upon every wight . . .
> And with hire fyrbrond in hire hand aboute
> Daunceth biforn the bryde and al the route.   *crowd*
>   (IV, 1723 . . . 8)

It is an extraordinary image almost of mythic power. Yet it consorts with sarcastic remarks about tender youth marrying stooping age.

The festivities finish and all rejoice save January's young squire Damyan

> So soore hath Venus hurt hym with hire brond,   *torch*
> As that she bar it daunsynge in hire hond.

(IV, 1777–8)

The poet, not quite seriously, as Expositor, sententiously addresses the perilous fire, the familiar foe, the servant traitor, that January is nourishing: to wit, his squire, Damyan, in love with his wife.

January and May go to bed. He fondles her and kisses her with his bristly chin. Chaucer creates an extraordinary tactile image of the stiff bristly old face nuzzling the young and tender one. So January labours till day, and then sits upright and sings full loud and clear, all full of fun, a comically disgusting sight.

> The slakke skyn about his nekke shaketh
> Whil that he sang, so chaunteth he and craketh   *trills*
> But God woot what that May thoughte in hir herte,
> When she hym saugh up sittynge in his sherte,
> In his nyght-cappe, and with his nekke lene;
> She preyseth nat his pleyyng worth a bene.   *bean*

(IV, 1849–54)

The apparently impartial plain description of domestic reality, by its selection of detail, combines the visible facts with the responses of January, May, poet and reader and thus forwards the story by implying motive. Although the poet refrains from comment, even claiming ignorance of May's mind, he forms our opinions and expectations. The poet as so often takes up an apparently objective attitude to his story which is actually not neutral.

Meanwhile, Damyan sickens. May in womanly kindness visits his sick-bed with her women (some of the action in this poem is a remote parallel to that in *Troilus and Criseyde*) and he secretly slips her a note, which when she has secretly read she tears up and puts down the privy. These domestic details effectively remove us from the realm of high romance. No such account is given of the disposal of Troilus's letters. Yet we need not think the tale bitter or harsh because of them. It works on the down-to-earth everyday domestic level of the adult comic tale, and though not glamourised shows no deep revulsion.

May is gentle and has pity, like Criseyde and all the best Chaucerian heroines. She writes a nice letter back, tucks it under Damyan's pillow, and secretly squeezes his hand. This is enough to cure his sickness.

January has made a walled garden so private and beautiful that Pluto the king of Fairy Land and his queen Proserpina 'and al hire fayerye' often visit it, and dance about the well-spring in it. Sometimes January makes love to May there.

But, says the poet in a familiar phrase, 'worldly joy cannot last for ever', and accuses Fortune with mock seriousness on January's behalf; for January suddenly becomes blind. He is also jealous. May brings it about that Damyan gets into the garden where alone the jealous January feels sure of May. One day, in June, January lovingly addresses May in words that are a witty parody (by the poet, not by January) of the Song of Songs, and brings May into the garden. She makes a hypocritically tearful declaration of her love for him, and as she does so signals to Damyan to get up a tree, as she had forewarned him in a letter. Meanwhile the Classical god and goddess Pluto and Proserpina enter and wrangle over the nature of women. May implies that she is pregnant and must indulge her fancy for green pears. 'Alas,' says January 'that I am blind and cannot help.' May is ready to climb on his back and up the tree where Damyan awaits – and there, says the poet, as he is a rude man, and cannot glose, he must say pretty plainly what happens.

When Pluto sees the wrong which May is doing January he miraculously restores his sight, and when January sees what the poet says may not be courteously expressed (though he does express it a few lines later) he sets up a great roaring. May is not one whit put out. Proserpina has in fact promised Pluto that she shall have an answer. May says she has been instructed that in order to restore January's sight she must struggle with a man in a tree. January has the impression that more than struggling has taken place but is assured that he only thinks so because the recovery of perfect sight cannot be immediate, and so he did not see quite straight. So January finishes up happy. We hear nothing of Damyan, nor how May feels. The focus is on an absurd sequence of improper events, not on characters, and the poet (hardly the Merchant) concludes, within a sense even greater impropriety

God blesse us and his mooder Seinte Marie.

(IV, 2418)

To end such a story so piously seems true Gothic and Chaucerian indecorum, giving a relish of worldly comedy, rather than blasphemy. The nucleus of the story is the traditional proposition spoken by Pandarus: 'Women ben wise in short avysement' (*Troilus*, IV, 936). A woman always has an answer.

The central episode called 'the Pear-Tree Episode' is well-known and has many variants. Its origin is probably ultimately in the East, but the twelfth-century learned Latin 'comedy' called *Lydia* gave it impetus in Europe. In some versions God and St Peter discuss the characters' actions. St Peter complains, and God says, in effect, 'You'll see how, if I restore his sight, she'll get out of it.' Chaucer articulates the story much better, connecting the delightfully humanised Pluto and Proserpina much closer to the action, making the whole story a stronger chain of cause and effect. The magical quality of the private garden is also Chaucer's invention, as well as the idea of adding the preliminary discussion of the charms of marriage, even though the material of that is quite traditional. To be sorry either for May at the beginning or January at the end, or Damyan at all, is to sentimentalise a coolly derisive but not embittered story – though the story is reasonably attributed to an embittered pilgrim. In *The General Prologue* we were given licence not to sympathise too greatly with the Merchant. The narrative is spoken by the poet, the general Chaucerian Expositor, and is beautifully adorned with a great variety of interesting description.

Yet this account of the poem given so far will not prepare the reader for the large and impassioned amount of critical discussion which the tale has caused. It has been described as deeply cynical, bitter, disillusioned, coarse, blasphemous, socially disorientated, commercial, and as an expression of a mercantile class in search of its own identity, or subjectivity. The most substantial, learned and powerful of recent accounts, with its own originality, is that of Professor Lee Patterson, who fits the tale into his account of Chaucer's development of subjectivity, and his attack on transcendental authority, patriarchy, absolute values.[3]

There is no space here for prolonged debate, though discussion of these issues enhances our appreciation of Chaucer and is intrinsically interesting. Our own attitudes and values inevitably become involved, tested, sometimes changed. Debate is far from barren. The fundamental issue can be quite simply stated: *Who tells the tale?* Professor Patterson takes it as a completely dramatic, self-standing expression of a fully characterised Merchant. The considerable Classical and Biblical learning, the sense of a courtly environment and what is regarded as a bourgeois outlook ('bourgeois' being as pejorative as 'transcendental', 'authority' and 'patriarchal'), the wit, parody and blasphemy, are all attributed to the Merchant as telling the tale. But there is no evidence for such a view. It is unhistorical. It goes against what little objective, stylistic and textual evidence there is. For example, the state of the manuscripts suggests that the tale may have been written for a different teller, as Cooper notes.[4] (*op.cit.* 202). Not all manuscripts have the Merchant's *Prologue*, and there are signs of revision. In the course of the witheringly ironical 'sermon' on marriage at the beginning of the *Tale* (IV, 1267–392), the speaker refers to the unhappy plight of unmarried men

> – I speke of folk in seculer estaat.
>
> (IV, 1322)

Earlier, he speaks, with reference to the 'worthy knight' who always followed his bodily delight without marrying

> As doon thise fooles that been seculeer.
>
> (IV, 1251)

Chaucer tends to put any self-characterising statements at the very beginning and end of his tales. *The Merchant's Tale* ends with the comment

> Now, goode men, I pray yow to be glad,
>
> (IV, 2416)

The references to 'secular fools' and the sermon-like address 'Now, goode men', would all fit a clerical speaker well. The Pardoner three times addresses an imagined congregation as 'goode men' (VI, 352, 377, 904), as does the Nun's Priest at the end of his tale (VI, 2402, 3640, and perhaps 3445). When such stylistic indicators are combined with the learned tradition from which this particular *fabliau*-like story comes, with the ecclesiastical tradition of misogyny, with the learned ecclesiastical and Biblical parody, and the substitution of figures of classical mythology for God and St Peter, the case for an ecclesiastic as the teller the tale was originally designed for is strong. If it is even granted as a good possibility, the case for presenting the tale as an analysis of mercantile subjectivity collapses. Nor is it helped by Professor Patterson's own argument that the strongest case for the tale as representing the Merchant's subjectivity is that he has no subjectivity, being denied it by the absence of an available class-identity (p. 338).

In arguing for the possibility of an originally clerical teller (the Monk is a favourite candidate) I do not wish to fall into the same interpretative trap of the dramatic principle, for four reasons. The first is that cultural circumstance in Chaucer's day made psychologically and dramatically expressive, independent characters unavailable to authors even so advanced as Chaucer, though the Wife of Bath and Pardoner, in their *Prologues* (not their *Tales*), come near. This general principle applies to the whole of *The Canterbury Tales*. Second, and consequently, such characterising traits as are built into the tales are light and superficial, traditional and external characteristics. Third, Chaucer could and did switch tales written for one speaker to another. *The Shipman's Tale*, where the speaker characterises herself as a woman at the beginning (VII, 11–12), and *The Second Nun's Tale*, where the speaker characterises himself as a man (VIII, 62) offer irrefutable examples. *The Merchant's Tale* may be another. The fourth reason is that even where Chaucer had a speaker in mind the sense of a dramatic identity significantly different from the poet's own poetic identity is weak and fluctuating. We see examples of it in many tales, most recently in this book in *The Clerk's Tale*. The dominating mind in all the tales is Chaucer's. This is true of all great artists, even those with a developed sense of dramatic independent character as in the English novel, but it is particularly true of Chaucer because of his historical culture. What is also true of Chaucer, and differentiates him from his contemporaries, is the extraordinary variety of the attitudes of mind and feeling, often apparently juxtaposing incompatible elements, which he himself displays. Our modern critical passion for unity and logic is often vexed by Chaucer's acceptance, and presentation, of inconsistent views and positions. Such inconsistencies have been regarded as artistic or moral flaws. But they may equally be regarded as the only way to present the otherwise totally baffling complexities of experience, even if we grant, what may not be true, that there is an underlying unity of experience to be grasped.

Returning to *The Merchant's Tale* with all this in mind we must see that if there is an historically conditioned mind driving the poem along, as there must be, it is Chaucer's. A number of points made by Patterson and others may be true of Chaucer the poet, though many other points fall away as irrelevant. Chaucer's chameleon-like spirit knew much of the merchant classes from which his family derived, and much of the royal court where he spent his life from early adolescence. As we know he was unusually well-schooled in Classical and medieval Latin literature and non-fictional works, as well as French. He could and did combine profound scepticism with profound devotion. He was a great poet, who took up various points of view, and a great satirist. *The Merchant's Tale* reveals a scepticism verging on nihilism. Reading it we may feel, as the Psalmist says, 'There is none that doeth good, no not one' (*Psalms*, XIV, 1). But these traditional generalisations are always confronted with others to different effect, or qualified in some way.

Many critics have found this a harsh and bitter tale, perhaps taking their cue from the Merchant's sour description in his *Prologue* of his own marriage, but it is a mistake to allow that to colour the tale too strongly. *The Tale* is no more cynical than *The Miller's* and *Reeve's Tales*, and much less violent and unkind (think of poor John the Carpenter's broken arm, and his jeering neighbours). The characters in *The Merchant's Tale* are not evil. January is a selfish, silly, lecherous old man but there is nothing unusual in that. May is 'of small degree' as the snobbish courtman who is writing the poem tells us, and 'no better than she ought to be' as used to be said, but she deserves some sympathy. If the story began its history as an antifeminist joke, nevertheless the woman gets away with it, to our amusement. All the characters finish up satisfied within the narrow context of the poem. We do not follow them outside its confines, but if we were to we should surely find that such athletic and enterprising young folk will not do too badly, and January will soon go to his 'long home', as the liturgy calls his grave, and to his immortal destiny. There is deceit in plenty, but no innocents suffer. We need not feel sorry for any of the characters. The wedding feast is a splendid festival. The parody of the Song of Songs is wonderfully witty and does no harm to that great work. Church and minor gentry are fair game for Chaucer's satire here as elsewhere in his poetry. In so far as the poem is class-specific it mocks, from Chaucer's superior position, minor gentry, but no characters are in any doubt about their identity, and May goes up in the world in several senses. It does not diminish the fascination and the poetry of this poem to refuse to hitch it to various general social forces. Though the names of January and May indicate the stereotypes of crabbed age married to fresh youth they are vividly realised and could equally well be John and Alison as in *The Miller's Tale* with only a little blunting of the ancient dictum about old men and young wives. There is no allegory, just as there is no self-revelation. There is some delightful fantasy, especially of Pluto and Proserpine as fairies, Pluto being presented, as Professor Mann remarks, as the only hen-pecked rapist in literature.[5] An epilogue to *The Merchant's Tale* is provided by the Host complaining about his own wife, but no lead to the next tale.

THE SQUIRE'S TALE

The Prologue to *The Squire's Tale*, as it is entitled in the Ellesmere and some other manuscripts, follows immediately the comment 'Heere ended the marchauntes tale of Januarie,' though nineteenth-century editors divided it into an Epilogue to *The Merchant's Tale* of 22 lines and then the remaining eight as introduction to *The Squire's Tale*.

A brief glance at one of the outstanding differences between manuscripts here will tell us important things about literary effect. It will be recalled that the Hengwrt manuscript was, as the experts Doyle and Parkes[6] assure us, probably the earliest of the manuscripts of *The Canterbury Tales*, copied in the very early fifteenth century, soon after Chaucer's death. The order of tales is different from that of the Ellesmere manuscript, and there are numerous other differences, though both manuscripts were probably copied by the same scribe, working under the orders of someone else now unknown. Hengwrt is much less splendid and some scholars believe it to be closer to the rough papers left by Chaucer, and so more authentic than Ellesmere which is more 'edited'. (All editors distrust other editors, not without reason.) This general situation reminds us that not only the order of the tales but also some of the very tellers were not finally decided by Chaucer. This makes it perilous to deduce a teller's character from any particular tale. As has been suggested above (p. 279) in most cases the tales come first and were allocated to more or less appropriate tellers, with a few exceptions.

In the case of the *Prologue* to *The Squire's Tale*, as Ellesmere calls it, we have the Host's comments arising out of *The Merchant's Tale*, mainly remarking on women's tricks and his own wife's shrewishness and other vices – standard misogynistic moaning – followed by an invitation to the Squire to say 'somwhat of love' as he is obviously an expert. The Squire politely agrees. All this is clearly right. In Hengwrt, by contrast, the same passage following *The Merchant's Tale* leads to *The Franklin's Tale*. The word 'Squier' is changed to 'Sire Frankeleyn' which does not scan (V, 1) and the words 'And sey somwhat of love' are changed to 'And sey us a tale' (V, 2) which also spoils the line's scansion and is feebler. This version is obviously wrong. Chaucer never wrote such unnecessarily lame lines which obviously derive from, as they weaken, the Ellesmere version, or rather, the common ancestor. Ellesmere here is clearly superior. In Hengwrt's present order, which anyway is probably disturbed from the original mess the scribe left it in, *The Squire's Tale* follows *The Man of Law's Tale* without that tale's endlink (also missing in Ellesmere) though the scribe left a space for it. Although *The Squire's Tale* begins abruptly without introduction in Hengwrt, and in an odd position, it is labelled 'the Squiers tale' and there can be no doubt that Chaucer meant to allocate that tale to him, as being suitable in subject-matter, though more of that later.

In Hengwrt *The Squire's Tale* is followed by *The Merchant's Tale*, and the speech about his son's bad behaviour given to the Franklin in Ellesmere is given to the Merchant in Hengwrt, who is thus deprived of the motivation of a bad marriage which Ellesmere gives him to tell his tale of another marriage. While the Ellesmere arrangement seems best at this point it is not impossible that Hengwrt represents Chaucer's earlier thoughts, which he modified, finally giving what he had first allocated by way of introduction to the Merchant to the Franklin, and developing the Franklin's speech a little. The moral is the slipperiness of texts, the specific slipperiness of the texts of *The Canterbury Tales* and the weak foundation for modern psychosocial theories about tellers based on the tales they tell. On the other hand the state of the texts suggests an openness of meaning. There is tremendous variation, much ambiguity. We are dealing with a work in process, not a completed finished product, even if Chaucer did hastily parcel up his pages in some sort of order and wrote some final words before death dealt him a dint.

To return to *The Squire's Tale* as we have it in the Ellesmere text and Skeat-Bradshaw sequence, after *The Merchant's Tale*, Chaucer was evidently looking for a change. *The Merchant's Tale* is a sort of anti-romance, like many other *fabliaux*, and perhaps Chaucer thought that a true romance would change and sweeten the tone without being too great a break. Obvious candidates were *The Squire's Tale*, though it was not yet complete, and *The Franklin's Tale*, or at least those tales which now go by those titles.

As the Host is now made to say, the Squire is the obvious person to tell a love-story, and so he starts in a vein of exotic romance and wonder. The metre is the five-stress couplet, and this and the control of the verse, the grasp of courtly situations, and the self-characterisation of the teller as 'a dull man' (V, 279) all show that it is a work of Chaucer's maturity. In view of the poet's self-characterisation it is likely that the poem was not written at first with the Squire in mind as the teller. Its interest in love and wonders suit the Squire but Chaucer's failure to finish also demonstrates that he has grown beyond an interest in youthful love, which is not surprising when we consider the predominance in *The Canterbury Tales* of stories of the adult dilemmas, comedies and tragedies, of married life.

The Squire's Tale is set in the romantic land of Tartary, on the edges of the known world, beyond Prussia. The noble king, Cambyuskan, holds a courtly feast on his birthday in March, and a strange knight comes with a horse of brass, a magic mirror, a gold ring and a naked sword. All have magic properties and arouse great wonder, with Chaucer showing his usual gently satirical contempt for the gaping crowd; 'Diverse folk diversely they demed' (V, 202). In the end horse and sword are dismissed by the poet somewhat peremptorily.

The story turns to the king's daughter, Canacee, to whom has been given mirror and ring. She is up early, on a beautiful morning, and the ring allows her to understand what the birds are saying. She hears the piteous story of a female falcon, betrayed in love. It was once a theme dear to Chaucer, as we have seen, and it is told with some vigour. After the complaint the poet promises to continue the tale to tell how the falcon won her love back, and how he will recount adventures and battles – very untypical Chaucerian subjects – but the story immediately fades out unfinished. Chaucer must have got bored with it. It was a mistake. The account of the falcon's lost love is pale and thin after the superb introductory descriptions of how the wonderful horse of brass came to the court, of the behaviour of the people, and of the court festivities. Despite Chaucer's usually rather *blasé* attitude to feasts, especially the food, which even appears in this tale, we get a delightful sense of the personal aspects of a great fourteenth-century court festival with the description of people high and low buzzing around the new wonders, the music, the orderly bustle of the feast, the wine, the form of dances, the secret interchange of looks, even to the hangover on the following morning. People are now a primary interest. The description of Canacee is both realistic and charming. She has not revelled the night away.

> She was ful mesurable, as wommen be,
>
> (V, 362)

and she rises fresh at dawn

> As rody and bright as dooth the yonge sonne.   *red-cheeked*
> (V, 385)

When she hears the misery of the falcon, she asks her

> Is this for sorwe of deeth or los of love?
> For, as I trowe, thise been causes two

That causen moost a gentil herte wo;
Of oother harm it nedeth nat to speke.

(V, 450–3)

Such a comment harks back to the dilemmas presented by Machaut, which Chaucer has now outgrown.

The poem shows Chaucer's mature awareness of and interest in the technical conduct of the story. He comments on how important it is to get to the 'knot' of a story, by which he probably means what we should call the 'point', and urges himself to get on with it (ll. 401–8). Earlier he had used the favourite rhetorical device of describing by refusing to describe and says of the courtly celebration

Heere is the revel and the jolitee	
That is nat able a dul man to devyse.	*describe*
He moste han knowen love and his servyse	
And been a feestlych man as fressh as May,	*festive*
That sholde yow devysyen swich array.	

(V, 278–82)

But the Squire is *just* such a 'feestlych man', so described, even with the reference to May, in *The General Prologue*, who the teller says he is not but would have to be to recount revel and jollity. The story-telling attitude here clearly dramatises the teller as the dull man ignorant of love, the *persona* that Chaucer himself as poet loves to assume, and whom the Squire is not. The passage is an example of Chaucer's usual 'ignorance formula', nothing to do with the Squire as a character but part of the poet's normal battery of narrative devices.

There is a possibility that an astronomical structure underlies the curious problem. There is no doubt that such a structure underlies *The Complaint of Mars*, as we have seen, for it is made obvious. Dr J. D. North has argued that such astronomical allegories underlie several other poems. He bases the argument on a number of mysteriously precise astronomical references that occur in many poems – for example, in *The Merchant's Tale* and in *The Franklin's Tale*. That these must have had significance for Chaucer is hardly to be disputed. They relate to Chaucer's scientific interests. In general they are likely to be additional enrichments rather than structural determinants – even if we could understand what structures they might represent. The problem is highly technical, but it does seem as if Chaucer in *The Squire's Tale* took the name of Cambyuskan's queen, Elpheta, from the name of a star, and that Cambyuskan has some relation to Mars. Chaucer may have ingeniously dabbled in some of these correspondences, rather in the spirit of composing a crossword puzzle, and then found it got too complicated, or at any rate had carried it as far as he cared to. How many people would have appreciated his ingenuity?

THE FRANKLIN'S PROLOGUE AND TALE

It may be that Chaucer, not wishing to finish *The Squire's Tale* began to think he would have another character cut it short, as the Knight had *The Monk's Tale* and the Host *Sir Thopas*. At any rate, the manuscripts follow the unfinished *Squire's Tale* immediately with effusive praise from the Franklin 'considering thy youth', which perhaps is meant to stifle any continuation. The Franklin wishes his own son were a man of such judgement as the Squire, and there seems no irony here.

> Fy on possessioun
> But if a man be vertuous withal.
>
> (V, 686–7)

Critics treat this admirable sentiment with derision, but there is no reason to think this traditional sententiousness as insincere, or only allow it to be poetry if taken to be ironical on someone's part. He wishes his son could learn 'gentillesse'. Perhaps the Franklin is presented as a bit of an old buffer. At any rate the Host rudely replies 'Straw for youre gentillesse', and abruptly calls for a tale. The Franklin responds peaceably, first disclaiming in a rather rhetorical manner any knowledge of rhetoric. He says he will tell a 'Breton lay', though it is little like the handful of earlier Middle English poems that may be claimed to be such. The action is, however, set in Brittany. The story is about *trouthe* and *gentillesse* and presumably the Franklin's earlier remarks about *gentillesse* and his son were given to account for the fact that it is he to whom the tale is attributed, and to link it with *The Squire's Tale*. Chaucer places the tale here for further variety. It is about love, as *The Squire's Tale* was meant to be, but about love, and the problems of love, in marriage, which at this stage of his life Chaucer found much more interesting than the sorrowful moo–ings of calf-love. He had already told several of the normal popular tales about love in marriage, which are all comic, and which culminate in *The Merchant's Tale*. After this it is time for sweetness and light, without evading the threats to happiness that life, and particularly love, offer. Hence *The Franklin's Tale*, one of Chaucer's most original poems, not comedy, not exactly romance, certainly not satire, nor irony, yet with elements of all these, and *pace* many recent critics unashamedly a celebration of *trouthe* and *gentillesse*.

In Armorica, now called Brittany, we are told, a knight called Arveragus fell in love with a lady, Dorigen, and served and suffered long. At last she, for his worthiness, and especially for his meek obedience, took pity on him and agreed to take him for her husband and her lord (of such lordship as men have over their wives). Apart from the touch of mature flippancy in the last remark this is the normal Chaucerian ideal of love leading to marriage, briefly dealt with in some dozen lines. In order to achieve full happiness Arveragus agrees that even as husband he will obey Dorigen except that in public, for honour's sake, he takes the 'name' of sovereignty. This is the first premise of the tale. The second premise is Dorigen's corresponding promise always to be humble and true to him. We begin where *The Wife of Bath's Tale* ends. The third, immediately arising out of the proposition of mutuality just expressed,

> That freendes everych oother moot obeye   *must*
>   (V, 762)

is that

> Love wol nat been constreyned by maistrye.   *constrained by force*
>   (V, 764)

So much for mastery, even sovereignty. The free spirit of love, which desires liberty, not to be a thrall, demands also patience, a high virtue, which conquers where rigour fails (as Griselda may be thought to illustrate). 'Lerneth to suffre' (V, 777), that is, to be patient – for like it or not, everybody in this world misbehaves at some time, for some reason, and every wrong that is received cannot be avenged. This sensible, sententious passage is the foundation stone of the story, and can only be taken as said by the poet. It is indeed part of the foundation of the whole of Chaucer's thought. Other characters and stories illustrate it. Not only Griselda overcomes by patient endurance: so does Palamon. Even Criseyde expresses this traditional pacific wisdom: 'Men seyn, "the suffrant overcomith", parde' (*Troilus*, IV, 1584).

Arveragus and Dorigen are happy, but the pursuit of honour requires Arveragus to go and dwell in England a year or two. It may

seem strange that after a long and passionate courtship, and at the
beginning of a happy faithful marriage, Arveragus should decide to
go away for so long. Once again we need to recall different cultural
obligations and different literary conventions. We are reading a self-
declared Breton lay which the poet himself distances as pre-Christian
(like *The Knight's Tale*), not a realistic modern novel. The assump-
tions of the society he describes are nevertheless those of his own, or
more so – current idealisations. The most important thing is to
recognise (again) the obligations of honour, that most powerful in-
frastructure of so many pre-industrial societies. As already noted
(above, pp. 224–5), there were those even in Chaucer's day who
were hostile to the notion of honour, notably in the Church. Even
in secular society there were those who disapproved. The classic
pros and cons of honour had to wait a couple of centuries before
being summed up by Shakespeare, somewhat extravagantly and very
wittily, in the persons of Hotspur and Falstaff (*I Henry IV*, I, iii,
202–8; V, i, 127–40). Honour itself, whatever might happen to
those who sought it, was of very long life, even to the wars of the
present century, but its apogee in the seventeenth century, and
Arveragus's own attitude, could he have articulated it, may be summed
up in Richard Lovelace's famous poem, *To Lucasta (Going to the
Warres)* beginning, in words that might be addressed to some mod-
ern critics,

> Tell me not (Sweet) I am Unkinde . . .
> To Warre and Armes I flie

and ending

> I could not love thee (Deare) so much
> Lov'd I not honour more.

It is also worth recalling that despite the pleasant mixed company of
the sexes in courtly circles in castles and gardens as in *The Franklin's
Tale*, and in Chaucer's own English society, men and women even
when married still lived in different social worlds in many respects,
with different obligations and duties. Chaucer himself, and his wife,
despite having children, like many married courtiers frequently
endured long separations, as indeed, until the recent advent of easy
air travel did many married people in the armed services, many
seamen and others, not infrequently for years at a time. So there is
nothing callous or absurd, within the conventions of his own or

even Chaucer's society, in the compulsion Arveragus feels to win honour beyond the seas.

Arveragus writes regularly to Dorigen, like many a serving soldier abroad, but she, like many a wife at home, is sad and in particular worries about the threat of the rocks on the coast to the safety of the ship in which Arveragus will eventually return. In a long speech she questions the wisdom of God in creating something so evidently evil and irrational.

> Eterne God, that thurgh thy purveiaunce   *providence*
> Ledest the world by certein governaunce,
> In ydel, as men seyn, ye no thyng make.   *in vain*
> But, Lord, thise grisly feendly rokkes blake   ·   *fiendish*
> That semen rather a foul confusion
> Of werk than any fair creacion
> Of swich a parfit wys God and a stable,
> Why han ye wroght this werk unresonable?
>
> (V, 865–72)

Her friends try to cheer her up, and on 6 May bring her into a beautiful garden, where all sing and dance save the melancholy Dorigen, and here when she is on her own a young squire, Aurelius, who has long loved her, expresses his feelings and asks for her mercy, or he will die. Dorigen is not in the least tempted to be untrue; nor is she shocked, and in order to make her refusal less harsh, though not less absolute, says 'in play' that she will be his love if he removes the rocks which she feels endanger her husband's life. 'It is impossible,' he says, and he must die. He goes home distraught and since these are pre-Christian times prays to the gods, then falls sick. Arveragus returns safely and he and Dorigen resume their happy life. Meanwhile Aurelius's brother remembers his studies at the university of Orleans, and they both go there where they meet as by magic a clerk who can perform magic deeds, and who will remove the rocks on the coast for a thousand pounds. All this is done, with much scientific comment from the poet about tides and astronomy, with the result that the magician produces, not the fact, but the illusion, to all people, for a week or two, that the rocks have disappeared.

Aurelius, with fearful heart and humble expression then courteously recalls to Dorigen how she plighted her 'trouthe' in the garden, and announces that he has fulfilled the condition. Dorigen is horrified. She goes home in fear and sorrow, and weeps and wails a day or two. She then expresses her sorrows in a long 'complaint' against

Fortune, formally introduced. She gives a long list of ladies who have committed suicide rather than lose their virtue.

> Why sholde I thanne to dye been in drede?
>
> (V, 1386)

And thus she laments, always intending to die rather than give herself to Aurelius. But she cannot bring herself to it. Arveragus, who has briefly been away, returns and asks the cause of her sorrow, which she immediately confesses. This husband, with cheerful face, says the poet

> Answerde and seyde as I shal yow devyse.   *tell*
>
> (V, 1468)

She must keep her promise, for

> 'Trouthe is the hyeste thyng that man may kepe'
> – But with that word he brast anon to wepe.   *he immediately burst out crying*
>
> (V, 1479–80)

After this agony Dorigen obeys, 'as if she were half mad' with sorrow, so that Aurelius has so much compassion on them both that he cannot bring himself to commit

> so heigh a cherlyssh wrecchednesse
> Agayns franchise and alle gentilesse.   *generosity; nobility*
>
> (V, 1523–4)

She thanks him on her bare knees. Aurelius curses the day he was born, hard put to it to pay his debt for which he has had no gratification. But he too vows to keep his 'trouthe', and asks the clerk of Orleans time to pay off his debt in full. The philosopher himself will not be outdone in *gentillesse* by knight and squire, and releases him from his debt. The tale ends with the question, who was the most generous?

It is as usual a traditional tale with many folktale elements, adorned with considerable though not burdensome scientific knowledge about tides, and deepened by philosophical questioning. The central narrative episode is a version of what folklorists call the Rash Promise – examples are stories such as that of Jephtha (*Judges*, XI), or, with a happy ending that of Rumpelstiltskin. Chaucer probably carved the essential elements of this story out of a much longer one in Italian prose, by Boccaccio, in his series on 'questions of love' called *Il Filocolo*, though there is another version of the same story in the *Decameron*. But Chaucer made considerable changes.

Stories of this kind do not rely on plausible motivation or consistent illusion, as we have seen. The characters are clear-cut types with recognisable human feelings, but the power of the story lies in its inner structure, based on, but not 'imitating', real-life situations, and usually concerned with personal relationships and the values which govern behaviour. The obvious examples are fairytales and Biblical parables, which often contain implausible elements, combined with surface realism, in order to make important points.

What is the point of *The Franklin's Tale*? Obviously, at the level of conscious values, to teach the importance of love, freedom, patience, generosity, *trouthe*. But it would not do this if the inner structure were not powerful. It is built on paradoxes, composed of opposite but complementary compulsions which both support and oppose each other, and in so doing create interest and illustrate the nature of life. Honour, *trouthe*, love, safety are part of each other, yet are also in conflict.

The structure of *The Franklin's Tale* rests on Dorigen's love for her husband, her consequent fears for his safety from the rocks in the sea, and her paradoxical and good-natured jest to Aurelius that if he can remove the threat to her husband she will give herself to Aurelius. The proposition is self-contradictory, and the impossibility of removing the rocks guarantees the impossibility of her loving Aurelius. That is why Dorigen allows herself to make the joke, to soften her refusal. (Unlike Criseyde she *can* say no, but sentimentalises it a little.) She knows the true hardness of the rocks and of the world. When Aurelius produces an *illusion* that the rocks have disappeared he reveals an unsuspected relationship between the rocks, and love, and faith. The structure of events shows that the physical materiality of the world, as represented by the rocks, may be harsh, but if you deny it you lose the spiritual values of love and faith. You cannot have advantages without disadvantages, or without risk. The rocks do not *symbolise* honour; that is either too materialistic a view or not materialistic enough. They represent *rocks* – harsh physical materiality. They also represent the price you have to pay for honour: physical danger for the husband, physical chastity for the wife.

The story goes further, when, none of them knowing that the rocks are covered only by magical illusion, Dorigen's husband, Arveragus, says she ought to keep her word and give herself to the squire

Aurelius. Arveragus sacrifices his own feeling of his own honour, as reputation, to its deeper aspect as *trouthe*, which is loyalty, keeping one's promises, integrity, an inner value. There is no extravagance of sacrifice. Arveragus would not have Dorigen's unfaithfulness known, but the nature of unfaithfulness is the opposite of solitary. Dorigen's *trouthe* to her husband conflicts with her *trouthe* to her own plighted word. The survival of society depends on individuals keeping their promises, but which of two conflicting promises should be kept? Chaucer reveals the ambivalence of deep values, or that values good in themselves may be incompatible with each other – a good Gothic point illustrated again in *The Clerk's Tale* and in *Troilus*. *The Franklin's Tale* also includes propositions about appearance and reality. When the sea apparently covers the rocks, appearance takes over from reality. Physical reality is harsh and dangerous, but it is better not to conceal it from oneself, or worse, spiritual, dangers ensue; and then moral integrity, represented by Dorigen's faithfulness as a wife, may be shipwrecked. Reality is better than illusion, even when painful.

The happy ending reflects the 'moral optimism' of Chaucer, of Gothic feeling, of the Romance *genre*, and of Christianity; of the faith (in the Boethian language of *Truth, Balade de Bon Conseyle*), that 'trouthe thee shal delivere'. The adherence of Arveragus and Dorigen to *trouthe* calls forth in the others the *gentillesse* which we are told in *The Wife of Bath's Tale* derives from Christ, the type of self-sacrificing love.

Another major point in the story is the *connectedness* of all experience, whereby Chaucer reveals his traditional, archaic feeling for the unity of experience, as against the fragmentation of experience which is characteristically modern. In *The Franklin's Tale* we see that the moral laws governing behaviour have some connection with the physical laws governing matter. Disturb one and you disturb the other. Dorigen attempts to change the environment irresponsibly. She does it in jest, so the outcome is only a fantasy, and is redeemed. The modern world does indeed change the environment on a scale quite as large as Dorigen envisages, and ecologists now begin to warn us of the consequential but unforeseen and dangerous effects. Magic is the technology of folktale. Chaucer puts into Dorigen's mouth a very modernistic accusation of God for allowing all the suffering, danger and evil in the world. In modern thought the recognition of evil often leads to the denial of the existence of God, the denial therefore of value and purpose in the universe independent of mankind's preferences. Of course, if objective value is denied, evil also cannot exist – it is just another irrational purposeless accident for which nothing and nobody can be blamed. Good and evil are themselves inextricably linked. One cannot exist without the other. The story structure of *The Franklin's Tale*, like that of *The Clerk's Tale*, illustrates this traditional notion. It is notable that the danger from the rocks, and Dorigen's questioning, are entirely original with Chaucer. He articulates modern feelings and insights. The answer to all this questioning is the assertion, and exercise, of the archaic complex of moral qualities evoked at the beginning of the tale. In these matters Chaucer carries further, and deepens, the concepts of honour already examined in connection with Criseyde (above, p. 224). *Trouthe* meaning faithfulness, integrity, promise-keeping, is the part of honour which takes its origin from inner integrity, not outward social reference. The balance between the inward and the outward pulls of honour makes it a potentially ambivalent quality, with an element of inherent self-contradiction. When the self-contradiction becomes too strong, for Chaucer the inner pull, personal integrity, *trouthe*, should prevail.

One of the strangest things of many strange things in modern Chaucer criticism is that this penetrating and generous-spirited tale has been read as totally ironical, a cynical send-up of a silly old Franklin who is obsessed by social climbing. Such a reading is produced by applying novelistic assumptions to traditional literature, and by adopting anachronistic attitudes that disregard or are ignorant of the historical nature and value attributed to chastity, honour, bravery, etc. The cynical reading also bases itself on Dorigen's long, formal complaint, which is regarded as so long, and in the end so irrelevant to her situation, as to be self-evidently silly and therefore a mockery of Dorigen. This judgement itself assumes that Chaucer never nods. It is indeed the case that Dorigen's complaint to some extent gets out of Chaucer's control. It is on a subject he was always inclined to dwell on. A list is always attractive to him. But there is no signal whatever that Chaucer *intends* Dorigen to be made to look ridiculous: at worst there is a minor artistic failure.

The general interest of this extraordinary and original, yet traditional tale is so great that there is no space here to comment on its wealth of knowledge and the felicity of diction.

The Franklin's Tale concludes a long and fascinatingly varied but connected series that can reasonably be held to begin with *The Wife of Bath's Prologue*, and which, though it also contains *The Friar's Tale*, *The Summoner's Tale* and *The Squire's Tale* is sometimes called The Marriage Group, and is believed to conduct a kind of debate about marriage. It might as well be called the '*Trouthe* and *Gentillesse*' group. Certain themes do recur, and three out of the seven tales do indeed deal with married people, with *The Wife of Bath's Tale* in addition commenting on sovereignty in marriage. There is good evidence that Chaucer in his maturity is interested in marriage as little 'high' literature has been until the twentieth century, though the international medieval comic tale deals often with the subject and reflects Chaucer's own interest. But to refer to a 'Marriage Group' or 'Marriage Debate' is to impose a desire for systematic thought and exposition on Chaucer which the whole of *The Canterbury Tales*, from *The General Prologue* onwards, shows him avoiding. Chaucer, more influenced by systematic scientific thinking than any other major English poet, seems specifically to reject systematisation of human relationships and moral concepts. His modernity is profound and exceptional, but partial.

NOTES

1. Lee Patterson, *Chaucer and the Subject of History* (Madison, 1991), 290–321, with much more space than I can afford, has a particularly valuable discussion. See also Anna Laskaya, *Chaucer's Approach to Gender in* The Canterbury Tales (Cambridge, 1995).

2. The disdain of medieval intellectuals for literature, in contrast with the Humanists of whom Petrarch was the great forerunner, is noted in the Introduction to Sidney's *The Apology for Poetry*, edited by G. T. Shepherd (London, 1965), 17–22.

3. Lee Patterson, *Chaucer and the Subject of History* (Madison, 1991), especially 322–49.

4. Helen Cooper, *Oxford Guide to Chaucer*: The Canterbury Tales (Oxford, 1989).

5. Jill Mann, *Feminist Readings: Geoffrey Chaucer* (London, 1991), 66.

6. *The Canterbury Tales: A Facsimile and Transcription of the Hengwrt Manuscript, with Variants from the Ellesmere Manuscript*, edited by Paul G. Ruggiers, Introductions by Donald C. Baker and by A. I. Doyle and M. B. Parkes (Norman and Folkestone, 1979).

Chapter 21

The Canterbury Tales III: Family Honour; You Find what you Seek

THE PHYSICIAN'S TALE

The Physician's Tale is quintessential connoisseur's Chaucer of his own time, which is perhaps why it is generally disliked or ignored. Here is no expression of the genial modern man-of-the-world for whom anything goes. It is pure fourteenth-century Chaucer. Its roots are deep in human history, yet it is told with a fully Gothic sensibility to beauty, pathos and paradox. Racial memory, patriarchal authority, the preservation of the purity of family, the recourse to death – what could be more alien to late twentieth-century sensibility? Anybody can enjoy the comic tales. They are no less rooted in basic human feelings, but they are marginal to the real demands of the preservation of social life, because the joke is that those demands are evaded. *The Physician's Tale* confronts them head on. As much of its time and tradition as it is, so offensive to liberal anti-patriarchal egalitarianism and modern sexual freedom, it nevertheless, as will be shown, reaches out to concerns that are still ours today, if we will have a little patience to unravel the tale, appreciate its assumptions, see it in its historical situation, and recognise the laws which control it. It will be worth spending more space than usual on this neglected tale. We may not like it, but in coming to understand it as the product of a related but distant culture we learn something which may be to our advantage. A superficial reading of the poem, as usual with Chaucer, is easy.

The Physician's Tale can be taken on its own. Chaucer (and it must be Chaucer, no Narrator) never finally decided how it would fit into the *Canterbury Tales* sequence. It has no headlink or Prologue. It is firmly tied to *The Pardoner's Prologue and Tale* by the beginning of the *Introduction* to *The Pardoner's Prologue and Tale* and the conjunction obviously aims at variety and contrast. The end of *The Pardoner's Tale* has no further link. Both tales have a simple traditional but very different core, elaborated in Chaucer's normal manner. The folktale structure gives the basic poetic power; each story is extreme in very different ways.

The Physician's Tale is written in Chaucer's mature style of the five-stress couplet lines, fully realised and closely controlled. No pilgrim-voice is even hinted at. There is no characterisation of the teller except as revealing one of the poet Chaucer's serious deeper concerns: the bringing up of children and the hatred of injustice and exploitation. These are traditional human concerns and the story attracted such dissimilar writers as Boccaccio and Gower, whose versions are quite independent. The tale is quite clearly attributed to the Physician by a headline in the Ellesmere manuscript and an appropriate but emblematic miniature of him in blue hood and red coat, perched awkwardly (like most of the figures) on his horse, inspecting a half-full urinal, an unlikely activity on his pilgrimage, but a main method of medieval medical diagnosis. In the *Introduction to The Pardoner's Prologue and Tale* the Host refers to the urinals typical of physicians. Another line after the end of the tale tells us that 'Heere endeth the Phisicien's tale,' followed by words of the Host to Physician and Pardoner. This apparently incongruous pair form a kind of floating fragment.

The Physician's Tale embodies a profound human paradox concerned with the fundamental nature of society. In evolutionary terms what is vital is the survival of society as a whole. Society is made up of individual members, who have desires which it is the function of society to satisfy, but in evolutionary terms (and others too) the survival of the group may involve sacrifice of the desires of individual members. In other words, some general social compulsion may come into conflict with individual desire. In this respect evolution, like God, is no respecter of persons (2 *Samuel*, XIV, 14; *Acts*, X, 34), or of 'subjectivities', is non-egalitarian, and achieves only rough justice. The general evolutionary law of long-term group survival, variously active in various societies, must override what is good and socially desirable in the short term for the individual. Since modern science and technology have apparently freed us from most social constraints they may well appear alien to us now. But this is an extraordinarily recent development.

The heart of *The Physician's Tale* is a dreadful paradox produced by conflicting compulsions. Virginius, the admirable father, loves his supremely beautiful and virtuous fourteen-year-old daughter, Virginia, with fully protective patriarchal love. She is lusted after by an unjust judge, Appius, who intends to abduct and enslave in order to rape her. Since might is right in this story's archaic world (not so different from our own), Virginius, powerless against the judge, is forced against his will to exercise the only power left to him to fulfil his deepest obligation, to preserve his child from the disaster of what was then no cynical joke but literally considered to be a fate worse than death. Thus,

> With fadres pitee stikynge thurgh his herte
> Al wolde he from his purpos nat converte
>
> (VI, 211–12)

he says to her

> Ther be two weyes, outher deeth or shame . . .
> O deere doghter, endere of my lyf . . .
> For love, and nat for hate, thou moste be deed.
>
> (VI, 214 . . . 25)

We have to recognise that this is an honour-driven society. Shame is a component of honour.

The modern objection to this is that Virginius expresses his own grief – not, 'How terrible for you,' but 'How terrible for me.' In Virginia's response Chaucer squeezes every drop of pathos from the way she asks her father for mercy as she lays her arms about his neck in a manner familiar to fond parents 'as she was wont to do' (233) and asks, is there no grace, no remedy? (236). But there is none. Is Virginius hard-hearted, selfish, egotistic? Not, certainly, as he is presented in terms of the story. His agony increases as does the reader's discomfort when Virginia asks for time to 'complain' (not in the modern sense, but to 'mourn') her own death, quoting the case of Jephthah's daughter.

We should take a moment to consider Jephthah's and some comparable stories. The story of Jephthah, like that of Virginius, Virginia and Appius, was widely known in the Middle Ages. Jephthah, an Israelite military leader, vowed to God, if he were granted victory in battle, to sacrifice the first living creature to greet him on his return (*Judges*, XI, 30–1). His daughter was the first. Jephthah laments in terms similar to Virginius: 'Alas, my daughter, thou hast brought me very low, and thou art one of them that trouble me.' He grieves for himself, not explicitly for her. He makes more explicit the obligation upon him: 'for I have opened my mouth unto the Lord, and I cannot go back' (*Judges*, XI, 35). His daughter accepts the compulsion he is under, only asking for two months in which to 'bewail her virginity', after which without further repining she returns to her fate, which then is annually lamented (*Judges*, XI, 36–40).

Virginia in *The Physician's Tale* refers to Jephthah's daughter as an example of being given time to mourn, but in the economy of the tale Jephthah's story is an important parallel. Jephthah's daughter 'bewails her virginity' not as a matter of regret that she has had no sexual experience but as a precious asset which she would have brought to marriage and is now to be wasted by death. By contrast, in a later culture which values virginity equally but differently, Chaucer represents Virginia also recognising that her father has no alternative, but thanking God that she dies a virgin. Medieval high culture took over the Judaic and New Testament supreme value attributed to virginity and even heightened it, as the Wife of Bath cheerfully recognises (just as she also represents the average sensual woman's acceptance of a lower rank in virtue for the sake of greater personal pleasure). In classical, medieval and many other cultures chastity was regarded as the intrinsic quality of a woman's honour, and the demands of honour constituted an inexorable demand, here as elsewhere in Chaucer's work. Furthermore, a daughter's, like a wife's, honour, was part of the father's honour, and for both men and women honour was, or should be, dearer than life, as in various forms it has been so judged even in the twentieth century.

To return to Jephthah, his story has to be seen in the light of the passionate Jewish commitment to the family and of parents to children, along with the Solomonic injunction 'he that spareth his rod hateth his son' (*Proverbs*, X, 13). The story of Abraham and Isaac is familiar (*Genesis*, XXII). There are numerous Old Testament references to the sacrifice of children for the greater cause of the benefit of Israel (*Exodus*, XXII, 29; *Isaiah*, LVII, 5; *Ezekiel*, XX, 26): some of these were condemned by *Jeremiah*, VII, 31, but the case of Jephthah was not regarded as contrary to the worship of the Lord as it achieved its purpose of Jephthah's victory. His sacrifice was necessary but peculiarly painful to him, and the story emphasises that she was his only child. His grief is not in doubt but he has no alternative and she resigns herself to death. For Chaucer the Old Testament had historical validity, and divine sanction, though some medieval commentators condemned Jephthah's vow.

The situation was known in other ancient cultures. In Greek mythology Agamemnon fell under the necessity of sacrificing his daughter Iphigenia, as told in Aeschylus's play *Iphigenia in Aulis*. This story would not have been known to Chaucer but variants of the theme are common in folktale, and the point is that, as the wide

distribution of the stories shows, the interest of the theme was not
peculiar to Chaucer, or to medieval Christian culture. It is multi-
cultural. He derived his own version of the story mainly from Jean
de Meun's brief account in *Le Roman de la Rose*, which Chaucer
follows in referring to the Roman historian, Livy, as its source.
Chaucer himself may have consulted Livy's much longer account, as
did Gower and Boccaccio for their own independent versions. But
Chaucer as usual modified the tradition. He stripped the story down
to its barest essentials in order to heighten the effect. Virginia's *fiancé*,
for example, is not mentioned. For Livy the sacrifice has a political
point – it provokes a popular uprising. In other respects Chaucer
amplifies, as is his way, the human and personal interest, expanding
the delay in execution and the talk between Virginius and his daugh-
ter, all heightening the emotional tension and the pathos. Chaucer
insists on the historical truth of the story. In view of the nature of
the story this does not seem to be ironical. A story could be told
with new detail appropriate to the way the teller sees the story, as
is traditional from Biblical narratives onwards (for example, the
four Gospels). He remarks, rather unusually for him, as Professor
Cooper notes,

> this is no fable
> But knowen for historial thyng notable
>
> (VI, 155–6)

'Real history' for Chaucer seems to have been Roman history. He
makes virtually the same remark in his account of Cleopatra, *Legend
of Good Women*, 702. As in that case we cannot but wonder if
Chaucer 'doth not profess too much', and a modern reader may
suspect irony. Rather, perhaps, he was encouraging himself to
believe something so unusual. Yet as will be shown, something like
the actual situation was not impossible in Chaucer's England, despite
his *penchant* for pushing situations to extremes. He seems to have
made a clear distinction between 'fable', which is false, and 'history',
which is true, implied again in *The Prologue to the Parson's Tale*.

In *The Physician's Tale* Chaucer is touching, at its deepest level, on
a dreadful dilemma common to all societies, and recognised for
millennia in Judaic and European, perhaps all successful cultures. It is
when a society, to survive, must paradoxically deny the happiness
and even the life of some of the individuals who make it up. This is
common enough even in successful modern societies which have
had to risk sacrificing their young, usually young men, in order to

survive a hostile attack. The young men (I was one of them) acqui-
esce in the compulsion felt by society to sacrifice them, or risk
sacrificing them, but there is no greater grief than that caused to the
parent by the death of a grown child, except when the father himself
has to administer the death-blow.[1] It is the most poignant form of
the clash between natural personal feeling and a social need irresist-
ibly imposed by ingrained conviction and external necessity. All the
characters in the story recognise both the pain and the inevitability.
What makes it even more painfully paradoxical is that society also
depends on the young for its survival. That this particular situation is
unusual ('notable' as Chaucer says) makes it paradoxically more typi-
cal and the more memorable. It affects us all, and especially parents,
who must at times, though not so extravagantly, deny their chil-
dren's desires and be cruel to be kind. (This is perhaps a poem, like
a few others – Pearl, Shakespeare's King Lear – which can only be
fully appreciated by parents, or even more narrowly, by fathers of
daughters. Younger readers will have to wait.)

The grief of a father over a son is projected theologically in the
doctrine of the Trinity, with especial reference to the sacrifice of the
Son by the Father, they, with the Holy Spirit, being both three and
one. Modern atheists object that for a father to sacrifice a son is
no true sacrifice, but that is the expression of a modern atomistic
individualism which would be incomprehensible to earlier cultures,
especially the passionate paternalism of the Judao-Christian tradition.
The Father suffers through the Son, being at one with him. The
same pattern operates in the non-Jewish ancient tradition repre-
sented by Livy.

The particular social circumstances of the story may seem suffi-
ciently strange to the modern reader to distance the actual dilemma,
because of the generally accepted modern view that chastity is of no
importance, and because of the modern weakness of the sentiment of
honour. The circumstances were not so entirely strange in medieval
England, and Chaucer also modernises them to suit his own time.
There are touches of legal language. The actual legal procedures of
presenting a Bill in late fourteenth-century England are followed
by Chaucer, when Appius gets Claudius to present a Bill alleging
that Virginius wrongfully detains Virginia. The procedure becomes
unjust only when Appius prevents Virginius from giving his side of
the case or invoking 'compurgators' – witnesses, or trial by jury, or
trial by combat 'as a knight' (193). The unjust judge thus perverts the
course of justice, and since he is governor of the region there is no
higher court which can be appealed to. It does not seem that Chaucer

was indirectly criticising the actual course or concepts of justice in England in his own day. The general unpopularity of lawyers (a phenomenon not unknown in later centuries, including our own) and underlined in the Peasants' Revolt has but a faint reflection in Chaucer's sarcasms about self-enrichment in the portrait of the Man of Law in *The General Prologue*. The injustices he recounts in his tale are treated with indignation but not satire.

The essentials of Virginia's case might occur even in Chaucer's England. His own father had been abducted at the age of 12 in order to be forced into a marriage which happily for English literature was eventually foiled. Chaucer himself was placed in 1387 on a commission to enquire into the abduction of a young heiress. Hornsby notes an even closer analogue in real life, 'a bill presented by William Burton before the chancellor in 1420 [which] complained of the abduction of his seven-year-old daughter and claimed that the girl had been ravished and detained "wrongfully, and against law, right and good conscience, and against the will of the said suppliant"'.[2] In this case the false plea of the churl Claudius is matched by the presumably true plea of the father, but Burton's daughter had already been abducted and raped.

Virginius is compelled to act by the cultural obligations of patriarchal honour and female virginity. Nor are these concepts utterly remote from our own time. It is recorded that an Arab 'father murmured "Quiet, little one, Die, my daughter, die" as – to save his honour – he killed the child for walking home from school with a male classmate'.[3] Another story is told from Afghanistan of a Muslim father shooting his daughter to save her from being raped by soldiers. Modern Western indignation needs to understand the 'otherness' of other cultures before being easily unleashed.

Chaucer tells the story because it is shocking, but shocking in a way that is different from modern cultural expectations. Yet there is a common human element to be reckoned with. The story is historical for Chaucer, and may interest us not least because it is a most extreme example of a dilemma that affects all parents, and particularly fathers in traditional patriarchal communities. (If the community were matriarchal then mothers would endure the same problems.) The central character is not the daughter but the father, just as in *King Lear* the father not the suffering virtuous daughter is the central character. Virginia is another Cordelia. That, incidentally, is a good reason why the claim that *The Physician's Tale* should be associated with *The Legend of Good Women* must be dismissed. Virginia is a necessary character but not the centre of interest. It is in order to heighten the tension of the story that Virginia is described as so hyperbolically exemplary a daughter.

> And if that excellent was hire beautee
> A thousand foold more vertuous was she.
>
> (VI, 39–40)

The rhetorical device of the description of the lady, which Chaucer could use both seriously, as of Blanche the Duchess, and parodically, as of Alison in *The Miller's Tale*, was never deployed in a more heightened manner. The portrait may not please independent modern women, as it praises not only all Virginia's great qualities, but emphasises how docile, modest and restrained she is. No midnight discos for her. And Chaucer adds, as old-fashioned people may still, that indulgence in amusements make children precociously ripe and bold – they will become bold enough when married (61–71). There seems no joke intended in this last remark, but a cool assessment that any kind of virtue in the world is rare enough. It redeems the portrait of virtue from any conventional sentimentality.

The remark leads Chaucer into further observations on the theme of bringing up children concerning those who have lords' daughters in their charge, and so to further warning of parents to control their children strictly. It is the kind of meditative reflection on the essence of a story that Chaucer is fond of. A parallel example is the apparent digression on the need for patience near the beginning of *The Franklin's Tale* (V, 761–90), or that on the futility of caging a wild bird in *The Manciple's Tale* (IX, 163–86). Such commentary is intrinsic to Chaucer's leisurely narrative style. Here it is relevant to the general theme of the nature of parenting and more specifically, in the ancient tradition (again offensive to modern sensibilities, especially those of the young), to the need for strict parental control. We may well attribute this interest in parental care to Chaucer the man, bearing in mind that at the height of his powers he started to translate the treatise on the astrolabe 'for little Lewis my son', aged ten (above, p. 153). Although *The Physician's Tale* does not rely on the expression of a personal subjectivity, and the views given are orthodox, we may well detect a personal earnestness in these addresses to governesses and noble parents, forthrightly expressed. They are part of the story as relating to Virginius's stern and deeply painful duty. At the same time Chaucer does not give the same sense of personal participation in the tale as he sometimes does elsewhere. There are no extravagant apostrophes and exclamations on the part of the narrating poet, no 'colour'. It is a serious tale and the poet plays no games with it. He took it too seriously for that.

As is customary in Chaucer's tales, with rare exceptions, the actual events are briefly told. They are the foundation but the interest of the building is created by commentary and the expression of feeling. The *Tale* ends with a moral statement about sin attached only to the final outcome which does not concern Virginia or Virginius. The wicked judge takes his own life when imprisoned, the moral being that your sin will always find you out. This is serious traditional wisdom. We only wish it were more often true.

It does not console us for the suffering of Virginius or Virginia, but nothing could, any more than we can be consoled for Cordelia's fate. *The Physician's Tale* presents a striking example of a terrible problem to which any solution must be distressing. In its minor way it is the equivalent of one of Shakespeare's 'problem plays'. One of these, *Measure for Measure*, also centres on what is for the modern Western mind the incomprehensible value set on female chastity but we should remember that this cultural incomprehension dates only from the late twentieth century, and is largely the product of sophisticated medical technology. The ideal was crucial to such poets as he who wrote *Sir Gawain and the Green Knight* and his sources,[4] very obviously to Spenser and Milton, and was strong up to the middle of the twentieth century. In the current state of Western society we might even learn something from the lessons of control and self-restraint.

The modern view, represented by Professor Lee Patterson, is that the tale shows 'Virginius's self-regarding commitment to female chastity' and his 'self-regarding cruelty' (p. 369). In a way this is of course true, since the family's honour is indeed the father's. He condemns *The Physician's Tale* as 'fraudulent or counterfeit hagiography'. In order to save Chaucer the poet from such deceit the story, thus judged by totally alien assumptions, has to be attributed to the character of a fraudulent Physician. What would be the point of this is not clear, nor is there any evidence. The tale is Chaucer the poet's, speaking in the terms of serveral thousand years of human, not only medieval Christian, culture. It has nothing to do with hagiography in any way.

The logic of Professor Patterson's judgement is that the only decent thing for Virginius to have done would have been to allow his 14-year-old daughter to be abducted, enslaved and raped, meanwhile saying how very, very sorry he was for her, and that chastity after all is not important, and if she has a baby it will probably soon die. Or to save himself the distress of seeing her fate, Virginius might have committed suicide. This would have done Virginia no good, have abandoned his wife, and been entirely selfish. Either of these other courses were humanly possible. They would have presented a weak, cowardly father. He would not have resisted cruelty and injustice and the story would be reduced to yet another casual incident of oppression and brutality to women of which history is full. Lack of action would also, by its cowardice, have failed to bring the unjust judge to justice, as he was by the incensed people rising up against him and his associates.

To conclude: *The Physician's Tale* is not one of Chaucer's most attractive tales. It is a grim anecdote about how a higher obligation may force a man to do what is against his own nature and is deeply painful to him. It is about honour and our duty to our children focused in an extreme historical example. What Chaucer himself – or any of us in parallel situations – would have done in such a situation is beside the point. The tale offers only the reflection that sin is punished, not that suffering is compensated for. It is a harsh lesson, but the twentieth century, like the fourteenth, offers ample material to apply it to, once we make the necessary cultural translation. The *Tale*, like most of *The Canterbury Tales*, comes very effectively to closure – no more uncertainties or inconclusiveness, though the Host's response as usual carries us to further thoughts about the story.

THE PARDONER'S PROLOGUE AND TALE

At the end of *The Physician's Tale* the Host has a section labelled in the Ellesmere manuscript, 'words to the Physician and Pardoner' in which he curses the 'false churl and false judge' and laments the death of this simple maid who 'bought her beauty too dearly', the poet thus building in the somewhat facile expression of pity for Virginia which some critics miss in the *Tale* itself. 'So piteously was she slain.' The Host's response is natural and proper, if characteristically inadequate. Here, as elsewhere, we see the medieval and later tendency to take the characters in stories literally, as persons. It is the first, natural human response to stories about people, and if we do not start with it we miss the first basic element of stories. That there is also a deeper understanding, not necessarily as allegory, should go without saying. The Host then turns to the Physician, addressing him with friendly impertinence, using medical terms with some malapropisms. The tone thus slides from the seriousness of the *Tale* to lightness. The Host feels the need for a 'draught of moist and corny ale' or for a 'merry tale' and with more rudeness contemptuously calls on the Pardoner, 'Thou beel amy' (VI, 318) (as it were, 'my fine fellow'). But first the Pardoner says he must eat and drink 'at this alestake', the usual sign of a low-class tavern. The 'gentils', who are distinguished from the 'churls' being the more refined though not precisely defined members of the group, cry out against being told 'ribaldry' which they expect from the Pardoner. Their wish is an important part of the medieval audience's requirement of literature. They cry

> Telle us som moral thyng, that we may leere   *learn*
> Som wit, and thanne wol we gladly heere.   *knowledge*
> (VI, 325–6)

'Lordynges', begins the Pardoner, and with this vulgarism establishes the fictional level at which he speaks his *Prologue*. Here begins one of the most entertaining and original passages of *The Canterbury Tales* as the Pardoner reveals all the dirty tricks of his trade, in how he preaches. His *Prologue* lightly parodies a popular sermon with such familiar addresses as 'Goode men and wommen' (VI, 377) but his material is the astonishingly cynical revelation of his deceit, and after boasting of how ruthlessly he plays upon his simple country congregations, he finishes up by saying

> For though myself be a ful vicious man
> A moral tale yet I yow telle can.
> (VI, 459–60)

Jean de Meun in his part of *Le Roman de la Rose* had begun the satirical device by which a villain 'confesses' with glee rather than penitence the treachery he practises (cf. the English *Romaunt*, 6153ff.). Such 'confession' possibly stems from the increasing pressure for real confession after the Lateran Council 1215–16, which must have promoted greater self-awareness and more introspection. There was a developing individuality and self-consciousness in English literature in the fourteenth century, somewhat behind French and Italian, and of a rougher cast. Langland uses something like the same method in *Piers Plowman* as Chaucer does with the Pardoner in the series of confessions of the Seven Deadly Sins, where again the sense of boastful enjoyment outweighs penitence and repentance. This development of self-consciousness thrives more on sin than on virtue. It is really boasting rather than confessing. It has no repentance. We would not enjoy anyone 'confessing', or describing their own virtues for several obvious reasons – the process would be boastful and thus self-contradictory and the very act would deny virtue. Boastful confession of wrongdoing, at least in literature, also lends itself to comedy, as well as satire, and has an air of confidential conspiratorial friendliness which cannot but be seductive. We see the same phenomenon when Shakespeare's villains confess their villainy. When Richard III before becoming king says to the audience 'I am determined to prove a villain,' though it seems to be intended as serious and true self-characterisation, the audience is inclined to laugh in sympathy. Today distinguished men in their memoirs boast of the misdemeanours of their younger or even not-so-young selves to general applause. It is a long-standing phenomenon, though more apparent in some periods. There is an old comic tradition which allows the swindler, the trickster, the coward, the betrayer of women – Falstaff is the supreme example – to confess his faults and win amused admiration and sympathy. Although such a tendency is inherent in human nature – ancient Greek comedy is an example – it may have developed greater self-awareness in the Middle Ages.[5] There were increasingly complex ways of presenting the, or a, self, going beyond the recognised stereotypes. In this European development Chaucer participates and his presentation of the Pardoner is one of its triumphs.

A Pardoner was not a clerk in holy orders, though he had always some ecclesiastical standing. A Pardoner was licensed, or should have been licensed, to sell pardons for sins when they were properly repented of in order to relieve the sinner of time in purgatory after death, and with his money to support good ecclesiastical causes on earth – like the hospital of Rouncivale at Charing Cross in London, where the Pardoner comes from via Rome with pardons all hot. A Pardoner was the medieval equivalent of a fund-raiser without the obligation to account for his takings. Granted the premises the system was reasonable, but granted also the temptations it was wide open to abuse, and was fully abused. So the Pardoner, who preaches that greed for money is the root of all evil, ironically exemplifies the evil he preaches against, and is presented as aware of it. In his *Prologue* he tells us that he preaches like a cleric in the pulpit while the simple people sit before him in church and

> Myne handes and my tonge goon so yerne   *eagerly*
> That it is joye to se my bisynesse.   *activity*

Of avarice and of swich cursednesse
Is al my prechyng . . .

(VI, 398–401)

With his long hair, wild gestures, charisma, high income, ability to
sing loud popular love-songs (*General Prologue*, I, 472), and uncertain
but avid sexuality, he is the equivalent of a modern pop-singer. If
blandishment fails he will 'spit out his venom' (VI, 421). He boasts
that he will not work but will take money and goods from the
poorest though their children starve for it. His pleasure in his own
expertise, 'joy to see', though detestable, witnesses also to that
Chaucerian savouring of outstanding examples of human behavi-
our which combines appreciation of 'the thing in itself' with moral
freedom for the reader and perhaps for the author. Chaucer allows
the Pardoner as it were to realise himself, or more accurately,
creates a self-realising character – yet that very self-realisation is self-
condemnation.

The Pardoner has many a tale with which to enliven his
preaching,

For lewed peple loven tales olde   *ignorant*
(VI, 437)

(Chaucer jesting against himself and his reader) and does indeed
come up, as he promises, with a moral tale, one of the most striking
of all the varied *Canterbury Tales*: the tale of the three 'rioters' who
went out to find and kill Death, and found him indeed.

It is in origin, like most of *The Canterbury Tales*, a folktale of
worldwide distribution and great age, equally effective today, a
'transhistorical' anecdote testifying to certain universal human traits,
greed, treachery, wildness, so destructive as to be self-destructive.

The story is so striking partly because of its neat pattern. The
three drunken young thugs lurching out to kill 'this thief men call
Death' find a heap of gold. Forgetting their first intention, two
remain on guard while the third goes into town to buy food and
drink to keep them going until nightfall when they can remove it.
The two plan to kill the third for his share. He poisons the food and
drink in order to get theirs. They kill him, eat and drink and die.
They have all found Death.

So it is another story about Death, concluding in death. Its power
lies in the ambiguity inherent in the way the 'riotours' absurdly
personify Death as something external, an enemy and a thief of life

(as we all do sometimes); whereas it is internal, intrinsic, general, incurred by evil doing, as with Adam and Eve, sought by ourselves, though that is not the whole of Chaucer's version, as will be seen. The story also offers an image of a society as presented by the three comrades without mutual trust, faith or truth. By implication it justifies by contradiction what would now be called 'civil society'. A premise for the survival of society is that promises must be kept: a truth well known and often in practice denied. In the story that premise is imaginatively and morally, if negatively, vindicated to our ironic satisfaction.

The structure and message are universal but Chaucer's own individual version both develops it and gives it touches of local realism and dramatic speech, while at the same time maintaining, especially in the earlier part, our sense that it is still the Pardoner speaking, with his moral quotations, and use of 'lordynges' (VI, 573). The chief development in the actual story is in the enigmatic figure of the old man whom the three 'riotours' meet when they rush out, seeking Death. In many versions of the tale they meet someone who has spurned the pile of gold but directs them to it. Chaucer improves on this. The 'riotours' who exemplify all the vices, and are sometimes called 'hasardoures' (gamblers), having plighted troth of brotherhood to live and die for each other (which latter in an ironical way they do), rush out, meet and threaten, in a way all too familiar with young thugs, an old poor man. He would all too gladly die. Death will not take him. He is bound to walk restlessly,

> And on the ground, which is my moodres gate   *mother's*
> I knokke with my staf, bothe erly and late
> And seye 'Leeve mooder, leet me in'.   *dear mother*
> (VI, 729–31)

Mother earth is also, it seems, mother death – a strange and moving image – built up, such is Chaucer's genius, from a passage in the well-known Latin schoolbook, the first poem of the sixth-century, Maximian's *Elegiæ*, describing old age as longing for death. Death here is a longed for, but rejecting, mother. To the young men's bullying demands the old man, after a dignified reproach quoting Scripture, points to where death indeed may be found, 'up that crooked way, in a grove, under an oak'. So they rush to their doom. The imagery of death is not consistent. The old man is not an allegory, or symbol, or death itself, but an expression of weary, experienced old age, and another view of death.

Chaucer enhances the tale in other quite different ways, by the setting in Flanders (not popular in England), where people wildly celebrate under the constant threat of plague.

Most of all he enhances the story by setting it within the Pardoner's own narrative, in the canting raving tones of the popular preacher as he condemns sins, breaking into the calculatedly hysterical scream of the pop-singer though with a very different message, quoting St Paul weeping, and saying he weeps himself to tell of gluttonous sinners, that

'They been enemys of Cristes croys,	
Of which the ende is deeth. Wombe is hir god.'	*belly*
O wombe! O bely! O stynkyng cod,	*bag*
Fulfilled of dong and of corrupcioun!	
At either end of thee foul is the soun.	*sound*
How greet labour and cost is thee to fynde!	*provide for*
Thise cookes, how they stampe, and streyne, and grynde,	
And turnen substaunce into accident,	*turn essence into attribute*
To fulfille al thy likerous talent.	*lecherous desire*
	(VI, 532–40)

There is an element of caricature by the poet here in creating the Pardoner's character. The reference to the foul sounds that come out of either end of the belly is certainly meant for a laugh, especially as medieval people, including Chaucer, always found mention of the breaking of wind remarkably funny. Similarly extravagant is the variation of style from concrete realistic homely bags of dung to the scholastic witticism of cooks changing the real essence of food into secondary qualities (the reverse of what it was thought the priest does in the Mass, changing the 'accidents' of bread and wine, their physical qualities, into the Real Body of Christ). The poet is a bit carried away here, perhaps, as he is when he allows the Pardoner to refer to the adulteration of French wine by Spanish, and thus to the drunken man who thinks he is in Cheapside when he is 'really' in Spain (VI, 563–71), a knowledgeable joke for the vintner's son. These witticisms are jokes between the poet and the audience: the Pardoner's character is a mere vehicle here which we need in no sense take seriously.

Most extraordinary of all is the daring which causes the Pardoner, abruptly changing his tone, to end with 'And lo, sires, thus I preche' (VI, 915), and then try to sell his confessedly bogus relics to the pilgrims, starting with the Host as 'moost envoluped in synne' (VI, 942). By a comic irony the Pardoner has deceived himself about his audience. Harry Bailly replies with a violence of expression which surely reflects Chaucer's own most severe satire. The Host would like, he says, to cut off the Pardoner's testicles and enshrine them in a hog's turd – he, at least, unlike many modern critics, does not believe that the Pardoner is a eunuch. This with other coarse insults makes the Pardoner too furious to speak, until the Knight courteously prays them to be reconciled and

> Anon they kiste, and ryden forth hir weye.
>
> (VI, 968)

The Pardoner is so vivid, and so satirised, partly because he remains a 'flat' character. His feelings and motives are all stereotypes, and the more telling for being so. We know nothing of his personal history or of any real interior life, and could Chaucer have provided them they would have blurred the outline, the comedy, the satire and the moral. What we have is yet a wonderfully complex portrayal created by Chaucer's mature art: a virtuoso, many-layered performance.

NOTES

1. Goefrey Gorer, *Death, Grief and Mourning in Contemporary Britain* (London, 1965).
2. J. A. Hornsby, *Chaucer and the Law* (Norman, Oklahoma, 1988), 155.
3. Lama, Abu-Odeh, 'Crimes of Honour and the Construction of Gender in Arab Societies' in *Feminism and Islam: Legal and Literary Perspectives*, 141–93 edited by Mai Yamani (Ithaca, 1996).
4. Derek Brewer, Introduction, *A Companion to the* Gawain *Poet*, edited by Derek Brewer and Jonathan Gibson (Cambridge, 1997), 16–17; in the same title, see Elisabeth Brewer, 246–9 and Nicholas Watson, 300–4. For a modern view, see Jane Gilbert, 66–9.
5. Derek Brewer (ed.) Introduction, in *Medieval Comic Tales*, 2nd edn (Cambridge, 1966).

Chapter 22

Chapter 22

The Canterbury Tales IV:
A Gift Returned; Virginity and
Martyrdom; Parody and Prudence;
Flattery and Reversal

THE SHIPMAN'S TALE

The actual tale told by the Shipman begins with a paragraph about
rich merchants which though fairly impersonal in actual style is
clearly written from a woman's point of view:

The sely housbonde, algate he moot paye:	*simple; always must*
He moot us clothe, and he moot us arraye.	*must*
	(VII, 11–12)

The story is yet another example of the 'international medieval
popular comic tale', and it exists in many variants, both written and
found orally in recent times virtually all over the world.

The theme is known to folklorists as 'the lover's gift regained'. In
Chaucer's version the wife of a rich merchant of Saint Denis near
Paris is kept somewhat short both of money and sexual satisfaction.
The merchant is friendly with a smart young monk of 30, who
frequents his house. Like the Monk in *The General Prologue* he is an
'outrider', a kind of steward or estate-manager. (Chaucer shows no
knowledge of, or interest in, life *inside* monastic cloisters.) The wife
tells the monk that she has incurred a debt of the vast sum of a
hundred francs. He promises to help her, and fondles her. The
merchant must go to Brugge (or Bruges) but before he goes the
monk borrows a hundred francs (a very large sum). In the mer-
chant's absence the monk seduces the wife at the price of the hun-
dred francs, which he gives her. The merchant on his return calls
first upon the monk, for he wants the money. The monk remarks
that he has paid it back to the wife. The merchant on his return
greets his wife fondly and they go to bed and make love vigorously.
But then the merchant gently reproaches his wife for not telling him

about the returned debt. She dismisses the charge lightly and says she had not realised it was repayment, but a gift, and she happens to have spent it on clothing, but she will repay him in bed. The merchant has anyway made a great profit, so he has to rest content.

In a sense the tale is antifeminist, and most versions present the wife unfavourably, but Chaucer gives it a twist that makes it sympathetic to women, good-humoured, and not ungenerous. All these tales bear witness to a layer of common European secular adult culture of relatively middling folk, who relish an improper joke provided it does not go too far; who accept the ordinary morality of society but find it amusing to indulge fantasies of breaking it, provided order is reasserted. Much the same layer exists today, indulgent of dirty jokes, of financial trickery up to a point, but outraged by any real assault on conventional moral standards. On the whole it seems very sensible and tolerant, recognising where fantasy starts and stops. In general the humour is derisive, not satirical in the sense of seeking to correct by ridicule, but not sympathetic either. Such is in general Chaucer's attitude as we have seen with *The Miller's Tale* and *The Reeve's Tale*, and as we shall see again. But he does bring a modifying gentleness and feminist sympathy as well, which we can see well in the strangely attributed *Shipman's Tale*. He also brings the marvellous realism of description of setting, action, character and psychology which we have come to expect. He paints a genre-picture of the merchant in his counting-house with his wife walking in the garden, like a seventeenth-century Dutch picture, exquisite with the poetry of everyday detail, yet never encumbered by excess detail. The precision of accounting for money is also a part of Chaucer's arithmetical interest (above, p. 18).

THE PRIORESS'S TALE

The mood changes through the link which tells of the Host's gentle and respectful words to the Prioress, switching from his mock respect and brusque 'thous' to the Shipman, to polite 'ye' and 'yow' to her, who freely and courteously agrees to tell a story. Her Invocation to the Blessed Virgin is fully in character and establishes the mood of pious exaltation in which the tale is told. There can be no doubt that this tale was written with the teller in mind.

The story is just as much a folktale as the preceding comic popular tale and really just as secular, but it illustrates secular affective piety and parental love, which are as much part of the secular culture as amusement at sexual impropriety.

The story is set in Asia, in a great city, though it evokes at the end the equivalent story of England's little Hugh of Lincoln. A seven-year-old child's widowed mother teaches him a special reverence for the Blessed Virgin, and then

This litel child, his litel book lernynge	
As he sat in his scole at his prymer	*primer*
He *Alma redemptoris* herde synge	*Loving (mother) of the Redeemer*
And as he dorste, he drough hym ner and ner,	*dared; drew nearer and nearer*
And herkned ay the wordes and the noote,	*tune*
Til he the firste vers koude al by rote.	*knew off by heart*
	(VII, 516–22)

The repetition of the word 'litel', like the same device in *The Man of Law's Tale* (*CT*, II, 834–61) effectively emphasises the pathos. The child asks a slightly older friend what the anthem means, and then determines to learn it before Christmas. He sings it as he goes home daily through the Jews' quarter. This is the point of placing the story in Asia; there were no Jewish communities in England from the thirteenth to the seventeenth centuries, which saves the gentle Prioress from an otherwise ugly anti-Semitism. She is talking about bogeymen. The Jews take the child's song as an insult, and murder him. The whole of the story up to here is told with remarkable realism. The dialogue between the two little boys will convince any parent. In other versions of the story, which was very popular in the Middle Ages, the boy is ten years old. By making him only seven, Chaucer increases the pathos, but also the realism, and he is extremely accurate about the child's academic schooling. All hangs together; a boy of seven is more innocent than one of ten, more docile and eager to learn. With all this, we still see the child from outside and, as it were, from above. We do not, as with nineteenth-century authors, attempt to enter into his view of the world. We do not feel with him; we feel with the mother, her joy in the child implied by her terror when he does not come home from school. After his murder a miracle follows:

This gemme of chastite, this emeraude,	
And eek of martirdom the ruby bright,	
Ther he with throte ykorven lay upright,	*on his back*
He *Alma redemptoris* gan to synge	
So loude that al the place gan to rynge.	
	(VII, 609–13)

His miraculous singing leads to the discovery of his body, and he explains that it is a miracle of the Virgin, who will fetch his soul when he actually dies. He is given a splendid burial. The last description of his mother comes before the explanation of the miracle, though after the discovery of his body, and tells how she lay swooning by his bier. There is no word of consolation for her. The Jews are put to death by torture.

There is naturally no psychological or other probability – it is, after all, a *miracle*. The poem draws its full strength from a pattern and a story which can hardly be called realistic in its total effect, though it employs realistic methods and materials in part. The force and beauty of the tale are based on the realistic description of the 'little clergeon'. Chaucer excels in natural pathos, especially of children. On this foundation are built the walls and roof which are largely supernatural. In terms of language we move from realistic dialogue and description to the idealising and more metaphorical phrases 'gem of chastity', 'emerald', 'bright ruby of martyrdom'. We move from playground to altar, and each strengthens and sets off the other.

Chaucer's treatment of children falls in with the general pattern of his art: his amazing juxtapositions of the comic and the pathetic, the realistic and the idealistic, the bawdy and the sincerely devout, the natural and the supernatural. The general pattern of development from nature to supernature is also found in *Troilus and Criseyde*.

The Prioress's Tale is an exemplary traditional religious tale which wonderfully appealed to high and low in Chaucer's day, as its reception among the pilgrims shows, but which has aroused varied response in modern times. Some critics, conscious of the appalling crimes of anti-Semitism in the twentieth century, have wished to attribute a similar repulsion to Chaucer. They argue that the Prioress must be satirised because after the ecstatic praise of the Blessed Virgin's mercy the story refers to the cruel punishment of the Jews. But the story, though it suits her, is not a dramatic soliloquy, and such a reading is another example of the rejection of the straightforward, traditional, 'naïve' reading in favour of an anachronistic modern critical literalism. By seeing irony and using deconstructive techniques we can turn the story inside-out, make it suit modern critical prepossessions, and destroy its 'alterity', its valuable 'otherness'. We have in fact to accept that Chaucer as a poet shares with his gentle Prioress the normal love of children and hostility to the Jews of medieval culture. The story-structure is another demonstration of the closeness of love to suffering, of Gothic pity and pathos, of the sad truth that to love the innocent and defenceless may lead to hatred of their oppressors. Nor is such a combination of love and hatred solely Gothic – only this particular version of it; it is very easily translated in the twentieth century into political terms, whereby those who are obsessed with a good cause will readily commit atrocities on its behalf worse than the original offence. Artistically speaking we notice again in Chaucer's adaptation of a popular tale a sort of artistic extremism, achieved partly by greater realism, as of the child, partly by more exalted religious fervour at the end. He twists our feelings several notches higher up than do other versions of the story. But in recognising the pathos we should not forget that the final point of the story is, after all, triumph and gladness.

The popularity of the tale is illustrated by its appearance in five independent manuscripts probably meant for devotional readers.

SIR THOPAS

Even the Host is sobered by this story of miracle, but begins to jest and, says the poet, for the first time 'looked at me'.

'What man artow?' quod he,	*art thou; said*
'Thow lookest as thou woldest fynde an hare	
For evere upon the ground I se thee stare.	
'Approche neer, and looke up murily.	
Now war yow, sires, and lat this man have place!	
He in the waast is shape as wel as I;	
This were a popet in an arm t'enbrace	*puppet*
For any womman, smal and fair of face.	*slender*
He semeth elvyssh by his contenaunce,	*not human*
For unto no wight dooth he daliaunce.'	*he does not chat with anyone*
	(VII, 695–704)

This precious though self-mocking glimpse of Chaucer the man recalls and is consistent with the self-description in *The House of Fame* (above, p. 124). He is plump, abstracted in manner, keeps himself to himself, and is patronised by more self-assertive men. This is surely one side of the truth, and perhaps to Chaucer's contemporaries the most obvious. There was another side: that of the pilgrim-author who tells us at the beginning of *The General Prologue*, if only for verisimilitude, that he had before nightfall spoken to every one of 29 pilgrims and had been accepted into their company (I, 30–2); and there is as well the solitary reader reproached by the Eagle in *The*

House of Fame who was as desperately eager to hear stories of real people as he was to read books late at night. There is a genuine modesty and introvertedness in Chaucer's authorial make-up, which is compensated for by an at times incompatibly powerful set of feelings, shown by extravagant apostrophe of characters in a story, a deep sense of pathos, irresistible attraction towards women. Moreover, by the very art of telling, the apparently unassertive poet also dominates his readers and controls their feelings and ideas. The whole set of contrasts of attitudes in him is perhaps the basis of his irrepressible sense of absurdity.

The latter now triumphs. The great learned European poet he knows himself and as we know him to be (though he is not presented as such on the dramatic level inside the fiction), can only offer a 'rhyme' he learnt long ago. He goes back to his origins in the English stanzaic tail-rhyme romances, and begins the tale of the Flemish knight *Sir Thopas*. It is the funniest parody in English. It is full of clichés, beginning

Listeth lordes in good entent	
And I wol telle verrayment	*truly*
Of myrthe and of solas;	
Al of a knyght was fair and gent	*nice*
In bataille and in tourneyment	
His name was sire Thopas.	
	(VII, 712–17)

Gent and *verrayment* are typically vapid words of the English romances. This 'doughty swain', with red and white checks and saffron yellow beard, is a good archer and wrestler – rather old-fashioned, though not impossible qualities for a knight.

Ful many a mayde, bright in bour,	*bower*
They moorne for hym paramour,	*in love*
Whan hem were bet to slepe:	*it were better for them*
But he was chaast and no lechour	
And sweete as is the brembul-flour	
That bereth the rede hepe.	*bears the red rose hip*
	(VII, 742–7)

The bathetic comment about it being better to sleep, the comparison with the common bramble flower, i.e. the dog-rose, and its red hips are all part of the cumulatively ridiculous effect, as, one fears, is the knight's chastity. (A very different attitude is found in *Sir Gawain and the Green Knight*.) The jog-trot metre makes the traditional description of spring, the knight's love-longing without a lady, the riding out into Fairyland, fighting a giant, ceremonially putting on his armour, sleeping in it in the open, all delightfully absurd. Chaucer's lack of sympathy with certain traditional literary topics, and with mythic romantic narrative, is well illustrated. The elaborate description of arming, for example, is a commonplace of epic and romance from Homer, through Virgil, medieval European romances, down to twentieth-century Yugoslav folk-epic. It is superbly handled in *Sir Gawain and the Green Knight*, which in alliterative metre treats seriously all the elements which Chaucer mocks, and is as great a poem, in its different way, as any that Chaucer wrote. Chaucer's 'modernism' is nowhere better seen than in his mockery of traditional romance, and surely his taste was shared by many readers. Yet the list, itself a parody of a rhetorical commonplace, of 'romances of price', which he quotes at the end, and the very act of parody, suggests that for many of his courtly readers these romances had been favourite reading. Several appear in the Auckinleck Manuscript (above, p. 56) and as he implies here, Chaucer had read them with great pleasure when he was young. He had grown up on them (above, p. 55) and out of them. He also takes the opportunity of some comic satire at the expense of Flemish knights, who were not thought much of generally, and that his father-in-law, the herald Sir Payne Roet, was Flemish, may have added some extra zest.

The poem, being a parody, is a good example of 'two voices' in poetry, or of two levels of understanding. One is within the fiction and certainly to be attributed to the plump, shy ignorant *persona* of the pilgrim-Chaucer, also fully within the fiction. At this literal level the poem is a genuinely feeble attempt. At the other deeper level, in reality outside the fiction, the poem is a most amusing parody of what it pretends to represent. The work of art in its unity straddles both fiction and reality, as the poet does, and for its full effect both levels must be appreciated. Indeed the second level cannot be perceived without seeing first the primary literal level. So with the poet: he is both inside and out. We murder to dissect, to divide too clearly the poet inside from the poet outside the poem.

The burlesque romance which Chaucer attributes to himself as Pilgrim takes us a stage further in his self-awareness and self-representation. It is paradoxically high art, and its mockery evokes the critical clichés, which like most clichés have some degree of truth, of the 'subversive', 'the carnivalesque' (undermining the higher spiritual levels of existence by the materialistic lower, in emphasising

Thopas's effeminacy) and even 'the transgressive', by mocking the chivalric ideal. Parodic, burlesque, jesting verses, from lyrics to such *jeux d'esprit* as *The Turnament of Tottenham*, no doubt existed in English before Chaucer, but never so skilfully and never so self-directed. Chaucer has something of the clown in him, bringing comic disaster on his own head, and all farcical comedy of this kind implies two persons in one. In every clown there is a sense of another person inviting you to laugh at the impersonation of himself. Hence the traditional melancholy of clowns in actual life, which Chaucer may well have felt.

Whatever implicit criticisms of his own self and his culture, alongside evident satire of inferior imitations of his own culture and art, that Chaucer the poet may have wanted to make, they are limited. He also exerts complete control. As so often, from *The Book of the Duchess* onwards, he goes to the edge and draws back. He directs our laughter. This is vividly illustrated by what follows.

THE TALE OF MELIBEE

Within the fiction the Host cannot stand this feeble poem and calls on Chaucer to stop rhyming. A little plaintively, but courteously, the pilgrim-Chaucer agrees, and says he will tell a 'little thing in prose', 'a moral tale vertuous' (*CT*, VII, 937–40), and goes on most interestingly as already noted to comment on variable verbal accounts of the same material, as seen in the Gospels, and uses it to excuse any variation he may employ in quoting proverbs. Literal accuracy, a very modern concept, always interested Chaucer, as we have seen in his address to his scribe (above, p. 271) although verbal variation of a given story is a characteristic of traditional literature which he himself makes full use of. Proverbs are also a form of the 'sententious' style which characterises popular and traditional literature, and which Chaucer, like Shakespeare, was so fond of that many of his phrases which sound like proverbs were probably actually invented by him. The teachers of rhetoric recommended the use of proverbs. Proverbs were well thought of by both learned and popular writers. They only fell from esteem in the seventeenth century, when Neoclassical standards created other assumptions about the need for originality and the avoidance of what was 'low'.

The Ellesmere scribe, or rather perhaps his superior, who commissioned the illustrations, evidently thought that *The Tale of Melibee* was much more significantly Chaucer's than *Sir Thopas*, for the miniature of Chaucer is placed at the commencement of *Melibee*, not *Thopas*. We may well take the hint and attribute it to Chaucer's serious interest. In the *Prologue* to the tale he calls it 'a litel tretys' (*CT*, VII, 957) which rather removes it from the dramatic narrative scene, although a few lines before (953) he has addressed his pilgrim audience wearing his pilgrim hat, so to speak, calling them 'lordynges alle'. He puts the word 'lordynges' in the early part of the treatise itself into the mouth of wise elderly counsellors (*CT*, VII, 1020, 1035) which rather suggests that he was writing the work with the Canterbury pilgrimage in mind. The date of composition is uncertain but there is nothing unreasonable in accepting the treatise as a product of the late 1380s or even later.

It is customary to pass somewhat hastily over the *Melibeus*, not least because reading takes some time and, for a modern reader, calls for more of that patience which the work rather lengthily recommends than is usually available. It is barely fiction, has only the slightest thread of narrative, and gives good traditional moral advice. It deserves consideration if only because Chaucer thought it did by including it in all its length in *The Canterbury Tales*.

The piece derives ultimately from the Italian layman and judge, Albertano of Brescia, written in Latin as a treatise of consolation and advice to his youngest son in 1246. It had European popularity and Chaucer translated fairly closely from the free-est of four French translations, made around 1340 by Renaud de Louens. It is in the tradition of 'wisdom literature', constantly quoting 'Solomon', i.e. the Old Testament books, Proverbs, Ecclesiastes, Ecclesiasticus, and then occasionally the New Testament, along with Seneca, Ovid and other Classical Latin authors, showing how the two moral traditions had assimilated each other. Chaucer took all these quotations over from the French. His only additions seem to have been in christening the daughter of Melibeus 'Sophie', i.e. Sophia, Wisdom, and an expansion of style towards the end in introducing many verbal doublets. Small as they are they are another indication, apart from sheer length, that Chaucer took the work seriously.

It deals with major problems that *mutatis mutandis* are still with us. The thin thread of story says that Melibeus's daughter was attacked by three enemies and harmed – signifying temptations offered to wisdom through the world, the flesh and the devil. Melibeus wants revenge. He calls a council to advise him. For any veteran of hundreds of committees there cannot but be a certain savour in the satirical characterisation of prejudiced counsellors, the account of debate, the conflicting advice, the shouting down of 'thise olde wyse' by the young Turks who cry 'war, war', and the majority vote of the council in favour of the wrong decision, desired by the chairman, Melibeus, himself. This nowadays somewhat specialised taste for debate was more widely shared in the Middle Ages. So too was relish for the arguments of Dame Prudence against the vote for revenge. Much of the discussion consists in pitting one accepted adage against another equally accepted. These 'conflicted' views are as such worth pausing over. They remind us that European culture was never monolithic: it has been a 'dialogic' culture since the Greeks and never more so than in the later Middle Ages.

The topics discussed range widely, from vengeance and war to the worth of women, which is agreed to be high. Though Prudence always defers to her rash and irascible husband, she can feign anger at him to bring him to submission. Other topics are the good sense of keeping riches, the need to love God first, to observe the law, and so forth. Not a few accepted adages have a strong worldly wisdom, not to say cynicism – none the less sensible for that. The value of 'old experience' is praised against rash youth. It is argued that to consult all and sundry is foolish because most men are fools, so only a few counsellors should be chosen, and in the end it is Melibeus's decision alone. Democratic discussion and majority rule are seriously thought to be full of dangers and folly. After long discussion Prudence prevails on her husband to forgive and be reconciled to his enemies. Since these have earlier been identified as the World, the Flesh and the Devil, the allegorical story would seem to have become a little muddled, but there may be some unconscious pragmatic wisdom of compromise even here, and Melibeus says earlier that he does not claim to be of 'the number of perfect men' (*CT*, VII, 1520). And Melibeus's problem is still with those countries who suffer from organised political terrorism.

From a literary point of view we can hardly agree with those critics who see *The Tale of Melibeus* as the core of *The Canterbury Tales*. But it is an explicit expression of the same culture, and inevitably much of the moral advice overlaps with that which is explicit or implicit in other tales. The highest importance is given to the preservation of 'the honour and worship' of Melibeus in this world (*CT*, VII, 1760). Honour is said to be more important than wealth, and this reminds us yet again of that underlying structure of honour which is the implicit motivation of many of Chaucer's tales and not least of *Troilus and Criseyde*. On a different aspect of comparison we note that Dame Prudence even uses a phrase closely similar to one of the Wife of Bath's, when in the course of repudiating a whole series of venerable slanders of women she mentions the accusation that they are 'riotous' and continues, with admirable restraint,

And sire, by youre leve, that am nat I.

(*CT*, VII, 1088, cf. III, 112)

The whole piece shows that the traditional complex value system, especially in relation to public affairs, implicit in *The Canterbury Tales*, is more explicit in the *Melibeus* and has actual political implications, though Chaucer is as discreet as ever. The general argument, even because not democratic, favours peace. The *Melibeus* repays analysis in terms of social anthropology and perhaps even political action. It verges on advice to princes. Perhaps Chaucer, like Richard II, and Gower, favoured a policy of peace with France. But the work cannot be dated exactly and does not need claims of specific relevance to have its own value. *The Tale of Melibee* was popular apart from its place in *The Canterbury Tales* and is found separately in five manuscripts, in one case along with *The Parson's Tale*, its religious counterpart, and in another with *The Monk's Tale*, which dealing with the falls of public figures has some obvious affinity, and which we move to next. These tales obviously appealed to serious-minded readers rather than to the seekers after light fiction.

The Tale of Melibee always disturbs modern critics, and some think it must be meant to be funny, despite its popularity in the fifteenth century, at least with serious-minded people, attested by the five manuscripts in which it is separately preserved. Admittedly monks and other serious-minded readers may be slow to see a joke, especially in so long-winded a collection of traditional and still sensible wisdom. In fact, the idea that the *Melibee* is comic is itself absurd, and not relevant to Chaucer.

The style has been condemned as 'clogged'. Two lines are quoted by Professor Helen Cooper from the French which Chaucer, whose style became more expansive towards the end of the piece, renders in English in seven lines, full of doublets and repetitions, which Professor Cooper believes must be parodic in intention. In another example the French text offers obedience by Melibeus's foes in the following terms:

et vous prions a genoulx et en larmes que vous ayez de nous pitie et misericorde.[1]

(and we pray you on knees and in tears that you may have pity and mercy on us).

This becomes in Chaucer

> bisekynge yow that of youre merciable pietee ye wol considere oure
> grete repentaunce and lowe submyssioun and graunten us foryevenesse
> of oure outrageous trespas and offense
>
> (VII, 1820–5)

These are not cases of parody. They are examples of an English high
style later made familiar in Cranmer's sixteenth-century *Book of Com-
mon Prayer* and worked towards in many an English fifteenth-century
sermon of the kind which translated passages from Latin.[2] Chaucer
omits the concrete French terms for 'knees and tears' in favour of
the high abstract and spiritual word 'merciable' to reinforce 'pitee'.
He doubles 'grete repentaunce' with 'lowe submyssioun', expands
with 'graunten us foryevenesse', and both heightens and doubles
with 'our outrageous trespas and offense'. It could be argued that
such language is suitable only in addressing God, so that Chaucer is
being absurdly extravagant, but at the end of a long treatise of
progressively heightened and reinforced language, taken along with
Chaucer's characteristic taste for hyperbole, it can only be deliber-
ately and seriously intensified. By this time in the treatise we are
within the religious sphere: those speaking are the foes of man, the
World, the Flesh and the Devil, conquered by Melibeus who now
symbolically represents God. Consider as a parallel a portion of
Cranmer's General Confession, from both Morning and Evening
Prayer, partially translated from Latin, but with Cranmer's own char-
acteristic and traditionally English heightening and doubling:

> We have followed too much the devices and desires of our own hearts.
> We have offended against thy holy laws . . . But thou, O Lord, have
> mercy upon us, miserable offenders. Spare thou them O God, which
> confess their faults. Restore thou them that are penitent . . .

and the Absolution, that God

> hath given power and commandment, to his ministers, to declare and
> pronounce to his people, being penitent, the Absolution and Remission
> of their sins

Cranmer's prose is better: he combines repetition with variation and
progress, but it is the same kind of style, exalted and emphatic. It is
essentially oral in origin, and finds little sympathy or comprehension
today, inside or outside the Church of England. Cranmer has been
accused of addressing the Almighty and merciable Father as if he
were a medieval king. Chaucer might be accused of the same fault,

in so far as Melibeus is supposed to be a man. But if we cannot understand high language as appropriate to high subjects we fail to understand an essential element of medieval literature and culture. The attitudes and the language in which they are conveyed are as intrinsic a part of the medieval English mentality as are Melibeus's regal and godlike wrath (1695–1700), his human concern for honour above riches (1760), and his divine and human mercy (1875–80) in the name of God 'so free and merciable' (1885), for which last phrase there is no basis in the French. Whether we like or approve such language and attitudes is a quite different matter. Understanding may not lead to forgiveness but it requires an effort of imaginative sympathy.

The Host is too eager to say how different his own wife is from Prudence, the wife of Melibeus, to comment on the tale. And indeed comment would only remind us of the extreme unrealism of the long prose treatise delivered on the way to Canterbury. In the Host's case, the joke of the masterful man mastered by his wife is an old and good one. The Host's remark about his bossy wife provides welcome relief after the ponderings and ponderousness of *The Tale of Melibee*. Chaucer may have introduced this new element in the Link because he was abandoning the well-used device of contrasting tales. The Link itself provides the contrast both to the preceding and to the following tale. The description of the Host's termagant wife also underlines one of the themes of the *Melibee* – the relationship between husband and wife – which becomes more and more prominent as the *Tales* proceed. The Link amusingly reveals the Host as a hen-pecked braggart and an ignoramus, but also notes that the pilgrims have now come near to Rochester. He speaks impertinently to the Monk. The Link is a vivid fragment of roadside drama and the Host expresses a traditional anti-clerical jest, addressing the fat monk with impertinent comments on his potential as a 'tredefowl'.

The worthy Monk takes 'all in patience' and, rather out of character from his portrait in *The General Prologue*, promises a series of tragedies of which he has a hundred in his cell, giving a definition of tragedy (actually from Boethius) as memorial of 'the harm of those who stood in high degree' and fell, usually to death. It is a classic story pattern, though the Monk's high tone allows for no laughter beside death.

THE MONK'S TALE

Chaucer here adapts the character of the Monk to the nature of the stories that Chaucer wishes to tell. He is now a patient, worthy, learned monk and the poet takes the opportunity, through him, of giving us the definition of tragedy just referred to. Medieval tragedy does not necessarily include death, but death is traditionally seen as one of the greatest tragedies that can, and must, befall a man. The modern notion of tragedy as an ennobling spectacle is not found here. Rather it is pathetic. At times it may be a salutary warning.

The idea for *The Monk's Tale* is mainly based on a Latin work of Boccaccio's, *De casibus virorum illustrium*, which itself is very Gothic in its mingling of Biblical, Classical, legendary, historical and modern instances. It is rather archaic, with its disregard for different kinds of story, or different historical periods. But Chaucer drew on a great variety of sources for his actual subjects, which range from Satan, through Hercules and Samson, Nero and Julius Caesar, to Chaucer's contemporaries Peter of Cyprus and Bernabò Visconti, whom Chaucer considers worthy men foully betrayed (though we regard them as cruel tyrants). All are treated much as if they had lived around the same time in the same conditions. Repetition is of the essence. What they have in common is the fall from high to low, which is the work of treacherous Fortune. The image of Fortune's Wheel, rather than specific ill deeds, dominates the stories. Fate, not individual responsibility, causes men's fall. There is no subjective guilt, or sympathy, on Chaucer's part, except of a general kind, such as a courtier might well feel, for the horror of the falls especially of the modern men whom Chaucer may well have met, with the exception of the story of Hugelino of Pisa.

The most moving and pathetic of the stories is that of the death of Count Hugelino of Pisa and his three small children, which Chaucer took from Dante. Parenthood and small children always evoke an easy pathos from Chaucer, as *The Prioress's Tale*, and the stories of Constance and Griselda, all illustrate.

How far Chaucer himself began to feel uneasy about the quality of *The Monk's Tale* is impossible to tell. Since the modern instance of Bernabò must be later than December 1385, when he was killed, Chaucer was content to work on the poem in full maturity. He must have worked intermittently on various poems simultaneously. In this one he may have been attracted by the need to exercise his ingenuity over the rhymed stanza, which is more difficult than the rhyme royal. Perhaps he got tired of it all the same, but with ever-flowering ingenuity covered it by having the Knight interrupt:

'Hoo' quod the Knyght 'good sire, namoore of this!'

(VII, 2767)

The Knight goes on a dozen lines to say that he much prefers to hear of men going up in the world, as poor men favoured by fortune and becoming prosperous. This generous attitude to upward social mobility seems typical of the Knight, and presumably of Chaucer, but not of the culture generally, which required men to remain in that station of life to which God was presumed to have called them. In another mood Chaucer himself could condemn 'wrastlynge for this world' which 'axeth a fal' (*Truth*, 16). However this may be, the Host supplements the Knight's courteous and reasoned request with rude comments on the dullness of the stories. He asks for a tale of hunting, reverting to the character of the Monk as portrayed in *The General Prologue*, which Chaucer has so casually abandoned. The Monk, not surprisingly, in a huff, refuses to play, and the Host, nothing abashed, 'with rude speche and boold' calls out to the Nun's Priest, 'thou preest', who rides on a horse 'bothe foul and lene'. He cheerfully agrees, 'This sweete preest, this goodly man sir John' (*CT*, VII, 2820) as the poet calls him with rare if also slightly patronising approval. Again, there will be no subjective individualisation, no dramatic appropriateness in his tale, which is perhaps the best of all the tales, a perfect poem, a wonderful mixture.

THE NUN'S PRIEST'S TALE

The poem and the story start immediately and simultaneously with the description of a poor widow, living a simple life in patience with her two daughters, on a bare, if healthy, diet of plenty of milk and brown bread, eggs and fried bacon, and 'hertes suffisaunce'. She has a glorious cock, Chauntecleer, whose brilliance outshines all comparison and who rules the roost with seven wives, of whom his favourite is Pertelote.

Chauntecleer is the hero of this well-known story, which is the conflation of two even older stories. The first is Aesop's Classical fable of the fox and the crow. The crow in the tree has a piece of food in his beak. The fox flatters him into singing, upon which he drops the food. It is a crisp and amusing anecdote illustrating perennial truths about flattery and keeping our mouth shut, and the non-human actors make the human point all the more memorably. Another similar story first found in the eighth-century work of Alcuin of York tells how a wolf catches a cock and runs off with it until the cock flatters the wolf into opening his mouth to show off his beautiful voice, thus allowing the cock to escape. Each story is about the dangers of flattery. These two stories were first combined in the eleventh century with characters of wolf and partridge, and become popular. In the twelfth-century Latin poem *Gallus et Vulpes* some unknown genius finally created Cock and Fox as they have become familiar. Thus, traditional stories may grow and be improved. For all the learning with which the *Nun's Priest's Tale* is adorned, it is another admirable folktale. The chase of the fox with the cock in its mouth became a favourite topic for illustration in manuscripts and on capitals and misericords in churches. The fox himself became a widely known rascally character, the subject of many stories in French and Latin.[3] Chaucer must have known several versions, and probably took the main outline from one section of the enormous French *Roman de Renart*. That is, however, literally only a part of the whole story. The actual plot takes up about one-tenth of the narrative, though the plot is fundamental to the nature of the whole poem.

The underlying pattern is one of reversal, which by simple repetition of the same kind of incident gives pleasure, but with the reversal of the incident, so that fox flatters cock, then cock flatters fox, gives extra aesthetic and moral pleasure. The fox's reputation for cunning, based on natural observation, makes him more suitable than the wolf as one character, while the cock, so commonplace a creature, so 'cocky', as we say, by nature, makes him amusing in his temporary discomfiture, and fittingly triumphant in his final escape. The cock is also notoriously sexual, and is symbolically associated with fertility, self-renewal, resurrection. That does not make him or his story allegorical in Chaucer's version but indicates the resonances which the story-pattern may subconsciously arouse, and makes him suitable for such a fable of variety, quick-wittedness and survival. In the predominantly rural Middle Ages, cock and fox were extremely familiar, and also natural enemies. *Gallus et Vulpes* also introduced the episode of the chase after the fox who is carrying off the cock in his mouth. It is only briefly mentioned but the seed flowered in the fourteenth and fifteenth centuries in popular art, and especially in Chaucer's poem. There are two essential figures, the woman chasing (usually shown with 'her distaff in her hand') and the fox with his prey; hunter and hunted. This image of the chase set between the two main acts of reversal which make up the plot helps to tie them together as cause and effect, but is also in itself an image of reversal, for the fox who was the hunter becomes hunted, and by a woman, who is not a natural hunter, but is carrying the image of female domesticity, the distaff. When so many others join the chase it becomes a cluster of potent images, a rush together of excitement joining many different individuals in one spontaneous desire. It both witnesses and contributes to the breaking down of boundaries, the rush to freedom, but also the rush to reassert the natural order, to prevent theft and punish the criminal. It has a certain ambiguity. We share both the bloodlust and desire for revenge of those who chase, and the temporary triumph and final fear of the offender. The whole episode is transitional, crossing and recrossing boundaries so as both to refresh and reassure us. Yet it is also a comedy: that is, by the medieval definition, a story with a happy ending. Death is ingeniously deflected with incurable optimism. And Chaucer's version is packed with memory of other stories, jokes, sententious wisdom undermined and at the last minute justified.

No poet anywhere so richly fulfils the potentialities of this whole narrative sequence as Chaucer. One thing he does not give us, and that is, an allegory, though many critics wish to extract one. The author of *Gallus et Vulpes* tells the story in 136 lines, but adds a further 152 elaborately allegorising the traditional tale. The cock's dungheap is penitence, the beating of his wings while he crows, says the author in a triumph of bathetic ingenuity, signifies teachers who add gestures to keep their audience awake while being addressed. The fox signifies Satan, etc. All this illustrates a habit of mind common to clerics in the Middle Ages and to some critics today, but it is alien to Chaucer's secular and artistic interests. He does indeed enrich and elaborate the structure, but by adding associative, metonymic details, by hyperbole (the colours of the cock), and by adding from the mouth of the learned cock the grim little anecdotes of the murdered traveller whose body is found in a dung-cart, the voyager drowned when his ship mysteriously sinks, the murder of the seven-year-old Anglo-Saxon royal saint, Kenelm, all of whom could have avoided their fate by attending to the warnings of dreams. Chauntecleer's wife robustly and equally learnedly declares his own warning dream to have a merely physical nature – probably overeating, but he defies her and her list of appallingly powerful laxatives. All this expands the nature of reversals, fundamental to the poem, with the juxtaposition of contrasts; death side-by-side with laughter; courtly barnyard fowls and poor humble human beings; 'marital' argument; rhetorical parody; traditional mockery of women – yet women, in the form of Chauntecleer's Pertelote and six concubine hens are adored. A neat illustration of several of these elements is Chauntecleer's own joke after praising (in comical poultry terms) the beauty of his beloved Pertelote, quoting

Mulier est hominis confusio –	*Woman is man's trouble*
Madame, the sentence of this Latyn is,	*meaning*
'Womman is mannes joye and al his blis'.	

(VII, 3164–6)

This is also a joke between Chaucer and his audience, perhaps at the expense of any ladies present, who were much less likely to know Latin, though this Latin is easy enough to guess.

By naturalistic standards there are inconsistencies of narrative and point of view, but no reader was ever puzzled by them because they are inherent in traditional story-telling.

Although so comical, the main action of the story is postponed to the end because Chaucer embellishes the talk between cock and hen, exemplifying husbandly pomposity and wifely brisk good sense with all the panoply of his usual learning and rhetoric. All the subjects of Chaucer's most serious thought are here. The comedy is in the neatness of the disproportion. Chaucer plays with serious ideas; while pretending to treat his frivolous 'matter' seriously, he treats serious matters frivolously. Thus, he ponders yet again the problems of pre-destination and foreknowledge, but they arise out of the concern of a farmyard fowl who has dreamed about a fox. This does not mean that he is satirising concern with the problem of predestination, but that it was so much a part of his thought that he enjoys it whether serious or light-hearted. This kind of joyful burlesque is the play of the mind, taking the same kind of exercise for pleasure, without concern for ultimate causes, as it normally takes when seriously at work. The attitude to rhetoric is an outstanding example. The poem is in the best sense of the word 'rhetorical', using all the devices of persuasive elaborate language, yet Chaucer also mocks and parodies the chief rhetorical author he knows, Geoffrey of Vinsauf, in an affectionate way.

The poem is written with marvellous versatility, and every line might serve as example. At one extreme we have the absurdly learned fowls, with the parody of rhetoric; at the other their naturalistic behaviour, the way the verse can imitate the clucking of a hen (as well as a loving hen-pecking wife)

Pekke hem up right as they growe and ete hem yn.

(VII, 2967)

and in between, again Pertelote, in her farcically scornful words to Chauntecleer

Have ye no mannes herte, and han a berd?

(VII, 2920)

The poem comes towards its conclusion with some lines of senten-
tious wisdom derived from the tale about not yielding to flattery and
keeping our mouth shut which wrap up the beast-fable joke of
talking creatures and are true and pleasant enough (VIII, 3430–7).

Chaucer then turns to, or perhaps on, his readers, perhaps a trifle
defensively. 'You good men, who think this is a silly trifle about a
cock and a hen, Taketh the moralite' (VIII, 3440). He is saying, as it
were, 'So you see, there *is* a message in an apparently trivial story'
and he goes on to quote St Paul's saying that all is written for our
doctrine, adding the possibly contradictory words 'Taketh the fruyt
and lat the chaf be stille' (VIII, 3443), which can mean 'read the
allegorical core and disregard the literal sense', which is not at all
characteristic of Chaucer's usual attitude, or it may mean the oppo-
site – or it may mean both. Chaucer knew that stories have literal
and symbolic meanings, and sometimes allegorical meanings. There
is no reason why he should not have thought the obvious 'morals'
he has uttered were not perfectly good, as indeed they are. But
perhaps he also felt the need to justify so much art and skill on an
apparently simple story, as he may well have felt about equally
artistic and much more morally dubious *fabliaux*-tales.

As with most of what are almost certainly his later and most
mature poems, like the *fabliaux* themselves, there is no doubt about
the firmness of closure here, even with the somewhat enigmatic
references after the story has come to its satisfying conclusion. Chaucer
adds another puzzle a couple of lines later, when after a slightly odd
version of the traditional prayer that often concludes a poem to God,
'if it be thy will',

As seith my lord, to make us alle goode men.

(VII, 3445)

Who is meant by 'my lord' is unclear though the reference must be
religious.

Though the poet himself mocks such platitudes (3205–13) ending
with a joke mocking both Arthurian literature and women, we can
easily accept the final sensible if commonplace 'morality' without stop-
ping or starting there in our appreciation. There is a self-justifying,
self-referential quality of sheer fun in the poem. It has no designs
on us. The poem is about itself yet it links up with many themes,

ideas and attitudes in the rest of *The Canterbury Tales*. It is a wonderfully Gothic mixture and form, digressive yet associative, full of juxtaposed contrasts and reversals, an exercise in sheer play, an acrobatic form of poetry, rejoicing in itself, which may be a reason why Chaucer had at the end a moment's misgiving about it.

The Nun's Priest's Tale has no subjectivity attributable to the Nun's Priest. It is the poet Chaucer who refers, for example, to

O Gaufred, deere maister sovereyn

(VII, 3347)

meaning the rhetorician Geoffrey of Vinsauf, apostrophe being one of his favourite rhetorical devices. There are some fifteen first-person references in the poem, quite characteristic of Chaucer's general manner, some jesting. The warning about false flatterers (3225–30) could on the other hand be taken quite seriously. It is twice addressed to 'ye lordes'. There are three addresses to 'goode men' as the audience (3402, 3440, 3445). None of this suits the fiction of the pilgrimage, and the poem seems to me to have been probably an independent though late piece which Chaucer thriftily inserted into *The Canterbury Tales*. The very lack of characterisation of the chaplain to the Prioress allowed the most characteristic of Chaucer's mature poems to be attached to him. The probably cancelled Epilogue, which appears in only some manuscripts, testifies to the fluid state of general organisation in which Chaucer left *The Canterbury Tales*. But here we come to another stop.

NOTES

1. Helen Cooper, *Oxford Guide to Chaucer*: The Canterbury Tales (Oxford, 1989), 321.
2. Diana Borstein, 'Chaucer's *Tale of Melibee* as an Example of the *Style Clergical*', *Chaucer Review* 12 (1977–8), 236–54; Derek Brewer, 'Some Observations on a Fifteenth-Century Manuscript', *Anglia* Band 72 (1955), 390–9.
3. K. Varty, *Reynard the Fox* (Leicester, 1967) discusses the many aspects of the fox with copious medieval illustration.

Chapter 23

The Canterbury Tales V: Spirit and Matter; Restraint and Repentance

THE SECOND NUN'S PROLOGUE AND TALE

The Second Nun's Prologue begins the Fragment numbered eight in the Ellesmere order and is not connected with any preceding tale. It has already been discussed as *The Life of St Cecilia* (above, pp. 131–2). It comes after *The Nun's Priest's Tale*, and is followed by *The Canon's Yeoman's Prologue and Tale*, and here we may merely note its placing, and the lesson it has of the ongoing, fluid state of *The Canterbury Tales* in many of its stages before its firm but abrupt conclusion. *The Canon's Yeoman's Prologue*, clearly with its *Tale* an inspired afterthought, begins with a reference to *The Life of St Cecilia*, so there is no doubt that Chaucer meant to link the two in piquant contrast. But he had hesitated. In Hengwrt (written, it will be remembered, by the same scribe as he who wrote Ellesmere, at an earlier stage, or with a different version, of Chaucer's order of tales) *St Cecilia* with the simple title 'The Nonne' comes after *The Franklin's Tale* after a blank half page, and before *The Clerk's Prologue and Tale*, with no link. So Chaucer clearly intended the already written story of St Cecilia to be told by the Nun who accompanied the Prioress as her chaplain. But Hengwrt does not include *The Canon's Yeoman's Prologue and Tale*. It must have been written, but not included, because it was an afterthought and presumably stored elsewhere, away from the bundle of texts from which the Hengwrt scribe copied. (There is no reasonable doubt that *The Canon's Yeoman's Tale* is genuine.) At some stage it was realised that *The Canon's Yeoman's Prologue and Tale*, because of its beginning, was intended by Chaucer to follow the *St Cecilia*, and so it was inserted in the more splendid, and more edited, Ellesmere manuscript. Chaucer, as already noted, had written *St Cecilia* for a man, but had not had time to make the necessary adjustments at the beginning – unlike the situation with *The Knight's Tale*, whose beginning he had adjusted. There seems no doubt that he would ultimately have adjusted the story of

St Cecilia to the Second Nun – second, that is, after the Prioress. Attribution to a woman teller is suitable because of the subject-matter, though the very possibility of change shows that there was neutral ground shared by both sexes.

THE CANON'S YEOMAN'S PROLOGUE AND TALE

The Canon's Yeoman's Prologue is certainly late, mature work, and as certainly linked to *The Second Nun's Tale*. It was composed so late that though there can be no doubt of its authenticity on grounds of sheer style, manner and greatness, even if it did not get into all the manuscripts. The Canon and his Yeoman are described as coming up on horses sweaty with the haste they have made to join the pilgrims. They are clearly a happy afterthought of Chaucer's. The *Prologue and Tale* seem to be motivated partly by his interest in alchemy, partly by his strong suspicion that it was bogus, partly by the fascination of tricky or downright dishonest practices and persons. That led to thinking about those who had been deceived, and fed his lately discovered vein of self-revelatory speeches or soliloquies. Hence, the Canon's Yeoman's long and passionate outburst. The whole fitted into Chaucer's mature interest in the world and people around him, and in the scientific and philosophical problems which lie beneath the surface.

The Canon's Yeoman's Prologue makes a fascinating little drama on its own. First we see the sweaty horses, and the strange canon who had ridden so fast, apparently for no more than the pleasure of the pilgrims' company.

> He hadde ay priked lik as he were wood   *spurred; mad*
> A clote-leef he hadde under his hood   *burdock-leaf*
> For swoot, and for to keep his head from heete.
> But it was joye for to seen hym swete!   *sweat*
> (VIII, 576–9)

That last line is pure Chaucer, pure pleasure in essential animated life of whatever kind, such as leads him elsewhere to write of a 'manly man', 'a wommanliche wyf', a 'horsly hors'; and to praise the pilgrim Yeoman for dressing his tackle 'yeomanly'. The Canon's Yeoman, in answer to the Host's questioning, at first praises the Canon's 'heigh discrecioun', his judgement, and says the Canon if he wished could turn the very ground to silver or gold. He is, in other words, an alchemist. Why then, asks the Host, is he so shabby and dirty, 'so sluttish'? At this the Canon's Yeoman breaks into quite another vein.

Of the Canon he says he is too clever by half; they live in squalor, and his own face is strangely discoloured because of his work at the alchemical furnace, where the Canon's experiments are false and always fail. The Canon comes up on this conversation and tells his Yeoman to be silent, but the latter now has the bit between his teeth. The Canon flees away for sorrow and shame, while the Canon's Yeoman begins his tale by disburdening his heart of all the lost labour and deceit of 'that slidyng science', of which Chaucer shows considerable knowledge, satirically deployed. Chaucer must have studied it, though there is no reason to suppose that he had himself ever been seduced by it. The Canon's Yeoman is a somewhat different case. He is bitterly disillusioned about alchemy.

> Whoso that listeth outen his folie,   *wishes to show*
> Lat hym come forth and lerne multiplie.   *practise alchemy*
>   (VIII, 834–5)

He describes the infatuation of men so desirous of the fabled riches to be won by alchemy that they reduce themselves to poverty and ill-health in their mad pursuit. He drives the lesson home by a wonderful *chiaroscuro* sketch of the experimental shop of his master the Canon – the materials, the explosions, the disappointments, disagreements and arguments of the experimenters. Chaucer takes a great delight in the list of strange and resounding names of chemicals and processes. The Canon's Yeoman after showing the ill-success of his own Canon then proceeds to tell of the downright trickery of another alchemical Canon, describing a confidence trick which Chaucer may have learned from life, though a few comparable anecdotes have been noted. It is too complicated a plot for an orally based folktale, but it is very much of the same nature as the medieval international comic tale. The dupe is laughed at, and though the trickster, the 'cursed Canon', is condemned, there is no serious satirical and didactic purpose. The narrative of the complicated conjuring trick is a masterpiece of clarity and ingenuity. The interest and aesthetic satisfaction normally founded on a shapely and complex plot are here based on the convolutions of the confidence trick itself, which is of course related to the characters of the subtle alchemist and his stupid victim. We smile at the ingenuity of the trick, and the disappointment of the dupe, who is an idle and selfish priest on whom we need waste no sympathy.

The tale is rounded off with a hundred lines of consideration of the pros and cons of alchemy, where it is Chaucer rather than the

Yeoman who is speaking. There is a characteristic avoidance of an extreme position either for or against. Alchemy, though never intellectually so respectable as astrology, was nevertheless a well-established and accepted science. Chaucer's objections to it are not scientific; he is prepared to believe that the experts are right. In so far as he objects, he objects on practical and religious grounds. First, it is no good for the non-scientist to practise alchemy, because he is too ignorant:

> Lat no man bisye hym this art for to seche,
> But if that he th'entencioun and speche
> Of philosophres understonde kan.   *scientists*
>   (VIII, 1442–4)

And second, since, according to Plato, scientists are sworn not to disclose or write the central secret of their art, because it is so dear to Christ, that He does not wish it to be generally known,

> I rede, as for the beste, lete it goon.   *advise*
> For whoso maketh God his adversarie,
> As for to werken any thyng in contrarie
> Of his wil, certes, never shal he thryve,
> Thogh that he multiplie terme of his lyve.   *practise alchemy all his life*
> And there a poynt, for ended is my tale.
> God sende every trewe man boote of his bale.   *remedy for his evil*
>   (VIII, 1475–81)

As with *The Pardoner's Tale* the actual narrative is a jewel within a rich setting of comment and example, as well as of realistic description, dialogue and character. There are occasional touches which suggest a special audience, and since we know from Chaucer's poem to Bukton that at least *The Wife of Bath's Prologue* circulated, perhaps separately, in Chaucer's lifetime, it is quite possible that he used various Canterbury poems to suit special occasions, even if he designed them originally for inclusion in the Canterbury series. He may have been called on for special recitals and have produced individual parts of *The Canterbury Tales* on such occasions.

In this last of the comic tales we see, appropriately enough, in the subject of alchemy, the height of Chaucer's interest in what may be called the 'materiality' of matter. Many popular comic tales are based on the intransigence of matter to emotional or spiritual pretentions – the equivalent of a dignified man slipping on a banana skin, or having a custard pie thrown in his face. *The Miller's Tale* and *Summoner's Tale* are particularly good examples of human dignity comically reduced by brute materialism. The human condition itself, seen as a spirit stuffed into a bag of skin and bones and dung, is in this respect a comic anomaly or, from a different point of view, a tragic one. Alchemy, however, was built on the premise that matter somehow could be made to obey laws similar to those of the spirit. It was fundamentally unlike modern science because its intellectual system was really an analogy of psychological and emotional structures, which is why the modern psychoanalyst Jung found it so interesting to study. (That alchemy led to modern chemistry is pure accident, and alchemy may have in reality held the development of real chemistry back, for chemistry developed much later than physics.)

Alchemy is based on the notion, ultimately, that matter behaves as if it were like mind and feeling. It is archaic, and scientifically confused. It is also morally confused. Its practitioners were either almost literally half-baked idealists, like the Canon's Yeoman, or swindlers, like the Canon in his story, or simply stupid, greedy men, like the priest in the story. It might be said that *The Canon's Yeoman's Prologue* and his long after-speech set out to reveal the confusion of mind and matter involved in alchemy, and to show that it must be ridiculous. In so doing, matter and mind are distinguished. The confusion is a perversion of the connectedness that *The Franklin's Tale* shows validly exists between matter and mind, because alchemy is followed in a spirit of selfish acquisition, not of *trouthe*. *The Canon's Yeoman's Tale* itself, the comic anecdote, is a story of a trick whose comedy lies in the revelation of trickery, the disappointment of greed, and the implicit reassertion of clear social, intellectual and moral rules which have been foolishly muddled and infringed by those who have thus been appropriately punished. The confidence trick is itself a clarifying comment on the nature of alchemy. The comic contradiction which is both presented and sorted out is summed up in the pregnant line

Bitwixe men and gold ther is debaat.

(VIII, 1389)

The style at first also plays the game of spiritualising matter by using alchemical terms so freely, but the story of trickery is very lucidly explained. The comic story and the discussion of alchemy each come to the same conclusion: have nothing to do with alchemy. The style in every sense makes this plain: avoid 'multiplying'.

This cautious attitude may be seen to develop further in the following tale by the Manciple, though it is on a very different subject. Caution is carried still further again in *The Parson's Tale*. If we are right in assuming that this was Chaucer's final decision about the sequence of tales, he is indeed moving towards the end of the general story both of the *Tales* and his own life.

THE MANCIPLE'S PROLOGUE AND TALE

The next tale stands on its own, not yet connected with other tales, but it begins in the *Prologue* with a reference to 'Bob-up-and-down' which may be a facetious reference either to Harbledown, or to 'Up-and-Doun Field' near Boughton, in either case no more than a mile from Canterbury, and an unrealistic place to start even a short story. There is some entertaining comedy between the Manciple and the drunken Cook. This is the longest of the links between tales, which there has been too little space to discuss, and a word or two more on this one must serve as example.

The links are self-evidently mature writing of *The Canterbury Tales* period and clear evidence of Chaucer's delight in the Human Comedy of character. Their immediate function is to articulate the sequence of stories as managed by the Host, but they do more than that. They are genuinely dramatic in the tradition of knock-about comedy but extraordinarily rich and innovative. The interplay of characters and comments in Boccaccio's *Decameron* is much simpler, though it shows that such a device was 'in the air'. The links are ultimately based on the mixture of good fellowship and mutual antipathy which characterises all human company, sharpened by Chaucer for dramatic purposes. The Host provides personal comments on the tale that has been told. He is the first of Chaucer's critics of the individual tales and often, like most critics, is superficial and somewhat beside the point. Chaucer might be said to use him as a gentle satire on his less perceptive readers, but what he likes or dislikes about tales may not be a bad index of popular taste, and is a salutary contrast in many cases to modern reactions. (Chaucer also uses the Host at the beginning and end of *Sir Thopas* for a little self-reflective jesting with further critical echoes and re-echoes, but not in *The Manciple's Prologue*.) This *Prologue* and the following *Tale* drift about various placings in various manuscripts of *The Canterbury Tales* with the result that textual scholars isolate them as one 'fragment', but they seem from internal evidence to be joined fairly firmly to *The Parson's Prologue* and *Tale*. For example, Hengwrt precedes *The*

Parson's Prologue and *Tale* with *The Tale of Melibeus* as already noted, but its version of *The Parson's Prologue* still begins with the reference to the Manciple in the first line. (But *The Manciple's Prologue* and *Tale* in Hengwrt come much earlier between *The Nun's Priest's Tale* and *The Man of Law's Tale*.) The Ellesmere order which we are following here seems to represent Chaucer's latest thoughts, and reasonable confidence about the order is important if we are to trace what appears to be a dominant line of thought in Chaucer's last years. At the same time the variations in order between these two good manuscripts must remind us that all systematic theories remain tentative.

To accept the Ellesmere order does not necessarily mean that the *Prologues* and *Tales* we are considering were composed in the order in which we now have them. Some critics would see *The Manciple's Tale* as earlier work because of its curious structure, while *The Parson's Tale*, a devout prose meditation, largely translated, could have been intermittently worked on for a number of years and only accidentally incorporated in the *Tales*. But *The Manciple's Prologue* must be fairly late, as suggested, apart from style and subject-matter, by its absence from a number of manuscripts. In the *Prologue* the Host calls on the Cook for a tale, though he is too drunk to tell one. The Cook had started a tale far back in the pilgrimage, following *The Reeve's Tale*, though it had not got far (above, p. 291). Chaucer had perhaps halted *The Cook's Tale* because it was going to be insufficiently varied from the two preceding *fabliau*-like tales. If he had only cut it out completely we would have had no evidence of a change of plan, nor any sense of inconsistency in the request to the Cook here for a tale. At that earlier date he had postponed a final decision.

The quarrel between Manciple and Cook has no traditional basis and is not prepared for in any way. A pause has apparently come in the tale-telling. The Host remarks on how sleepy the Cook is and roughly calls on him for a tale. The Manciple butts in to say he will excuse the Cook because his breath stinks so horribly. (It might be thought that medieval people who had so much livestock about even in towns, and such poor sanitation, were immune to bad smells, but that seems not to have been the case, as we see here. One of the torments of Hell, says the Parson, will be the foul stench (X, 205–10) and sin, especially lechery, stinks (e.g. X, 840–5)).

The Cook, who is drunk, is furious and falls off his horse – there is great shoving to and fro to get him back up again, all good knockabout comedy. The Host excuses the Cook – who also has a cold in the head – and reproaches the Manciple for reproving the

Cook, saying that one day the Manciple might be caught out in his own false dealings. The Manciple agrees, and half maliciously offers the Cook more wine to drink, to the amusement of the Host, who praises somewhat improbably Bacchus, the classical god of wine, and urges the Manciple to tell a tale.

All this is pure comic invention in the tradition of popular comic tale, which is the only genre in which Chaucer, like Shakespeare, appears to be able to invent, and to do without a source.[1] Drunkenness is a constant source of comedy in Western Europe for many centuries. It makes men into fools, and is powerfully, if unconsciously, symbolic of our relation to the material world, both as we conquer it and it conquers us. Here drunkenness provokes rancour but, as the Host remarks, then turns rancour into love and accord (IX, 97–8). The nature of the comedy is popular in the strict sense, appealing to all classes, derisive, realistic. Those who laugh are superior to those who are laughed at, morally, socially and in clarity of mind. Those who are laughed at are degraded – the Cook falls into the mud and is helpless. Dirt and drunkenness make him incapable of speech. His chief foe, the Manciple, though not physically degraded, is nevertheless taunted by the Host with his own dishonesty, which he calmly admits, a lightly satirical touch which is a miniature of the Pardoner's self-revelation. Both these are relatively low-class characters. They are churls, and behave badly, but they do not threaten the reader or hearer, so they arouse no anxiety and consequently no serious hostility. This, like most of Chaucer's comedy, is observation by the high of the low, who are brought lower. Like all comedy it is about contrast, human dignity contrasted with drunken folly in the mud, unctuous distaste for the physically disgusting checked by having to acknowledge its own dishonesty. There is no grotesque, Rabelaisian 'carnivalesque' reversal, no world-upside-down. The little episode is realistic, vivid, conservative not radical, like so much of Chaucer's humour: the humour of confident, personally fastidious courtiers, who observe the goings-on of their inferiors with amused disdain. Yet it ends with harmony restored.

The tale which it prefaces is different: less genial and, as Chaucer tells it, rather odd. There is little sense of any personality that the Manciple might have, but the poem is clearly put into the mouth of a speaker, as will be seen, and the word 'lordings' (IX, 309) towards the end recalls the sense of a pilgrim-speaker. Yet even at the beginning the speaker has a certain impersonality. It is not in any way specific to the Manciple's character or job. Several versions of the plot were available to Chaucer but he went directly to Ovid, though he thoroughly medievalised his protagonist, Phebus, who was originally the Classical god associated with the sun. The *Tale* begins abruptly, hardly in character of the Manciple, not represented in *The General Prologue* as a learned man:

> Whan Phebus dwelled heere in this erthe adoun
> As olde bookes maken mencioun
>
> (IX, 105–6)

he was the most lusty bachelor, (i.e. young knight), best archer, and did many a worthy deed. He was fulfilled of *gentillesse*, honour and perfect worthyness. Phebus has a beloved wife, who in his absence betrays him with a much less worthy man. A white crow, kept in a cage, and capable of speech, tells Phebus what has happened and in a passion Phebus kills his wife with an arrow. Then he deeply regrets his impatient anger, and condemns the crow evermore to be black and to have a discordant cry.

This rather strange tale has received considerable attention from critics who do not much like it and take it as a fully dramatic speech by an unpleasant man, though also as a story circling around the concept of 'language' and what language corresponds to. The tale was several times told in the medieval period, though not as being about language. Chaucer's version as usual is very original, has trimmed down the story to its essence, then added various considerations to it in the best rhetorical manner.

Ovid tells the story in *Metamorphoses* II, 531–632 as yet another fable of change, how the raven became black, with little explicit moralisation. As is the way of traditional literature other versions vary detail and emphasis. Chaucer may owe some of his changes to French and English versions, including Gower's brief account in *Confessio Amantis*, III, 804–5, under the heading of Anger, though the point even with Gower is, as in most versions, the folly of disloyal tale-telling. Gower uses the phrase 'Mi sone', characteristic both of the priest's address and of medieval instructions to boys.

It is important to notice that in these medieval versions there is no misogyny. Despite the general obsession with honour in the form of the wife's faithfulness, which is shared by Phebus, all these versions concern only the tell-tale, the gossip or 'jangler'. Neither Phebus nor his wife is much blamed. There is a sort of worldly wisdom not dissimilar to that of the *fabliaux*, but also an entirely medieval emphasis on the supremacy of loyalty (in this case of servants to masters), *properly interpreted*, i.e. so as not to upset them, different from loyalty in marriage as a part of honour.

Chaucer's version can be assumed to be roughly contemporary with Gower's, around 1390, and its lateness is significant. It is longer and more complex than Gower's. With Chaucer the lady, unnamed, is Phebus's wife, not lover as in some versions, and despite his own beauty, youth and great skills, while he lives as a knight on earth, he is jealous of his wife and by implication tries to restrict her. This leads Chaucer into a digression saying that you cannot keep a bad woman in – nature will out. A bird in however golden a cage and well fed would prefer in a rough cold forest

> Goon ete wormes and swich wrecchedness.   *to go*
> (IX, 171)

So also a cat, or a she-wolf to the same effect, though the Manciple (or Chaucer) says he speaks this only of lecherous men who always prefer lower creatures to their wives, and indeed the bird and cat examples are male. But the principal example is Phebus's wife, who prefers 'A man of litel reputacioun', said twice, in almost the same form (IX, 199, 253). The digression, a reflection on the action of a kind familiar in Chaucerian narrative, risks an antifeminist implication which is absent from earlier versions.

It is followed by another unusual digression of great interest, and like the first not altogether consonant with the usual underlying message of the tale. It is a comment on worldly and hence linguistic judgements being biased in favour of class and success, as against morality and truth (a transhistorical phenomenon if ever there was one). The Manciple remarks that an upper-class woman who commits adultery is called 'a lady, as in love', while a poor woman is called the lover's 'wenche or his lemman' (IX, 220): both contemptuous words for Chaucer. We should not attribute too much class-bitterness to this because it is immediately followed by a comparable example of a 'tyrant' who kills and burns and destroys everything and is called a 'capitayn', while one who does similar but far less damage is condemned as an outlaw or a thief (IX, 223–34). The point is exactly the same, and not class- or gender-specific. Though these are traditional criticisms, and remind us that medieval culture has many strands, they nevertheless come across with considerable sharpness. Chaucer is not *becoming* disillusioned: he always was, as his Boethian lyrics written in his maturity clearly illustrate.

Some critics have thought that the heart of *The Manciple's Tale* lies in these comments on the conflict between social, linguistic convention and moral verbal truth, believing that the poem is 'about language', but that is only part of it. The comments 'lady/wench', 'captain/thief' are preceded by the Manciple's comment

> The wise Plato seith, as ye may rede,
> The word moot nede accorde with the dede.
> If men shal telle proprely a thyng
> The word moot cosyn be to the werkyng.
> I am a boystous man . . .

> (IX, 207–11)

A great deal of medieval and Chaucerian linguistic theory is packed into these few lines, with the added interest of the self-description of the speaker as 'boystous' and the question of how far who is the speaker modifies, by character and intention, what is said. Is it the poet or the Manciple who is the 'boystous' man who quotes Plato and other old books? Boistous is an interesting word. It comes from French *boiteux* meaning 'lame'. Chaucer uses 'boystous' only here, and 'boistously' once only, in *The Clerk's Tale* (IV, 791), where it means 'harshly, rudely'. 'Boystous', coming into more general use at the end of the fourteenth century, has a range of meanings, 'rough, ignorant, rude'. None of this applies strictly to Chaucer or the Manciple, but the contemporary author of *Pearl* (i.e. the *Gawain*-poet) applies it in humility to himself (*Pearl*, 911), and once also to Christ's cross (*Pearl*, 814), these also being the only two uses in all his works. The author of the mystical contemporary prose work *The Cloud of Unknowing* applies it to himself. It would suit Chaucer's own self-deprecatory self-presentation. In the Manciple's mouth it is perhaps equivalent to the Franklin's disclaimer of rhetorical ability ('Have me excused of my rude [i.e. rough] speche' he says (V, 718) and 'boystous' sometimes goes with 'rude' in this sense.) But as the Manciple's use goes along with the radical, aggressive comments about 'lady/wenche' and 'captain/thief' the word may also suggest the suppressed resentment of a man having to serve superiors who are less clever than he. Perhaps Chaucer at times, with his fundamental scepticism, also felt such resentment. The Manciple's reference to Plato is an inconsistency in characterisation which shows we should not push dramatisation of character too far.

A brief note must be made of the concept of language expressed by the Manciple. This concept is not special to Chaucer or the Manciple, and like the nature of the characterisation applies to the rest of *The Canterbury Tales*. For the 'word' to accord with the 'deed', or be 'cousin' to the 'working' is very different from the view that became dominant from the seventeenth century to the twentieth that a 'word' ought to correspond with a 'thing', the 'thing' being preferably material. This is a view that no informed person now holds, but which still unconsciously underlies much 'commonsense' discussion of the highly complex relations between language and what language represents or 'means'. That the word must be cousin to the deed is still important for a 'correspondence theory' of truth in language – now impugned by many literary scholars who claim to believe that language and poems are self-contained, independent of any external truth, entirely relative, depending only on the critic's own view. The medieval view asserts that there is something we can speak about 'out there', which is not purely our own mental invention. This is a sort of 'literalism' which is strong in Chaucer from *The Book of the Duchess* onwards. It is an aspect of the contemporary medieval scholastic theory of Nominalism (above, pp. 151–2). However, language in this medieval theory is not tied to material objects, nor is the material physical universe the ultimate reality. In medieval thought there is a fluid relationship between words and meaning, and there is room for other aspects of language, as performance, persuasion, rhetoric, drama, etc., important to our understanding. The sheer power of language to move us is recognised. And this has a curiously negative illustration in the tale we are considering, which makes the question 'What is truth' as difficult as jesting Pilate found it. To this extent the poem is indeed about language.

We return to the story. What is its central concern? It goes on to report the brutally blunt language in which the crow tells Phebus that for all his beauty, song and watchfulness (*waiting*, IX, 252) over his wife he is deceived

For on thy bed thy wyf I saugh hym swyve.

(IX, 256)

Here the word is all too close a cousin to the deed, the language of a 'boystous' man. Then the story continues in the way already noted. As in other versions the crow is condemned for his 'false tale' (IX, 293) which was not false but true. Chaucer omits the pathos of the wife's pregnancy. The crow is further punished by being deprived of his once beautiful song and is turned black, as Phebus says 'in tokenynge that thurgh thee my wyf is slain' (IX, 302) – though it was Phebus's own rash anger that killed her. The crow is then consigned 'to the devil' (IX, 307) – a nicely anachronistic colloquialism.

The actual plot thus concludes in death, shame, banishment and grief, all as a result of someone telling an unwelcome truth. We may recall stories of messengers being executed for bringing kings unwelcome truths. Not unrelated in feeling is the widespread folktale of the faithful dog rashly killed by his master though he has saved his child.[2] These are all stories of the bitter irony of circumstance, but that of the crow has an intriguing structure, whereby the virtuous deed is not only ill-rewarded but unwanted and its truth denied – with further implications of our desire for a fool's paradise and our regret at hasty deeds.

The Manciple's Tale concludes in a very curious original way with 50 lines of which the first two give the moral

> Lordynges, by this ensample I yow preye
> Beth war and taketh kep what that ye seye.   *be wary and watch*
> (IX, 309–10)

The word 'Lordynges' ensures that we know that the Manciple is speaking. In the last 44 lines of the tale the Manciple tells us, sententiously and repetitiously, quoting Solomon, David and Seneca by name, what his 'dame', his mother, taught him, which is exactly the same moral: keep your mouth shut, pretend not to hear slander. In 44 lines the words 'My sone' are repeated 11 times. Is this repetitious message a parody, satirising the very injunction to silence? So some think, but it does not seem very funny.

The key to the passage, which has not been noticed, lies in the line

> Thus lerne children whan that they been yonge.
> (IX, 334)

Instruction of youth is in some way reflected. Although the closing passage is a tissue of commonplace wisdom and the address 'My son' is found in Chapter 23 of *Proverbs* and other 'wisdom literature', the closest parallel is the instructional piece *How the Wise Man Taught his Son*, beginning

> Listnith lordingis and ye schulen here . . .

Of its 19 eight-line stanzas giving miscellaneous good advice, including strong emphasis on guarding the tongue, nine begin with the words 'And sonne' and four others include the phrase. The good advice includes kind treatment of a wife. The advice is given by a father not a mother (though a parallel piece tells how *The Good Wiif tauȝte hir Douȝtir*) but the Manciple (or Chaucer) seems unquestionably to be invoking this model. There are a number of such elementary instructional pieces, the manuscripts dating from the fifteenth century but the texts earlier.[3]

The effect of this doctrinal little epilogue is to insist on the familiar medieval message attributed to the story, reinforced, apparently seriously, by recall of teaching received in youth, though narrowly concentrated on speech. It has not been much approved of by critics. It has yet another interesting implication, again in some ways contradictory to other tendencies within the poem. The Manciple invokes his mother as the source of wisdom. Although there are indeed learned and didactic women in medieval narrative they are usually saints, and no other case is known to me in medieval literature (though there must have been many instances in life) of instruction by a mother, though the Wife of Bath has been taught a thing or two by her mother not included in the instructional manuals (III, 576). For Chaucer there are three medieval images of the feminine: one, the beloved virginal young lady; the second, the rather ambivalent wife; the third, the wise protective instructive mother, summed up in the Blessed Virgin Mary. *The Manciple's Tale* invokes the second and third.

Wordsworth thought the poem worth translation (though friends astonishingly thought it too immoral to publish) and wrote about it, 'The formal prosing at the end and the selfishness that pervades it flows from the genius of Chaucer, mainly as characteristic of the narrator whom he describes in the Prologue as eminent for shrewdness and clever worldly Prudence.' And of the central episode he wrote 'How could the mischief of telling truth, merely because it *is* truth, be more feelingly exemplified? The Manciple is not, in his understanding, conscious of this . . . Then how vividly is impressed the mischief of jealous vigilance, and how truly and touchingly in contrast with the world's judgments are the transgression of a woman in a low rank of life and one in high estate placed on the same level, treated.'[4]

This is perceptive appreciation, though the dramatic characterisation seems to me to be less strong than Wordsworth claims. Other critics share his condemnation of the cold and negative morality expressed, but this is to deny both the morality and the good sense of the advice given. It also forgets the medieval obsession, probably justified, with the dangers of slander and malicious gossip, referred to by Chaucer a number of times. Moreover *The Manciple's Tale* has subtle implications about activist, simplistic morality. It is not obsessed with honour, chastity or total openness. It does not encourage a devastating truthfulness at the expense of personal relationships. It does not encourage enthusiasm for morality at the cost of community and loyalty.

Finally, though not least, *The Manciple's Tale* is so emphatic, so clearly placed significantly before *The Parson's Tale*, which is so obviously meant to end the series, the pilgrimage being now virtually accomplished, that it is worth digging a little deeper into this powerful rejection of 'tale-telling', which is how loose speech is often described in the little educational treatises referred to, and elsewhere.

The plain moral, not to 'tell tales', seems to be one that Chaucer is ready to apply to himself. He is indirectly telling himself to 'shut up'.

> My sone, be war, and be noon auctour newe   *new teller*
> Of tidynges, wheither they been false or trewe.
>
> (IX, 359–60)

Never to repeat a story whether true or false is a strange message from the author of *The House of Fame*, so eager for tidings, let alone the author of *The Canterbury Tales*, but we may also recall from *The House of Fame* the disdain shown for the falseness of Fame in both senses of 'worldly fame' and 'rumour', and we remember also the claim to independence from what the world may think of us.

The Manciple twice says 'I am noght textueel' (235, 316), that is, well-read (though quoting Plato, which is attributable to the medium rather than to realistic characterisation). The only other time this word is used in Chaucer is in the immediately following *Parson's Prologue*, where the Parson also claims not to be 'textueel'. If any one was 'textueel' it was Chaucer himself, but in his divided consciousness, where old is set against new, unified against specialised, contemplative against analytic, it begins to look as if the old, the 'archaic' contemplative element, dependent on few texts, is beginning to get the upper hand of the discursive, widely ranging more modern element. *The Manciple's Tale* perhaps unconsciously reflects Chaucer's deepening distrust, as he gets older, of undue verbalisation, of irresponsible story-telling. *The Parson's Tale* shows that distrust becoming decisive, and *The Retractation* shows it as conclusive. *The Manciple's Tale* has not only many implications in itself; it tells us something about Chaucer's own pilgrimage of the mind, the approaching end of his quest, of the coming closure of *The Canterbury Tales* (which like most deaths may seem premature), of Chaucer's mind to many secular interests, and ultimately, of course, of the story of his life.

THE PARSON'S PROLOGUE AND TALE

The first line of *The Parson's Prologue* gives us another neat illustration of the slipperiness of attribution of teller to tale. It begins

> By that the Maunciple hadde his tale al ended
>
> (X, 1)

and thus clearly attaches the two tales, of Manciple and Parson together, as in the Ellesmere manuscript. But Hengwrt has 'maunciple' written over an erasure, and in fact the preceding tale in that manuscript is *The Tale of Melibeus*. Other manuscripts instead of 'maunciple' write 'yeman', 'marchaunt', 'Frankeleyn', and as we have seen there is no strong reason why *The Manciple's Tale*, derived from a Latin source, stuffed with clerical wise commonplaces should not have been attributed to any one of several other characters on which the reader may like to speculate.

At all events the Manciple seems to have been Chaucer's final choice quite specifically as prelude to the Parson. *The Parson's Tale* is a contrast as being in prose and less worldly, even more didactic, but in not being a story it follows the injunction against tale bearing not inappropriately, especially the sententious moralising at the end of *The Manciple's Tale*, if in a different spirit. Before we come to *The Parson's Tale* – which is no tale at all in our sense of the word but a religious meditation and instruction on penance – there is *The Prologue to the Parson's Tale* which also seems late work and which is full of interest. To start with, it was obviously designed for the closing part of the pilgrimage, but there is some inconsistency in the details which are given of the journey. There were some necessary adjustments that Chaucer never got round to making. The astronomical timing described in *The Parson's Prologue* shows that it was about four o'clock in the afternoon, on 20 April, whereas the Manciple's tale, begun only a mile from Canterbury, was started explicitly in the morning. There is also an oversight in the astrology.

In *The Parson's Prologue* the Parson expresses a rigidly hostile attitude to 'fables', which for Chaucer are at best fictions, at worst lies, to be contrasted with true 'storial' material (*Legend of Good Women*, 702), of Cleopatra, and of the Physician's story of Virginius (VI, 155–6), but says he will tell of 'morality and virtuous matter' in order to give lawful pleasure. But he is a Southern man

> I kan nat geeste 'rum, ram, ruf' by lettre,   *tell tales*
> Ne God woot, rym holde I but litel bettre: *rhyme*

And therfore, if yow list – I wol nat glose –   *if it pleases you; deceive*
I wol yow telle a myrie tale in prose.   *pleasant*
(X, 43–6)

The Parson's condemnation of alliterative verse which often tended towards solemn edification, *and* of rhyme, in which many pious works are written, is surprisingly severe. It can only be explained by assuming that in Chaucer's mind prose was coming to be thought of as the only vehicle for serious, non-fictional writing, and that verse was becoming associated only with fiction, and usually secular fiction. This actual situation was not fully realised in English till late in the sixteenth century, but Chaucer is here as usual in advance of his age. At the end of the Parson's 'tale', the distrust of fiction becomes complete. On the other hand, the Parson must still at this stage, before his tale, be allowed some dramatic freedom and autonomy. Chaucer need not have agreed wholeheartedly with the words he puts in the Parson's mouth, though it would not seem that he is mocking the Parson.

The Parson likens their journey to the perfect glorious pilgrimage which is called the heavenly Jerusalem. On the whole this seems more like another late thought of Chaucer's, and a further turning away from the secular realism of daily life, rather than an early plan finally reverted to. All the pilgrims, including the Host, are glad to hear him, though the Host asks, very sensibly, that he should speak 'in little space'. Many of the themes touched on in the *Tales* are summed up in this long tract. The Parson reminds his hearers of the Day of Judgement, and the torments of Hell. God orders and controls all things, and a man's first duty is self-mastery. Honours, wealth, delights, even love of family, though good in themselves can seduce him from his eternal destiny. There is a long passage about the Seven Deadly Sins, where many things are held up to condemnation, as 'superfluitee of clothing and horrible disordinat scantness'; great households (such as John of Gaunt's, though Chaucer does not say so); 'bakemeats and dishmeats, burning with wildfire and painted, and castled with paper' (as they were in court festivities), and so forth. The commonplace that Christ is the only source of 'gentilesse' is reiterated. One of many shrewd remarks is that inordinate desire for knowledge or glory may be regarded as a form of avarice. Extortion and oppression are roundly condemned, and while 'degree' is upheld, it is a lord's duty to give his dependants cause to love him. Throughout there is a continual insistence on 'reason'.

The immediate source of this powerful diatribe against the joys of life is unknown and there seems no reason why we should not attribute to Chaucer himself sufficient conviction to have compiled it from traditional elements themselves well known, mainly deriving ultimately from thirteenth-century Latin originals repeated in part by subsequent writers. Chaucer may well have also worked, as was his custom, from French texts of the same tradition. Opinions vary on the style. The great expert, Professor Wenzel, regards it as frequently uninspiring and awkward, with some errors, though some of his examples are unconvincing. Professor Cooper rightly remarks that the treatise is 'relentlessly expository' but not consistently drab. The chief point must be that Chaucer himself took it seriously. He was well acquainted with this type of literature, but it is important to realise that for a layman to write such a work was highly innovative, even though sermons had been written in English continuously from the Old English period onwards.

In religious as in scientific prose Chaucer was among the leaders. If *The Parson's Tale* is not the first instance of a layman writing a religious piece in English, then probably the prose treatise *The Two Ways*, by Chaucer's friend and poetic disciple, Sir John Clanvowe, is actually the first, but composed under Chaucer's influence at a very similar date around 1390. Clanvowe's treatise has some touch of Lollardry; not so Chaucer's, but each is essentially a devout layman's serious attempt to come to terms with the self-discipline, the social codes, the asceticism and other-worldliness of monk-dominated medieval Christian spirituality. Much of it seems more sour and more absolute than is necessary for laymen or than would have been endorsed by the great medieval theologian, St Thomas Aquinas, who seems to have made more allowance for natural affections. The whole mixed 'Gothic' nature of *The Canterbury Tales* implicitly juxtaposes *The Parson's Tale* with other tales which though they may, as Chaucer later expresses it, 'sownen into synne', qualify and modify *The Parson's Tale* by implicitly or explicitly expressing a quite reasonable different view of a decent life and social norms. Even the international popular comic tales imply, by the laughter caused by the infringement they describe, the sensible rules of quite a good society. One kind of writing is comic and fantastic, the other serious and devout, but neither sermon nor comic tale can be a *total* statement of a world-view, even if *The Parson's Tale* implicitly claims to be.

Its nature, with the inevitable (for this type of work) emphasis on sin does in fact make it quite a wide-ranging survey of much ordinary human behaviour. There are therefore a number of echoes of remarks made or things done in other tales, but it is not a commentary on the tales as such. It represents the common moral baseline of the culture which all tales start from but it cannot be comprehensive, and being ecclesiastical it inevitably omits secular or even scholastic modifications of absolute injunctions. Nevertheless, it provides important insights, and even gives us glimpses of the social world of the times.

The claim by *The Parson's Tale* to absolute assent need not worry us because no one need now take literally the devotional injunctions of six hundred years ago, when social and intellectual conditions were so different. For *us* the tale must be a kind of fiction, because the passage of time turns all documentation, even lists of stores, into fictions. On the other hand, it would be grossly anachronistic to believe that this strenuously devout work was in any way consciously fictional, or ironical, or not serious, to Chaucer. We must not confuse our fictions with his, or allow modern abstruse speculation about the nature of reality to confuse a perfectly clear literary-historical situation. The works of Chaucer, so multiple in point of view, conducted on so many fictional levels, are powerfully attractive to speculations about the nature of fictions, of the relation between word and deed, of teller to tale. Such speculations should not wantonly obscure the broad historical truths about which there cannot be reasonable doubt. One of these truths is that such a devotional work as *The Parson's Tale* was serious and literal in intention. There is no question of a Narrator, stupid, ironical, anti-Christian, or even Christian. Nor is the *persona* of the writer important here. He is virtually invisible – simply the accepted producer of the text on which we focus all our attention without regard for the speaker. There is equally no sensible doubt that the *Retractation*, in which Chaucer 'revokes' all his secular works, is serious, literally meant, by Chaucer the man. We shall return later to it.

First, we may here, almost at their end, cast an eye back over *The Canterbury Tales* as a whole. Their protean variety defies summary: they have to be seen as a Gothic miscellany. The dominant impression is of liveliness. The fundamental image of pilgrimage is one of movement, opening horizons, changing forms. The portraits of *The General Prologue*, both traditional yet broken into new possibilities, reflecting both ideal and real people, are characteristic of the whole. And the place the poet gives himself in *The General Prologue* is equally representative. He is perfectly at home even in that place of transience, an inn. He is familiar with all classes, friendly to all, in no sense a rebel or an Outsider. Yet a part also of him is withdrawn, as an observer outside the group, a little aside. He is not Knight, Clerk, Parson nor Ploughman. He alone of all the pilgrims is of undescribed status and has no function, no work, attributed to him. Yet he is there, partly inside; not only as an invisible omniscient author but part of his own subject-matter. He occupies socially and artistically a perfectly secure but marginal, exploratory, even transitional position. Transition is often that brief period when experience is most intense, when we are momentarily conscious of two states of being, related yet different, between which we move, conscious of both states, appreciative of both, as we cannot be when we are firmly ensconced in the one or the other. This transitional quality may well be as much inherent in everyone's experience as is that other different experience, of the archaic timeless moment, of intense peacefulness and rest, which we often imagine in the past or in the future, and so rarely, if ever, experience in the present. Chaucer sought such archaic stability of felicity in Boethius. He did not find it at the end of his early poems, and only doubtfully at the end of *Troilus*. He may have found it at the end of *The Canterbury Tales* and of his life, but if so it was only by rejecting that peculiarly transitional, ambivalent willingness to be in two worlds at once, to accept both of two apparently incompatible points of view, which is the source of so much of his liveliness and his humour.

Moments or periods of transition are peculiarly intense experiences. To explore them is one of the underlying motifs of Chaucer's poetry. It is one of the sources of his resistance to, or reluctance for, closure, in his earlier poems. We have noted too in them, that while there is a readiness to go to the edges of worldly experience, there is also a certain caution about going beyond. Even Chaucer's religious poetry is a poetry of this world, of faith as ethics, like his prose, not a poetry or prose of mysticism. His interest in the stars is a modern, astronomical interest. He does not wish to be 'stellified', or go beyond the stars, though he accepts on faith that there is such a country beyond the stars. His thisworldliness is part of his modernity and charm. Towards the end of his life there seems more willingness to accept limitation, and in his work to accept closure. In the comic bawdy tales there is as it were a line drawn firmly round the action and the people, despite their comic relationship to everyday life, and their apparent realism. There is inherent in their nature a strict limitation of sympathy, a refusal to explore consequences, a necessary disregard of effect and affect, on which the comedy depends. Comedy may be subversive, even 'carnivalesque' on occasion, but too careful consideration of its implications may check our laughter if laughter is the primary consideration. Laughter's true place is as an adjunct, which is why it may accompany death, and why satire needs an independent target. Serious subjects too may admit, or demand, closure, and that is one reason why the *Retractation* sounds an apparently final note. But even that may require some qualification from the nature of Chaucer's, and not only Chaucer's, culture and nature as we shall see.

It remains to survey briefly his later years, and a few of the shorter poems, some of which express that more settled view of life, for which Boethius and much Christian teaching strove.

NOTES

1. Derek Brewer (ed.) *Medieval Comic Tales* (Cambridge, 1996).
2. A. Aarne and S. Thompson, *The Types of the Folktale* (Helsinki, 1961), Tale Type 178A.
3. The most convenient collection is still *Manners and Meals of Ancient Times*, edited by F. J. Furnivall, *Early English Text Society* 32 (1888). For general discussion of such 'courtesy books' see J. W. Nicholls, *The Matter of Courtesy: Medieval Courtesy Books and the* Gawain-*poet* (Cambridge, 1985).
4. *The Poetical Words of William Wordsworth*, edited by E. de Selincourt and Helen Darbyshire (Oxford, 1947), IV, 471.

Chapter 24

Closure and Beyond

The outlines of Chaucer's career after 1386 can be clearly traced. Much the same pattern of courtiership and public service as before is repeated.

Having lived in Kent since 1385 and been free from office since 1386, he presumably devoted himself to his writing and to his duties as Justice of the Peace. Doubtless the exercise of such duties further enriched his knowledge of men. He did not enjoy or endure a stationary tranquillity for long, for in July 1387 he was granted protection for a year to go to Calais in the retinue of Sir William Beauchamp, although as his name does not appear on the list of Sir William's Controller it is not certain that Chaucer went, or if he went, how long he stayed. Also in 1387 the payments to his wife ceased, and it is probable that she died in that year. Perhaps the loss of her annuity caused Chaucer to live beyond his income, for he began to be sued for debt in April 1388, and sold his crown pension for a lump sum about the same time. Other matters made the first half of 1388 unpleasant. The 'Merciless Parliament', controlled by the barons hostile to the court and Lancastrian factions, sat from 3 February to 4 June 1388, and pursued the leaders of the court party with relentless hostility. Sir Nicholas Brembre, formerly Lord Mayor and one of Chaucer's colleagues as a Collector of Customs, who was leader of the Victualling guilds and the most important leader of the court party in the City, was tried, found guilty and executed in February in a barefaced travesty of justice not to be condoned by his own violent and unscrupulous character. Thomas Usk, Chaucer's admirer and also a member of the court party, was executed early in March. After a long and bitter struggle, Sir Simon Burley, the principal leader of the court party and one of Richard's tutors, was condemned and executed on 5 May. Richard risked his very throne in his opposition to Burley's fate; his queen is said to have gone on her knees to Richard's uncle, the surly and quarrelsome Duke of Gloucester, to save him; but to no avail. With him perished three other knights of his party. Truly, 'the wrastling for this world axeth a fal', as Chaucer writes in the poem *Trouthe,* with its envoy to his friend, Philip Vache.

Burley's death seems to have slaked the Merciless Parliament's desire for blood, and the tension of hostility relaxed. Richard had no choice but to lie low and make friends. A year later, in May 1389, Richard made a dramatic gesture of self-assertion, and after ridding himself of some of his main enemies began to appoint some of his own nominees. Chaucer was small fry, but it may be that he owed his next official post to Richard's new ascendancy. On 12 July 1389 he was appointed to the responsible position of Clerk of the King's Works. Since Gaunt was not in the country until October of this year, it cannot be to his influence that Chaucer owed the appointment. As with his position at the Customs, the clerkship was not a sinecure, a reward for mere courtiership. He had general responsibility for repairing and maintaining the Tower, Westminster Palace and other royal buildings, and was granted wide powers to obtain materials, control expenditure and in some cases to impress workmen. In 1390 he was given a special assignment to erect scaffolding for the jousts at Smithfield, and another for repairs to Saint George's Chapel, Windsor. In the same year he served on a commission led by Sir Richard Sturry (another of the court party and one of those friends who favoured Lollardry). The commission's task was to survey the walls, ditches, bridges and sewers along the Thames between Greenwich and Woolwich. In September 1390 Chaucer was robbed no less than three times in four days. On one of these occasions he was assaulted and beaten, and seems to have lost 20 pounds of the king's money, with some of his own.

This is evidence that he had real work to do, being in charge of the king's money, the loss of which he was excused. He gave up the Clerkship eight months later, on 17 June 1391, probably because of his appointment, made before 22 June 1391, as subforester of the king's park in North Petherton, Somersetshire. He was apparently appointed by Sir Peter Courtenay, who was Constable of Windsor Castle while Chaucer was in charge of the repairs to Saint George's Chapel. (Sir Peter Courtenay seems also to have been a knight agreeable to the king.) So far as is known Chaucer retained this office to the end of his life, and it was obviously less arduous than the Clerkship of Works. Its value is unknown.

Whatever travelling was required by the subforestership, Chaucer retained his dwelling at Greenwich, which may be the 'solytarie wildernesse' of which he complains in the *Envoy to Scogan.* His favour remained strong at court and he received in January 1393 a gift of ten pounds for good service; in February 1394 an annuity of 20 pounds; and in December 1397 the grant of a butt of wine yearly. During these years he often borrowed small sums of money in advance from the Exchequer, and in 1398 was sued for debt, though this was an action probably arising out of transactions during his clerkship, since he was sued by the widow of one of his former subordinates. His favour at court again stood him in good stead, and he was able to obtain letters of protection against this suit for two years. We do not know the outcome of the affair. The chances are that he was not poor, though he may have lacked ready money at times. The dilatory methods of the Exchequer (often badly in arrears with payments) and the general shortage of currency in the fourteenth century could easily account for small borrowings.

During these later years Chaucer seems also to have established firmer relationships with John of Gaunt's son, Henry, Earl of Derby, and afterwards Henry IV. At Christmas 1395 and in February 1396 Chaucer delivered ten pounds to Henry, and received a valuable scarlet robe, trimmed with fur, as a gift. No one at this time thought of Henry as future king. Chaucer had always been associated with the Lancastrian faction, especially through his wife, although his main associates and interests seem to have lain with the court party. Moreover, Gaunt had been much out of the country in the past few years. Now Gaunt had returned, and although Henry had been associated (in the absence of his father) with the baronial party in the year of the Merciless Parliament, he seems, by virtue of his Lancastrian affiliation, to have become by 1396 a member of the new court party in which his father was active. To be loyal to Henry was not yet to be disloyal to Richard. Chaucer's friends, Scogan and Bukton (if the latter was Sir Peter Bukton from the Holderness mentioned in *The Summoner's Tale*), were also close adherents of Henry of Derby. Two other friends of Chaucer similarly had a footing in both court and Lancastrian factions: Sir Lewis Clifford, who brought Deschamps' poem in praise of Chaucer from France; and Sir John Clanvowe, the probable author of the Chaucerian poem *Cuckoo and Nightingale* and the prose tract, *The Two Ways*. Both these were distinguished men and favoured the Lollards.

Apart from such of the *Canterbury Tales* as were written in this last decade of the century and of Chaucer's life, there are some minor poems which may belong here. They make a mixed bag. *Trouthe, Gentilesse, The Former Age, Lak of Stedfastnesse, Fortune*, all express in varying degrees a keen sense of 'This wrecched worldes transmutacioun', with its corollary that

No man is wrecched, but himself it wene,
And he that hath himself hath suffisaunce.

(*Fortune*, 25–6)

The power of mind, the need for self-sufficiency, for internalised
values, are again emphasised. *The Former Age* praises the archaic past,
expressing a longing for peace and calm, finishing

Allas, allas! now may men wepe and crye!
For in oure dayes nis but covetyse,
Doublenesse, and tresoun, and envye,
Poyson, manslawhtre, and mordre in sondry wyse.

(60–3)

The strain of contemplating the actual world is always severe, but
these poems emphasise evil rather than joy. They have none of the
readiness of earlier works to see the good, and to hold good and
evil together. But they are beautiful and moving poems with many
memorable lines.

There are also two humorous poems to younger friends, Scogan
and Bukton. To Bukton, perhaps on the occasion of his marriage,
Chaucer writes mockingly of marriage, bidding him 'read the Wife
of Bath'. In the *Envoy to Scogan* he asks in pretended dismay:

Hastow not seyd, in blaspheme of the goddes,
Thurgh pride, or thrugh thy grete rekelnesse,   *rashness*
Swich thing as in the lawe of love forbode is,
That, for thy lady sawgh nat thy distresse,   *because*
Therfore thow yave hir up at Michelmesse?

(15–19)

He gravely reproaches him, for the god of love may extend his
displeasure with Scogan to include those who are 'hoary-headed and
round of shape'; once more the image of the portly Chaucer arises
before us, now grey-headed. He makes an interesting reference to
his poetry

That rusteth in my shethe stille in pees.
While I was yong, I put hir forth in prees;   *thrust her eagerly forward*
But al shal passe that men prose or ryme.

(39–41)

There is a note of melancholy here, but it is followed by a reference
to his distance from the head of the stream of grace and honour and

worthiness, by which he presumably means the king's court. He says he lives in 'solitary wilderness', 'as dull as death', and desires Scogan to keep him remembered 'where it may fructify' – perhaps in the mind of the king, or of Gaunt, or of Gaunt's son.

The handful of short poems of this period includes also the delightfully witty *Merciles Beaute*, in which Chaucer commits with exquisite skill the very 'crime' of which he had accused Scogan. After praising the beauty of his lady, and complaining in the usual terms that her lack of pity will be his death, he concludes:

Love hath my name ystrike out of his sclat	*slate*
And he is strike out of my bokes clene	
For evermo; ther is non other mene.	*way*
Sin I fro Love escaped am so fat,	*since*
I never thenk to ben his prison lene;	*prisoner*
Sin I am free, I counte him not a bene.	*not worth a bean*
	(34–9)

This shows an agreeably carefree spirit in age. The requests in *Scogan* and *Fortune* may suggest that by this time Chaucer's active life as a 'working courtier', so to speak, was over. No such poetical requests for favour have survived from his earlier, more active years. It may be that the favours he undoubtedly received are to be associated with these poems.

Towards the end of the decade King Richard became more and more unpopular, while divisions increased within the court party. The most famous of these quarrels was that between Gaunt's son, Henry, and the Duke of Norfolk, which in 1398 culminated in the abortive trial by combat at Coventry and the exile of both. John of Gaunt died in February 1399, and Richard, who was badly in need of money, confiscated the whole of the huge Lancastrian inheritance. This confiscation, combined with many other acts of extortion and despotism, thoroughly alarmed everybody. When Richard set sail for Ireland in May 1399, complete with minstrels and crown jewels, to crush the Irish revolt, he left behind him his own country ripe for rebellion. When the new Duke of Lancaster arrived in England to claim his rights such numbers of Richard's discontented subjects hastened to join Henry that many had to be sent home again for lack of food. Even Henry's eventual seizure of the Crown did not destroy his popularity.

In the last five years Richard had completely alienated the affections of his subjects from the great lords to the London rabble, and many of his most loyal and efficient officers stayed on to serve his successor equally loyally and efficiently. It must have been a relief to serve a king more capable and less capricious than Richard, while Henry's claim to be the true successor of Henry III together with the façade of legalism of Richard's deposition were a sufficient sop to the conscience of most. There can be little doubt, too, that Henry's might helped to confirm whatever seemed shaky in his right. Richard's cause attracted few martyrs, and the Revolution was achieved with remarkably little fuss and bloodshed. Henry IV was received as king by Parliament on 30 September 1399, being in the official terms which Chaucer repeats,

> conquerour of Brutes Albyon,
> Which that by lyne and free eleccion
> Been verray kyng.

Chaucer, an old man as the times went, and with a lifelong association with the House of Lancaster, acquiesced in the change, as did many a 'civil servant' and courtier at the middle to higher levels of courtly society. He addressed the lines just quoted to the new king in a poem entitled *The Complaint of Chaucer to his Purse*, a graceful punning request for reward as witty as anything he ever wrote. There was nothing servile or unusual in such a poem by a court poet, and doubtless other courtiers, less talented, were accustomed to make similar requests in plain prose. As noted much earlier in this book, such demands were part of the system by which a great man or a king obtained and paid for the services of the retinue which was as necessary to him as he was to his dependants. Henry IV was careful to obtain support wherever he could, and was as inclined to foster the arts as Richard had been. It is pleasant to record that he speedily granted Chaucer an annuity of 40 marks on 19 October and a few days later confirmed Chaucer's former grants from Richard. The ostensible reason for this confirmation was that the earlier letters patent from Richard had accidentally been lost, but maybe as a practised courtier Chaucer felt it would be no bad thing, while Henry was in a giving mood, to have new letters under the new seal.

In December 1399 Chaucer took a lease of a house in the garden of Westminster Abbey. His last recorded payment from the Exchequer was on 5 June 1400, and on 25 October 1400, according to the inscription formerly on his tomb, he died. He was buried in the Abbey. This may have indicated that he was held in special honour by the king, for the Abbey was primarily a burial place of royalty.

(The first commoner to be buried in the Abbey was John Waltham, Richard's Treasurer and Bishop of Salisbury, who had died as recently as 1395. This signal honour was paid to him as a mark of Richard's special regard, and many people had objected.) Unfortunately the chronicler Walsingham, who tells us about Waltham, does not notice Chaucer's death, so we do not know what people thought. But it is certain that for some years Chaucer had been recognised in both the English and French courts as the great poet of England.

The final honour (if such it be) of his burial gives a greater, indeed an ironic interest, to the last chapter of all his writing, the *Retractation*. This short passage of prose comes at the end of the *Tales*, but refers to the whole of his life's work, and in it he asks mercy and forgiveness of Christ for just those 'translations and indictings of worldly vanities' which had earned him fame. He revokes them in some detail – *Troilus and Criseyde*, *The House of Fame*, *The Legend of Good Women*, *The Book of the Duchess*, *The Parliament*, *The Book of the Lion* (now lost), those *Canterbury Tales* which tend towards sin, 'and many a song and many a leccherous lay'. He gives thanks for his translation of the *Consolation*, saints' legends, homilies and other books of morality and devotion.

There seemed something morbid to the earlier critics about this wholesale and as we feel unnecessary denunciation of the secular works, and some scholars are still reluctant to accept it as the intended conclusion of *The Canterbury Tales*. It appears in 28 of the 55 complete manuscripts including Ellesmere (Hengwrt has suffered physical loss of the final pages so is not a witness either way) and there is no reasonable doubt of its authenticity. After the repudiation, or rather, 'withdrawal' (retraction) of the secular works – Chaucer does not deny responsibility, quite the reverse – he concludes with a prayer to Christ and his Mother to send him grace to bewail his guilty deeds and to 'graunte me grace of verray penitence, confessioun and satisfaccioun to doon in this present lyf' (X, 1087–90). The prayer fits absolutely with the tone and message of *The Parson's Tale* of penitence, and transcends, as *The Parson's Prologue* has already suggested should happen, the worldly details of the pilgrimage, transforming them into the aim to reach that other city of which Canterbury is but a shadow, the heavenly Jerusalem.

The Retractation derives from that strand of extreme otherworldliness in traditional Christian culture which goes back as far as the epistles then attributed to St Paul. The Epistle to the Ephesians condemns 'corrupt communications' (IV, 29), 'filthiness, [and] foolish talking [and] jesting, which are not convenient' (V, 4), while the Epistle to

Timothy condemns 'profane and old wives' fables' (IV, 7). Chaucer knew his Bible well, though he read it in Latin, and these quotations are from the King James Version of 1611.[1] The importance of this ascetic strand in the complex tapestry of Chaucer's life and works cannot be denied, but should not be exaggerated. The condemnation is not part of the Gospels, and goes against much natural human conduct. Yet both its modicum of good sense and its ascetic severity are an important part of Chaucer's dualistic culture. It was always part of his mind. Among the Parson's pretty comprehensive list of venial, i.e. minor and pardonable, though dangerous, sins are included being a talker of idle words or 'vileynye' (X, 375), and he makes a passing contemptuous reference to a 'jape or tale' (X, 1020–5). No man (nor woman neither) can avoid such sins, but they have to be repented of, and so Chaucer does. His repentance is not neurotic but part of that decent, ethical, practical, narrowly puritanical vein in medieval Christianity which *The Parson's Tale* so extensively represents. Its very narrowness could through those same doctrines of penitence so remorselessly urged upon us accommodate human inconsistencies of behaviour, and even make them (once repented of) acceptable.

In *The Retractation* Chaucer abandons all his roles except that of a sincere writer or translator of religious works in English. He is still a writer, his most enduring role.

That very well-known medieval schoolbook, *The Distichs of Cato*, has an aphorism to the effect that the end seldom accords with the beginning (i. 18).[2] We might bear that in mind thinking of *Troilus and Criseyde* and of *The Retractation* as at the end of *The Canterbury Tales*. It is not worth while straining too hard to prove logical consistency and artistic organic unity in Chaucer's works, because they do not always exist.

Yet *The Retractation* is in many respects a fitting close to *The Canterbury Tales*. From the purely narrative point of view it provides a surprise for which, we can now see by hindsight, as in the *dénoument* of a detective story (the archetype of plots) some clues have previously been given, both in Chaucer's life and works, and in the sections of *The Tales* immediately preceding *The Retractation*. It has strong verbal and psychological links with *The Parson's Tale* and *The Manciple's Tale*. Within the structure of the pilgrimage it is much better, though less realistic, than what could only have been the anticlimax of a 'soper at oure aller coste' (I, 799). How could Chaucer, of all poets, with his *blasé* courtier's disdain even for a 'kynges feeste', have represented with any effectiveness the much more humble

supper of this motley band of pilgrims in an inn? In a wider sense
The Retractation reaches a conclusion that allows *The Canterbury Tales*
to image the curve of a whole life, as so much narrative does (above,
p. 101). It represents an end to a lifelong quest, a kind of death. But
that death was not for Chaucer a final end, a snuffing out of a
pointless life, as it must be for so many modern readers. It represents
a closure in this world, but a firm hope, by its very nature as
assertion with repentance, of continuing what has always been, if not
always recognised as such, the ultimate end of all the seeking, ques-
tions, questioning; the heavenly Jerusalem, where all things shall be
made plain in glory, an ultimate closure that also means eternal life.

> Repeyreth hom fro worldly vanyte
> And of youre herte up casteth the visage
> To thilke God that after his ymage
> Yow made; and thynketh al nys but a faire
> This world, that passeth soon as floures faire.
>
> (*Troilus*, V, 1837–41)

Chaucer knew, as in his late poem to his friend, Henry Scogan, that

> Al shal passe that men prose or ryme.
> Take every man his turn as for his tyme.
>
> (*Scogan*, 41–2)

Chaucer has had his turn and takes his leave, his immortality lying
not in his works, even the religious ones, but elsewhere, in himself.
He may say, with Criseyde,

> But al shal passe; and thus take I my leve.
>
> (*Troilus*, V, 1084)

He goes without repining, if not without repentance, because, as
Theseus so grandly says,

> What maketh this but Juppiter the kyng,
> That is prince and cause of alle thyng?
>
> (*The Knight's Tale*, *CT*, I, 3035–6)

There we may leave Chaucer's works, to renew themselves and their
readers for some time yet to come, before all shall pass away. Both
their remoteness and their immediacy make their appeal. To read
them is always to embark on a new voyage of discovery, where

among other strange things we may discover ourselves within a
certain community of spirit, that allows that 'diverse men and women,
diversely they speak', while excluding the ignorant – 'They demen
gladly to the badder ende' (*The Squire's Tale, CT,* V, 223).

It would be pointless after so long a book to attempt to summar-
ise the greatness and diversity of Chaucer's work. It is the supreme
example of the Gothic spirit in English literature, even in European
literature. Despite the variety, even the inconsistencies, there is every-
where in his poetry and in his non-scientific prose the imprint of
his mind, recognisable if ultimately indefinable. Part of its uniqueness
is the balance between the spoken and the written word. Chaucer's
poetry is as it were a script for himself, more than the poetry of any
other poet, even where, as great artists, they put their own stamp on
what they have produced.

When we 'read Chaucer', that expression takes on more meaning
than the normally convenient brief designation of a particular body
of writing. We ourselves have to act out in our imaginations his own
script. It is we, as readers, who hold or do not hold together the dis-
parate points of view we allow ourselves to entertain. It is we who
imitate the reading poet-in-his-audience, who project our ironies,
to take responsibility for all the various things that may be said, or
hinted, or even thought. In a curious way this highly dramatic and
least egotistical or assertive of writers sucks us up more completely
into his own world than any such varied monsters of egotism as
Donne or Milton or Wordsworth. And yet we are still the audience,
too. Thus, we are made to embody multiple points of view, bound
together in unity of story, story-teller, audience. As he says when
all is ready for Criseyde to come to Pandarus's house:

Us lakketh nought but that we witen wolde	*We lack nothing; know*
A certeyn houre, in which *she* comen sholde.	

(III, 531–2)

We are all joined together in the reading, under the eager guidance
of Chaucer the Expositor, who shares, yet manipulates our feelings.
How far is this Master of Ceremonies himself or an actor? The
degree of acting varies during the course of his works, and some-
times he speaks more in his own voice, and with one voice, than at
others. The uncertainty is part of the interest, and as we have seen,
readers' opinions may differ.

Chaucer's family continued and prospered in the fifteenth
century. His son, Thomas, who had received favours from Richard,

continued to receive them from Henry throughout a distinguished career. He married about 1394–5 and his daughter eventually became Countess of Suffolk.

Chaucer's poetic reputation also flourished. In the middle of the sixteenth century it was even fashionable for courtiers to 'talk Chaucer'. Only about the eighteenth century did he become thought of as predominantly a comic, even a ribald poet. Throughout the nineteenth century his works continued to attract the attention of men and women of general education and interests.

At the end of the twentieth century we have seen an unprecedented flourishing of scholarly and critical interest, not only in Britain, nor only in the United States of America, where the lead in Chaucer studies has been firmly established in the second half of this century, but also notably in Japan, and wherever in the world there has been an interest in English historical literature and culture. We are today on the brink of further developments in the form of versions, more or less faithful, created for other media than the spoken or printed word. Such rewriting, even when grotesquely alien in spirit from what Chaucer wrote, is nevertheless fully in the medieval, even Chaucer's, tradition, though his aim was never to coarsen or degrade. It is also possible to hear Chaucer's works spoken, recorded in their original pronunciation. The survival of great historical works of art enriches all who care to take advantage of their availability. Surely Chaucer would have been pleased.

NOTES

1. Derek Brewer, 'Chaucer and the Bible' in *Philologia Anglica*, edited by K. Oshitari *et al.* (Tokyo, 1988), 270–84.
2. Quoted in *Sir Gawain and the Green Knight*, edited by T. Silverstein (Chicago, 1984), l. 499.

Select Bibliography

There are a number of specialist bibliographical studies of work on Chaucer which are not recorded here but which are invaluable for research. *A Variorum Edition of the Works of Geoffrey Chaucer*, General Editor, Paul G. Ruggiers, Norman, Oklahoma, has been in process for many years, 'vaster than empires and more slow', and the individual volumes, covering separate works, including separate Canterbury Tales, are notably helpful. Journals devoted mainly to Chaucer appear regularly: *The Chaucer Review*, published by The Pennsylvania State University Press, quarterly, 1975– ; *Studies in the Age of Chaucer*, published annually for the New Chaucer Society, currently by The Ohio State University, Columbus, 1978– ; *The Chaucer Yearbook*, published by Boydell and Brewer, 1997– . The Chaucer Bibliographies is an important ongoing series, General Editor T. Hahn, published by Toronto University Press covering substantial sections of Chaucer's work. More general surveys of studies in English literature contain sections on Chaucer. Further bibliographical information will be found in many of the works cited below and in a number of selective bibliographies. What follows is a highly selective list covering the major aspects of Chaucer's work, ranging from some books of general significance that have been referred to in the course of this book to specialist articles that have also been referred to. Within the sub-sections below there are inevitably some overlaps which have been ignored. In some cases one entry has had to stand for a number of books which might have been cited. Many valuable studies have had to be omitted from the following basic list.

Place of publication is London or New York except where otherwise indicated.

BIOGRAPHY

Brewer, Derek (1978) *Chaucer and his World*, reprinted 1992, Cambridge.
Crow, M. M. and Olson, C. C. (1966) *Chaucer Life-Records*, Oxford.
Howard, Donald R. (1987) *Chaucer and the Medieval World*.
Pearsall, Derek (1992) *The Life of Geoffrey Chaucer: A Critical Biography*, Oxford.

EDITIONS

The Canterbury Tales (1958, revised 1990) edited by A. Cawley (Everyman Library). With Introduction and glosses on page. A new edition is in process.

The Equatorie of the Planetis (1959) edited by D. J. Price.

The Parlement of Fowlys (1976) edited by Derek Brewer, Manchester.

The Riverside Chaucer (1988) edited by Larry D. Benson, Oxford.

The Book of the Duchess (1997) edited by Helen Phillips, 3rd edn, Durham Medieval Texts.

The House of Fame (1994) edited by Nicholas Havely, Durham Medieval Texts.

The Legend of Good Women (1995) edited by Janet Cowan and George Kane, East Lansing, Michigan, and Woodbridge.

BIBLIOGRAPHIES

Benson, Larry D. (1974) 'A Reader's Guide to the Writings of Chaucer', in Brewer, Derek (ed.) *Geoffrey Chaucer* (Writers and their Backgrounds), reprinted 1990, Cambridge.

Crawford, W. R. (1967) *Bibliography of Chaucer 1954–63*, Washington.

Griffith, D. D. (1955) *Bibliography of Chaucer 1908–1953*, Washington.

Hammond, Eleanor P. (1908) *Chaucer: a Bibliographical Manual*, reprinted Gloucester, Mass., 1933.

Leyerle, John and Quick, Anne (1986) *Chaucer: a Bibliographical Introduction*, Toronto, Buffalo, and London.

Lorrayne, Y., Baird-Lange and Schnuttgen, Hildegard (1988) *A Bibliography of Chaucer, 1974–1985*, Hamden, Conn., and Cambridge.

Magoun, F. P. Jr. (1961) *A Chaucer Gazetteer*, Chicago.

CONCORDANCES

A New Rime Index to The Canterbury Tales (1988) edited by M. Masui, Tokyo.

Benson, Larry D. (ed.) (1993) *A Glossarial Concordance to the Riverside Chaucer*, 2 vols.

Tatlock, J. S. P. and Kennedy, A. G. (1927) *Concordance to the Complete Works of Chaucer*, reprinted Gloucester, Mass., 1963.

DICTIONARY AND DISCOGRAPHY

A Chaucer Glossary (1979) complied by N. Davis, D. Gray, P. Ingham and A. Wallace-Hadrill, Oxford.

Bowden, Betsy (1988) *Listeners' Guide to Medieval English*.

FACSIMILES

Works   *Geoffrey Chaucer The Works 1532: with Supplementary Material from the Editions of 1542, 1561, 1598 and 1602* (1969) edited by Derek Brewer, Menston.
Cambridge University Library MS Gg.4.27. (1980) edited by M. B. Parkes and R. Beadle, Cambridge.

Boece   *Boecius De Consolacione Philosophie, Translated by G. Chaucer* (1974) Amsterdam.

Earlier poems   *Bodleian Library MS Fairfax 16* (1979) edited by J. Norton Smith.
Manuscript Tanner 346: Bodleian Library Oxford University (1980) edited by Pamela Robinson, Norman and Cambridge.
Manuscript Pepys 2006: Magdalene College Cambridge (1985) edited by A. S. G. Edwards, Norman and Cambridge (earlier poems and some separate Canterbury Tales).
Bodley 638, Bodleian Library, Oxford (1982) edited by P. Robinson, Norman and Cambridge.

Ellesmere   *The Ellesmere Chaucer* (1911) Manchester.
The Ellesmere Manuscript: Chaucer's Canterbury Tales: A Working Facsimile (1989) Introduction by Ralph Hanna III, Cambridge.
The New Ellesmere Chaucer Facsimile (1995) edited by Daniel Woodward and Martin Stevens, Tokyo and San Marino.

Hengwrt   *The Canterbury Tales: A Facsimile and Transcription of the Hengwrt Manuscript with Variants from the Ellesmere Manuscript* (1979) edited by Paul G. Ruggiers, Norman and Folkestone.

Troilus   *Troilus and Criseyde: Geoffrey Chaucer. A Facsimile of Corpus Christi College Cambridge MS 61* (1978) edited by M. B. Parkes and Elizabeth Salter, Cambridge.
St John's College Cambridge LI (1983) Introduction by R. Beadle and J. Griffiths, Norman, and Cambridge (*Troilus and Criseyde*)
Morgan 817 (Olim Campsall) Pierpont Morgan Library (1986) edited by Jeanne Krochalis, Norman (*Troilus and Criseyde*)

SOME GENERAL STUDIES

Bakhtin, M. (1979) *Estetika slovesnogo tvorchestva (The Aesthetics of Verbal Creation)*, Moscow.

Bakhtin, M. (1996) *Rabelais and his World*, translated by Helen Iswolsky, Cambridge, Mass. and London.

Brewer, Derek (1980) *Symbolic Stories*, Cambridge, reprinted 1988.

Brooks, Peter (1995) *Reading for the Plot: Design and Intention in Narrative*.

Cooper, Kate (1996) *The Virgin and the Bride: Idealized Womanhood in Late Antiquity*, Cambridge, Mass.

Douglas, Mary (1966) *Purity and Danger: an Analysis of Concepts of Pollution and Taboo.*

Duby, G. (1980) *The Three Orders: Feudal Society Imagined,* translated by Arthur Goldhammer, Chicago and London.

Gellner, E. (1988) *Plough, Sword and Book: The Structure of Human History.*

Gellner, E. (1994) *Conditions of Liberty: Civil Society and its Rivals.*

Gorer, Geoffrey (1965) *Death, Grief and Mourning in Contemporary Britain.*

Gurevich, Aaron (1992) *Historical Anthropology of the Middle Ages,* edited by Jana Howlett, Cambridge.

MacQueen, J. (1985) *Numerology: Theory and Outline History of a Literary Mode,* Edinburgh.

Mauss, M. (1954) *The Gift,* translated by Ian Cunnison.

Miller, William Ian (1993) *Humiliation,* Chicago.

Taylor, Charles (1989) *Sources of the Self: the Making of the Modern Identity,* Cambridge.

HISTORICAL AND CULTURAL STUDIES

Aers, David and Staley, Lynn (1996) *The Powers of the Holy: Religion, Politics and Gender in Late Medieval Culture,* Pennsylvania.

Barber, Richard (1978) *Edward, Prince of Wales and Aquitaine,* Woodbridge.

Barber, Richard (1995) *The Knight and Chivalry,* Woodbridge and Rochester, N.Y., revised edn.

Barber, Richard and Barker, Juliet (1989) *Tournaments: Jousts, Chivalry and Pageants in the Middle Ages,* Woodbridge and Wolfeboro, N.H.

Barnie, John (1974) *War in Medieval Society.*

Brewer, Derek (1988) 'Chaucer and the Bible', in *Philologia Anglica: Essays presented to Professor Yoshio Terasawa on the Occasion of his Sixtieth Birthday,* edited by K. Oshitari *et al.,* Tokyo, 270–84.

Brewer, Derek (1989) 'Chaucer's Anti-Ricardian Poetry', in *The Living Middle Ages: A Festschrift for Karl Heinz Göller,* edited by V. Böker, M. Markus and R. Schöwerling, Stuttgart and Regensburg.

Brewer, Derek (1992) *Chaucer and his World,* 2nd edn, Cambridge.

Bumke, J. (1991) *Courtly Culture: Literature and Society in the High Middle Ages,* translated by T. Dunlap, Berkeley.

Burrow, John Anthony (1986) *The Ages of Man: A Study in Medieval Writing and Thought,* Oxford.

Chambers, R. W. (1924) 'Long Will, Dante and the Righteous Heathen', in *Essays and Studies* 9, 50–69.

Dickinson, J. C. (1979) *The Later Middle Ages* (An Ecclesiastical History of England).

Duffy, Eamon (*c.* 1992) *The Stripping of the Altars: Traditional Religion in England, c. 1400–c. 1580,* Yale.

English Court Culture in the Later Middle Ages (1983) edited by V. J. Scatterwood and J. W. Sherborne.

Given-Wilson, Chris and Curteis, Alice (1984) *The Royal Bastards*, London.

Green, Richard Firth (1980) *Poets and Princepleasers: Literature and the English Court in the Late Middle Ages*, Toronto and London.

Hornsby, John Allen (1988) *Chaucer and the Law*, Norman, Oklahoma.

Justice, S. (1994) *Writing and Rebellion in England in 1381*, Berkeley, Los Angeles and London.

Manly, J. M. (1926) *Some New Light on Chaucer*, reprinted Gloucester, Mass., 1959.

Manners and Meals of Ancient Times (1888) edited by F. J. Furnivall, *Early English Text Society* 32.

McFarlane, K. B. (1972) *Lancastrian Kings and Lollard Knights*, Oxford and New York.

McKisack, M. (1959) *The Fourteenth Century*, Oxford.

Nicholls, J. W. (1985) *The Matter of Courtesy: Medieval Courtesy Books and the Gawain-poet*, Cambridge.

North, J. D. (1988) *Chaucer's Universe*, Oxford.

Ormrod, W. M. (1989) 'The Personal Religion of Edward III', *Speculum* 64, 849–77.

Patterson, Lee (1990) *Literary Practice and Social Change in Britain 1380–1530*, Berkeley and Oxford.

Pollard, W. F. and Boenig, R. (1997) *Mysticism and Spirituality in Medieval England*, Cambridge.

Popular and Practical Science of Medieval England (1994) edited by Lister M. Matheson, East Lansing.

Rand-Schmidt, Kari-Anne (1993) *The Authorship of the Equatorie of the Planetis* (with facsimile) Cambridge.

Rickert, E. (1948) *Chaucer's World*, edited by C. C. Olson and M. M. Crow.

Rooney, Anne (1993) *Hunting in Middle English Literature*, Cambridge.

Russell, John *Boke of Nurture*, see *Manners and Meals*.

Smalley, Beryl (c. 1983) *The Study of the Bible in the Middle Ages*, 3rd edn, Oxford.

Strohm, Paul (1989) *Social Chaucer*, Cambridge, Mass. and London.

The Age of Chivalry (1987) edited by Jonathan Alexander and Paul Binski.

Thrupp, S. (1948) *The Merchant Class in Medieval London*, Ann Arbor and Toronto.

Varty, K. (1967) *Reynard the Fox*, Leicester.

Wack, Mary F. (1990) *Love-sickness in the Middle Ages*, Philadelphia.

Wilkins, Nigel (1996) *Music in the Age of Chaucer*, 2nd edn, Cambridge.

LITERARY HISTORY

Brewer, Derek (1983) *English Gothic Literature*.

Boitani, P. (1982) *English Medieval Narrative in the 13th and 14th Centuries*, Cambridge.

Burrow, J. A. (1982) *Medieval Writers and their Work*, Oxford.

Ford, Boris (ed.) (1983) *The Pelican Guide to Medieval English Literature*, Harmondsworth.
Pearsall, Derek (1977) *Old English and Middle English Poetry*.

SOME CONTEMPORARIES

Brewer, Elizabeth (1997) 'The Sources of *Sir Gawain and the Green Knight*', in *Companion to the* Gawain-*poet*, Cambridge, 243–55.
Burrow, J. A. (1971) *Ricardian Poetry*.
(*Gawain*-poet) *The Poems of the* Pearl *Manuscript* (1978) edited by M. Andrew and R. Waldron.
A Companion to the Gawain-*poet* (1997) edited by Derek Brewer and Jonathan Gibson, Cambridge.
Gilbert, Jane (1997) 'Gender and Sexual Transgression', in *Companion to the* Gawain-*poet*, Cambridge, 53–69.
Godden, M. (1990) *The Making of Piers Plowman*.
Gower, John (1900) *The English Works of John Gower*, edited by G. C. Macaulay, *Early English Text Society*, Extra Series, LXXXI–II, 2 vols.
Langland, William (1987) *The Vision of Piers Plowman. A Critical Edition of the B-text*, new edn., edited by A. V. C. Schmidt.
Langland, William (1995–) *A Parallel-text Edition of the A, B, C and Z Versions.*
Piers Plowman: An Edition of the C-Text (1978) edited by Derek Pearsall.
Sir Gawain and the Green Knight (1984) edited by T. Silverstein, Chicago.
Watson, Nicholas (1997) 'The *Gawain*-poet as a Vernacular Theologian', in *Companion to the* Gawain-*poet*, Cambridge, 293–313.
Wynnere and Wastoure (1991) edited by J. W. Conlee in *Middle English Debate Poetry*, East Lansing.
Yeager, R. F. (1990) *John Gower's Poetic*, Cambridge.

LANGUAGE AND METRE

Baugh, A. C. (1959) *A History of the English Language*, revised edn.
Baum, P. F. (1961) *Chaucer's Verse*, Durham, N. Carolina.
Brewer, Derek (1988) 'Orality and Literacy in Chaucer', in *Mündlichkeit und Schriftlichkeit im Englishen Mittelalter*, ScriptOralia 5, hrsg. W. Erzgraber und Sabine Volk, Tübingen, 85–120.
Burnley, J. D. (1980) *Chaucer's Language and the Philosopher's Tradition*, Cambridge.
Burnley, J. D. (1989) *The Language of Chaucer*.
Elliott, R. W. V. (1974) *Chaucer's English*.
Jones, Charles (1972) *An Introduction to Middle English*.
Kökeritz, H. (1962) *A Guide to Chaucer's Pronunciation*, Stockholm and New Haven, Conn.
Pinker, Steven (1994) *The Language Instinct*, Harmondsworth.
Roskow, G. (1981) *Syntax and Style in Chaucer's Poetry*, Cambridge.

Ten Brink, B. (1901) *The Language and Metre of Chaucer*, 2nd edn, revised by F. Kluge, translated by M. Bentinck Smith.

SOME GENERAL CHAUCER STUDIES

Acker, Paul (1994) 'The Emergence of an Arithmetical Mentality in Middle English Literature', *The Chaucer Review* 28, 293–303.

Aers, David (1980) *Chaucer, Langland and the Creative Imagination*.

Aers, David (1988) *Community, Gender and Individual Identity: English Writing 1360–1430*, London.

Boitani, Piero and Mann, Jill (1986) *The Cambridge Chaucer Companion*, Cambridge.

Brewer, Derek (1974) *Geoffrey Chaucer* (Writers and their Background), reprinted 1990, Cambridge.

Brewer, Derek (1982) *Tradition and Innovation in Chaucer*.

Brewer, Derek (1983) 'Arithmetic and the Mentality of Chaucer', in *Literature in Fourteenth-Century England*, edited by Piero Boitani and Anna Torti, Tübingen, 155–64.

Brewer, Derek (1984) *Chaucer: the Poet as Storyteller*.

Burrow, J. A. (1986) *The Ages of Man: A Study of Medieval Writing and Thought*, Oxford.

David, A. (1976) *The Strumpet Muse*, Berkeley and Los Angeles.

Donaldson, E. Talbot (1970) *Speaking of Chaucer*.

Ganim, John (1990) *Chaucerian Theatricality*, Princeton, N. J.

Grudin, Michaela O. (1996) *Chaucer and the Politics of Discourse*, Columbia, S. Carolina.

Howard, D. R. (1976) *The Idea of the Canterbury Tales*, Berkeley and Los Angeles.

Kean, P. M. (1972) *Chaucer and the Making of English Poetry*, 2 vols.

Kelly, Henry A. (1975) *Love and Marriage in Chaucer*, Ithaca.

Kelly, Henry A. (1997) *Chaucerian Tragedy*, Cambridge.

Kittredge, G. L. (1915) *Chaucer and his Poetry*, Cambridge, Mass.

Knapp, Peggy (1990) *Chaucer and the Social Contest*.

Koff, Leonard Michael (1988) *Chaucer and the Art of Storytelling*, Berkeley and Los Angeles.

Mann, J. (1973) *Chaucer and Medieval Estates Satire*, Cambridge.

Muscatine, C. (1957) *Chaucer and the French Tradition*, Berkeley and Los Angeles.

Patterson, Lee (1987) *Negotiating the Past: The Historical Understanding of Medieval Literature*, Madison, Wisconsin.

Patterson, Lee (1991) *Chaucer and the Subject of History*, Madison, Wisconsin.

Payne, Robert O. (1963) *The Key of Remembrance. A Study of Chaucer's Poetics*.

Robertson, D. W. Jr. (1962) *A Preface to Chaucer: Studies in Medieval Perspectives*, Princeton, N. J.

Rowland, Beryl (ed.) (1979) *Companion to Chaucer Studies*, revised edn, Oxford.

Spearing, A. C. (1972) *Criticism and Medieval Poetry*, revised edn.
Spearing, A. C. (1993) *The Medieval Poet as Voyeur*, Cambridge.

GENDER CRITICISM

Dinshaw, Carolyn (1989) *Chaucer's Sexual Poetics*, Madison, Wisconsin.
Ellmann, Maud (1984) 'Blanche' in *Criticism and Critical Theory*, edited by Jeremy Hawthorn, 99–110.
Hanson, Elaine Tuttle (1992) *Chaucer and the Fictions of Gender*, Berkeley, Los Angeles and Oxford.
Lama, Abu-Odeh, 'Crimes of Honour and the Construction of Gender in Arab Societies', in *Feminism in Islam* (1996), 141–93, edited by Mai Yamani, Ithaca.
Laskaya, Anne (1995) *Chaucer's Approach to Gender in* The Canterbury Tales, Cambridge.
Mann, Jill (1991) *Feminist Readings: Geoffrey Chaucer*.
Martin, Priscilla (1990) *Chaucer's Women*.
Masculinities in Chaucer (1998) edited by P. G. Beidler, Cambridge.
Medieval Masculinities: Regarding Men in the Middle Ages (1994) edited by Clare Lees, Minneapolis and London.

SOURCES AND ANALOGUES

Aarne, A. and Thompson, S. (1961) *The Types of the Folktale*, Helsinki.
Benson, Larry D. and Andersson, T. M. (eds. and trs.) (1971) *The Literary Context of Chaucer's Fabliaux*, Indianapolis.
Brewer, Derek (1996) (ed.) Introduction, *Medieval Comic Tales*, Cambridge.
Brewer, Derek (1997) 'Retellings' in *Retelling Tales*, 9–34, edited by T. Hahn and A. Lupack, Cambridge.
Bryan, W. R. and Dempster, G. (eds) (1941) *Sources and Analogues of Chaucer's Canterbury Tales* (reprinted 1958).
Havely, N. R. (1981) *Chaucer's Boccaccio*, Cambridge.
Hertog, Erik (1991) *Chaucer's Fabliaux as Analogues*, Leuven.
Lewis, C. S. (1964) *The Discarded Image*, Cambridge.
Miller, R. P. (ed.) (1977) *Chaucer Sources and Backgrounds*.
Minnis, Alastair (1982) *Chaucer and Pagan Antiquity*, Cambridge.
Spearing, A. C. (1976) *Medieval Dream Poetry*, Cambridge.
Teseida (1941) by G. Boccaccio, a cura di A. Roncaglia, Bari.
Wimsatt, J. I. (1982) *Chaucer and the Poems of 'Ch'*, Cambridge.
Windeatt, B. A. (1982) *Chaucer's Dream Poetry: Sources and Analogues*, Cambridge.

THE SHORTER POEMS

Benson, L. D. (1995) 'The Beginnings of Chaucer's English Style', in *Contradictions*, edited by T. M. Andersson and S. A. Barney.

Frank, R. W. (1972) *Chaucer and* The Legend of Good Women, Cambridge, Mass.

Hardman, Phillipa (1994) '*The Book of the Duchess* as a Memorial Monument', *The Chaucer Review* 28, 205–15.

Minnis, A. J., Scattergood, V. J. and Smith, J. J. (1995) *The Oxford Guides to Chaucer: The Shorter Poems*, Oxford.

Palmer, J. N. (1984) 'The Historical Context of *The Book of the Duchess*', *The Chaucer Review* 8, 253–61.

Salda, Michael Norman (1992) 'Pages from History: the Medieval Palace of Westminster as a Source for the Dreamer's Chamber in *The Book of the Duchess*', *The Chaucer Review* 27, 111–25.

Shippey, T. A. (1996) 'Chaucer's Arithmetic' *The Chaucer Review* 31, 184–200.

TROILUS AND CRISEYDE

Barney, Stephen A. (ed.) (1980) *Chaucer's* Troilus: *Essays in Criticism*.

Barney, Stephen A. (ed.) (1993) *Studies in* Troilus: *Chaucer's Text, Meter and Diction*, East Lansing.

Brewer, Derek (1990) 'The History of a Shady Character', in *Modes of Narrative: Presented to Helmut Bonheim*, edited R. M. Nischik and B. Korte, Wurzburg.

Brewer, Derek (1996) 'Some Aspects of the Post-War Reception of Chaucer: a Key passage, *Troilus* II, 666–79', in *Expedition nach der Wahrheit; Poems, Essays and Papers in Honour of Theo Stemmler*, hrsg. S. Horlacher und M. Islinger, Heidelberg, 513–24.

Brewer, Derek (1998) 'Troilus's "gentil" Manhood', in *Chaucer's Masculinites*, edited by P. Beidler, Cambridge.

Critical Essays on Chaucer's Troilus and Criseyde *and his Major Early Poems* (1991) edited by C. David Benson, Milton Keynes.

Essays on Troilus and Criseyde (1979) edited by Mary Salu, Cambridge.

Lewis, C. S. (1932) 'What Chaucer Really Did to *Il Filostrato*', *Essays and Studies* 17, 65–75; repr. in *Chaucer Criticism* (1961) edited by R. J. Schoek and J. Taylor, Notre Dame, Indiana, 16–33.

Mann, Jill (1980) 'Troilus's Swoon', *The Chaucer Review* 14, 319–35.

Muscatine, Charles (1948) 'The Feigned Illness in Chaucer's *Troilus and Criseyde*', *Modern Language Notes* 63, 372–7.

Salter, Elizabeth (1966) '*Troilus and Criseyde*: a reconsideration', *Patterns of Love and Courtesy*, edited by J. Lawlor, reprinted in Benson, C. D. (ed.) (1991) *Critical Essays on Chaucer's* Troilus and Criseyde *and his Major Early Poems*, Milton Keynes.

Shultz, James A. (1991) 'Medieval Adolescence: the Claims of History and the Silence of German Narrative', *Speculum* 66, 519–39.

The European Tragedy of Troilus (1989) edited by Piero Boitani, Oxford.

Wetherby, Winthrop (1984) *Chaucer and the Poets. An Essay on* Troilus and Criseyde, Ithaca and London.

Windeatt, Barry (1992) *Oxford Guides to Chaucer: Troilus and Criseyde*, Oxford.

THE CANTERBURY TALES

Benson, C. David (1986) *Chaucer's Drama of Style: Poetic Variety and Contrast in* The Canterbury Tales, Chapel Hill and London.
Bornstein, Diana (1977–8) 'Chaucer's *Tale of Melibee* as an Example of the *Style Clergial, The Chaucer Review* 12, 236–54.
Brewer, Derek (1955) 'Some Observations on a Fifteenth-Century Manuscript', *Anglia* Band 72, 390–9.
Brewer, Derek (1994) 'Chaucer's Knight as Hero, and Machaut's *Prise d'Alexandrie*', in *Heroes and Heroines in Medieval English Literature: A Festschrift Presented to André Crepin*, edited by L. Carruthers, Cambridge, 81–96.
Cooper, Helen (1989) *Oxford Guides to Chaucer: The Canterbury Tales*, Oxford.
Critical Essays on Chaucer's Canterbury Tales (1991) edited by Malcolm Andrew, Milton Keynes.
Keyser, G. A. (1978) 'In Defence of the Bradshaw Shift', *The Chaucer Review* 12, 191–201.
Koff, Leonard Michael (1988) *Chaucer and the Art of Storytelling*, Berkeley, Los Angeles and London.
Kolve, V. A. (1984) *Chaucer and the Imagery of Narrative*, Stanford, California.
Leicester, H. Marshall Jr. (1990) *The Disenchanted Self: Representing the Subject in The Canterbury Tales*, Berkeley and Oxford.
Manly, J. M. (1959) *Some New Light on Chaucer*, Gloucester, Mass.
Mann, Jill (1973) *Chaucer and Medieval Estates Satire*, Cambridge.
Owen, Charles A. (1991) *The Manuscripts of* The Canterbury Tales, Cambridge.
Patterson, Lee (1991) *Chaucer and the Subject of History*, Madison.
Pearsall, Derek (1985) *The Canterbury Tales*.
The Ellesmere Chaucer: Essays in Interpretation (1995) edited by Martin Stevens and Daniel Woodward, San Marino, California and Tokyo (Companion to New Ellesmere Facsimile).

RECEPTION

Brewer, Derek (ed.) (1978) *Chaucer: The Critical Heritage*, 2 vols.
Eighteenth-Century Modernizations from The Canterbury Tales (1991) edited by Betsy Bowden, Cambridge.
Spurgeon, C. F. E. (ed.) (1914–24) *Five Hundred Years of Chaucer Criticism and Allusion 1357–1900*, 3 vols.
The Poetical Works of William Wordsworth (1947) edited by E. de Selincourt and Helen Darbyshire, Oxford.

RECORDINGS

A sensitive reading aloud is itself an act of critical interpretation and many versions are now available. See Betsy Bowden (1987) *Chaucer Aloud: The Varieties of Textual Interpretation*, Philadelphia.

Some readings in the original pronunciation

Troilus and Criseyde (abridged) Argo ZPL 1003–4.
The General Prologue, Argo PLP 1001.
The Knight's Tale, Argo ZPL 1208–10.
The Miller's Prologue and Tale, CUP Cassette 211859.
The Wife of Bath, CUP Cassette 212197.
The Merchant's Prologue and Tale, CUP Cassette 211875.
The Pardoner's Tale, Argo ZPL 1211.
The Nun's Priest's Tale, Argo PLP 1002.
The Wife of Bath's Prologue and Tale, Argo XPL 1212/13.

The Chaucer Studio Recordings now contain many recordings of medieval English literature in original pronunciation, including Chaucer. Apply to Paul R. Thomas, Department of English, Brigham Young University, Provo, Utah 84602–6218, USA; or Tom Burton, Department of English, University of Adelaide, South Australia 5005, Australia.

Index